DATE DUE

GAYLORD			PRINTED IN U.S.A.

Social Capital, Trust and the Industrial Revolution, 1780–1880

Although research has shown that high levels of social capital and trust promote economic growth, low crime rates and improved labour relations, little work has been done on the historical impact of this essential resource. David Sunderland's incisive monograph is an attempt to reset the balance, seeking to demonstrate how social capital played a crucial role in the industrial, social and political changes of the late eighteenth and nineteenth centuries.

Dr Sunderland takes a comprehensive approach, examining the forms of behaviour, institutions and strategies that contributed to the formation of trust, the circumstances that could lead to its rise or fall, the presence of distrust and the relationship between trust and power. He shows how social capital levels fell due to the economic and social upheavals of the period and how they later recovered, and suggests that trust itself was a form of power.

This book will be of great interest to undergraduate and postgraduate historians, in both the UK and the USA, interested in the eighteenth and nineteenth centuries. It will also be illuminating for students interested in economic and political history, as well as sociologists and political scientists.

David Sunderland is a Lecturer in International Business at the University of Greenwich Business School, UK. A previous book, *An Economic History of London, 1800–1914*, is also available from Routledge.

Routledge explorations in economic history

Social Capital, Trust and the Industrial Revolution, 1780–1880

David Sunderland

Routledge
Taylor & Francis Group

LONDON AND NEW YORK

First published 2007
by Routledge
2 Park Square, Milton Park, Abingdon, Oxon OX14 4RN

Simultaneously published in the USA and Canada
by Routledge
270 Madison Ave, New York, NY 10016

Routledge is an imprint of the Taylor & Francis Group, an informa business

© 2007 David Sunderland

Typeset in Times by Wearset Ltd, Boldon, Tyne and Wear
Printed and bound in Great Britain by TJI Digital, Padstow, Cornwall

British Library Cataloguing in Publication Data
A catalogue record for this book is available from the British Library

Library of Congress Cataloging in Publication Data
A catalog record for this book has been requested

ISBN10: 0-415-41668-X (hbk)
ISBN10: 0-203-96432-2 (ebk)

ISBN13: 978-0-415-41668-9 (hbk)
ISBN13: 978-0-203-96432-3 (ebk)

For my mother, Mrs Betty Sunderland, who taught me perseverance

Contents

Acknowledgements

This book owes its existence to the Economic and Social Research Council, which financed the three-year project on which it is based (grant no. R000238347), and to two individuals. First to Professor David Jeremy, who recruited me to the project, compiled much needed reading lists, through our many discussions helped to advance my ideas, and read and commented on the finished manuscript. He is the embodiment of all the positive aspects of trust. Secondly, the book owes much to Professor Avner Offer, my ex-supervisor at Oxford University, who, through his example, showed me that history could and should be far more than a collection of facts, figures and dates. My understanding of trust and social capital has further benefited from living in Manchester and my frequent visits to Knaresborough, North Yorkshire. Both places, in very different ways, have demonstrated to me the importance of these concepts. Help and suggestions have also come from Professor Douglas Farnie, Dr Geoffrey Tweedale and Professor Peter Cain, who first directed me to Fukuyama's seminal monograph.

A great number of libraries and archives were used during the research of the book. I would therefore like to thank the staff of the John Ryland's University and Deansgate libraries, the Manchester Central Library and Local Studies Centre, Manchester Metropolitan University All Saints and Aytoun libraries, the British Library, the Bolton Local Studies Centre and Archive, the Lancashire Record Office, the Bodleian Library, Chetham's Library, the National Archive, Blackburn and Accrington Libraries, and the Manchester Record Office. I am also most grateful to Brian Farris of Bolton for allowing me to use the local data that he collected and recorded so carefully, and to Manchester Metropolitan University Business School, which hosted the ESRC project.

Finally, research is a lonely business and I would like to thank Dr Geoffrey Tweedale, Mary Tweedale, Professor David Jeremy, Jean Jeremy, Philip Burbidge and Mari Momose for their friendship. It was much appreciated.

Introduction

For many years, economists referred to three forms of capital: financial capital, physical capital (that is fixed and moveable resources) and human capital (which comprises knowledge and technical skills). To these has been added another form of resource, termed social capital. This has been defined as 'the glue that holds society together'. More specifically, Putnam describes it as the 'features of social life – networks, norms and trust – that facilitate co-operation and co-ordination for mutual benefit'. Like other forms of capital, it produces great economic and social returns. Researchers have linked high levels of social capital with improved economic performance, better educational outcomes, low crime rates, increased judicial efficiency, more effective government, social peace and a healthier population.[1]

Of the three attributes that comprise social capital, by far the most important is trust, which can be defined as an expectation, expressed in action and disappointed or fulfilled, that a partner will honour his implicit or explicit obligations. The importance of trust, the formation of which largely depends on the existence of co-operative norms and networks, cannot be exaggerated. All relationships, whether social, economic or political, are subject to the principal–agent problem. Individuals are rational and self-interested and will attempt to maximise their welfare.[2] A person entering a collaboration therefore faces two dangers. First that the potential partner will hide or falsify information, particularly about his abilities, before it begins. And second that, once in the relationship, he will not keep his side of the negotiated or assumed bargain and will take action that will maximise his own interests to the detriment of the collaborator, a practice known as moral hazard. Given these dangers, a person will only enter a relationship if he trusts that the other person will honour his obligations. If this confidence does not exist, then the collaboration will not take place and the benefits, both to himself and the wider society and economy, will be lost.

The concepts of social capital and trust have a long history. Both Adam Ferguson and Charles Montesquieu acknowledged the importance of civil society, in the 1840s Alex Tocqueville discussed at length the close relationship between voluntary associations and democracy in America, and the ideas have much in common with Marx and Engels's concept of 'bounded solidarity', Simmel's 'reciprocity transactions' and Weber's 'enforceable trust'. The modern theories were largely developed by Pierre Bourdieu and James Cameron and later Robert Putnam and Francis Fukuyama.[3] Since the publication of these authors' seminal works, social capital and trust have been used in a wide range of academic disciplines, including political science, philosophy, economics, anthropology, sociology and management studies, and have been adopted by politicians of all political hues. For those left of centre, they affirm the importance of generosity and collective action in the solving of social problems, and for proponents of laissez faire they hold out the promise that market failures can be overcome with little State intervention or expenditure.

Despite these historical precedents and its popularity, however, trust has largely been overlooked by historians, for whom the most important theoretical construct is often power. History is interpreted as a never-ending battle to gain, maintain and, if possible, increase one's holding of this supposedly valuable commodity. Social historians thus concentrate on the elite's apparent interminable quest for hegemony, political historians focus on party political conflict and those interested in business history tend to be preoccupied with competition. Trust is sidelined, and, where its existence cannot be denied, it is often reinterpreted in power terms. The growing co-operation between the classes in the mid-nineteenth century, for example, is supposedly the result of working-class capitulation in the class war or the creation of a deferential workforce. Religion, education and 'respectable' leisure pursuits, meanwhile, which can be interpreted as attempts by the middle class to raise working-class morality, are regarded as tools of social control.[4]

The historians who have written about trust can almost be counted on the fingers of one hand. A collection of articles originally published in a special edition of the *Journal of Interdisciplinary History* on the influence of social capital in different periods and in various countries appeared in book form in 2001, Craig Muldrew has recently discussed the importance of the concept in credit relationships in the early modern period, and it has been used in two articles on nineteenth-century banking and the Staffordshire potteries respectively. Trust also plays an important, though largely unacknowledged, role in E. P. Thompson's and his followers' work on the moral economy, in writings on working-class solidarities and in a number of recent books on nineteenth-century labour relations. One of the main components of social capital, the network, has faired better. Business, kinship, neighbourhood, friendship, social and migration networks have all been discussed at length, but few of the authors have examined the feelings of trust and loyalty that bound members together. Similarly, a fair amount has been written on the use of gifts and social signals, such as etiquette and respectability, though little has been devoted to their use in the development of trust relationships.[5]

This book seeks to fill the gap in the historiography of late eighteenth-century and nineteenth-century trust. The period was a time of great economic, social and political change, in which social capital played a major role, and its importance was widely acknowledged by numerous contemporary writers, and, later, by groups such as the Owenites, Chartists and Christian Socialists. The social commentator John Holland, for example, wrote in 1795 that 'without doubt there would be an end to the whole intercourse of society if the children of men could not in general depend on one another', and a writer of one of the most popular conduct manuals of the period believed that it was 'impossible to stir a step' without 'trust and dependence'.[6] It is further hoped that an investigation of how trust functioned in the past will throw new light on how it operates today.

The study seeks to discover the forms of behaviour, institutions and strategies that contributed to the formation of trust, the circumstances that could lead to its rise or fall, the presence of distrusts, and the relationship between trust and power. The existence and growth of social capital is traced through the use of written sources, such as etiquette and business manuals, statistics that reflect trust levels at second hand and information gained from an extensive range of historical, sociological, and economic books and articles. In addition, two data-bases were constructed. To discover the average lifespans of businesses, deter-mine the extent of business relocation and diversification, and so on, and thus throw more light on commercial social capital, the names, addresses and occu-pations of all of the 12,222 people listed in trade directories appertaining to the Lancashire cotton town of Bolton during the years 1778–1861 were collected. The analysis of this data appears in Chapter 9 'Business trust'. Similarly, to determine the trust benefits of the membership of formal networks and to find out the identity of members and how they networked, the names, and, where given, the addresses of those who belonged to 300 formal networks that met in Bolton during the same period were obtained from membership lists. This information was then combined with the trade directory findings and data on political allegiances drawn from poll books. The results of the analysis of the database constructed is recorded in Chapter 3, 'Formal networks'.

The book is roughly divided into four parts. The first two chapters discuss the development of trust within and between the classes. Chapter 1 examines a number of ways in which the middle classes built social capital. The first section looks at the media used to indicate trustworthiness, namely the code of etiquette, the mores of respectability, dress, language and household objects, and consid-ers the fraudulent use of these signals. There is then a discussion of some of the other means of generating confidence that were adopted – the giving of gifts, the acquisition of a good reputation and interaction with peers at domestic social gatherings, and, outside the home, at the theatre, the concert hall, the museum and the art gallery. Despite these initiatives, intra-class animosity continued to exist, and the final part of the chapter examines the mutual suspicions that were held by the various sub-groups that made up this class.

The investigation of social caste continues in the following chapter, which considers some aspects of working-class and inter-class trust. The lower orders generated social capital through the adoption of mores of respectability, the establishment of neighbourhood, leisure and employment networks, the mem-bership of friendly societies and trade unions, and the reciprocal exchange of gifts. They, nevertheless, suffered from intra-class acrimony and were the victims of middle-class distrust, though, from the 1850s, improvements in the economy, the perceived permanence of the capitalist system and various other factors brought the two classes closer together.

The second part of the book takes a closer look at the networks in which trust was formed. Chapters 3 and 4 explore formal networks. The trust benefits of belonging to these associations, the means by which they created loyalty and the nature of their members are discussed in Chapter 3, and the various ways in which philanthropic, religious and educational networks built trust and their contribution to the generation of social capital is explored in Chapter 4. The following chapter discusses informal networks and the importance of intermediaries, and examines some of the arenas in which these associations were most likely to develop and be maintained, namely the pub, the shop, the pageant and the funeral. It then goes on to examine some miscellaneous determinates of trust – demography, in particular migration, the built environment, income and happiness levels, and the local and national media.

The next three chapters survey other types of loyalty. Chapters 6 and 7 investigate the influence the State had on trust through the political system and those institutions that sought to sanction those who acted opportunistically. Chapter 6 examines how and why the social contract, the trust relationship between the ruled and their rulers, changed over time; discusses how the bonds of loyalty between political representatives and their electorates were established; and investigates the role played by local government networks in the generation of social, personal and other types of trust. This is followed by an examination of the State's attempt to raise social capital through improvements in the criminal and civil legal system and via changes in the way communities were policed. Chapter 8 concentrates on three other forms of trust. Much of the chapter is devoted to a study of kinship, which seeks to identify its benefits to family members and the wider society and to determine whether this form of social capital, the primary socialization of co-operation norms and trust within marriage became more or less important during the period. Geographic trust, the attachments between the inhabitants of towns, regions and countries is then discussed, followed by a short section on changes in masculine self-confidence and male bonds.

The final part of the monograph considers the commercial world. Chapter 9 looks at businesses and explores the increase in commercial distrust, attempts to determine why the rise was not as great as in other spheres, and seeks to determine those behavioural and corporate factors that promoted business confidence and trading success. It concludes with a brief examination of the importance of business networks, specifically trading associations, professional societies and networks based on trade, credit and shared directorships. The following chapter turns to labour relations, exploring how changes in labour demand and various other determinants caused many putting-out employers to exchange their trust bonds with workers with ones based on power, and many factory masters to adopt an autocratic followed by a more democratic relationship with their operatives. The various methods adopted by manufacturers to promote loyalty are then analysed, including the introduction of wage lists, the recruitment of friends and relatives of existing employees, and the provision of paternalistic gifts. The chapter ends with an examination of the master–servant relationship and the part played by both parties in the sanctioning of inappropriate behaviour.

The book ends with a Conclusion that puts forward the theory that trust levels changed over the period under investigation. At the end of the eighteenth/start of the nineteenth century, environmental change caused trust to fall, though the extent and the timing of the decline varied between spheres. Action by the individual, the community and the State, along with further socio-economic change, then caused social capital levels to rebound, though the extent and timing of the upswing was again not uniform. The conclusion also discusses the possible existence of cycles of trust, links the early nineteenth-century trust crisis with the present-day dearth of social capital, and considers three other propositions advanced in the book. First, that the rich and powerful could gain more trust more easily than their less well-off colleagues. Second, that, although both society and the individual wished to generate sufficient integrity to permit action and promote social peace, neither wanted to eliminate self-interested behaviour or immorality completely. Third, that levels of trust varied between towns and regions.

The character of trust

It is important that the reader knows something of the basics of trust generation and understands the meaning of terms borrowed from economics and sociology that are used in the book. The following pages therefore describe the various forms of trust that exist and the most important factors that propagate co-operation, look at trust relationships and examine power, the antithesis of trust. More detailed theory is introduced, where appropriate, in the chapters that follow. To ease understanding and future referral, the factors that lead to the generation of trust are listed as bullet points.

Forms of trust

Trust can be one sided, where only one party trusts the other, or two sided, when there is mutual trust. If two sided, each actor must be both trusting and trustworthy. To be trusting, a person must obtain affirmation about the behaviour of the other party, and to be trustworthy he must provide assurance about his own actions. Most people participate in a multitude of trust relationships, which change over time and involve varying degrees of loyalty. People have trust or confidence in themselves, in their families, the fellow members of their social class, those who reside in their local community, town, region and nation, and, if religious, in their god. In the economic field, trust exists between directors or partners, traders, and owners and their workers, and, in politics, the ruled ideally trust their rulers, with whom they form a social contract in which each side agrees to fulfil certain obligations and trusts that the other party will deliver their side of the bargain (Table I.1).[7] In the case of social classes, communities and

Table I.1 Types of trust

Type of trust	Description
Trusts classified by the identity of those involved in the trust relationship	
Business trust	Between trading partners or members of an industry or business community.
Employer–employee trust	Between a master and his workers.
Geographic trust	Between inhabitants of a town, region or country.
Inter-class trust	Between members of different classes.
Intra-class trust	Between members of the same class, e.g. middle-class trust.
Kin trust	Between family members. Includes husband–wife, parent–child and sibling trust.
Masculine trust	Between males. Derived from conformity to internalised social norms of manly behaviour.
Neighbourhood trust	Between neighbours, i.e. residents of a particular street(s) or community. A form of geographic trust.
Political trust	Between the ruled and their rulers.
Self-trust	An individual's trust in his or her own capabilities, i.e. self-confidence.
Social contract	A reciprocal trust relationship between rulers and the ruled in which each side agrees to fulfil certain obligations and trusts the other party to deliver their side of the bargain.
Spiritual trust	Between an individual and their god.
Worker trust	Between employees of a company or between all workers.
Trusts classified by the factors leading to their generation	
Affluence trust	Related to the wealth of a potential collaborator.
Ascribed trust	Arises from the shared characteristics of agents, e.g. ethnicity, religion, education.
Status trust	Related to the status of a potential collaborator.

the like, the trust will be anonymous, in that it will allow group members to engage in a wide range of co-operative activities and exchanges with strangers.

Generation of trust

A number of factors are involved in the development of trust.

- *Self-interest.* A person will trust someone to perform an act if he is aware that the trustee's self-interest is advanced by the action. This is the most basic form of trust.[8]
- *Shared attributes.* Trust further arises where two people have similar characteristics, such as gender, family, ethnicity, class, religion or other attributes, the mutual confidence generated being known as ascribed trust. Such shared features produce feelings of solidarity and enable people to gauge the honesty of potential partners from personal experience or the ethical culture associated with the common background. Individuals also tend to be unwilling to ascribe the negative character of untrustworthiness

to their peers, and, by extension, to themselves.[9] To ensure that others recognise the possession of the common characteristics, they are often signalled through clothes, accent and the like. For those who wish to form relationships, such signals reduce information collection costs. An upper-class accent, for example, immediately indicates the social background of the speaker and removes the need to obtain this information through questioning, which would be time-consuming and could generate distrust. To be effective, therefore, the signals need to be noticeable and easily identifiable. To avoid their fraudulent use, transmission media is costly or difficult to acquire and the knowledge of their meaning is often restricted. An upper-class accent, for instance, is not easily learned and the design of a school tie is generally only known to those who were educated at the establishment in question. As will be discussed later, for members of the Victorian middle class, ascribed trust was generated by their shared upbringings, educations, beliefs and leisure activities, and signalled through etiquette, the 'mores' of respectability, accent and language.

- *Possession of trust attributes.* These are characteristics that indicate trustworthiness and can be inherent or related to an individual's lifestyle or achievements. Inherent attributes include: gender – men tend to trust other members of their sex more than women; age – the old tend to be believed more than the young; and physical appearance – it is said that the ugly are less trusted than the beautiful. Lifestyle and achievement traits include the possession of long-term friendships and close family ties, participation in team sports, membership of clubs or a church, and wealth and status. People who are wealthy are deemed to have less need to behave opportunistically, and, in the early nineteenth century, providential economics further asserted that goodness was rewarded by riches, and, for those with a high social status, dishonesty could lead to the loss of their social position.[10] As with shared characteristics, the possession of these attributes is signalled through dress, language, objects and the like. The middle-class Victorian living room, for example, typically contained heavy, ornate and expensive appearing furniture, family portraits, a prominently displayed family bible, and often sporting cups and invitations to social events.

  Perhaps the most important trust attribute is a reputation for trustworthiness. Reputational information is obtained from those who have themselves had or know others who have had dealings with the person concerned in the past, and, because it is a valuable commodity, it is generally exchanged only between those who have close relationships. To build a reputation, an individual must act in an honourable manner, protect his name when it is threatened by false or true accusations, and associate with a large number of people who themselves have good reputations. These will inform others of his integrity and the very fact that they deal with him will suggest that he is honest.[11]

- *Long relationships.* Long associations, beginning with minor transactions involving little risk or trust, enable agents to monitor their counterparts for dishonesty, discover their capabilities, and lead to the development of emotional attachments that facilitate trust. After the first successful transaction, each partner will attribute the resultant emotion of satisfaction, happiness or excitement to the relationship, and the partner's positive behaviour to his personal traits and character, leading to the development of feelings of liking and attachment. These emotional pay-offs will become stronger after each successful transaction and will encourage each partner to be more honest and add to the costs of ending the relationship if minor infractions occur.[12] Generally, the trust generated will be stronger if the relationship involves face-to-face meetings. Personal interaction helps to build emotional bonds, facilitates gossip and the exchange of information regarding the honesty of others, and permits non-verbal communication, which reduces the risk of misunderstanding and allows more accurate appreciations of integrity.

• *The exchange of gifts.* The Victorian era was replete with gifts. The middle class showered their friends with dinners, teas and ornaments, businessmen offered fellow traders price discounts, loans, tools and letters of introduction, and many employers gave their workers meals, outings to the seaside, libraries and recreational facilities. Gifts indicate regard, that is recognition and consideration, which ranks high among the sources of human satisfaction. For Adam Smith, 'to be observed, to be attended to, to be taken notice of with sympathy' was the prime motivator of 'all the toil and bustle of the world'. Gifts also transmit other signals. The initial present denotes the strength of the giver's desire to form a relationship and his trustworthiness – there is no guarantee that the offering will be reciprocated and the giver therefore risks a loss. If it is reciprocated, the return gift signals both the recipient's willingness to enter into the relationship and his own trustworthiness. More reciprocal exchanges then occur, fostering feelings of gratitude and indebtness that strengthen the ties between the parties, and, through their sheer predictability, stabilise the relationship.[13]

  Two special types of gift are the free gift and the critical life situation gift. Free or philanthropic gifts are given in the knowledge that there will be no direct return from the often unknown beneficiary and are well publicised. Examples are the recreation grounds and libraries that Victorian industrialists often gave to their home towns. The gifts signal to the community the giver's trustworthiness and may be reciprocated by individual members of the society. They can therefore reap extremely high rates of return. Critical life situation gifts, on the other hand, are provided when the recipient is going through a particularly traumatic period. In nineteenth-century working-class communities, they took the form of information, small sums of money, pawnable items, domestic paraphernalia and the completion of tasks. Neighbours, for instance, would care for the children of women giving birth, nurse or complete the household duties of the sick, shop for the elderly and lay out the dead. Because of their relatively high value, the gifts require the presence of large amounts of social capital before they are given and reciprocation generally involves a gift of equal worth, which is provided when the giver is undergoing a similar critical life situation. In very high-trust communities, the present may be provided to a member of the community who lacks the means to reciprocate. The bequest will be given because the benefactor, who will advertise his contribution, will expect and receive reciprocation from another member of the community and may lose his own reputation if he fails to act. The recipient of the gift, in turn, will be expected to reciprocate in some way and at some later date to a further community member, failure to do so causing him to be deemed untrustworthy and ejected from the gift network.[14]

- *Social and personal norms and institutions and routines.* Social and personal norms determine people's willingness to resort to opportunism and to trust each other. Social norms are rules of conduct common to all the members of a group and can be split into society norms, which relate to the code supposedly held by a whole society, and network norms, which are often radically different and are followed by those who belong to that network. In early Victorian Britain, for example, for the respectable working class there was a social norm that acted against public drunkenness, but a friendly society network norm that permitted and expected heavy drinking at annual dinners. People conform to social norms partly because the rules are internalised and they suffer psychological pain in the form of guilt or shame if they do not comply with them. Internalisation occurs through primary socialisation, that is in the parent–child relationship, and secondary socialisation, which takes place within a variety of agencies, including schools, peer groups, the church, and so on. Compliance is also encouraged by others in the society or network, who constantly monitor their colleagues' behaviour and apply sanctions, such as disapproval, ridicule and, in extreme cases, ostracism on those who ignore the rules. Their development is driven by moral, cultural and ideological discourse, the opinions and actions of community and network role models, whose beliefs are widely noticed and imitated, and by broader social and economic trends.[15] Nineteenth-century moral norms, for instance, were arguably weakened by the new political economy of Adam Smith and David Ricardo, and by the metropolitan social codes brought to provincial towns by national newspapers and professional authority figures.

Personal trust and moral norms are exclusive to the individual, determined by conditioning, early attachment experiences, learning over time and perhaps genetic inheritance. They are supported by emotional rewards and punishments in the form of peace of mind and guilt, though the latter can be depressed. Individuals can censure negative memories or reframe immoral occurrences, attributing responsibility to others or mentally reducing the actual damage caused to the other party. Most people possess a number of personal norms of differing intensity, the adoption of which depends on the potential returns from a relationship.[16] The average middle-class Victorian male, for example, maintained a high trust norm for family members and close friends, but weaker ones for lesser kin, acquaintances and strangers.

Formal institutions are norms of behaviour that are recorded and must be followed, such as laws, property rights and the rules of professional associations. Individuals who flout these codes suffer sanctions, such as imprisonment or expulsion from the organisation. The institutions thus discourage opportunistic behaviour, reduce the uncertainties involved in human interaction and create order and thus promote trust. To be effective they must possess both legitimacy and power. Related to institutions are routines, ways of behaving that are habitually followed by networks and organisations. These are based on formal rules, but also on past decisions, tacit knowledge and norms, and are only modified if the environment changes. In the Victorian shipbuilding industry, for example, negotiations regarding new orders always conformed to a set routine. Meetings between the owners of the firms involved would be followed by further meetings attended by middle managers to decide the details of the contract, and both owners and managers sought to drive a hard but a fair bargain. As with institutions, the tendency for an organisation to behave in the future as it did in the past again engenders trust, allowing people to accurately predict behaviour and outcomes, and the routines often incorporate trust norms.[17]

- *Networks*. The main arena for the generation and transference of trust is the network. Networks can be formal, involving connections with a specific organisation, such as a church, political party or trade union, or informal, comprising relationships between friends, neighbours, kin, and so on. They can be bonding networks, whose members possess similar characteristics as in family groups; bridging associations, containing people who have dissimilar identities, such as choirs; or linking networks, where there are large imbalances in member power, as in the employer–employee assemblies that set the wages of cotton operatives from the 1830s.[18] Whatever the form, within a grouping the shared characteristic of membership, long relationships and the exchange of gifts generates strong intra-association trust. Members also build self-confidence, sometimes obtain status, exchange reputational information and the trust norms of the other groups to which they belong, and develop the network's own norms, which, in turn, are passed onto other groupings and to society in general. The amount of trust created by an association is determined by the trust and moral norms of the society in which it is embedded and the characteristics of its members, its purpose, the regularity of its meetings and the opportunities for social interaction. Size is also important. In small groups, each member connects with a large proportion of his associates, can easily monitor their actions and characteristics, and can effectively apply sanctions for moral hazard, leading to the development of strong norms.

The transference of group trust norms to other associations and the rest of society again depends on the purpose of the network, the strength of its norms and the connections of its members. Victorian evangelical churches, for example, will have disseminated far more trust than sporting clubs. Associations, however, do not invariably spread harmony. They can also reduce trust or even generate antipathy. High trust in one network can 'crowd out' its presence elsewhere. Nineteenth-century Irish migrants, for instance, possessed little wider communal feeling, as they preferred to socialise with each other rather than with natives of the town in which they settled. Likewise, members of one network may distrust counterparts in groups with opposing interests. There will exist little ascribed trust, stringent trust norms in an association often reduces the extent to which members are able to trust outsiders, and groups sometimes adopt relatively low standards of moral behaviour in their dealings with strangers, who are distrustful of them as a result. In the early 1800s, the Anglican and non-conformist churches were almost continuously at loggerheads. In some circumstances, though, social capital, phoenix-like, may rise out of such animosity. An association's dislike of another network can increase intra-group trust. The antipathy Baptists felt towards the Church of England will have strengthened intra-congregation solidarity. Similarly, competing groups that develop a mutual abhorrence of a third party greater than their own inter-group distrust will often forget their differences in order to oppose the joint adversary. In the 1850s, for example, Anglican and Nonconformist distrust of the Catholic Church caused the two denominations to come together.[19]

Within each association are inner networks, smaller informal groupings of members, which arise from the tendency for individuals to interact more with people who are similar to themselves than with those who are dissimilar.[20] They are based on age, class, gender, occupation, religion, ideology or length of membership, and generate differing amounts of trust, though the strength of the trust in each inner-network will be higher than that which exists for the association as a whole. Most Victorian churches, for instance, contained two distinct inner networks – the middle-class fee-paying pew holders and the less wealthy who sat in the free seats, each of which was in turn split into further cliques and factions. Beyond but connected to many networks are groups of supporters – those who contribute to charity appeals, attend fund-raising activities and football matches, view processions, and so on. The presence of the network promotes much sociability and trust among these people, who can be regarded as extra-members.

Networks are ultimately initiated by individuals, who need to possess initiative, organisational ability, and, since there is no guarantee that the new association will develop networking value, a good trust reputation in order to attract the first recruits. In return for their efforts, founders improve their reputations and gain strong links with other members. Ordinary members tend to be male, middle class and middle aged, and a disproportionate number will have a propensity to co-operate and trust. A person's sense of self or self-confidence is influenced by their dispositional characteristics. Collaborative and honest individuals therefore seek out networks in the knowledge that they will provide an arena where they can fulfil their co-operative and trust needs and thus increase their levels of self-esteem. Most will possess a limited number of memberships, as each network connection is costly in terms of time, and, if contact is not maintained, the trust generated begins to wane. If possible, the memberships will be in diverse networks, which increases the range and amount of information that can be obtained and improves the individual's attractiveness as a network contact to others.[21]

Trust and power relationships

Few trust relationships are unchanging. As time passes and the environment and each partner's needs alter, disagreements inevitably occur that can flare into major conflict. Usually, trust survives. Each partner forgives the other's unacceptable behaviour and eventually participates in the renegotiation of the trust contract. Such commitment is motivated by self-interest. Relationship entry costs are high. Much time has to be spent discovering the reputation of prospective partners, building emotional bonds and providing gifts – the amount invested depending on a range of factors, including the expected returns and the partner's trustworthiness and ability to trust. Given these sunk costs, individuals are averse to abandoning relationships; a reluctance that is encouraged by other factors. The cost of maintaining established associations is low and exit and replacement costs can be high. The breaking of the emotional bonds that developed may be painful, and a danger exists that any new partner will prove to be unscrupulous. Most people, consequently, only abandon associations when the return is close to zero or the other person acts opportunistically.

In theory, a person will act opportunistically and threaten a relationship when the benefit from moral hazard is greater than the perceived long-term return from the continuation of the association and the psychological costs of duplicity. In reality, much unscrupulousness occurs for far smaller short term returns, as many people are inter-temporally inconsistent. Faced with a small gain available in the short term and a superior reward obtainable in the distant future, they choose the inferior option, the achievement of which is relatively certain. When opportunism takes place, the innocent party often reciprocates the moral hazard. In the nineteenth century, for instance, buyers cheated by suppliers sometimes provided them with sub-standard goods. To Adam Smith, 'the law ... as every man doth, so shall be done to him' was 'dictated by nature', retaliation forcing the 'offender ... to repent of his injustice' and causing others 'through fear of the like punishment ... [to] be terrified from being guilty of the like offence'.[22] Such reciprocation also enables the victim to wholly or partly recoup his losses and provides him with an emotional reward that offsets the anger generated by the duplicitous act, which would otherwise provoke him to end the relationship. The likelihood of revenge largely depends on the injured party's ability to reciprocate, the costs involved, the moral norms of the society/network to which he belongs and his own personal norms.

In many cases, duplicitous behaviour can easily be predicted before a relationship commences. People, nonetheless, enter associations and trust opportunists, even when they have access to information that strongly suggests that all is not as it appears. In the 1850s and 1860s, thousands bought commercial equity despite voluminous evidence that many company promotions were fraudulent. Explanations for this tendency are legion. Individuals appear to be psychologically pre-disposed to optimism. As today, millions of working-class Victorians gambled convinced that they had a good chance of winning. Likewise, they tend to be over confident in their judgments, believing them to be correct to a much greater degree than is actually the case. They are also the victims of recency, halo and framing effects. Recently obtained information tends to have a greater impact on judgment than older knowledge. One positive trait in a potential collaborator, such as a pleasant personality, can disproportionately guide evaluations, and outcomes can be excessively influenced by the way in which a choice is framed or presented.[23] The result is that any information received before a decision to commit is made is too often interpreted in a biased way and trust is bestowed on those unworthy of it.

Power relationships appear to be the antitheses of those based on trust. Power arises out of unequal dependencies, that is where one actor is dependent on another for particular benefits. The party with the resources has power over the dependent partner and can force him to carry out acts that are contrary to his preferences and interests. The extent to which the dominant party can take advantage of his power, however, is dependent on two factors – the value the weaker partner places on the benefit he desires and the nature of the alternatives; whether they are numerous, easily obtainable and adequate substitutes.[24] If alternatives are widely available, the use of power will cause the weaker partner to enter an association with a supplier willing to treat him fairly. Bolton cotton masters, for example, were unable to treat workers as badly as their counterparts elsewhere because the town possessed many other alternative sources of employment in the engineering, bleaching and mining industries. Likewise, if the dependent actor places little value on the benefits, he will conclude that they are not worth the cost and will withdraw from the relationship without seeking a replacement. In both cases, the stronger party loses his own return from the association and is faced with significant disruption expenses and the cost of finding a new partner. He will therefore in future limit his use of power, and, if many alternatives are available and the weaker partner attaches little value to the benefit, will abandon the use of force completely.

The President of the Bolton Hesperus Literary and Christian Association in 1863 believed that there were 'two roads, either that of despotism or of confidence'.[25] In reality, the division between trust and power is not as straightforward as it first appears. Without power there would be no need for trust; both partners in a trust relationship generally have at least some power, but opt not to use it. Trust itself can be a form of power. Weaker partners in relationships with a dominant actor may form bonds of trust with each other in order to increase their collective strength against the power holder. A good example is the nineteenth-century trade union movement. Trust can also be signalled by the abandonment of power. A dominant party, who, despite his resources, treats co-partners fairly, in doing so, demonstrates his trustworthiness. In the same way, people in trust relationships often give the other person gifts of power or vulnerability. For instance, they may disclose information that reveals their goals or intentions and could be used against them. Such gifts, by raising the vulnerability of the information givers, signal their trust of the recipient and act as a test of his trustworthiness. The powerful, meanwhile, can sometimes obtain trust far more easily than the powerless, having greater access to networks, superior knowledge of trust signals, and so on. They may even be more willing to enter trust relationships, aware that they can always resort to dominance if the feelings of mutuality dissipate.

1 Middle-class trust

The various building blocks of middle-class trust are considered throughout the book. The formal networks in which the class spent so much of their free time are discussed in general terms in Chapter 3, their involvement in philanthropy, the church and political networks in Chapters 4 and 6, and the confidence they generated in their professional lives is investigated in Chapters 9 and 10. This introductory chapter concentrates on a number of basic methods of raising trust that were adopted in all spheres of their lives, though the enthusiasm with which they were taken up was dependent on status and income. The first section examines how trust was signalled to others through etiquette, the mores of respectability, language, facial features, and household objects, and examines how the transmission of fraudulent information was prevented. The second section then discusses three other ways in which confidence was raised – the provision of gifts, the establishment of a good name, and attendance at a range of informal social gatherings held in the domestic sphere and at places of entertainment and culture. The middle class, of course, was not a homogeneous mass. It comprised numerous sub-groups, which had distinctive political and religious beliefs. Such differences inevitably led to disagreements and distrust, and the final section briefly discusses these divisions and seeks to understand why they became less important as time passed.

Trust signals

Etiquette

The code of etiquette promoted trust in a variety of ways. It firstly identified followers of its strictures as members of the middle class and thus engendered ascribed trust. Second, it involved the reciprocal exchange of gifts of regard, which facilitated the growth of loyalties and attachments. Although the gift of 'graceful behaviour towards others' had no monetary value, it nevertheless 'pleas[ed] others because it indicat[ed] respect for their personality'. The code also advocated honesty in every aspect of life, and may have increased self-esteem, Samuel Smiles famously claiming that politeness 'gives tenfold more pleasure to ourselves' than to others.[1]

Etiquette broadly covered three types of signal – conduct, appearance and language. Conduct or outward behaviour involved acting at all times in a manner that was compatible with one's rank in society and incorporated honesty as its highest ideal. 'The true gentleman', as Smiles reminded his readers 'has a keen sense of honour – scrupulously avoiding mean actions. His standard of probity in word and action is high. He does not shuffle nor prevaricate, dodge nor skulk; but is honest, upright and straightforward.' Practitioners were to adopt this behaviour in all their dealings whether 'in the cottage, in the court [or] in the daily and hourly performance of social services' and with superiors, equals or inferiors. Such sincerity was particularly important in contacts with the poor, as 'if you take pains to mortify [them] ... it is an insult that will not readily be forgiven'.[2]

As regards their actual actions, to ensure that their gifts of regard appeared authentic, students of etiquette were advised to behave naturally and unselfconsciously with ease and spontaneity. They were also to act simply in a conservative, restrained and down to earth manner, since 'men ... distrust the showy extravagance which is meant to dazzle, but seldom deceives and never increases social respect'. Emotion was to be concealed. There was a danger that it would display an individual's actual beliefs and lay him open to exploitation, for, having discovered someone's true feelings, a dishonest man 'has the springs of the affections at his command and may wind them up or let them down at pleasure'. Equally, there was a temptation for people to use the expression of emotion for their own advantage, for instance to obtain concessions that would otherwise not be given. Emotional people, furthermore, were generally distrusted, as they were thought more likely to make irrational decisions than phlegmatics, and shows of emotion could give offence. 'To live pleasantly with each other' people must 'at least appear to be kind, friendly, disinterested, obliging' and have 'the command of [their] tempers and countenances', even in the most extreme circumstances. 'On receiving an affront', for example, a person, if he 'could not be justified in knocking the offender down ... must not notice the offence'.[3]

Appearance largely involved dress, from which it was thought one 'may form some opinion of a man's sense and character'. Although, for women, cosmetics were also an issue. A painted face signalled a propensity towards concealment and hid that most accurate indicator of female purity and modesty, the blush. As with conduct, the most important aspect of attire was uniformity. To signal membership of the middle class and generate ascribed trust, women had to follow a strict dress code and choose clothes that were suitable to the occasion, the time of day, the season and where they were to be worn, whether in the town or country and inside or in the open air. They thus had to possess a relatively large wardrobe and be able to devote a great deal of time to their appearance, requirements that further signalled wealth. Men followed a similar, though far less complex, code. Formal dress was the black suit or tails, which was de rigueur when visiting a person of rank and at formal events. On other occasions, a frock coat was worn, the tails of which indicated the wearer's age, gravity and

social position via their length. Generally, fashion and frivolous and gaudy ornaments were to be avoided. The latter indicated a desire to disguise one's true
self, and 'in a man of business' suggested extravagance, 'which never fails to be
attended by ruin', and 'levity of mind and effeminity of manners'. Individual
items of clothing had to blend and thus signal a rational and ordered mind, not
be too 'beggarly', which would indicate poverty, and be clean. 'He who is not
thoroughly clean in person will be offensive to all he converses with' and would
particularly displease women 'tacitly accusing them of vanity and declaring that
... [he] thought them not worth that respect which everybody else [pays them]'.[4]

Language, whether used verbally or in its written form had to be straightforward and simple. Students of etiquette were advised to state exactly what
they were thinking and feeling, provided that their words would not damage the
other's regard. They should therefore 'never say an ill-natured thing nor be witty
at the expense of anyone present' and 'agree to differ and when ... [men] do
differ, bear and forbear ... [as] there are circumstances in which words are
blows and inflict wounds far less easy to heal'. Nor, on the other hand, were they
to flatter. 'A young lady, however beautiful she may be, is in society never
referred to as more than "nice" ... a steak cut from the most tender cut of beef
and broiled in its juices is found "nice". No one describes someone as "excel-
lent".' Hyperbole led to suspicions of hypocrisy and was found 'disturbing,
because it forces others either to voice the same high-toned sentiment or else to
make obvious the gulf that exists between them and the enthusiast'. Accent was
similarly important. Dialect-free speech generated ascribed trust among other
members of the middling classes, especially those from the South-East, and was
acquired through interaction with those who spoke 'better english' and the
employment of elocution teachers.[5]

The vocabulary adopted had to be plain and unpretentious. Words were
chosen for their simplicity. So, for example, 'buy' was better than 'purchase',
'rich and poor' superior to 'those of large and small means', and 'begin' prefer-
able to 'commence'. Foreign and Latin phrases and business terms were to be
avoided. All suggested a desire for obfuscation. Foreign words brought to mind
the distrusted foreigner and commercial language evoked the dishonesty of the
counting house. An 'elegant' manner of speech was also to be adopted; 'gracefulness of speaking [was] ... as essential as gracefulness of person, ... [as]
nobody can attend with pleasure to a bad speaker'. It was thus recommended
that people speak 'deliberately and distinctly', constantly vary the tone of their
voice and use language in a grammatical manner. 'Course and vulgar language',
which generated 'hate and revengeful feelings', was to be especially avoided, as
was the temptation to hog the conversation, for 'those that talk much cannot
always talk well and may oftener incur censure than praise [since] few people
care to be eclipsed'.[6]

A drawback of the use of politeness as a trust signal was that it was subject to
hypocrisy. To generate trust, the honest had to pretend 'to feel what ... [they
did] not feel, to believe what ... [they did] not believe, to practice what ...
[they did] not practice'. The dishonest, meanwhile, could easily fake the signals,

concealing 'their true intent under a specious show of sincerity and serpent-like glide into men's confidence only to dart their venom with greater certainty'. Such hypocrisy was a natural part of Victorian life. The German V.A Huber found England to be thoroughly imbued with double standards, and the Revd Lamb believed that cant 'penetrat[ed] and permeat[ed] everywhere like the air we breathe'.[7]

Several attempts were made to act against this deceitfulness. In the mid-eighteenth century, there developed the ethos of sensibility, which sought to reconnect manners with moral virtue and urged its followers to empathise with others and possess at all times 'sympathetic and generous feelings of the heart'. Such sympathy was to be demonstrated through expressive actions, such as sighing and weeping, and the provision of practical help. The creed evolved from the writings of the Scottish moral philosophers and the new theories of physiology and was spread via the periodical and the novel.[8] As with politeness, however, the doctrine was corruptible. Adherents adopted its strictures for their own self-advancement, and when, in the 1780s, its leading supporters were revealed to be duplicitous, its popularity began to decline.

Further attempts to link politeness with morality were made in novels and plays, which satirised the fop, a narcissistic and morally vapid male who was committed to fashionable manners, and, in the late eighteenth century, in conduct books. Unlike etiquette manuals, which became popular in the 1830s and initially were only concerned with protean identity, these taught manners within a fundamentally moral framework, stressing sincerity, character, that is inner qualities of morality, and the importance of emulating the behaviour of role models. Character also played an important part in the code of manliness, which became popular from the mid-nineteenth century. The doctrine emphasised manly vigour, frankness in both action and speech and the adoption of high personal moral norms, and was adopted by both the middle class and respectable workingmen, thus generating much inter-class trust.[9]

Not surprisingly none of these initiatives completely eradicated hypocrisy. Minor duplicity was generally tolerated. Such insincerity involved few costs, either for the victim or the dissembler. It was largely used 'for the purpose of avoiding the suspicions or merited ill will of other men; sometimes for the purpose of obtaining the confidence of others, without any settled design to make it the means of committing any positive and particular injury'. In such cases, even if the victim suspected that the 'untruths of expression or of action' were 'base coin', he was unlikely to break up the relationship. He continued to receive its benefits, there was always a possibility that he had misinterpreted the suspect's motives, a harsh reaction would discourage others from forming bonds of trust with him and would contravene the norms of etiquette, and the gifts of regard, though insincere, like 'sugar candy to the coffee of life', probably gave him pleasure. For the dissembler, meanwhile, failure to indulge in minor duplicity could lead to distrust. On a basic level, 'if every man told his neighbour what he really thought of him, the world would soon be an arena of pretty general conflict'. A refusal to follow the hypocritical conventions of etiquette would also lead to ascribed distrust. As depicted by Walter Bagehot, there would be 'a gentle murmur of "most unfortunate ideas", "singular young man", "well intentioned I dare say; but unsafe, sir, quite unsafe"'.[10]

Hypocrisy that was used for 'acts of gainful fraud' was far less acceptable, and, from the 1840s, etiquette books began to warn against the misuse of their codes of politeness and to provide methods by which the dishonest dissembler could be identified. Readers, for example, were advised to distrust those who claimed friendship, particularly those who 'profess the most … [and] if their advances are sudden, extraordinary or without plausible foundation'. Harmful immoral behaviour, however, was relatively rare, as the rewards were small and the potential costs could be high. Trust signals alone were used to determine trustworthiness only for 'innocent frolics'. For 'serious matters', signals were augmented by other evidence of trustworthiness, including the views of others and personal experience. Costs included lost reputation and cognitive dissonance. Hypocrisy is easily spotted. To quote Nietzsche, 'one can lie with the mouth, but with the accompanying grimace, one nevertheless tells the truth'. There was therefore a high chance that the dishonest would be found out – 'something strikes someone; an unpleasant idea is somewhat reluctantly admitted; it is kept secret; but somebody else hinting something like it, it finds words, and, by and by, the thing is discovered to have a lodgement in many minds'. Depending on the nature of the act, the culprit would then be subject to the sanctions of gossip, insults or exclusion, and would lose his trust reputation, 'suspicion will attach itself to [his] future conduct; truth will obtain for [him] no credit, no integrity, no confidence'.[11]

At the same time, some hypocrites will have suffered psychological costs, which will have damaged their self-esteem. Many will have been haunted 'by tormenting fears of exposure' or suffered from cognitive dissonance, the disutility that arises when behaviour clashes with social and personal norms. Others, though, will have escaped such torments. Not all hypocrites will have believed in the moral codes of honesty and honour, and some no doubt circumvented dissonance through self-deception. Dissemblers will have rationalised their behaviour by changing their beliefs, trivialised or provided excuses for the actions, distorted the circumstances that led to the inconsistency, or misattributed the dissonance to something other than the moral discrepancy. Ironically, those who were most successful at such self-delusion will have been less likely to have been discovered acting hypocritically, as self-deception will have made it easier to deceive others.[12]

Although rare, immoral hypocrisy, nevertheless, did occur, but, as today, often failed to be punished by social sanctions. One reason could be that there was a fear that penalties against gross hypocrisy would lead to a fall in trust. Punishing dissemblers would merely cause fewer people to follow the ethical code and discourage others from advocating its tenets, reducing the numbers who would hear about and adopt them. A more likely explanation is that sanctions were only applied if the behaviour threatened the trust reputation or myth of the social group. If the actions were known or were likely to become so by others outside the social circle then they would be punished. If not, group members would turn a 'blind eye', aware that the very act of chastisement would draw others' attention to the recaltricant behaviour. Such a response, itself hypocritical, would particularly occur if the immorality did not harm other members of the group and if the degenerate colleague possessed power or resources that could prove useful to the clique Also, turning a 'blind eye' constituted a gift and group members would expect reciprocation if they themselves broke the moral code.

Other trust signals

Etiquette was not the only indicator that signalled the possession of shared and confidence-raising characteristics. Respectability, facial features, household objects, language and other cues were also relied upon. Respectability, a close cousin of the code of manliness, involved sobriety, hard work, sexual continence, piousness and obedience of the law, and was signalled through regular church attendance, membership of societies that promoted respectable behaviour, and by verbally informing others of one's beliefs and way of life. As with etiquette, however, the respectable were prone to hypocrisy, abandoning their supposedly strongly held views in private. Such disrespectable behaviour was particularly adopted by young unmarried men, who, not yet embarked on careers, had little need for repute, and by older men, who had well-established reputations that could withstand gossip, and, close to retirement, had relatively less to lose if their good names were tarnished. Those with occupations that took them away from their local environments, for example commercial travellers, were also prone to such behaviour, as their misdemeanours, committed far from home, were unlikely to have an impact on their reputations. The misconduct largely occurred in districts or towns some distance from the miscreant's home, where he was unknown, or in voluntary associations, for example gentlemen's clubs and freemasons' lodges. Here, moral norms were relatively lax and the common breach of respectable codes reduced the likelihood that fellow members would reveal an individual's activities to the outside world.[13]

As with etiquette, such behaviour generally went unpunished, provided that it did not become known to others outside the social circle to which the offender belonged. Many may also have believed that the transgressions had a beneficial effect on social trust. The misbehaviour provided a valuable release from respectability, reinvigorating individuals' adoption of the respectable code in their everyday lives, and, as will be discussed later, played an important role in the generation of masculine and intra-associational trust.

The way in which the trustworthiness and other characteristics of individuals could be derived from a study of the human face and head was explained by the 'sciences' of physiognomy and phrenology. Physiognomy linked facial features with character traits. So, for example, the size and shape of the forehead was thought to indicate the intellectual capacities of an individual and the bottom half of his face his emotional nature. The science was popularised in the 1770s by John Casper Lavater, whose theories were developed by Alexander Walker in his 1834 book on the subject. Phrenology confined itself to the shape of the head and the indentations found on skulls, which again were related to character traits, including trustworthiness. Developed in the eighteenth century, the science was promoted through life-sized casts of heads and handbooks.[14]

Both theories reached the apex of their popularity in the 1850s and 1860s, aided by the invention of photography, which allowed the accurate depiction of features, and the rise of the newspaper and the novel. Lavater's book was 'thought as necessary in every family as even the bible itself' and its findings were widely believed. Charles Dickens, for example, on being given a plaster cast of a murderer, remarked that the man possessed 'a style of head and set of features, which might have afforded sufficient moral grounds for his instant execution at any time, even had there been no other evidence against him'. If Dickens was prepared to end a man's life on the basis of his head and countenance, it would seem likely that these factors played a large part in decisions to trust and therefore influenced who attained social and commercial success. A 1850 phrenological and physiognomical study of the members of the Manchester Exchange found that nowhere in England was there 'such a collection of clever heads'. And it is interesting to note that contemporary portraits of worthies suggest that a large proportion had facial features that, according to physiognomy and phrenology, indicate honesty, honourable behaviour and intelligence.[15]

Household objects carried a variety of signals, though these changed over time and their strength varied according to the social and religious background of those who viewed the articles. The signals encouraged guests to trust the owner, heightened his neighbourhood trust reputation, strengthened his bonds of loyalty and attachment with others, and raised his self-esteem (Table 1.1). The most important signals were carried by large or expensive items. The beauty, variety or convenience of these objects gave guests the gift of pleasure and enabled them to provide hosts with reciprocal gifts in the form of complimentary comments, and displayed the wealth and status of the householder, generating the trust associated with these attributes. The monetary value of articles could be easily judged and social status could be determined by the kind of items owned and whether they conformed to the existing canon of taste. To further emphasise wealth, furniture was often heavy and ornate, imitated aristocratic styles, and was highly polished.[16] Some fixtures and fittings, such as dining tables, pianos, punch bowls and crystal decanters, also reflected the extent to which the householder socialised and his adoption of codes of etiquette. A large dining table, for example, indicated that he held many dinner parties and possessed many network connections, which increased the chances that he would be trustworthy. Objects given by friends, relatives, business associates or employees, meanwhile, demonstrated to visitors that such relationships existed and were strong, and were a daily reminder to the householder of the importance of the bonds and the need to maintain them. These gifts, along with expensive furniture and

Table 1.1 Objects and their associated trust signals

Object	Trust signal
A large collection of family portraits or photographs.	Householder was married and had a family, which, in itself, endowed him with a certain amount of trust. His bonds of kinship were strong and kinship networks were extensive.
Portraits of royal figures and china celebrating royal anniversaries, famous victories, etc.	Signified patriotism, a form of trust.
Items of local manufacture or paintings depicting local scenes.	Implied identification with and faith in the local community.
Traditional furniture and collections of classic literature or art.	Denoted a conservative outlook and a tendency towards risk aversion.
Sporting cups.	Demonstrated owner's masculinity, boosting masculine trust, and his ability to be part of a team and to work co-operatively.
Signs of presence of pets, e.g. bird cages, dog baskets.	Compassion for animals and therefore probably for humans.
Photographs of fellow members of voluntary associations.	Indicated membership of the societies and all that entailed as regards trust.
Heirlooms, portraits of previous generations of the family.	Suggested inter-generation kinship trust was strong; enabled owner to free ride on forebears' wealth and status trust.
Large and many clocks.	Signified a punctual, ordered and efficient person who deserved competence trust.
Decanters, toddy ladles, etc.	Indicated the householder consumed alcohol, raising masculine trust.
Photographs of employees.	Demonstrated good employer–employee trust relationships.
Framed local maps.	Indicated identity with and commitment to the local community.

furnishings and mementoes of their owners' past lives and minor achievements, furthermore, acted as daily tangible boosts to their self-confidence, reminding them of their ability to form co-operative relationships, and their possession of the skills and talents that enabled them to purchase or acquire the objects.

Furniture was also a means by which the middle class could identify bona fide members of their class. To be used, many household goods required fore-knowledge and a certain learned manual dexterity, which was only possessed by those who had previously come across such objects. Desks often contained concealed drawers, and required a deep knowledge of a variety of knobs, ratchets, cranks or keys. Handwork/writing tables had reversible and bi-functional surfaces and would topple over if not manoeuvred around with sufficient grace. To sink into and arise from an armchair with finesse often required great physical control. Conversely, other items of furniture were specifically designed to facilitate naturalness and sociability. The shapes of desk chairs and day beds produced bodily positions that appeared both relaxed and unaffected; while game tables forced players into close proximity by their small size.[17]

For the very rich, wealth and the related trustworthiness was signalled through conspicuous leisure, which was made even more conspicuous if it was spent in philanthropic activities, public service or the pursuit of some hobby that reaped publicity. Like the middle class, the rich also made others aware of their wealth and status through conspicuous consumption. Large houses were bought 'to announce the great man within' and given names that generated trust; many, for example, were named after royalty, local notables or saints. Opulent furnishings were purchased, works of art collected, which additionally generated trust with fellow collectors and the aristocracy and the Southern gentlemanly elite, and a large number of servants employed; all 'quack advertisements and assumptions on the question of merit'. Likewise, children were given expensive educations and costly private carriages were bought, body weight was allowed to become excessive and attempts were made to obtain a title, preferably a knighthood.[18] Care, however, had to be taken not to give the impression that money was being squandered, as, by exposing the contrast between the different returns from productive capacity, this expenditure could easily damage employer–employee trust. Large employers thus resided away from the urban area at the end of private roads and commuted to town in their less lavish carriages.

Language was used to signal trust in a number of ways. 'Where the speaker [had] some appreciation of not being believed on his bare statement', he often sought to 'convince others by swearing the truth of it'. Ascribed trust was generated by individuals imitating the speaking style of listeners, and, in voluntary associations, by members adopting network political or business jargon or the trust redolent language of the family. Freemasons were 'brothers' and a newly established lodge the 'daughter' of a 'mother lodge'. Ascribed class trust was denoted through the use of certain words and expressions, 'gig' for 'carriage', 'stole' for 'shawl' and 'serviette' for 'napkin', or the adoption of upper-class, public-school or Oxbridge slang, unintelligible to the lower classes, for example 'hipped' for depressed, 'sapping' for working hard and 'oak' for door. In the wider world, members of the elite sought to use language to shape social norms, constantly using the imagery of 'caring', 'altruism' and 'empathy' in social policy discourse. Labels were attached to the various working-class divisions that clearly denoted their trustworthiness – the 'respectable poor', 'roughs', the 'residuum' and the 'submerged tenth'. It also seems likely that there existed class and kin linguistic codes learnt in childhood that generated kin and class trust, but limited inter-class socialisation. In close-knit working-class family units, with shared assumptions, histories and interests, the code was probably highly restricted with a limited range of syntactic alternatives, a narrow lexis and a strong metaphoric element. Between middle-class kin, on the other hand, a more elaborated code appears to have been used, involving more straightforward discourse and containing little unarticulated or implicit meaning.[19]

Further trust generators

Miscellaneous methods of raising intra-class trust included social sanctions, the exchange of reciprocal gifts, the building of reputations, and social interaction in formal and informal networks. Middle-class sanctions for immoral behaviour were designed to punish the offender and to issue 'a warning to others'. The sanctions ranged from the 'cut', the failure of colleagues to acknowledge the offender's presence, to total 'expulsion from unspotted society', and could carry a high psychological cost. The miscreant was 'often cowed and crushed ... to stand solitary and alone, destitute of friends, avoided and scorned, none to sympathise with or to sustain him – it is a fearful doom'.[20]

Among the middle classes there was a constant exchange of gifts. Their form varied. In trading circles, popular presents included the business meal, price discounts, credit, contract completion guarantees given to employers of colleagues, loans of money and tools, the provision of jobs for relatives or friends, and letters of introduction, which facilitated trust between the recipient and the person to whom the letter was addressed. In social circles, they were often ornaments or pictures, which constantly reminded a recipient and others of his trust relationship with the giver, and beverages and foodstuffs, which incorporated signals of sociability and permitted easy reciprocity in the form of an invitation to consume or drink the offering.[21]

Social gifts were generally inefficient, in that they were not goods or services that the recipient would have preferred and had little resale value. Such inefficiency deterred 'gift collectors', those who would accept offerings with no intention of reciprocating or entering into a trust relationship, and, in some cases, was related to the social norms of the gift. On the birth of a child, for instance, it was the custom for fathers to distribute cigars. Gift inefficiency also permitted the form of the present to carry additional messages regarding the giver and his view of the receiver, which generated more trust, and the type of relationship that he wished to establish. The books of poetry increasingly given to lovers as the century progressed, for example, incorporated signals regarding the giver's intellect and sophistication, his estimation of the intellect/sophistication of the recipient, and, if the poetry was of a particularly romantic nature, the kind of relationship that he wished to form. Bonding power could be further increased by an expression of the reasons for presenting the gift. The 'principle of good nature and compassion' that prompted the father of Thomas Turner, a Sussex shopkeeper, to give him a small present, for example, was regarded by Turner 'as a thing of greater value than ... the worth of the present'.[22]

The actual size of the gifts exchanged, the timing of gift giving and the manner of presentation were all determined by social norms. Those norms associated with gift size related to the resources of the giver and the needs of the recipient. Where giver and recipient possessed similar resources, it was generally regarded as important that the presents exchanged were of equal value, particularly in the early stages of the relationship. Thomas Turner, for example, obsessively recorded the cash value of the gifts he received and gave, in July 1755 taking care to reciprocate a present of two carp with '1lb sugar and 6 fish hooks, value about 9d'.[23] Conversely, if the donor and receiver had imbalanced means, asymmetry of gift size was less important, with the bonding power of the exchange laying in the reciprocity rather than the size of the offering. The fact that a poor person received from a richer partner a gift more expensive than the one he gave was not significant, indicating neither levels of trustworthiness nor power.

As regards timing, reciprocity was generally delayed, though again tended to be more rapid in the early stages of a relationship. Many presents were given at set times – at holidays, for example Christmas or New Year, or to mark important stages in the recipient's life cycle, such as birthdays or marriages. Such gifts derived additional meaning and bonding power from the occasion celebrated, and were particularly useful in the maintenance of mature trust relationships. Failure to reciprocate inevitably created distrust. In 1800, the Norfolk parson John Woodeforde wrote despairingly of a neighbour that he was ' merely interested for himself . . . he never makes any kind of return for the same, not even the smallest present to my person'. Equal care had to be taken when presenting the gift. The donor was advised to avoid 'clog[ging] his grant with disagreeable conditions', delivering 'a pompous harangue concerning what he was about to do', making the recipient 'feel that he is a slave' until he reciprocated, and, if the gift was a future action, promising more than he intended to perform. To advertise his generosity, where possible, he was to present the gift in the company of others, and never 'lose an opportunity of becoming the historian of his own good deeds'.[24]

The importance of reputation was well known in early nineteenth-century Britain. It was generally acknowledged that there was 'no securing or accomplishing anything without reputation – the confidence of fellows'. A good character facilitated the formation of trust relationships, enabled an individual to gain access to and obtain the benefits of informal and formal networks, and could determine the outcome of court proceedings. Although legally irrelevant, both criminal and civil trials to a great extent revolved around assessments of character. Its loss, on the other hand, could have catastrophic and long-term affects. The person would 'always be liable to suspicion', and would increase his chances of being the victim of opportunism, as 'others will have the boldness to pilfer on the presumption that [if caught, the victim] will be understood to be the thief' and their own good character would remain untarnished. Reputation was most fragile at the start of a career, but then gradually took 'root and [became] established on a solid foundation of good conduct and success'. It was thus important for those at the start of their business lifes to devote time and energy to building and protecting their name. Later, they could take a more relaxed approach and even act opportunistically, as, by then, their reputation would be so strong that 'if anything dishonourable were to be said [about them], it would not be believed; [indeed] it would be laughed at by all who know them'.[25] Such a reaction would also discourage people making accusations, since by doing so they would run the risk of damaging their own good character.

To obtain a good reputation, the young had to behave honourably (or at least appear to do so), associate with the trustworthy, promote their qualities to others and protect their name when it was threatened by true or false accusations. As 'a man is known by the company he keeps', the young were advised to form relationships only 'with persons as . . . honestly disposed as [themselves]' or who had 'property to preserve and characters to endanger', and to avoid even minor interaction with the dishonest, as 'speaking to a certain person or . . . exchanging cards [can] sometimes be most injurious'. Association with the trustworthy would enable them to free ride on the other person's reputation, cause them to assimilate his personal trust norms, and reduced the likelihood that they would act dishonestly, since, wishing to maintain their reputations, both parties would act as ' a mutual check on [the] other'. Promotion of an individual's trust qualities could be undertaken by the person concerned or by his friends, one of the reciprocal gifts of trust relationships often being an understanding that each party would 'hawk the good qualities' of the other 'in all companies, . . . bring back word of all that has been said', and defend them when their honesty was queried. Those who advertised themselves and used a 'little varnishing and daubing, a little puffing and quacking', however, ran the risk of engendering distrust, excessive puffery providing 'the strongest proof of . . . vanity, conceit and folly'.[26]

Reputation had to be protected not only against true but also false accusations. For the young, there was a danger that someone would 'malignantly circulate a lie' or 'jestingly or thoughtlessly direct the shaft of calumny'. Such behaviour was generally regarded as unacceptable, 'no less venal . . . [than] stealing money and goods', and perpetuators, if discovered, ran the risk of damaging their own good names. Nonetheless, false as well as true accusations continued to be made and victims often had little option but to defend themselves. In the eighteenth and early nineteenth centuries and particularly among the landed gentry, defence often involved the duel, which discouraged false accusations and reaffirmed the masculine trust reputations of the duellists. From the mid-1750s, however, this method of defending one's honour became less popular. Clerics attacked it, claiming that it was against Christian doctrine, and the new urban elite argued that duellists' immunity from the law damaged the authority of government. It also fell foul of the new code of politeness, in which honour was synonymous with virtue; the reformed ideal of masculinity, which stressed sensitivity and refinement; and a growing public intolerance of violence.[27]

Reputation was thus generally protected by other means. Those who were slandered demanded that the accuser retract his allegation, revealed to others the actual or supposed self-interested reasons behind the smear, or destroyed by fair means or foul the reputation of the culprit and thus reduced the credence of his allegations. Others retaliated by damaging the reputation of the accuser's family, encouraging friends to exclude him from their networks, taking action that would affect his livelihood or by seeking legal redress. No action was taken only if the slanderer had 'no influence; [and] what he has said will do . . . no harm' or if he was well established and defence would fail and further damage the accused's own reputation.[28]

Social interaction occurred in religious, political, philanthropic, sporting and other formal associations, discussed elsewhere in the book, and in informal networks. Outside these spheres, individuals sought to protect themselves from opportunism by restricting their interaction with others, a practice which 'violate[d] every good feeling' and did much to depress social capital. A German visitor to England in 1832, for example, found that its inhabitants possessed 'a haughty aversion . . . to addressing unknown parties', and, that if an attempt were made to 'address them, they receive it with an air of insult'. To further protect themselves from moral hazard and low-value associations, many followed the etiquette of relationship formation, which determined that the process should comprise three stages. The first was the introduction, without which there could be no conversation. The introducer, known and trusted by both parties, 'certif[ied] to each the respectability of the other' and provided some guarantee of trustworthiness.[29] To give added protection, both acquaintances, but particularly the superior partner and women, possessed the right of recognition, the option of renewing the acquaintanship at the next meeting. If this did not occur, then the other party, gentleman or inferior was expected to keep his distance.

The introduction was followed by an exchange of cards or calls. To indicate their interest in advancing the association, a person either left his calling card, that is gave the card to the new acquaintance's servant, or paid a proper call, which was then reciprocated. The practice enabled those in relationships to 'govern and determine their acquaintances and intimacies', the association ending when one partner no longer called or left cards, and gave some guarantee that each party possessed affluence and ascribed trust, as calling consumed a great deal of time, which was available only to the wealthy. It also allowed each associate to monitor the other's house, furnishings and behaviour and thus further determine their class and resources, and, as the calls and cards acted as gifts, helped to generate trust. As with all gift giving, the timing of the calls and delivery of cards was crucial. The social superior, had the right to make the first call or card drop, and, if both were social equals, age and civil condition determined precedence. This first call/card delivery had to be returned promptly within a few days. Thereafter, the amount of time that elapsed between calls/cards was dependent on the intimacy of the relationship, though at least one call or card delivery had to be made each season.

If one of the acquaintances wished the association to move onto the next level of familiarity, an invitation to a domestic or non-domestic entertainment was made. Invitations were sent out well ahead of the event and guests gave a prompt reply, attributing a refusal to a conflicting engagement in order to avoid giving trust-damaging offence. Two consecutive refusals generally indicated that the other party did not wish the relationship to advance. Domestic entertainments included the ball, at which 'dancing alone is the amusement'; the rout, which comprised 'a crowd of persons in full dress assembled to pay their respects to the lady of the house' and to which, to avoid 'tedium', there may be the 'occasional introduction of music and dancing'; dinner parties, card parties and conversaziones, at which the guests discussed serious issues, such as literature, art and politics; and the musical evening, where those invited participated in music making. The mistress of the house, meanwhile, called on friends; attended 'at homes', small tea parties; became part of informal card clubs at which bridge was usually played; or, in rural areas, went on walks in the countryside, during which berries or mushrooms were picked. Each gathering served a specific group, thus maximising the benefits of networking, and had an explicit trust-building role.[30] Balls were for the young and for the generation and maintenance of weak relationships, particularly romantic liaisons; routs were for older guests and created weak to mild trust; card parties, dinner parties, conversaziones and musical evenings were designed to foster and sustain strong bonds; and 'at homes' and so on facilitated female companionship. The friendships made at such gatherings often eased access to formal networks, whilst the connections made at voluntary associations sometimes led to invitations to domestic get-togethers.

The most important assembly was the dinner party, which in middle-rank households developed from the light supper at the end of the eighteenth century, and, by 1830, was 'particularly in vogue amongst the higher classes'.[31] The parties served various trust functions. They first promoted fraternisation amongst the guests, in particularly between couples. Wives of those in a trust relationship were given the opportunity to form parallel bonds that supported and monitored the male union, and to determine and report back to their husbands their views of the trustworthiness of their colleagues. Their other halves, in turn, were able to judge whether colleagues' spouses were likely to prove an advantage or a hindrance to their competence.

To encourage sociability, hostesses were advised to invite approximately ten to 12 guests, as 'a very large party is not likely to be so lively and sociable as one of moderate size ... when a table is very long, the conversation ... at one end must be lost at the other'. Likewise, it was recommended that alcoholic drink should be allowed to flow liberally, the room to contain 'the works of the poet, the dramatist, the novelist and the traveller' to 'afford topics for ... transitory conversation', and that the seating plan should mix guests by gender, age and personality, so that the 'conversation may be as varied as the party, uniting the sense and experience of age with the vivacity and originality of youth'. Guests were to be those who could provide high networking returns, plus individuals who possessed the looks or talent to attract such people or who could provide charming or witty conversation. Occasionally, high value guests would be excluded if 'their general behaviour is reserved, distant and repelling ... [and they] check the freedom of conversation, restrain the buoyancy of joyous feelings and ... by a look or word cast a chilling influence'. To prevent distrust, 'those ... who are known to be disagreeable to each other' were to be invited to separate dinners; the dining room had to be harmoniously decorated, with plants and flowers blending 'in colour with one another and with the furniture'; and, if the conversation appeared 'likely to turn upon subjects known to be unpleasant to any of their visitors', the host was urged to 'skillfully' alter its direction. To permit gender networking, after the meal, the ladies withdrew, and, to maintain the value of the information exchanged, it was generally understood that 'what one hears or sees at a party is as confidential as what one hears or sees in a Masonic lodge and woe unto him who blabs!'[32]

Dinner parties, second, created trust between the host and his guests. The dinner acted as a gift, made more powerful by the fact that it occurred in the family home, which was reciprocated by the guests' gifts – their agreement to attend and usually a small present given to the host or hostess. The meal also allowed the party giver to demonstrate to his visitors his wealth and status and the related trustworthiness through the food and drink served, the etiquette observed, and the house and room in which the party took place. The US Ambassador in 1861 noted that 'dinners must be just so, ... the plate of silver, the wines of the same quality and growth, not because each person takes pleasure in the display, but because everybody else does the same thing'.[33]

Outside the home, interaction occurred in the theatre, the concert hall, the art gallery, the museum and at public dances. Here, trust relationships were formed and maintained and acquaintanceships made that facilitated access to closed formal networks and domestic informal sociability. In the case of the theatre, middle-class attendance was relatively rare until the 1850s and 1860s. Theatres were associated with drunkenness and prostitution, and plays were believed to inflame the passions and to be an insincere form of entertainment based wholly on pretence. Thereafter, middle-class audiences increased, as an interest in the performing arts and culture became a sign of respectability and therefore trustworthiness. Theatre-goers, nevertheless, continued to be concerned at the insincerity of the dramatic form, demanding, for example, that actors be dressed in clothing that accurately reflected the characters of the people they played and the time period depicted.[34]

Cultural events raised social capital in other ways. The ability to spare the time to attend a theatre or concert and pay the high entrance fee demonstrated patrons' affluence trust, which could additionally be signalled through dress, the manner of arrival and the purchase of expensive programmes. The theatre and concert hall kept people from 'the casinos and the gin palaces', and the melodramatic play provided a release from 'respectable' behaviour, allowing the audience to savour forbidden emotions, which ultimately strengthened their adherence to moral norms. Plays also provided 'useful moral lessons ... implant[ing] ... and foster[ing] ... the seeds and energies of moral good'; if based on local events, could generate town trust; and often demonstrated the strength of sanctions. The actions of villains were usually motivated by a desire to revenge themselves against those who had acted opportunistically and caused their families to be 'cast asunder'. Contemporary paintings, meanwhile, often incorporated moral messages, and it was believed that art 'softened' 'angry and unsocial feelings' and that portraits of national and local worthies generated national pride and self-confidence and provided an 'incentive ... to noble actions [and] good conduct'. Museums, again, promoted national identity and acted as 'antidotes to brutality and vice'.[35]

To maximise networking returns, access to these places of entertainment was restricted. To associate with those who patronised the theatre, concert hall or gallery, an individual had to be available in the early evening, or, in the case of galleries, weekdays and saturdays, be able to afford the high ticket prices and associated costs, and possess a degree of social competence. As regards public concerts, even greater exclusivity was assured through the establishment of sub-scription societies, which had a limited membership and a substantial annual fee that covered the cost of attending all of the forthcoming season's perfor-mances.[36] Ticket prices were also used to ensure segregation within the concert hall or theatre. The bourgeoisie were generally to be found in the stalls, and those able to afford to sit in a box could use separate entrances and socialise during intermissions in special areas.

Intra-class distrust

Although succeeding in generating general social capital, the above stratagems failed to prevent all distrust. The petty bourgeoisie had little in common with the elite, who were riven by political and religious divisions that bred dislike and even hatred. Splits were intensified by dissimilar educational backgrounds; membership of different formal networks, many of which restricted access to those who supported a particular party or professed a certain faith; business competition; and migration to the suburbs, where small religious and political enclaves grew up. Other divisions were founded on kinship – with distrust between individual families arising from past interactions; disparities of wealth – the rich being suspicious of their less wealthy neighbours; occupation – the various economic sectors often having divergent interests; leisure – Conservat-ive society favouring the hunting, shooting and racing world of the aristocracy, whereas Liberals preferred rational recreations, such as attendance at lectures and churchgoing; and social lineage. The landowners who had established the first mills in urban towns believed themselves to be superior to the early indus-trialists, who, in turn, were disdainful of those who enriched themselves at a later date. General intra-class trust was further dissipated by the reduced popular-ity of the town house, which, with its communal garden and proximity to the urban amenities, promoted far greater social interaction than the suburban villa, which generally had enclosed private grounds, and, a distance from the nearest town, required most journeys to be undertaken by carriage.[37]

Groups that particularly distrusted each other were the urban and rural elites, 'the proprietor of land' regarding 'those engaged in manufacture with an eye of jealousy and distrust', and the upper middle class/old petit bourgeois and the new and burgeoning army of white-collar workers. One of the reasons for the urban elite's distrust of the landed aristocracy, particularly after the French Revolution, was the latter's louche morals, which many believed had a damaging influence on the moral norms of the lower orders and could provoke social unrest. The upper middle class/old petit bourgeois, meanwhile, were convinced that white-collar workers were inherently dishonest, and, through their imitation of dress and manners, posed a threat to upper middle class reputations. Great care, however, was taken to maintain good relations.[38] To gain the trust benefits of public service and committee membership, the elite needed the support of rank and file association and party members. Likewise, lacking the money to fulfil their obligations to the community and thus maintain the social contract, they had to rely on such people to fund their charitable associations and to provide poor law and council finance.

Over time, these middle-class divisions became less important, though the rate at which this occurred varied from town to town and depended on a multiplicity of factors, such as the nature of the urban economy, the size of the elite and the structure of local government. Explanations for the healing of the various rifts include the diminution of religious and political distrust discussed later in the book, the growth in joint business dealings, greater inter-marriage, the increase in the number of formal networks that were open to all, the adoption of similar leisure activities, and, from the 1880s and 1890s, a shared public school/Oxbridge education. Trust between the urban and rural elites was facilitated by the introduction of social and cultural attributes other than birth as criteria of gentility, the purchase by businessmen of landed estates, and urban demands for water, building land and places to deposit sewage, which encouraged the establishment of co-operative relationships with landowners.[39]

Conclusion

To a great extent, the middle class was a closed society. Those outside the class had great difficulty gaining the confidence of its members. Not only had they no ascribed trust, but they also lacked sufficient funds to purchase the correct clothes, household objects and gifts, and to attend middle-class cultural events. Moreover, they were information poor. Although etiquette manuals provided some indication as to how trust relations were generated, class outsiders had no understanding of the deeper nuances of etiquette, dress or social behaviour. On the other hand, those born and bred in privileged circumstances were fluent in the trust language of the class and thus had access to its resources. Provided that they followed its code of politeness, participated in social events and adopted a respectable way of life, they would be regarded as honest individuals. Some, however, had a greater chance of being trusted than others. Those who were personable and extrovert, conformist and possessed the correct facial and skull features had a higher probability of being regarded as people of integrity than the introverted, the rebellious, and those with few social skills and the 'wrong' faces or heads. More significantly, the powerful and rich could gain more trust more easily than their less well-off colleagues, being able to afford the correct wardrobes, household objects, gifts and domestic entertainments. Trust, as will be seen in later chapters, was thus in many ways merely another tool of those with pecuniary and social power that they used to make themselves still more powerful.

The adoption of the various indicators of trust, of course, did not necessarily mean that a person was not deceitful. The signals could be and were faked. Such hypocrisy, however, was generally tolerated. It was usually innocuous and most people had no wish to disturb the trust myth, that their society possessed high levels of integrity. As again will be discussed later in the book, the support of this myth was a crucial goal of communities and governments who were well aware that, without it, social and business intercourse and the concomitant bene-fits would diminish. Only where behaviour was socially damaging and threat-ened the myth was it punished. Although even then, if it was known only to members of the culprit's social circle or family, the circle/family would some-times turn a 'blind eye', conscious that sanctions would draw the attention of others to the behaviour and that their association with the reprobate would damage their own reputations.

2 Working-class and inter-class trust

Working-class trust is discussed throughout the book. Chapters 3 and 4 examine the somewhat limited involvement of the poor in formal networks, Chapter 8 looks at the trust that existed within families and Chapter 10 investigates the relationship between workers and employers. This chapter concentrates on two general ways of raising confidence – the adoption of norms and the membership of a variety of informal and formal associations. The first section describes how workers followed and signalled their adoption of either non-respectable or respectable norms and became involved in neighbourhood networks. These comprised most of the families living in a community, were almost wholly managed by women and generated trust through the exchange of gifts. Their strength largely depended on the presence of competing kinship loyalties and levels of residential mobility and prosperity. The second section looks at other working-class associations: leisure and employment networks and the friendly society and the trade union. All generated trust, but could equally breed division and disunity. The final part of the chapter discusses class antagonism. Until mid-century, the relationship between the working and middle classes was often acrimonious. Thereafter, the sustained economic upswing and various other factors inaugurated a period of relative social peace.

Personal and community trust

Personal trust reputations among the non-respectable working class were generated in communities and by individuals following neighbourhood norms of trustworthiness. These were exclusive to the community and were often the reverse of middle-class norms – those who failed to frequent pubs, for example, were regarded with suspicion. Trust reputations were closely guarded as they affected the individual and his family's prosperity, in particular their ability to obtain credit and neighbourhood gifts. Any insinuations as to one's lack of honesty that had been made in public were therefore challenged, and disturbances and fights were common, with the aggrieved party continuing to defend himself until his accuser retracted his words or compensated him.[1]

A proportion of the working class sought to conform to the middle-class norms of self-sufficiency, economic continence and moral rectitude and attain a 'respectable' reputation. The adoption of such norms generated middle-class approval and trust, as a 'respectable' working man could be expected to be honest and was unlikely to find himself in financial straits and thus tempted to act immorally. For the respectable, such trust could reap large benefits, including heightened employment opportunities, access to charitable funds and entry to middle-class networks, and, if the individual valued middle-class respect, high self-esteem. On the other hand, such people were distrusted by the non-respectable and were often unable to participate in neighbourhood exchange networks. The privacy norms of respectable behaviour limited interaction with neighbours and the devotion of a large part of their earnings to the maintenance of their status meant that they lacked the means to give and reciprocate gifts. They thus obtained little help from neighbours, and may have been subject to sanctions if their non-participation was interpreted as an attempt to damage the network.[2]

Respectability was signalled by dress, home furnishings and leisure activities, all of which were pale imitations of middle-class practices and thus engendered middle-class appreciation and trust. Dress had to be clean, sober and of reasonable quality, and was particularly used as an indicator of respectability at Sunday church services and on other occasions when the middle class or fellow members of the respectable working class were likely to be present. Home furnishing signals were largely displayed in the front room or parlour, where guests were entertained and which was visible to those who passed the house. A good mahogany clock bespoke 'a considerable degree of regularity and providence', while sufficient cupboards or shelves indicated a desire for orderliness. Furniture was of good quality, often large and brash to increase the power of the signal, and well-dusted. The room itself was bright, ordered and tidy. Respectable amusements comprised activities that involved little contact with 'reckless, drinking, cowardly or dishonest neighbours', which could threaten status. Communal day trips and outings were popular, as were memberships of associations that promoted self-sufficiency, such as friendly societies and trade unions.[3]

The proportion of the working class that became 'respectable' is the subject of dispute. Some believe that respectable values and behaviour were found at all levels of the working-class and that they were an indigenous part of working-class culture. Others suggest that they were largely ignored by all but the skilled, who had little need of neighbourhood gifts and had most to gain from middle class trust. The confusion may arise from the tendency of some working men to adopt false respectability, taking on the behaviour and attributes of the respectable only on those rare occasions when they were in the company of the middle class. They could thus reap the benefits of middle-class trust, whilst retaining neighbourhood trust. In some cases, no doubt some members of the middle class were well aware of this role-playing. To maintain the trust of their colleagues, the pseudo-respectable often indicated that they were play-acting through subtle use of sullenness, irony or sarcasm, signals that were probably picked up by some of those they wished to impress. Victims, however, probably dismissed these signs, believing that pseudo trust by facilitating interaction was better than no trust at all.[4]

Neighbourhood trust involved those attachments that existed between the inhabitants of a particular geographical area and was based on shared characteristics and the reciprocal exchange of gifts. Residents also developed an identification with their local communities, linking their conception of self with their perceptions of their neighbourhood. Arising from common customs and a shared knowledge of past events, the identification contributed to resident self-confidence and generated a low level of trust for all community members whether or not they were personally known to them. As the social commentator Richard Parkinson wrote, 'though the name and the occupation of the individual might be unknown altogether, passing one's door at wonted hours, from meal to work . . . was of itself a sufficient testimony of character'.[5]

The level of neighbourhood trust generated and the general behaviour of residents, in turn, determined the community's trust reputation, non-residents' appreciation of the trustworthiness of inhabitants. In working-class areas, both trust levels and reputation were crucial to the living standards of residents. High trust and mutual aid would reduce the likelihood that they would fall into destitution, and a good neighbourhood reputation, on which they could free ride, would affect their personal standings and the way they were treated by other inhabitants of the town. Those who lived in streets with a poor reputation, for example, could have difficulty obtaining employment, credit at local shops and access to extra-neighbourhood networks.[6] Moreover, current reputation could influence the future standing and trust levels of an area. A street that possessed a good character would attract those who prized reciprocity and had the means to become involved in exchange networks and would thus retain or even improve its status.

The norms of reciprocal exchange and general behaviour were largely laid down and policed by women. An important gift was that of information, which was provided during gossiping sessions. Gossiping, additionally, helped to build strong relations between the participants and between the gossipers and those they talked about, and, involving some self-congratulation, increased self-confidence. Excessive gossiping, however, was sanctioned, as it was believed to lead to idling and thus to weaken kin trust and to involve the exchange of untruths, which would damage neighbourhood trust and negatively affect the community's reputation for trustworthiness. Other gifts included small sums of money, often lent for a few days, pawnable items, domestic paraphernalia, such as linens and clothing, and the completion of tasks. Neighbours, for instance, would care for the children of women giving birth or working full-time, nurse or complete the household duties of the sick, shop for the elderly and lay out the dead. In Manchester in the 1850s it was reported that 'factory operatives are almost invariably kind to each other in distress . . . [and] often pinch themselves to relieve the pressing wants of a neighbour'. The timing of reciprocation varied, though tended to be rapid during downturns, and, if a recipient was unable to return a gift, other members of the community would perform the task on her behalf. The recipient, however, would normally be expected to reciprocate in some way and at some later date to a further community member, and, if this did not occur, sanctions would be applied, and, in the last resort, the individual would be expelled from the network. Sanctions for non-reciprocation and behaviour that damaged a neighbourhood's trust levels or reputation included gossip, designed to injure the individual's personal reputation, and insults, attacks on his or her self-esteem. If these proved unsuccessful or an individual had behaved in a manner that posed a particular threat to a street's local standing or mutual trust, the perpetuator was subjected to 'rough music', a physical beating given by local youths or males. Victims of this form of punishment, which acted as a warning to others, included thieves, wife beaters, adulterers and paedophiles.[7]

The only exception to the norm of reciprocity were the old and widows, who were unable and were not expected to fully reciprocate.[8] The elderly were excluded from the ruling because of their past gifts to the community, and widows were exempted as there was a fear that, if they failed to receive aid, they would resort to begging, prostitution or the poor law and thus damage the reputation of the whole neighbourhood. Societies' sympathy for the elderly and those who had lost husbands also ensured that the neighbours who gave help gained a reputation premium. Generally, the non-reciprocity was concealed by the elderly and the widowed making very minor recompense, which, though failing to repay the help received, gave the impression of reciprocity. These 'mock' gifts maintained the pride and self-confidence of recipients, prevented givers gaining a reputation as an 'easy touch' and minimised the danger that non-reciprocation by these groups would be used as a precedent by others or encourage non-reciprocators to move into the community.

Neighbourhood trust levels and reputations were dependent on the presence of kinship loyalties, which could crowd out community trust, residential mobility and prosperity. Residential mobility, the movement of people to other neighbourhoods within the same or in another town, disrupted exchange and trust relationships in the area of departure, with similar relations taking time to develop in the place of destination. Indeed, where movement was frequent, many may not even have bothered to enter trust and exchange networks, as the costs involved will have exceeded likely rewards. The overall affect of migration on neighbourhood trust, however, was probably relatively minor. Most of those who relocated moved short distances. The reputation of those who moved to adjacent neighbourhoods probably travelled with them, and it seems likely that even those streets with high turnovers had exchange networks composed of permanent residents, and that these may have given new entrants limited membership, allowing them to reap low cost benefits. Garroch's study of Paris also suggests that neighbourhood trust formed far more rapidly than sometimes assumed and was more dependent on personality, behaviour and industriousness than on long residence and familiarity with personal histories.[9]

As regards the prosperity of residents, during downturns, all neighbourhoods experienced a fall in trust. Poverty increased needs, but reduced the ability of networks to meet these new demands, non-reciprocation became more common, and petty crime levels soared. In normal times, those streets that contained a large proportion of poor or respectable residents also possessed weak networks. Both groups lacked the means to give and reciprocate and the respectable often preferred to enter exchange networks composed of people like themselves. [10] These offered more appropriate and less costly gifts, and, because the respectable were geographically scattered, extended over several neighbourhoods.

From mid-century, neighbourhood trust weakened, the result of changes in the built environment, middle-class attempts to dissipate such trust, the arrival of a more family-orientated lifestyle, and the rise in real incomes and greater state social provision, which reduced the need for reciprocal exchange. Until the 1850s, working-class housing was located in enclosed courts, culs de sac and alleys, and residents could thus monitor every aspect of their neighbours' lives and accurately assess trustworthiness and note the possession of characteristics similar to their own. There was also much sharing of hallways, toilets and sculleries, which again permitted the testing of co-operativeness and trustworthiness. This cellular pattern then gave way to an open and encapsulated layout. Houses possessed their own private yards and were laid out in streets and monitoring became more difficult, inevitably weakening trust. [11]

At the same time, the middle class sought to dilute community loyalties. The crowd action that enabled the working class to ensure the fair operation of the social contract (the reciprocal relationship between rulers and the ruled) was highly dependent on the social co-ordination that arose from the operation of exchange networks. A weakening of these associations and a fall in interaction would reduce the power of the working community to protest, enabling the elite and middle class to stretch or breach the contract with equanimity. It was also believed that neighbourhood gifts hindered the development of a work ethic and threatened inherent values of frugality and thrift, which were more likely to halt poverty and immorality than a gift exchange system. To diminish neighbourhood trust, slums were cleared and reliance on exchange networks reduced through the encouragement of working-class respectability, high levels of private charity and, in the North, the lax operation of the poor law. [12]

Other trust generating networks

Leisure

Neighbourhood trust was augmented by common membership of leisure, employment and other networks. At the end of the eighteenth and the start of the nineteenth centuries, the amount of time the working class devoted to leisure fell, reducing the number and breadth of trust relationships formed. In the pre-industrial period, unconstrained by factory hours, people worked at their own pace, taking frequent ad hoc holidays. During their time off, they pursued a range of activities, largely centred around sports and shared meals or parties that involved the exchange of trust strengthening gifts. Sports included cock fighting, bull baiting, fist fights and loosely organised games of cricket and football played on unenclosed fields or on common land adjacent to towns. Communal meals and parties occurred throughout the year and included harvest suppers provided by farmers to those who had helped to bring in the harvest; hunt suppers to reward those whose land the hunt traversed; rent night suppers, held on the evening tenants paid their rents and laid on by the landowner; and beef nights, parties organised by farmers on the night an animal was slaughtered and sold off to neighbours.[13]

With industrialisation, many of these activities disappeared. The increase in working hours reduced the amount of time available for leisure. In the 1820s, a typical working day was 12 hours, six days a week, and many even worked on public and religious holidays. Most workers thus had scarcely two hours per weekday and Sundays for the routine chores of life and recreation. Concurrently, enclosure, building and the denial of footpath rights by landlords caused the amount of land available for sport to diminish, 'operatives ... [becoming] like the Israelites of old, with the promised land before them, but forbidden to enter it'. Although, even where land was available, the low social trust of towns discouraged many, particularly the young, seeking it out; the negotiation of streets beyond one's own neighbourhood often being hazardous, if not downright dangerous.[14]

There were also various middle-class campaigns to eradicate certain leisure pursuits, in particular drinking, gambling, blood sports and prostitution, and to replace these with 'rational' recreations, such as churchgoing and gardening. The groups involved largely sought to raise social trust. It was believed that 'immoral' leisure activities prevented the working classes coming into contact with trust raising religious norms and values, took them away from the morally improving home, and actively encouraged immorality and distrust. It was claimed that gambling violated the spirit of 'fellow feeling', in that it involved 'the obtainment of pleasure at the cost of another's pain', and could lead to debt, which could prompt victims to turn to crime. Non-observance of the Sabbath resulted in 'idleness, fraud, prodigality, swearing, intemperance and other vices'. Blood and violent sports reduced social feeling and created a predisposition to surrender to base passions. Prostitution was associated with crime and led to the corruption of vulnerable men and the break-up of families. And excessive drinking weakened an individual's personal moral norms, reduced family income and prompted violence and criminal activity. The groups also wished to dilute neighbourhood trust, which was partly generated within the local hostelry and the street, and to raise church attendances.[15] Many of the societies were connected to churches and chapels, which hoped to prevent present and future worshippers drifting away to other leisure pursuits and developing non-church trusts. A movement away from a church would weaken the networking and reputation benefits of congregation membership, and, for Ministers, lead to a fall in salary and promotion prospects.

The groups campaigning for 'rational' recreation included the temperance movement, the Sabbattarians, who opposed all activities that occurred on a Sunday, the Owenites, and a variety of societies that wished to outlaw gambling and prostitution. Whatever their impact on working-class leisure pursuits, the groups' activities did much to generate middle-class and intra-class trust among their memberships. The temperance movement united evangelical Christians of all denominations and attracted both the working and middle class, although, at least in the early days, there was much friction between the largely middle-class moderationists and the total abstainers, who were mostly working-class activists. The most important Sabbatarian association was the 1831 Lord's Day Observance Society. This had an annual subscription of 10s per year and a largely middle-class membership, but acquired many working-class supporters through its campaign for the Saturday half holiday and its claim that people would be required to work a seven-day week if Sunday was lost as the day of rest. By mid-century, it had been joined by numerous similar societies, which in 1851 came together to form the Working Men's Lord's Day Rest Association. Having an annual subscription of just 1s. per annum, this attracted more artisans as members, but was again dominated by the middle class. The Owenites, by comparison, had a largely working-class following. The movement believed that making leisure a family affair was crucial to the restructuring of gender relations, which was seen as a necessary preliminary to the establishment of socialism. It was also felt that 'low and debasing practices', such as heavy drinking and blood sports, reinforced upper and middle-class perceptions of the masses as incorrigibly brutish and so undermined the movement's programme of political reform. To promote more family orientated amusements, therefore, social institutions were established, where lectures, concerts, tea parties and dances were organized.[16]

The campaigns of these groups were assisted by the appearance of the new mental illness of moral insanity. During the seventeenth and eighteenth centuries, madness was largely defined as the lack of or the derangement of reasoning. In the early nineteenth century, this definition was expanded to include an absence of morals. In the morally insane, 'the moral and active principles of the mind [were] strangely perverted and depraved; the power of governance [was] lost or greatly impaired; and the individual [was] found to be incapable ... of conducting himself with decency and proprietary'.[17] Symptoms were participation in theft, alcoholic or sexual excess, and it was believed that the illness was hereditary; those who descended into moral degeneration passing their habits of vice onto their children and succeeding generations. Not surprisingly, the appearance of the illness did much to spur on moralists and discourage individuals engaging in depraved behaviour. Following Foucault, it also divided the immoral from the rest of society, both metaphorically and, in some cases, physically. To prevent them creating social disorder or infecting others, many of those diagnosed to be suffering from the ailment were placed in asylums.

The rational recreations promoted included education and religious observance (discussed in Chapter 4), gardening, the use of parks, participation in brass bands, railway excursions, and visits to museums and art galleries. All promoted social interaction, allowed the elite to monitor and control activities, often permitted the inculcation of moral and trust norms, and, in some cases, involved the acquisition of skills, which raised participants' self confidence. Gardening was regarded as a source of physical and moral regeneration. It acted against idleness and extravagance, which could ultimately lead to crime, and kept workers 'away from the public house in the evening'. The result, according to the horticulturist Samuel Broome, was that 'very rarely do you find a man who is fond of flowers taken up for a misdemeanour of any kind'. To encourage the hobby, workers were rented houses with extensive gardens, allotments were provided, which were generally taken up by artisans, horticultural societies were established and annual prizes donated for the best shows of flowers or vegetables, though the latter often promoted dishonesty.[18]

Closely related to gardens were parks, which appeared from mid-century and sought to promote 'friendly conversation with ... neighbours', 'to keep [the working classes] away from the beer house' and to bring 'the inmates of the factory ... in collision with the middle classes' and thus cause 'a kindlier sympathy [to] arise between the two sections of society'. To ensure that they played host to 'sober and rational enjoyment', park users were subject to countless regulations, and, to prevent parks drawing people from the church on Sundays, many activities were banned on that day. In many towns, one of these pursuits was brass band music, another rational recreation. Bands were set up by employers, churches and temperance societies, drew players and audiences away from the public house, and, through the playing of music, dissipated listeners' feelings of alienation.[19]

Other recreations acceptable to the middle classes were sport and excursions. Team sports, such as football, bowls and cricket, were played informally, and, from the 1880s, professionally. By 1890, league cricket was well established and many towns had professional football teams. Participation fostered sociability and co-operation, left little energy for immorality, and raised players' masculine trust reputations and forced them to appreciate the importance of rules and norms. Spectators also socialised and developed town identities, though often cultivated rivalries with fans of opposing teams. Day trips or short holidays at the seaside were made possible by the high and rising real wages and low rail fares. The cost of excursions encouraged visitors to travel in groups and, by the 1860s, it had become the tradition in the summer for all the factories in a town to close down in a particular week and the workers to holiday at the same resort. Visits thus generated kin, neighbourhood and community trust and also geographic ties, as the residents of different towns inevitably met on the beach or at seaside churches. As with middle-class theatre attendance, the holidays acted as a safety valve, helping to ensure moral behaviour in the home environment.[20] Different trust norms operated at the seaside and minor immorality was accepted, though more serious depravity that would have a more damaging affect on trust were still frowned upon and penalised.

The impact the activities of those groups that promoted rational recreation had on social interaction and trust is debatable. Their actions generated a great deal of distrust. Mobs often broke up teetotal lectures, and, in 1855 and 1871–2, government public-house licensing restrictions led to riots. Opposition to these groups, though, again brought people and classes together. In 1855, the National Sunday League was formed to oppose the Sabbatarians' insistence that art galleries and museums should close on Sundays, and anti-temperance campaigners included working men anxious to preserve traditional entertainments, drink sellers, free traders opposed to state regulation and bon viveurs of all classes. As regards the groups' impact on working-class leisure, many of the new rational recreations proved extremely popular and a large number of 'immoral' pursuits disappeared or were less well attended, reducing sociability. Some, however, survived or were replaced by activities that were regarded as equally damaging to trust and moral norms. Pastimes that endured included attendance at the local public house and the civil pageant, discussed later in the book, some blood sports, such as cockfighting and bare-knuckle boxing, walking and promenading, and fairs.[21] A significant new pursuit was the music hall.

Workers walked with friends to and from work and in the evenings. The walk between the workplace and home was particularly leisurely and involved a number of attractions such as street bookmakers, hawkers and ballad singers. After eating and completing their household chores, the young, and, to a lesser extent, the old then again took to the streets to saunter and gossip with their companions, engage in banter and horseplay, flirt with members of the opposite sex and, later in the century, to window shop. Promenading, more formal walks, took place on Saturday evenings and Sunday afternoons. Participants wore their best clothes to signal their respectability and trustworthiness, and paraded at set times along central streets or in parks, occasionally stopping to talk to those they knew. They tended to be older than evening walkers, and, to maximise networking value, each socio-economic group paraded a particular route.[22]

Fairs retained their popularity until mid-century, when they began to disappear, and encouraged much sociability, promoted inter-class trust, though some were venues for burlesques that mocked the local elite, and fostered geographic cooperation. Former residents sometimes returned to a town specifically to attend, and they often included sporting contests between teams of local men and those from neighbouring settlements, which generated intra-town trust and a sense of belonging/identity for both the spectators and the players. To maximise networking returns, activities were generally organised for specific age groups, occupations and genders. Most, for example, had athletic races for young men, sack and other comic races for young ladies, tea-drinking matches for older women, and races for specific tradesmen.[23]

Music halls evolved from the 'free-and-easy', amateur musical entertainments held in public houses, and pub singing rooms, where professional singers entertained drinkers. They largely attracted a working-class audience of all ages and both sexes, though from mid-century the middle class increasingly began to frequent the better halls, and, in the provinces, there appears to have been a slight bias towards the young. Women also often made up a significant part of audiences, in particular unmarried females who attended in large groups made up of workmates, neighbours or family members. To maximise the value of networking, different halls catered for different socio-economic groups and the young tended to sit in the cheaper seats. Moral reformers regarded the halls as 'the very suburbs of hell' and claimed that they had a demoralising affect on the working class. Not only did they sell alcohol, but they opened on Sundays, were the haunts of prostitutes and corrupted the artistic tastes of audiences, making it impossible for them to enjoy more sophisticated moral fare. Not surprisingly, owners disagreed, claiming that only modest amounts of alcohol were consumed, prostitution was unknown, and that 'a good sentimental song' caused 'the heart ... [to] become subdued and ... baser feelings and passions [to] give way to ... sublime thoughts and actions'.[24]

Employment and other networks

Worker trust was formed within firms, friendly societies, trade unions and pressure groups. Inside firms, trust was primarily generated through social interaction, which mostly occurred during breaks; Thomas Wright, an engineer journeyman, in 1867 wrote of 'groups of workmen, who, at mealtime, gather together round the workshop stoves, and, in summer, in favourite places to have a chat'. Further trust was generated through gifts, norms and ritual. The presents exchanged took the form of information and ephemeral and critical life situation gifts. The information largely comprised news on the job market and employer trust reputations. According to Wright, most discussions with fellow workers centred on 'the characteristics ... and ... peculiarities' of bosses, whether they were 'an admirable master' and knew 'a good workman ... and will always pay such a workman well', or whether they were 'a duffer, the pecksniff of trade'. Ephemeral gifts were exchanged to mark milestones in a worker's life, and gained much bonding power from the occasion celebrated. On joining a workshop, a new recruit was expected to buy a round of drinks for his new colleagues 'as a token of his desire to cultivate their friendship and goodwill'. More drinks were bought when he ended his apprenticeship, earned the rank of journeyman, and each time he was promoted or became a father. If a workmate was ill, men would 'pitch into their work in the hardest style in order that they may give (him) a hand', and, during slumps, young single men would often volunteer for redundancy in order to ensure that older men with families retained their jobs.[25]

Norm inculcation occurred during apprenticeship. As part of his training, a workman learnt 'by the precept and example of his mates that he must respect the trade and its written and unwritten rules and that ... he must sacrifice personal interest or private opinion to what the trade has rightly or wrongly ruled is for the general good' and extend 'the hand of friendship to all fellow craftsmen, irrespective of position and appearance'. To ensure that he appreciated his workmates' norm sanctioning power, he was made the butt of 'practical jokes'; sent 'to the most ill-tempered man in the shop ... to ask him for the loan of ... some ... non-existent and impossible tool' or have 'the elbow of his hammer arm' jerked so as to 'cause him to hit his chisel hand'. Ritual highlighted worker closeness and emphasised norms and again occurred at milestones in a worker's life. In engineering workshops, marriage was celebrated by 'ringing in', which involved the groom's workmates banging their hammers on boilers and iron plates as he re-entered the workplace. The end of an apprenticeship, meanwhile, was marked by a variety of ceremonies and usually a speech by the workshop's senior artisan, in which the former apprentice was urged to 'hold out a helping hand to a brother workman in distress', and, in return, promised that he would 'never be in need of a friend'.[26]

The extent to which worker trust developed was dependent on the employees involved and the work undertaken. Those employed in small workshops, completing communal tasks, born locally and possessing similar characteristics and norms, or living in the same neighbourhood and with extra-work network connections will have had relatively high trust. As will those working for 'paternalistic' employers, who provided a large number of opportunities for sociability and whose trust norms will have been imbibed by their workforces. The employment by a manufacturer of the friends and relatives of existing workers also fostered strong attachments, with those who recommended a new recruit signalling the newcomer's trustworthiness to colleagues. Trust, on the other hand, will have been weak in those sectors and businesses that experienced a rapid turnover of staff, and in all firms during the first half of the century when business lifespans were relatively short. Brief worker relationships will have precluded the development of strong loyalties, though the constant movement of employees may have promoted extra-firm attachments. Later, as business lifespans lengthened, the period available for trust generation will have increased; spinners in the 1850s staying with a single employer on average for seven years.[27]

Little trust also existed between artisans and the rest of the working class. Artisans often had different norms and network connections to the non-skilled and unskilled, who, in sectors undergoing technological change, deprived them of their livelihoods. In some places, this distrust seeped into the community. Wright, for instance describes how 'artisan wives hold the wives of labourers to be of a lower social grade and very often will either not neighbour with them at all or else only in a patronizing way'. Similar suspicions existed between other groups or 'sections' of workers. Wright identified 'an educated and ... intelligent section and an uneducated and ignorant section; a political section ... and a non-political section ...; a sober steady saving section and a drunken unsteady and thriftless section; and ... a sectional difference of mode of life and feeling between the regularly and irregularly employed classes'. Between these groups there existed a 'degree of coolness and suspicious watchfulness', an 'antagonism of feeling' and a general 'distrustfulness'.[28]

Away from the working environment, worker attachments were established in local pubs, discussed in Chapter 5; the working men's clubs that began to appear from the 1860s; in 'camping shops', regular but informal meetings of workers, held in a pub or home in which topics of the day were discussed; and in friendly societies, trade unions and pressure groups. Friendly societies provided members with small sickness, unemployment and other benefits in return for a membership fee and were either formed locally or were branches of national affiliated orders. The latter became more common from mid-century, largely because they were better organised and less prone to collapse and they allowed migrating members to transfer their contributions from branch to branch. The societies grew rapidly and it is estimated that by 1850 one in three adult males was a member. Expansion was stimulated by industrialisation and urbanisation, which increased the seriousness and regularity of critical life situations, but caused neighbourhood and kinship networks to weaken and the help needed to survive these crisis to become more scarce. Membership densities thus tended to be relatively high in urban and manufacturing areas and in regions with high levels of migration; migrants having few nearby kin, lacking poor law settlements, and, because of their weak reputations, experiencing high levels of unemployment and finding access to charity and neighbourhood networks problematical. The State, aware of the trust advantages of societies, also encouraged their growth. A 1793 act offered them a rapid and cheap method of recovering funds from defaulting or bankrupt officers and exempted members from removal under the laws of settlement. Subsequent legislation sought to protect their capital stock by promoting actuarial soundness and the investment of funds in Trustee Savings Banks and government loans.[29]

For individual members, joining a society gave them help when it was most needed and some independence from economic forces, which may have increased their self-confidence; access to much useful information, particularly regarding employment opportunities; and trust relationships with other members. These were generally long lasting and therefore strong, as once someone had enrolled with a lodge it was usually disadvantageous, and, as they became older, almost impossible for them to move to another society. Members also acquired respectability and therefore trustworthiness. Society respectability arose from the presence of middle-class patrons, their insurance role, which reduced the possibility of destitution/immorality, their professed rejection of unrespectable behaviour, such as drunkenness, gambling and trade unionism, and their support of the established order. Lodges proclaimed their allegiance to 'Queen and country', sang the national anthem at meetings, publicly celebrated royal birthdays and marriages, and made large contributions to patriotic collections. Ironically, within meetings and away from the prying eye of the everyday world, very unrespectable behaviour often occurred, in particularly the consumption of large amounts of liquor.[30] As with middle-class networks, such conviviality acted as a safety valve and generated masculine trust. To signal their connections with associations and their respectability, members took part in society and civic parades and displayed framed membership certificates in the public areas of their homes.

On a macro level, societies contributed to neighbourhood, kin, geographic and inter-class trust. Friendly society literature promoted duty to the community and family, and a large proportion of association members lived in close proximity to each other. Forty-seven per cent of those who belonged to the Lancaster Lodge of the Unity of Oddfellows, for example, resided in a single council ward. Societies in areas with high levels of short distance out-migration, on the other hand, had a more widely dispersed membership. These societies thus promoted geographic trust (the trust between the inhabitants of towns, regions and counties), which, in regional and national associations, was further fostered by annual meetings, newsletters and fraternal visits from officials belonging to distant lodges. As regards class, members were predominantly labour aristocrats – artisans, tradesmen and skilled factory workers. Many semi-skilled and unskilled workers, though, also joined and most lodges included a handful of people with lower-middle-class occupations.[31] Societies therefore generated ascribed and a degree of inter-class trust. More importantly for the elite, by diminishing members' reliance on neighbourhood networks, they also weakened community bonds and the power of working-class crowd action.

Any trust formed, however, was at least partly offset by the division and disunity generated by the societies. Many clubs had age limits or restricted entry to those involved in particular trades and belonging to certain ethnic groups, and large numbers of working men were effectively barred from membership by their low or irregular earnings. Women members were equally scarce and there were few female-only societies. Women were unable to afford membership fees; until the 1882 Property Act, husbands had a legal right to their wife's society benefits; and females were believed to be less healthy than men and doctors were thus reluctant to agree to treat them at the usual flat society rate. Further friction was generated by attempts by the ill to join groups, people making duplicitous claims and by age differences; large numbers of veteran members, who made excessive use of benefits, could lead to younger colleagues having to pay high fees. Societies also regularly collapsed, leaving former members angry and resentful. Causes included poor organisation, the setting of unfeasibly low subscription rates, embezzlement, and, most commonly, economic downturn.[32]

The trust generated by trade unions was a response to the poor treatment of workers, discussed in Chapter 10. In industrial towns, unionism grew rapidly, particularly in those sectors where employer power was strong and vigorously used. As with friendly societies, trust was generated through the shared goals of members, social interaction and the reciprocal exchange of gifts. Social interaction rose during periods of unrest, and occurred at union meetings and the events, such as marches, organised by the union to signal their unity and power. Gifts took the form of sickness payments and so on, which additionally discouraged members from leaving the union or taking action, such as strike breaking or the acceptance of rates below the union standard, that could lead to their expulsion.

Unions built trust in individual firms and sectors and between sectors and towns. Inter-sectoral trust was generated and is reflected by the financial help given during periods of industrial unrest, and later by the formation of umbrella organisations containing union representatives from a variety of trades. As markets became regional, unions also expanded geographically, promoting the development of geographic loyalties. During strikes, moreover, shared circumstances and interests often created attachments and co-ordinated action between unions based in different towns.[33]

In their campaigns for improved working conditions, union and radical leaders, more ambitiously, also sought to improve moral social norms and generate social capital. Many subscribed to the eighteenth-century belief that commerce was an important moral agent, but believed that many of the ethical and social benefits of business were lost due to the unfair nature of commercial exchanges, in particular those between capital and labour. The radical William Thompson, for example, argued that the more exchanges were based on fairness 'the more man becomes dependent on man, the more his feelings become sympathetic, the more social he becomes, [and] the more benevolent'. This was a view echoed by the Spitalfield weavers, who called for adequate remuneration on the grounds that it was 'necessary to the support of that self-esteem, that honest and manly pride ... which constitutes ... that state of society in which ... the mass of the people can be expected to be virtuous and orderly'.[34]

The amount of trust generated, however, can easily be overstated. Mutual co-operation between unions in different areas rapidly dissipated when industrial relations returned to normal and local issues increased in importance. Many unions actively distrusted each other. Given the conflicting interests of their members, this is hardly surprising. In the early nineteenth century, for instance, members of the Millwright Society greatly distrusted those in engineering associations who were taking their jobs. There was also much distrust within unions. Before the employment of administrators, full-time union officials tended to be chosen for their administrative skills, the possession of which, along with their accumulated experience and ability to advertise their names within the organisation, ensured that many were annually re-elected. Unfortunately, these officials were hostile to strike action; a stance that created much rank and file distrust. Industrial disputes increased their workloads and diminished union finances, on which their own salaries depended, and they had no personal interest in improving working conditions or wages. Such men were also by nature conservative, often passionate believers in the benefits of co-operation and, inundated with administrative tasks, had little time to form trust relationships with their members with whom they often had little in common, being almost universally middle-aged respectable males. Conversely, 'courted and flattered by the middle class', living in 'little villa[s] in middle-class suburb[s]' and having regular face-to-face meetings with employers, many began to develop an identification with and a trust of the capitalist class.[35]

The most important working-class pressure groups were the Chartists and the Owenites. Chartism did much to promote interaction. Supporters socialised at meetings and demonstrations and the political excitement generated by the movement encouraged working men to join discussion societies. It also produced geographic trust, in that it was a national campaign with a common programme and a widely disseminated newspaper press, and advanced intra-class trust. Although some believe that the movement appealed principally to artisans, whose craft status and independence were being eroded by mechanisation, others argue that support was far more uniform. There is further dispute as to whether the campaign was an expression of class-consciousness and thus promoted working-class unity and damaged inter-class trust. Thompson believes that Chartist language was suffused with class imagery and attacks on the tyrannical middle classes and the new capitalist system. Jones, on the other hand, claims that Chartist argument was rather a critique of the existing political system and the aristocratic monopoly of power and thus did little to impair relations with the middle class.[36]

Owenism enjoyed far less support than Chartism. It attracted educated workers and those whose occupations suffered from the oversupply of labour, and had significant memberships only in Birmingham, Glasgow, Manchester and Paisley. Nonetheless, it promoted intra-class socialisation and its ideology had much influence on working-class trust norms. Believing that capitalist competition was inherently evil, the movement envisaged its replacement by an economy based on co-operation, which would unite all social classes and encourage the development of 'moral, social and sympathetic feelings'.[37]

Inter-class trust

In the early part of the century, the middle classes were generally highly suspicious of the lower classes – in Manchester there existed 'a wide gulf between the higher and social orders across which the scowl of hatred banish[ed] the smile of charity and love'. 'Prejudice, mistrust and apprehension' were generated by the perceived rise in crime, the supposed immorality of the working classes, the fact that unskilled males did not conform to the middle-class code of masculinity described later in the book, and 'by the parties being kept apart from each other'. The two classes belonged to dissimilar leisure networks, lived in different areas and worked apart, and there was little social mobility. There was also a fear of revolutionary activity among the poor, which was stoked by the French Revolution and the rise of popular radicalism, Luddism, Chartism and the disturbed industrial relations of the period, and some distrust may have been activated by migration. Incomers may have transferred their dislike of the rural gentry to the urban elite, and some believe that rural authorities, through the withholding of poor relief, may have encouraged the least deferential of their populations to migrate.[38]

From mid-century, it is generally accepted that inter-class trust improved, and, at least until the fourth quarter of the nineteenth century, there was a period of relative social peace. Militant 'independent' working-class political agitation declined, activists sought to reform rather than replace the capitalist system, many becoming supporters of Liberalism and Conservatism, and, as discussed in Chapter 10, labour relations became more cordial. There are numerous explanations for the new consensus. Some argue that it was related to the rise of the labour aristocracy, identified either as skilled and highly paid artisans or as those workers who wielded authority within the workplace, such as pacemaking cotton minders, engineering piecemakers and coal-mining clock weighmen. These aristocrats of labour supposedly assimilated the attitudes and moderate political viewpoint of the elite, which they then imposed on the rest of the working class. The theory, however, has a number of flaws. A labour elite had existed long before the 1850s, many labour aristocrats were actually at the fore-front of radical politics and it is argued that the thesis is based on suspect empirical evidence.[39]

Another explanation is that the transfer of control of the productive process from labour to capital brought about by technological change caused workers to be more dependent on employers as providers of work and to adopt a deferential attitude, which became internalised via paternalism. Through their provision of factory schools, reading rooms, and so on and their patronage of community associations, such as temperance societies and adult education institutes, employers altered the norms, values and beliefs of the working class to the extent that workers began to accept the elite's position of dominance and their own subordinate position as legitimate and morally right. As with the labour aristocracy thesis, however, historians have taken issue with this hypothesis. The empirical evidence on which it is based has been subject to intense criticism, and, as discussed in Chapter 10, not all employers were paternalists, workers were far from submissive, and paternalism itself can equally be interpreted as a reciprocal gift relationship, largely adopted to generate employer–employee trust.[40]

More likely causes for mid-century social peace were the strengthening of the social contract and the trust relations formed between managements and workers discussed in Chapters 6 and 10 respectively, economic and industrial change, and, to a lesser extent, the connections that were established between middle-class liberals and working-class radicals and the growth of the philosophy of sympathy. The sustained economic upswing, caused partly by railway construction, led to lower cyclical unemployment and higher real wage levels and forced radicals to accept that industrialised capitalism was a permanent feature. Rather than seeking to create an alternative order or obtain control over production, workers thus sought to change the system in their favour through gradual and piecemeal reform.[41] At the same time, the greater prosperity provided scope for the liberalisation of upper- and middle-class attitudes and permitted employers to improve their treatment of employees.

The involvement of workers in the reform process had its beginnings in the late 1830s when the first shoots of working-class and middle-class liberal co-operation began to appear. Both liberals and many radicals believed that poverty and distress were ultimately caused by the aristocratic control of Parliament and the passage of laws that benefited the landowning elite and their allies, but were detrimental to the urban industrial populace. Believing that reform would eliminate most social problems, some of the working class threw their weight behind the various middle-class pressure groups, their help being more than welcomed by the organisers, who generally adopted a mass platform, that is demonstrations and petitions. Any bonds created, however, were weakened by the resulting Act, which, as discussed later, actually reduced the number of working-class voters and was not followed by further expansion of the franchise as had been promised. Nonetheless, there was some working-class involvement in the Anti-Poor Law movement of 1837–8 and some support of the Anti-Corn Law League.[42]

The philosophy of sympathy advocated the cultivation of the human capacity to make links with others based on feelings and concern. Once a connection had been made, the sympathy would be reciprocated and a trusting relationship formed, with each partner avoiding 'whatever [would] give ... pain or be offensive' to the other party and adopting his ' tastes, sympathies or aversions'. The ideology caused many of the middle class to accept that they shared a common humanity with the poor, which generated ascribed trust, and encouraged some to form links with the less advantaged and to join humanitarian campaigns, which again fostered trust. The movements included the campaigns against capital punishment and in favour of prison and factory reform, examined later, and the campaign against slavery. The latter, though having no direct influence on domestic social relations, was nevertheless partly initiated by a desire to raise trust. Many nonconformist members believed that the unethical nature of the trade weakened domestic morals and would damage both their own and the nation's trust relationship with God.[43]

Conclusion

If anything, trust was more important to the working class than their middle-class counterparts. Their very survival depended on help from neighbours, work-mates, friends and kin and they thus developed strong ties with these groups within neighbourhood, leisure and work networks and in the informal family networks discussed in Chapter 8. Their successful creation of social capital, however, fuelled inter-class distrust. The middle class feared that the stronger bonds would increase the effectiveness of crowd action and stoke social and industrial unrest. There was also a belief that the networks in which the trust was generated produced externalities in the form of crime and lax moral norms, which weakened the social capital of the whole community. The elite thus sought to form stronger bonds of trust with the lower orders, and to establish new working-class leisure networks, which promoted more moral norms and where discontent with the capitalist system was less likely to ferment. Success, however, was only achieved in the 1850s when improvements in the economy, the perceived permanence of the capitalist system, better labour relations, the stronger social contract and the doctrine of sympathy inaugurated a new era of co-operation and social peace.

3 Formal networks

The first half of the nineteenth century was an 'age of societies', particularly in the new urban towns, which possessed the necessary critical mass of people from which associations could draw their members and had low levels of trust. In 1861, the *Bolton Chronicle*, the local newspaper of the Lancashire town of Bolton, remarked that there 'there are now more public meetings held and there is more public business transacted in a week than in a month when this [newspaper] was first published [in 1823]'. The rate of growth is difficult to determine. Most formal networks were ephemeral and left little trace of their existence. Some guide as to numbers, though, can be gained from references to networks in the local press. In Bolton, the various local newspapers mention 277 separate societies during 1823–49 and 417 during 1850–70. The proliferation of associations, to some extent, was an extension of the eighteenth-century expansion of informal networks. Able to fulfil the rising trust needs of the emergent industrial economy, however, these failed to meet the far greater requirements of full industrialisation. They were thus gradually superseded by formal societies, which produced more trust more efficiently by ensuring regular interaction and comprising larger and more diverse memberships.[1]

Roughly six types of voluntary association existed – those devoted to religious worship, cultural and scientific associations, business and property groups, political societies, philanthropic associations, and public service institutions, such as councils and Poor Law Commissions. Their formation was stimulated by one-off crises, such as epidemics, riots or economic slumps; the need to solve long term problems, for example crime or disease; fashion and the 'copy cat' effect, with the establishment of one society often promoting the formation of others in the same or in other towns; visiting public speakers, who frequently caused societies to be formed in their wake; the evangelical revival; and individual self-interest. To increase their private businesses, professional musicians often set up music groups, booksellers and printers promoted book clubs, and attorneys initiated prosecution societies. Various environmental changes also facilitated growth. The new transport system increased the number of visiting speakers who toured towns, newspapers increased the exposure of the activities of voluntary associations, and the spread of the clock and quarter watch and the adoption of uniform mealtimes increased attendances.[2]

Table 3.1 References to formal networks in Bolton newspapers, 1823–70

References	1823–49	1850–70	1823–70
One mention	48.7	56.3	53.3
Mentioned over a period of five or less years	20.2	31.9	26.9
Mentioned over a period of six to ten years	9.0	7.7	8.5
Mentioned over a period of 11 to 20 years	3.2	4.1	3.7
Mentioned over a period of over 21 years	18.8	–	7.5

Sources: Indices of the *Bolton Express*, *Bolton Free Press* and *Bolton Chronicle*.

Some indication of their lifespan and the amount of trust formed can again be derived from newspaper references. In Bolton, of the voluntary associations mentioned in the local press during 1823–70 over half were referred to just once, the proportion rising over time as the number of societies multiplied and competition for members intensified (Table 3.1). The disappearance of networks was often related to their functions or the reason for their formation. Once the purpose of a charity for the construction of a market hall was completed, the charity broke up. Associations set up to serve short-term needs for co-operation, for instance employers associations created to tackle labour unrest, faded away when co-operation was no longer required. Likewise, societies founded to permit the pursuit of a fashionable activity often saw their memberships dwindle when the popularity of the pastime waned. Closure could also be the result of economic downturn; legal changes – for example, the Six Acts led to the disappearance of many trade unions and political associations at the start of the century; inter-member distrust and conflict; the departure of a charismatic founder or leader; or a failure to recruit new members.[3]

Committees, however, rarely allowed their associations to disappear without a fight. Closure would cause them to lose the benefits that accrued to themselves, and, if they had been involved in the foundation of the society, the time and energy costs they had expended in setting it up. They therefore did all they could to ensure survival, making certain that membership trust benefits were high and costs low, and, if an association's function had been achieved, adopting a related purpose or goal. If they were unsuccessful, the death of the society did not necessarily mean the termination of member trust relationships. Many continued on an informal basis or were re-established when the ex-members joined another network or set up a replacement association.[4]

Trust benefits of formal networks

Voluntary associations benefited both members and the wider society. Those who belonged to formal networks reaped numerous advantages, which, in the case of the self-employed, had a marked impact on the longevity of their businesses. The individuals in the Bolton sample of association members who were listed in local directories during 1780–1860 traded or at least appeared in the directories, on average, for ten years, as compared with the three years of all directory entries. Committee members and those who were involved in public service and business associations seem to have received the greatest return, and females and those connected to philanthropic societies the smallest (Table 3.2).

For individuals, the advantages of network membership included improved reputations, material and information gifts, greater self-confidence and a range of lesser benefits. Members of voluntary associations raised their reputations merely by belonging to a group, which signalled sociability and that they were sufficiently trustworthy to be accepted by others. Their reputation would be further heightened if they were attached to a society that itself had a good reputation on which they could free ride. The ambitious thus sought to join groups that provided a public service or had a charitable or religious purpose or contained members whose status, wealth or reputation made them trustworthy. Those societies that offered sober, serious, ordered and morally elevating activities also allowed members to envelop themselves in the cloak of respectability, which was again a signal of trustworthiness.

Gifts took the form of physical goods and information. In the case of many associations, the material gifts were usually sickness, burial and unemployment insurance provided by the society and ultimately its members, which generated inter-member and member-association trust. As time passed, the range of benefits offered expanded. By the 1860s, the YMCA operated an employment agency and gave funds to aid emigration.[5] Within networks, members also helped colleagues on a personal basis. Those in financial straits due to unemployment or sickness were given money, clothes or food. Tradesmen were provided with loans and credit, and, when creditors threatened to foreclose, short-term advances, with the probability that this would occur further strengthening member reputations.

The information exchanged improved members' personal, family and, most importantly, business and professional lives. Business intelligence comprised information regarding reputations, the competencies and credit-worthiness of future trading partners and the characteristics of future employees, and more

Table 3.2 Business lifespans of identifiable Bolton voluntary association members, 1780–1860 (years)

	Business lifespan of association members (years)
All members	9.9
Females	5.7
Committee members	11.6
Members of church groups	10.1
Members of public-service groups	13.9
Members of business groups	13.9
Members of philanthropic groups	9.8

Source: Database.

general data on sector prices, markets, legal rights, political developments and technical change. Experience information, derived from doing or using, was also exchanged, helpful 'whenever any difficulty occurs that puzzles your own [knowledge]'.[6] The type of intelligence swapped was dependent on the degree of trust present between the parties involved. Where there was little loyalty, partners would impart public information or rumour that was widely available. Conversely, in close relationships more valuable private information not in the public domain would be exchanged, such as investment plans and production capabilities.

Any intelligence supplied took the form of a gift, which strengthened the trust relationship between the giver and the recipient, who would be expected to reciprocate, either in kind or in some other way. Often the information revealed the goals or intentions of the giver or his views of others and gave the recipient the power to use the information to the supplier's detriment. In such cases, by raising the vulnerability of the information giver, the gift also signalled his trust of the recipient and acted as a test of his trustworthiness. After receiving the gift, the beneficiary, in turn, could pass it onto others, strengthening his trust bonds with them. This, though, could reduce the value of the original gift, and, if more widespread distribution of the intelligence harmed the original provider, could prompt him to refuse to impart further information or to end the relationship. Only general information was therefore usually redistributed to others, with network members seeking to acquire 'a reputation for prudence and discretion' as regards more sensitive facts.[7]

The network conduit of information benefited business in a number of ways. Without networks, the intelligence exchanged would have been difficult and costly to collect, competition compelling 'each man to keep his thought and knowledge to himself, lest his neighbour, stealing a march on him, should manufacture cheaper than himself'. Indeed, experience knowledge may have been lost completely, such information being 'fugitive and evanescent ... like the morning cloud or the early dew, which soon passes away'.[8] Instead, this data was freely available to network members and greatly promoted economic growth. General intelligence facilitated the determination of business strategy and the monitoring of competition, reputation information reduced fraud and the cost of contract enforcement, and both permitted the operation of the credit system. The availability of such information prevented borrowers obtaining credit dishonestly, allowed creditors to monitor the businesses of borrowers and minimised the collapse of credit networks, which often occurred when a false rumour caused creditors to pull in loans.

The usefulness of the information was raised by its nature and the form of its delivery. Any intelligence supplied was likely to be understandable, important in the case of technical knowledge, relevant and shorn of any unwanted detail. Networks acted as a screening device, ensuring that 'facts, doctrines, opinions and arguments [were] thoroughly winnowed from their chaff' to leave 'nothing but the golden grain'. It could also be expected to be timely, received before non-network members and, more importantly, accurate. In the exchange of intelligence, there was always the danger that 'very imperfect and false' facts would be imparted. The information provider may have been given false intelligence, misunderstood it or be deliberately telling untruths. The latter could be motivated by 'vanity or . . . malignity', that is a desire on the part of the information holder to display his or her own importance or to encourage the recipient to act in a way that would benefit themselves. Networks, however, minimised these problems, as beneficiaries could check the accuracy of intelligence with colleagues and the trust norms of the network discouraged the opportunistic distribution of untruths. Oral communication, meanwhile, caused any knowledge procured to be 'easier digested' and to 'become more our own'; and allowed the information giver 'not only . . . [to] influence others, but . . . [to] aid his own intellect by giving distinct and forcible utterances to his thoughts', causing him to 'understand [himself] better [and] conceptions [to] grow clearer'.[9]

Networks increased self-confidence by allowing members to discover their capabilities through the performance of a skill or the achievement of a set goal, to compare their attainments with those of colleagues, to obtain the views of themselves held by others and to experience co-operation, which 'teaches self-respect [and] self reliance'. Network performance comparison raised the self-confidence of those who belonged to networks containing members with similar or lower achievement levels than themselves. Conversely, poor achievers who were part of high success networks probably suffered low self-confidence. Although, where the high performers were members of their own family, such people may have acquired a boost to their self-confidence by 'basking in the other's glory', and, to lessen the psychological costs of their sense of inferiority, they would eventually have left the network or, if their lack of success affected the confidence/reputation of other members, been ejected. The views of colleagues will have increased self-confidence where they took the form of praise and the demonstration of trust, and lessened it when they involved criticism and the display of distrust. The opinions may have been genuine, but, on occasion, were probably motivated by self-interest. It will often have been in the interest of fellow network members to raise or lower an individual's self-confidence. They may, for example, have provided praise to ensure that he completed a task in which they had a vested interest or to reduce the costs imposed on them by his depressed state and associated behaviour, or criticised or downplayed his achievements in order to increase their relationship power. Likewise, it seems likely that some low-esteem members will have exaggerated their lack of abilities to others in order to lower expectations of their performance of some action, to gain help in its completion or to avoid undertaking it. Such opportunism, if discovered, inevitably will have greatly damaged trust.[10]

Other important gains from network membership included affluence/status, masculine and kin trust, discussed elsewhere, and inter-member trust, which, in business circles, promoted trade, facilitated co-ordination and encouraged co-operation in the solving of problems arising from the trade cycle, over-capacity and labour unrest. Many formal associations also had an educative role, teaching members skills that assisted in the formation of trust relationships in informal networks. The discussions that preceded and followed meetings helped them to refine their conversation skills, manners and dress sense and to learn local codes of etiquette; singing in choirs improved their performance in the informal recitals that followed dinner parties; and dance classes gave them confidence in the ballroom.

Committee membership brought with it even more benefits, often at little cost as the duties were often light and many members attended few meetings. The great responsibilities of those who sat on committees suggested that they were trustworthy and the successful fulfilment of their associations' goals further increased their reputations, as did their inevitable appearances in the press.[11] They also gained from their interaction with fellow committee members and those on the committees of other associations, and could improve their relationships with people outside the network through the provision of gifts of membership and of patronage. Charity hospitals required doctors and attendants and charity schools needed schoolmasters and schoolmistresses, many of whom were relatives of friends or trading associates of those who appointed them.

On a macro level, networks stimulated social and political trust, and acted as an escape valve for trust damaging emotions. The social interaction that occurred in voluntary associations facilitated the generation of intra-middle-class and inter-class trust, and especially helped the business and non-business communities to come together, causing social approval to be bestowed on the role played by entrepreneurs and stimulating entrepreneurial activity. Having learned the advantages of loyalty and attachment, members of formal networks also became more co-operative in other areas of their life, and, in the process, influenced social norms. On the political front, societies contributed to the calls for and the establishment of the new social contract. Ordinary networks educated their members in the democratic arts of discussion, compromise, voting and self-government; generated feelings of duty and interdependence that encouraged a greater participation in politics; through debate, inculcated tolerance and respect for the opposing viewpoint; and, via their accounts and agendas, provided a discipline and a transparency that contributed to the development of standards of public probity. More political groups provided a training ground for future political leaders, expanded access to ideas and information, increasing government accountability and honesty, and acted as an early warning system, drawing the State's attention to societal problems that could threaten the social contract.[12]

As an escape valve, networks allowed members to act in an unrespectable manner, thus enabling them to maintain their respectability/trustworthiness in the outside world; to enter into close emotional and homo-erotic relationships, which elsewhere would damage their masculine trustworthiness; and, through their functions, satisfied the masculine urges to compete and to dominate others that would otherwise have acted against trust formation in other sectors. By seeking to outdo their fellow citizens with their sporting abilities, the excellence of their discussion papers, the skill of their musical performance or the size of their shallots, the members of philosophical groups, brass bands, vegetable societies and so on lessened the compulsion to display their superiority in the trading hall, factory floor and everyday social intercourse.[13] In the same way, the application of power by committee members lessened their need to dominate others in other spheres of their life.

As will be seen in the following chapters, formal networks also had a more direct impact on trust. Some specifically sought to minimise crime or attempted to alter those working-class leisure patterns that damaged familial and social trust. Others acted as the vehicles through which the gentry maintained the social contract and reduced the severity of the social unrest that occurred when the contract was broken. The elite fulfilled their obligations to the local populace through their involvement in charities, poor law commissions, councils and so on, used these and other associations to weaken working-class neighbourhood trust and the solidarity that made crowd action effective, and established voluntary yeomanry regiments to counter any agitation that actually occurred.

As regards the drawbacks of networks, within associations, personal animosities, political, religious and social differences could lead to discord, and the excessive drinking so important for conviviality could inflame tempers and trigger quarrels. Members of one network often distrusted counterparts in groups with opposing interests, and civic engagement could undermine fragile political institutions and the social contract or be a disguise for rent seeking and lead to the diversion of resources away from areas that would benefit the community as a whole.[14] Good networkers with high levels of social capital who achieved positions of power were also not necessarily equally well endowed with human capital. Their advancement thus often generated competence distrust, and, particularly in the business world, led to inefficiency, low productivity and inadequate innovation.

Other downsides were that attachment to trading networks could discourage businessmen from fully exploiting non-network business opportunities, intra-association trust could become so dense that it crowded out other trust, and strong group loyalties could even encourage members to support a colleague who had acted opportunistically towards someone from outside the network. Members, furthermore, often had little option but to adopt the norms and behaviour patterns of the group, as failure to do so reduced ascribed trust and damaged reputations. 'He who is a capricious, impracticable, dissatisfied member of his little club' was 'immediately set down as a bad member of the community in general, as no friend to regularity and order ... and one who is incapable of sympathy, attachment or cordial co-operation.'[15] Unfortunately, the norms and behaviours of a network were not necessarily efficient or applicable to every member's circumstances and were often influenced by association leaders, who were biased against certain behaviours or wished to discourage them for their own self-interested reasons. Many networks thus discouraged rapid growth, innovation and diversification.

Creation of trust

Intra-network and other forms of trust were generated though face-to-face meet-ings, debates, gifts, society names, rules, communal meals, rituals, processions, publications and annual meetings. Association names frequently directly or indi-rectly drew attention to the supposed trustworthiness of members. Friendly soci-eties were called the 'Brothers' Friend', the 'Honest View' and the 'Loyal Fox'. Freemason lodges often included the words 'friendship', 'harmony', 'concord' or 'peace' in their titles. Rules fostered trust in a number of ways. Many regu-lated behaviour during meetings. The members of the Little Hulton Society for the Prosecution of Felons were fined if found 'quarrelling ... or being disor-dered in liquor', and St John masons had to pay a 10s. fine and provide a formal apology if they ridiculed a fellow lodge member. Wishing to maintain their own and their members' reputations, some groups also punished acts considered immoral. Oddfellows found to be 'under the charge of felony or other disgrace-ful crime' and United Oddfellows discovered to be adulterers were expelled and their names circulated to all the society's lodges in the area.[16]

Other rules sought to increase the value of networking by fining those who failed to regularly attend sessions 'without a proper reason', requiring members to meet in the afternoon, which increased the likelihood of a middle-class mem-bership, ensuring that meetings stuck to the issues to be discussed and that members had sufficient time to socialise, and preventing information exchanged by society members being passed to outsiders by requiring oaths to be taken to this effect and banning visitors. To encourage the formation of business rela-tions, it was often laid down that, where possible, trading should occur only among those who belonged to the association. The rulebook of the Spectator's Twopenny Club, for example, directed that 'none of the club shall have his clothes and shoes made or mended but by a brother'.[17]

Communal meals allowed members to socialise, and, associated with family and other intimate gatherings, had strong trust connotations. Group dinners, teas and picnics were a regular occurrence, and, on feast and other significant days, many societies organised formal banquets attended by members, their families and high-status guests. Invitations to these formal meals benefited both the guest and association members, allowing the formation of attachments and permitting the society to free ride on the reputation of the visitor and vice versa. Tables were generally set out according to social status, maximising the value of net-working, and the meal eaten off the group's dinnerware, which often bore its crest and engendered feelings of solidarity. The splendour of the plate and the quality of the food also signalled to the guests the prosperity of the association and, by extension, its members, and generated affluence trust. Further solidarity was aroused by toasts and singing. Toasts acted as gifts to the people to which they were directed and, if to the King, reflected the patriotism of the participants, which again signalled loyalty. Many drew attention to the trustworthiness of association members, a popular Oddfellow toast being 'May Oddfellow lodges be distinguished for love, peace and harmony'. The songs were often written expressly for the association, involved numerous references to loyalty and co-operation and were sung in a way that stressed the importance of the group to the individual – solos followed by ensemble choruses. [18]

The consumption of drink during these meals and before and after meetings reduced inhibitions and promoted conviviality and trust, and permitted the establishment of a new social order based on the ability to hold one's liquor, which partly replaced the barriers of class, religion and politics that hindered the formation of trust relations. These barriers were further dismantled by the practice of serving alcohol from a communal bowl and the use of identical drinking vessels. When drunk, people also invariably acted badly. Non-disclosure of this behaviour could act as a gift that helped to bond drinking partners, whereas the threat of exposure could be used as a sanction that discouraged the breaking of promises. Gambling, though it could create distrust, similarly, reinforced links between members, with winnings often being regarded as inter-member gifts.[19]

Ritual was particularly practised in freemasonry circles and by friendly societies and occurred during the initiation of members and officers and the celebration of important events. It legitimised a society in the eyes of its members and the wider community, emphasised its norms, and reminded participants that they were subject to group sanctions if they acted in a dishonourable manner, with the various symbolic representations making the feelings of solidarity fostered during the ceremony easier to recall afterwards. The secrecy of many of the rituals also gave participants a sense of self-importance, raising their self-esteem, and could act as a test of trustworthiness; those who described the ceremony to outsiders being deemed unreliable. Freemasonry rituals, meanwhile, celebrated the virtues of manliness, generating masculine trust, and their semi-religious nature for non-church goers may have filled a spiritual gap and again strengthened self-confidence.[20]

Processions by societies were a common sight in the early nineteenth-century town. On feast days, groups marched to a local church where they and interested outsiders attended a special service, and then paraded to the formal dinner. Church attendance enabled the association to free ride on the trust associated with religion and the preacher to signal in his sermon the trustworthiness of the group and to promote harmony and solidarity among its members. Groups also marched to the funerals of departed members and the opening of sister or branch societies and at political, religious or civil celebrations, generally moving through areas of public space to stress their community attachment and loyalty. The processions generated intra-society trust, and, if associations paraded together, inter-society loyalty, and clearly signalled to spectators each member's connection with an association and its trust power. To strengthen these signals, smaller groups often took part in community marches, wore society regalia, carried flags and were accompanied by bands.

Publications comprised histories that highlighted longevity and charitable endeavours, printed copies of feast sermons, songs and poems, and, in the case of national organisations, newsletters that drew attention to the benevolence of the society and its members and generated geographic trust. Numerous administrative records also appeared, including membership lists, which signalled each member's connection to a group; audited accounts that demonstrated to the general public and potential recruits honest management; and annual reports, which included accounts, membership lists and a president's address that again lauded the group and its followers. Science societies, meanwhile, set up extensive correspondence networks, members creating much geographic trust by sending gifts of information and specimens to fellow enthusiasts.[21] Annual meetings and the related jamborees, similarly, created intra-society trust, signalled an association's transparency, accountability and honesty, and, through widely reported speeches, its benevolence. The meetings of national societies were attended by the representatives of auxiliary branches and generated much geographic trust, with a good speech by a branch delegate buffeting the competence trust reputation of both the branch and the town in which it was based.

Nature of members

Access to formal networks was difficult. To ensure high networking returns, some associations set size constraints and others restricted access.[22] Size limits were adopted by those associations that wished to generate strong inter-member trust and trust norms. The small number of members ensured that each had a relatively large number of social contacts with his colleagues and could easily monitor their actions and characteristics, and made sanctions for moral hazard easier to apply and more effective. Maximum sizes varied, but tended to be set at between ten to 30 members. Access restrictions were designed to exclude those who could add little value to a network and the untrustworthy. Many societies, for example, did not welcome businessmen whose firms were far smaller than those of existing members. Such owners would provide little useful information or resources, the size of their companies and their greater propensity to insolvency would damage the status of the network and the associated trust, and, by allowing them to gain the benefits of membership, existing members merely increased the likelihood that they would eventually become their competitors. Exceptions would be made only if a businessman was in a sector that was used by members, but was not well represented in the society.

Those regarded as untrustworthy were similarly rebuffed, as they would have reduced the trust returns of existing members. Their presence would have generated intra-network distrust, negatively affected the group's norms, damaged the reputation of the network and its members, and caused some people to quit, reducing possible networking gains. The value of their information and resources would also have been severely compromised by the possibility of dishonesty. They were therefore generally allowed entry only if their networking value was greater than the potential reputation and other costs. Those who were mistakenly admitted and acted opportunistically were either expelled or required to perform some act of penance, such as the provision of a public apology or compensation, the high cost of which discouraged repetition.[23] Such punishments were chosen with care, as excessive leniency would encourage other immoral individuals to gain access and too many ejections would deter the reputable from joining.

More welcome were friends and relatives of those who already belonged to a society. Existing members could be expected to vouch truthfully for a newcomer's honesty, as they would have some knowledge of his character and past actions and their own reputation would be damaged if he acted opportunistically. The new recruit, meanwhile, would be unlikely to resort to moral hazard, since by doing so he would damage his relationship with his sponsor and his social or kin reputation. He could also be expected to rapidly form attachments of trust with the rest of the society, being able to free ride on his nominator's good name and probably possessing similar characteristics.

Access to associations was restricted via charges and stringent application procedures. The ability to afford membership of a society indicated the likely value of a member to the network and his wealth and thus affluence trust. Charges usually involved an entrance fee and a quarterly or annual subscription, the size of which depended on the nature of the club, its material requirements and its exclusivity. Failure to pay subscriptions often resulted in dismissal, non-payment being taken as a signal of untrustworthiness or of straightened circumstances that could lead to insolvency. Many associations also had hidden charges. Members had to pay for monthly and annual dinners, buy gifts of drinks for fellow members and contribute to the charitable donations made by societies.[24]

Application procedures tended to become less stringent as the number of associations increased and the competition for members intensified, and, by the 1820s, in some cases had even disappeared. Practices varied between societies. Many specifically stated in their rules that access was restricted to the trustworthy. Other associations required aspirant members to earn more than a given sum or to go through a long and complex application process. The latter involved the applicant being proposed by an existing member(s) and the proposal being seconded and displayed in a public place. There was then sometimes an inquiry by officers into the applicant's background and a ballot of existing members, entry often being dependent on a majority vote. In some cases, the new recruit then had to serve a probationary period, during which his trustworthiness and networking value could be fully assessed and he was excluded from the privileges of the association.[25]

In Bolton, as elsewhere, members tended to be middle class and self-employed. Wage earners, mainly skilled operatives, were largely found in benefit societies and church groups. Of the self-employed, retailers and service providers, who had a relatively large number of customers, were the most frequent networkers, followed by those involved in textiles and other manufactures (Table 3.3). To maximise networking returns and ascribed trust, members of certain occupations often joined the same type of association or specific societies. Charitable networks appear to have been particularly attractive to professional and white-collar workers and church and public service networks to retailers and service providers (Table 3.4). As regards specific societies, 36 per

Table 3.3 Occupations of Bolton voluntary association members (percentage of total members)

	1790–1870	*1790–1829*	*1830–1870*
Textiles	18.6	26.1	14.6
Engineering/metals	8.1	4.9	9.6
Retailers and service providers	23.1	17.6	23.7
Bleachers	4.6	6.5	3.9
Other manufacturers	14.2	9.9	14.7
Professionals	13.8	11.8	14.6
Multiple occupations	5.7	5.3	5.1

Source: Database.

cent of members of the Bolton Cricket Club were bleachers, 35 per cent of Bolton Grammar School trustees during the period 1788–1879 were professionals, mainly lawyers, and 26 per cent of the Committee that organised the opening of the Temperance Hall in 1840 were shoemakers/curriers.

Given the large number of tradesmen in Bolton, a surprisingly small percentage were involved in voluntary associations, and, of these, the majority owned well-established, middling to large businesses that had relatively high growth rates. One explanation is that many of those with small incomes may have placed a higher value on consumer goods than on leisure goods and thus were unwilling to meet the costs of association membership and had to devote much of their leisure time to earning the money required to buy the objects desired. A more plausible reason is that new entrants and small traders had difficulty gaining access to formal networks, could devote little time and energy to networking, and had little need for association membership. The majority had relatively few trading relationships, which could be acquired and maintained through informal networks, and, because of the high levels of moral hazard and the damage opportunism could inflict on a small firm, they were reluctant to abandon trustworthy trading partners. Replacements were sought only if the

Table 3.4 Occupations of members of church, public-service, business and charity groups, 1790–1870 (%)

	Church groups	*Public-service groups*	*Business groups*	*Philanthropic groups*
Textiles	21.8	21.0	20.7	21.9
Engineering and metals	8.1	6.7	7.4	4.8
Retailers and service providers	20.4	22.5	12.9	12.4
Bleachers	4.0	6.4	9.8	8.6
Other manufacturers	14.1	9.6	8.0	8.6
Professional and white collar	14.2	17.3	17.7	32.4

Source: Database.

supplier/buyer ceased trading or acted unscrupulously, and new collaborators could again be obtained through informal networks and the trader's other business partners. These would also supply the small amount of information required, while reputations could be built though the adoption of an honourable business code and the avoidance of opportunism – reputations being spread via voluntary associations whether or not a trader was a member. As discussed in Chapter 9, small businessmen, moreover, had no wish to expand their firms, fearful of the accompanying fall in trust. They thus had no need for the multiple trading contacts, the widely known reputation or the large quantities of information that were provided by association membership and were essential for expansion and diversification.

At least in Bolton, the majority of voluntary association members were Nonconformists, supported the Liberal party, and were young and male (Table 3.5). The young made up a relatively large proportion of the urban population; had relatively high incomes; possessed more time for networking, especially if unmarried; starting out, had few trust relationships; and, denied the other signals of masculinity, needed to strengthen their masculine trust through male conviviality. Their involvement in associations was also encouraged by parents, who believed membership provided an education in conversation and etiquette and prevented their offspring mixing with the untrustworthy, and by the societies themselves. Youthful members had high attendance rates, ensured the long-term survival of the network, and provided older colleagues with access to the next generation of traders, with whom they would otherwise have little contact.

Certain associations catered specifically for the young, ensuring high networking returns and ascribed trust. A youthful membership was assured by a function that excluded the old, for example a sporting activity, or an age-biased access policy. New associations also tended to be dominated by the young, the old being reluctant to move networks and lose their sunk costs, and people, wishing to maximise returns, naturally drift towards institutions containing others in their age range. In some cases, associations even created offshoots specifically aimed at those in their teens; political clubs and freemason lodges, for example, often established 'junior' societies.[26] These ensured the long-term

Table 3.5 Gender and political and religious beliefs of Bolton association members

	Percentage of members
Supporters of Liberal Party	49.6
Supporters of Conservative Party	35.1
Nonconformists	79.2
Anglicans	20.4
Females	4.0

Source: Database.

Note
Some members split their votes between political parties.

survival of the association and maximised networking returns among the young and old.

Women were found in those societies that had religious or charitable goals, concerns in which they were thought to have a particular interest, or in associations that had a large female clientele. They were also well represented in various pressure groups and formed their own women-only societies. Pressure groups that had relatively large female memberships included the temperance and peace associations, the campaigns against the Contagious Diseases Acts and the anti-slavery movement, and, in the case of working-class women, Owenite and Saint Simonian socialism and the Chartist movement of the late 1830s and 1840s. Female members added to these groups' moral reputations, could play a large role in the collection of petition signatures and funds, and, in the case of the anti-slavery societies, as managers of household budgets, could make commercial boycotts effective.[27] For women, membership of associations that sought to protect their sex from male vices or the degradations of slavery also generated trust from other females.

Women-only societies took two forms – female auxiliary groups attached to national organisations or entirely independent associations. The auxiliary groups were pioneered by the missionary and Bible societies; the Bible Society in 1819 had 350 female branches and 10,000 women members. Their national organisations were generally managed by men, who created the rules of operation that were put into effect by the all-women local societies. The independent female associations mostly had philanthropic goals. There were also some female chartist groups and a number of women benefit societies, though these accounted for only 5 per cent of such societies in 1803–4 and many key players were male.[28]

Generally, formal networks contained few women, though working-class females appear to have withdrawn from the public sphere later than their middle-class counterparts – in the mid-nineteenth century as opposed to the late eighteenth/early nineteenth century. The cult of domesticity laid down that a woman's place was in the home. In large cities, a woman on the streets at night ran the risk of rape or being mistaken for a prostitute. Many could not afford association membership and subscription fees, having no or a low income, lacked the legal and financial skills required by committee members, and, because of their inferior legal status, were unable to perform important management tasks. The most important reasons for their exclusion, however, were trust related. Female members provided low networking returns. They possessed little useful business or general information, lacked the education necessary for intelligent conversation, and their presence created sexual competition and restricted male conviviality, eliminating the masculine trust gains of membership. Moreover, it was widely believed that they were inherently mendacious, owing to their 'sense of weakness, timidity of disposition and defective judgment'; disposed to be mutinous', as they 'stand in less fear of the law ... [and] presume the privilege of their sex'; and that their supposed tendency to gossip would lead to the widespread distribution of any information exchanged. There was also a more general distrust of women, and, over the century, a growing belief that they constituted almost an alien sex, quite different from that of the male. This differentiation and suspicion had a number of origins. Their withdrawal from the world of work; changes in accepted sexual behaviour that increased the import- ance of penetrative sex, which emphasized the male libido and female passivity; and new scientific and medical theories. These emphasized a 'two sex' model of reproductive development and suggested that women were mentally unstable and prone to insanity, especially at times of menarche and menopause, and that their intellectual development had been arrested to conserve their energies for childbirth and the rearing of children. Sexual differentiation was additionally perhaps a defensive reaction on the part of men to the more egalitarian political and sexual climate threatened by the French Revolution, and, later, to the revival of the female polemic and the improvement in the status of women that resulted from legal changes, better education and greater employment opportunities.[29]

Women, however, were as reluctant to join such societies as men were to admit them. Membership would reduce the amount of time available for neigh- bourhood and friendship networks, which provided relatively higher returns, and limit their access to such associations. Those who involved themselves in the public sphere would be less liked by other members of their sex, as their involvement would weaken ascribed trust, damage their personal reputations by forcing them to attend public houses and socialise with unsuitable members of the opposite sex, and threaten the myth of feminine virtue, from which women gained much power and which arose from their exclusion from the morally dam- aging public arena.

The majority of voluntary network members belonged to relatively few soci- eties. In Bolton, each member was connected to an average of 2.1 associations. Those involved in philanthropy appear to have been the greatest networkers and churchgoers the least enthusiastic (Table 3.6). 3.4 per cent of the sample had ten or more memberships and a number of individuals were connected to a large number of societies. The cotton manufacturer, bleacher and merchant Robert Heywood belonged to at least 39 associations, and the grocer, tea dealer and chemist James Scowcroft was affiliated to 34. Once an individual had gained access to one high-trust group, entry to others was eased, as the reputation of the society acted as a signal of his honesty (which could be vouchsafed by other multi-association members) and would burnish the reputations of the other associations he joined. The number of memberships held depended on the indi- vidual's goals, the size of his business and the economic sector in which he operated. Those who wished to gain strong, long-term trust relationships were affiliated to relatively few networks, and, within these, concentrated their time and energy on the establishment of relations with those with whom they wished to gain and maintain contact. This strategy was generally adopted by new busi- ness entrants and those operating relatively small companies, who required little information and relatively few trust relationships to expand, and, unable to dele- gate, had little spare time to devote to networking.

Large established business owners who wished to grow or diversify had

Table 3.6 Memberships and membership diversity in Bolton, 1790–1870

	Percentage of members with two or more networks	*Average number of association memberships per member*	*Average number of network areas per member*
All members 1790–1870	30.3	2.1	1.6
Members of church groups	27.5	2.3	1.6
Members of public-service groups	85.1	5.9	3.4
Members of business groups	61.0	4.5	2.7
Members of philanthropic groups	86.7	8.7	4.5

Source: Database.

Note
Network areas: the sample voluntary associations were split into twelve areas – the church, public service, business, education, temperance, politics, freemasons, charity/friendly societies, social groupings, non-official law enforcement, yeomanry and 'other'.

many memberships, and, within networks, made a large number of contacts. Those individuals in the sample who belonged to ten or more associations had an average firm lifespan of almost 19 years, just over half had multiple occupations and 17 per cent had diversified into another economic sector. Such masters required a large number of trust attachments and the strength of these relationships was relatively unimportant as moral hazard by one supplier/customer was unlikely to threaten the existence of the firm. Likewise, those in sectors where information had a high value or where businesses required 'less attendance than others and [gave] a man less occasion of application' also had numerous multiple network connections. Inevitably, there were constraints on the number of memberships that could be held. Each group had its own moral and social norms, and it was often impossible to simultaneously follow the codes of a large number of associations, especially in religiously and politically divided towns. There was also the problem of time. Benjamin Braidley, the Manchester cotton manufacturer, calculated in 1824 that he spent over 36 hours per week on 'matters totally unconnected with my own business', and many manufacturers devoted so much time to networking that they neglected their primary occupation.[30]

Such businessmen also had to make sure that that they belonged to diverse networks, and, within these, formed relationships with disparate members. In the sample, individuals on average belonged to associations in just 1.57 network areas, but those with ten or more memberships were affiliated to a mean 6.6 different types of associations (Table 3.6). Diverse memberships increased the range and amount of information obtained and improved the individual's attractiveness as a network contact to others. A variety of contacts was also important to those who wished to expand through diversification, and, where an individual had exclusive links with an individual with a specific demand and someone else with the skills to meet this need, new business opportunities could arise. Many businessmen took particular care to join one or two metropolitan networks, such as, in the North West, the Royal Exchange, the Manchester Chamber of Commerce and the Manchester Literary and Philosophical Society. Metropolitan formal associations possessed the latest technical and other information, had connections to government and financial networks, and contained the most able and ambitious entrepreneurs, who controlled relatively valuable resources and could provide introductions to traders in other regions and countries.[31] By joining such groups, businessmen thus gave themselves a head start over their more parochial counterparts.

Despite belonging to a large number of diverse networks, however, many sample individuals maintained strong relations with other multi-networkers by having more than one voluntary association in common. In 1849, for example, the Bolton cotton spinner Thomas Thomasson had two voluntary associations in common with the lawyer Thomas Lever Rushton, the grocer/malster George Binks and the spinners Thomas Cullen, John Entwisle and James Arrowsmith, and shared three networks with the spinner Robert Walsh, who, in turn, had two societies in common with the cotton manufacturer Joseph Bell, who shared two networks with the bleacher William Makant, who was a member of two voluntary associations that also contained Thomas Thomasson. Such strings of relationships also facilitated inter-network trust and ensured the rapid movement of reputation and other information between associations.

As for committee members, officers and patrons, these were generally elite businessmen or professionals. The status and affluence trustworthiness of such men added to the reputation of the association and their high networking value facilitated recruitment. Most committees also contained a clergyman, whose profession further burnished the society's reputation, and the relatives of previous committee members, the trustworthiness of whom could easily be assured. Officers tended to be local solicitors, bankers or accountants, whose professional skill and trustworthiness reduced the likelihood of mismanagement and who possessed much knowledge as to the suitability of recruits. Access to committees was restricted to the elite by pecuniary barriers and elections. Many charitable societies only allowed those who subscribed a certain sum to stand as a candidate, and elections were often uncontested and the result 'pre-arranged'. In all-elite voluntary associations, committee memberships and patron positions were often rotated, allowing each member to receive the trust benefits of office.[32]

Memberships over time

Memberships of formal networks peaked during upturns in the trade cycle. Believing that expansion would be successful, traders extended and diversified their firms and sought out the trust and information benefits of associations. The management of businesses was also easier, allowing owners to devote more time to networking. During downturns, participation rates often fell. Traders had difficulty paying fees and other costs and concentrated all their efforts on ensuring that their firms survived.[33] Between the peaks and troughs, memberships were generally of short duration. In Bolton, few were connected with a society for more than ten years, with member turnover rising over time as the number of formal networks multiplied. The lack of commitment was related to the high levels of migration and the benefits and costs of membership. Where costs were high, people left a society as soon as they had established the requisite connections and acquired a trust reputation. The relationships could be maintained, though at a lower level of intensity, outside the network and reputations once established took time to fade. If more connections were needed or a reputation required burnishing, they would then rejoin the association with which they had developed an attachment, or, if they required different contacts/information, attempt to become a member of another society.

In some cases, rapid exit occurred because the costs were higher or the benefits were lower than expected, both being difficult to determine prior to enrolment. Others found that they were unable to meet the costs because of an increase in family commitments or workload or an inability to pay the fees and the secondary costs of membership. They thus left, but then returned when their circumstances changed. [34] Those who remained in networks for long periods did so because costs were low, returns were high, trust benefits were offered that could not be obtained elsewhere, damaging exit sanctions were applied, or the maintenance of trust connections away from the association was difficult and costly. Association officials, who had few duties, thus tended to remain in their posts far longer than harder-worked committee members, and, as discussed below, the religious, who gained spiritual trust from attendance, tended to stay loyal to a church longer than a sportsman remained with a sports club.

Conclusion

Networks were and are the engine rooms of trust, improving the trust reputations of members, generating inter-group co-operation, and stimulating social, business and political trust. At the same time, they conferred on members and the wider environment other benefits that promoted individual prosperity and facilitated economic growth and social peace. Care, however, must be taken not to overstate their advantages. Voluntary associations could be the cause of much personal and social hostility and could slow or damage economic growth. Moreover, to ensure their own survival and expansion they were forced to restrict access to people who could provide high networking returns and enhance their reputations. Their benefits were therefore largely reaped by the middle class, and, in particular, by those who managed middling to large established businesses. Network membership and the concomitant trust thus served to maintain the status quo and to make those who already possessed power even more powerful.

4 Philanthropic, religious and education networks

The formal networks that had the greatest impact on trust were those that had philanthropic, religious and educational goals. All affected the middle and working classes, but to different degrees and in dissimilar ways. Although congregations contained both classes, with perhaps a bias towards the gentry, philanthropic groups were almost wholly middle class, though, through their actions, they generated inter-class bonds and sought to raise working-class trust. Likewise, at the start of the nineteenth century, the middle classes derived relatively more trust from education. As the century progressed, however, the expansion in the number of day and Sunday schools ensured that the offspring of the poor also derived at least some of the trust benefits on offer.

Philanthropic networks

Philanthropy varied between towns and took four forms:[1] the provision by individual philanthropists of money to wholly or partly finance public amenities, such as infirmaries, parks or churches; charitable trusts, which distributed money placed in trust funds for charitable purposes; charities that collected and gave away donations drawn from the local community; and non-charitable voluntary associations, for example cricket clubs, which occasionally gave or raised money for community causes. Charitable trusts were controlled by trustees and sometimes employed staff, and most charities possessed an organising committee, a number of active members (who performed the group's day-to-day tasks) and subscribers whose only commitment was to give money.

The trustees of charitable trusts largely came from the local elite and met a number of times per year. Charity committee members, title-holders and officers were similarly drawn from town gentry, who had many wealthy network contacts who could be inveigled on to make contributions, and trust reputations on which the societies could free ride. Such people were also unlikely to act fraudulently, as their wealth meant that they had little need for ill-gotten gains and criminal activity would carry a high reputation cost. As with other voluntary societies, a relatively small proportion of the elite held these posts. In Bolton, 30 per cent of those who had occupied one of these positions during the period 1780 to 1860 had played the same role in at least two other philanthropic organisations. A similar situation existed in Manchester, where, in 1804, 9 per cent of committee members served on three or more charitable governing bodies.[2]

Most of those holding higher positions were male. Women tended to be ordinary members and to act as helpers, visiting the households of the poor. Great armies of women were involved in this work. The Congregational Christian Instruction Society, for example, in 1835 fielded over 2,000 voluntary visitors. It was believed that women formed closer trust relations with working women than males, and could thus learn more about their circumstances, which, with their domestic knowledge, made them more able to distinguish the deserving poor from dissimulators. Male visitors also ran the risk of being the subject of gossip, which could tarnish their respectable and trust reputations, and women had more spare time to devote to these time-consuming activities. Female committee members were to be found only in the all-women charities, which focused on issues believed to be of interest to their sex, such as servant poverty and the care of orphans.[3]

A major reason for becoming actively involved in the provision of philanthropy was the wish to improve one's reputation. For philanthropist industrialists, gifts to the community signalled their trustworthiness by demonstrating their wealth and their empathetic and benign natures. The signals were largely directed at both present and future trading partners and existing and potential employees. That the gifts were not specifically aimed at workers and the business community only increased their symbolic power, particularly to the genuinely altruistic and trustworthy, who industrialists most wished to attract. Trust was further established with non-trading sections of the community, contributing to the development of pro-business norms and helping to establish a combined town and business identity with shared interests and aims. Such gifts also mitigated any distrust a master may have generated in the past as a consequence of a resort to power.

The gifts were 'free gifts', in that the philanthropist expected no direct return. This again increased their symbolic strength. Reciprocation, nevertheless, did sometimes occur; a clear indication that the gifts succeeded in the generation of trust. The return offerings were intended to strengthen the bonds of loyalty between the philanthropist and the community, but also to indirectly influence the recipient's future behaviour and self-actualisation. To receive a gift and public praise for one's virtues carried with it a responsibility to live up to the enhanced reputation and influenced one's view of oneself as a virtuous individual, which would again affect future actions. The gifts were bought with contributions from townsfolk, often contained inscriptions that made direct reference to the beneficiary's morality and integrity, and were presented at special ceremonies at which the donors gave speeches that again referred to the recipient's lack of self-interest, and so on. The presents themselves were either practical items, such as writing desks or Bibles, which would reinforce the philanthropist's self-view and remind him of his need to maintain his reputation each time he used them, or an article, for example a portrait or silver plate, that could be prominently displayed and would direct the attention of both the recipient and his guests to his virtuousness.[4]

Those involved in charities and trusts, similarly, gained a reputation for trust-worthiness. If possible, they became involved in well-established charities, upon whose reputation they could free ride, and organisations associated with education, medicine or children. The latter received relatively large amounts of publicity and involvement indicated the possession of high levels of compassion. To maximise their returns, many donors gave contributions to more than one charity. In 1822, 1825 and 1850 respectively, 36 per cent, 30 per cent and 43 per cent of subscribers to Bolton's Auxiliary Bible Society, Mechanics Institute and Society of the Protection of the Poor also gave donations to the Infirmary. Others increased gains by regularly changing their allegiance to particular philanthropic groups. Of those subscribing in 1845 to Bolton's Society for the Protection of the Poor and Infirmary respectively, only 63 per cent and 68 per cent gave funds five years later. Care, however, had to be taken to avoid over-generosity, as, according to a well-known business manual, once a businessman 'has the misfortune to be known as a charitable man, petitions will be thrust at him almost every hour of the day ... [and] his door will be besieged by the loudest and fastest talking, if not the most beautiful, of women'.[5]

Other benefits obtained by members of charities were affluence trust and a variety of privileges. Infirmary subscribers, for example, were allowed to recommend suitable patients for admission, a benefit that could prove useful in reciprocal gift exchanges. Members also gained self-confidence, spiritual trust, numerous close relationships, and opportunities for fraud. Self-confidence was raised by the emotional reward individuals gained from charity work, the sense of achievement felt when an organisation's goals were met, and, for committee members, the regard demonstrated by their successful election to their posts. For the religious, spiritual trust came from the ability to follow Christ's command to feed the hungry and clothe the naked and thus to strengthen their reciprocal relationship with God. Such work, along with grants for the construction of new churches, was also thought to facilitate the conversion of the poor to Christianity and its trusting values; the underprivileged having first to be raised from the depths of misery and deprivation if they were to heed the call of religion.[6]

The networking opportunities afforded by philanthropy could be extensive. Committee members interacted with colleagues and with ordinary members, who, in turn, had dealings with donors, who socialised at fund-raising events. Significantly, at least some of the members and subscribers will have been genuinely altruistic and trustworthy and will have made valuable trust partners. Fraud was generally restricted to trustees, whose activities went unmonitored. To prevent such behaviour, which damaged the subscriptions and trust reputations of other charities, trusteeship was often invested in an office or institution, for example the holders of a local church post or the local corporation, or in the heirs of a particular trusted or high status individual. Probity was further ensured through the setting up of Charity Commission enquiries, which sat almost continuously from 1818 to 1837, and, in 1853, the establishment of a permanent charity board; the commissioners and board members monitoring trusts for fraudulent behaviour and requiring the introduction and maintenance of good governance practices.[7]

People who became involved in philanthropy were not only interested in enhancing their own reputations. There was also desire to maintain the social contract, change working-class morals, diminish neighbourhood loyalties and improve other trusts. Charity was an important part of the social contract. In return for the social stability that was essential for economic progress, the elite, amongst other things, were obliged to give generously, particularly in economic downturns. The importance of these gifts in the maintenance of the contract is most clearly seen during the early 1860s cotton famine, when most Lancashire towns set up relief committees that paid the unemployed a cash benefit. As a result of this initiative, there was little social protest and many believed that the famine had actually increased social co-operation, laying the foundations for 'a better and more Christian feeling between the higher and lower classes, a feeling of love and charity'.[8]

In order to improve working-class morals, indiscriminate charity, that is money given directly to the poor by individuals, was discouraged, and applicants for assistance offered by professional charities were screened, with aid granted only to the 'deserving poor'. The strategy was designed to suppress mendacity and fraud by claimants. Giving money to those who pretended to be in poverty led to a weakening of general moral norms, and allowed such people to carry on living 'an idle, dissolute and vicious life', sapping the self-confidence, 'self-respect, self-help and self control' that would permit them to make a fresh start. They would thus continue 'to bring up their children in idleness, vice and crime' and to turn to criminal activities to supplement their handouts, with 'most of the petty depredations and robberies committed on our properties and on our highways [being] the acts of these vagrants'. Fraud, furthermore, weakened the reputation of the charity concerned and its ability to attract funds, and, for the religious, weakened the spiritual trust generated by helping the poor. The strategy also sought to reward those who adopted a way of life that would reduce the likelihood of immoral behaviour, and, in order to further encourage such conduct, assistance was accompanied by advice and tracts. The Domestic Missions, for example, gave recipients pamphlets designed 'to promote the order and comfort of their homes . . . and to shelter them from corrupting influences'.[9]

As regards neighbourhood trust, philanthropy provided an alternative to the critical life-situation gifts that bound neighbours together and thus contributed to the weakening of the crowd. To establish trust relations and encourage take-up, from the late eighteenth century, the elite and middle classes also began to adopt a more considerate and courteous code of behaviour towards recipients, generally abandoning their previous patronising and demeaning manner. Charity manuals of the period advise visitors to be 'courteous to the poor . . . it wins and instructs them', to exhibit humility rather than to 'say . . . I am more holy than thou', to develop friendly relations and 'a mutual intercourse of goodwill', and to wear plain simple clothes, as elegant dress would 'elicit feelings of envy or contradict the charitable expressions of consolation you will utter'.[10] Visits were to be regular, and, to encourage the poor to consider them true friends rather than alms givers, help was only to be offered a number of weeks after the first meeting.

Finally, a variety of other trusts were shaped by charity. High levels of giving and low levels of social unrest raised the reputation of a town, on which the elite could free ride when interacting with the inhabitants of other urban centres. The fact that the funds of charitable trusts often benefited a number of villages and townships, and, at least later in the century, that some local charities were part of national organisations strengthened geographic trust. As did the help received from other townships and regions during downturns. During the cotton famine, relief committees were established all over Britain and donations even came from abroad, prompting Richard Cobden to comment that the famine gave 'the whole country an opportunity of co-operating'. Charitable associations also promoted interaction among the middle class and, to a lesser extent, between the middle class and skilled working class, who occasionally gave subscriptions, and, in the case of large projects, generated town trust. The organising committees of such projects would attempt to involve the whole community in their activities. Fund-raising balls and dinners would be held, factory owners and foremen would be requested to canvass their work people for donations, friendly society and trade unions asked to solicit support from members, and, at the opening ceremony, the whole community would gather to celebrate the success of the campaign.[11]

The expansion of local charities came to an end in the 1880s. Thereafter, the number of philanthropic societies fell; some altering their goals to become pressure groups or fund raisers for research. Social investigations by Booth and Rowntree, along with the emerging ideals of New Liberalism, Labourism and Socialism caused many to feel that ad hoc giving was not the best way of overcoming poverty. Alternative sources of relief grew in importance – working-class institutional forms of protection, such as the friendly society and the co-operative movement, and, later, state and local government provision. At the same time, the elite gradually became less involved in the operation of charitable organisations. A similar retreat from public life occurred in the political sphere and was related to a variety of factors. The elite began to live beyond town boundaries and thus felt less attached to a particular urban centre, and many local networking benefits were no longer required. Good labour relations and social peace reduced the need to create social capital, business relationships were more often formed in local employers associations, and most elite manufacturers faced a regional or national market and thus obtained greater value from regional/national networks. In philanthropic circles, greater working-class contributions increased the number of middle and working-class representatives that sat on committees, which significantly reduced networking returns. Charity was also increasingly mediated through officials, reducing the trust kudos available, and bureaucratisation, prompted by the enlargement of communities/charities and the return of cyclical unemployment and a reinvigorated fear of claimant moral hazard, led to heavy committee workloads.[12]

Religious networks

Networks raising social capital

Religion generated personal trust for those who attended church and intra-congregation, kin, geographic and social trust. For worshippers, church attendance led to a closer trust relationship with God and greater self-confidence. The less successful could console themselves with the belief that, unlike their more flourishing but irreligious colleagues, they would receive a heavenly inheritance, and the self-esteem of especially working-class and female members was raised by their ability to adopt leadership roles and in some denominations to preach, and by their involvement in theological debate. Churchgoing also added to an individual's reputation for trustworthiness, the religious norms of honesty and co-operation being well known, and allowed them to free ride on the trust reputation of their fellow believers, with whom they could form close bonds. This networking aspect of church attendance was of particular importance to those in search of marriage partners and to businessmen, who used their place of worship to establish ties with employees and fellow traders. Indeed, many masters encouraged or even forced their workers to attend church.[13] A degree of interaction was thus assured, and committed Christians no doubt believed that the inculcation of religious norms would improve staff morality and that their action would provide employees with the gift of salvation and thus strengthen their own trust relationships with God and the converted workmen.

To ensure that their contacts with other worshippers were cost effective, churchgoers took great care in their choice of religious denomination and their place of worship. People tended to embrace the denomination and frequent the church that friends, other family members, workmates or fellow traders adopted and attended. In many industrial towns, the aristocracy and the oldest and richest families favoured Anglicanism and the smaller newer businessmen opted for non-conformism. As regards individual churches/chapels, concentrations of tradesmen are particularly noticeable. Of the 125 people who worshipped at Bolton's St Andrew's Presbyterian Church from 1855 to 1866 and for whom occupations are available, almost 60 per cent were shop owners/employees, joiners or servants. A list of the christenings performed at the town's St John's Church from 1849 to 1854 shows that 20 per cent of fathers and worshippers were weavers and a further 16 per cent involved in other areas of the textile industry, and Walmsley Old Chapel had a large number of members involved in the quarrying and stonecutting trades.[14]

Having joined a church, congregation members needed to maintain its reputation. A collapse in moral standing through the inappropriate behaviour of fellow parishioners or the minister would rebound on their own reputations and cause some congregation members to drift away to other places of worship, reducing networking returns. Congregations thus used sanctions to ensure that fellow believers adhered to the norms of the church and formed reciprocal trust relationships with ministers. Sanctions included gossip and social exclusion. In addition, sinners could be expelled and would face the ultimate punishment of hellfire. The Higher Bridge Street Methodist circuit in Bolton in 1822 expelled six members of its congregation – four for fornication and two for drunkenness, and, in 1823, banished another 13 for drunkenness, fornication, fighting and 'a suspicious act'. The Marsden Society of Friends from 1678 to 1860 cast out 81 members for among other things 'shameful acts, loose or scandalous conduct, for being a debtor, and deserting one's children'. Many churches particularly targeted business immorality, which could prove especially costly to worshippers. Some Nonconformist chapels investigated bankrupts for immoral behaviour, and the Society of Friends issued a code of commercial conduct to prevent members 'deviating from safe and regular methods of business' and expelled those who failed to abide by the code.[15]

Most ministers were unlikely to tarnish the reputation of their churches, aware that the diminution of the congregation or the loss of its trust would damage their prospects of promotion to a wealthier ministry and reduce pew rents and tithes, which heavily contributed to their salaries. To make sure that this was the case, congregations formed trust relationships with ministers, praising their abilities and providing them with gifts, such as Bibles and engraved addresses, usually on special occasions and anniversaries. They also often campaigned for the appointment of relatives of former incumbents, whose abilities were known and who would suffer a social cost in the form of family disapproval if they acted contrary to the values of their predecessors. The Revd J. Spencer, vicar of St Ann's church, Bolton until 1866, for example, was succeeded successively by his eldest son and youngest son, and Philipp Holland, the minister of Bolton's Presbyterian chapel, was replaced in 1789 by his cousin.[16]

In order to burnish their own reputations, worshippers gave money or time and energy to the church. The elite tended to become church officials, posts that additionally permitted closer contact with other elite members. Bolton Parish Church's list of wardens includes most of the leading business names of the town, and, as regards the partners of the local bank, it was 'said that future developments at the [business] were often discussed in the vestry after morning service'. A post as a church official also permitted greater interaction with ministers, who possessed much business-related information and could facilitate business alliances. Ministers were greatly trusted, often related to elite families, were members of voluntary association committees and performed chaplainry duties to networks. They thus knew a wide variety of people, who told them many things. The Revd James Slade, the Vicar of Bolton, for example, was related to the cotton manufacturing Bolling family, became president of Bolton's savings bank, a Great Bolton trustee, a member of the Pitt Club, Chairman of the Bolton Infirmary, and President of the First Temperance Society and the Bolton Association for the Deaf and Dumb, and sat on various turnpike trusts and on the committee of the Bolton Floral and Horticultural Society and the Exchange newsroom. Along with his fellow clergymen, he also performed chaplainry duties to the freemasons, the Ancient Order of Druids, the Church and King Club, the Pitt club, the Protestant Association and the Orangeman's Club.[17]

Turning to wider issues, intra-congregation trust arose from social inter-action, the exchange of gifts, and extra-church relationships. Worshippers socialised before and after services at a wide variety of social events, such as prayer meetings, Sunday teas and Christmas parties, and at numerous spin-off organisations, for example Bible and Missionary Societies, Book Clubs and Bell Ringing groups. If they were in need, they would be given gifts of prayer, cloth-ing, food, credit or even employment by their fellow churchgoers, and many ministers, wishing to gain the trust of their flock, established burial and sick societies and handed out patronage gained from their involvement in the volun-tary sector. Large numbers of worshippers at mainstream churches also lived in the same community and already knew each other. Neighbourhood and church trust thus often had a symbiotic relationship, each feeding off the other.

Generally, congregations comprised two factions – the middle-class fee-paying pew holders and the less wealthy who sat in the free seats. Although some trust will have existed between these two groups, it will have been far weaker than the attachments formed within them. The division between the camps was both physical and self-imposed. Seat holders tended to sit in their own blocks of pews, and in some churches, these were located in the body of the church, while the free seats were placed in the gallery. Even when there were opportunities for fraternisation, few members of the elite took advantage of them. James Taylor of the Unitarian Mosley Street chapel, Manchester, admitted in 1842 that he had 'always found a difficulty in uniting persons of all classes in any such meetings – the most educated and influential classes often keep away'.[18] Such behaviour, albeit unchristian, was perfectly rational. Middle-class worshippers had little in common with their social inferiors and would find the formation of relationships difficult. They also gained few information or other benefits from any bond established, which, given the social snobbery of the time, if known, could damage their ability to form trust liaisons with members of their own class.

Kin trust was promoted by Christian doctrine, which regarded the family as the primary source of social organisation, and through the involvement of family members in church activities, which, in turn, helped to generate intra-congregational trust. Families attended services together, took part in extra-church activities, and often held church offices. A father may have served as a deacon, the mother as a church visitor and the older children as Sunday school teachers. The degree of family involvement varied between denominations, but was especially high among Nonconformists. Twenty-six per cent of those who held seats at Bolton's Dukes Alley Independent Congregational Chapel from 1837 to 1854, for instance, were related to at least one other pew holder, and the list of interments at the town's Society of Friends burial ground from1825 to 1856 contains numerous family groupings.[19]

Geographic trust was generated by the dispersed nature of the congregations of the more obscure, smaller sects, links between churches in different towns and clergy networks. Unlike their mainstream counterparts, the smaller religious sects drew their worshippers from afar and the attendance at a central church by

churchgoers from surrounding villages and towns generated community affilia-
tions. Members of a church in one town were also often related to congregation
members in another town and there were more formal links between churches.
Nonconformist lay preachers and ministers regularly toured the churches in a
town and the surrounding district, members of the Bible, Religious Tract and
Missionary Societies often met colleagues from other conurbations and received
magazines summarising their activities, and the Society of Friends was constantly visited by members from afar. Similar links existed between clergymen,
who were often related. Sons followed fathers, uncles and grandfathers into the
church and daughters of ministers had a strong propensity to marry into the
clergy. Ministers also formed close friendships during training and regularly met
at meetings of denominational unions, local Nonconformist associations, and
societies to promote Nonconformist causes, such as the Peace Society and the
UK Alliance.[20]

The church contributed to social trust through its norms and values. Morality
norms, if internalised, caused churchgoers to behave in a more honest and kind
manner and to become involved in trust-raising philanthropy. The values of
industry and frugality preached particularly by the Nonconformists played a
similar role, reducing the likelihood that believers would find themselves in situations where they had to resort to dishonesty. As did more common values, such
as shared responsibility, mutual support and respect for the individual. 'Instead
of the mutual hatred and jealousy, which passion and selfishness excite'
preached the Nonconformist J. J. Taylor, 'Christianity substitutes those feelings
of kindness and sympathy and of reciprocal help and service'.[21] These norms and
values, in turn, were passed onto the irreligious sections of society though Christians' participation in the community, proselytising and the influence of ministers, who, through their positions as local dignitaries, magistrates and voluntary
association committee members, could win over both the general public and
those other notables who determined norms.

Trust limitations of the church

The church therefore can be seen to have played a large part in the generation of
trust of all kinds. Care, however, must be taken not to exaggerate its contribution. The social capital created was restricted to a demographically and socially
small section of each community, many of whom were not true believers, and
was offset by religion inspired distrust. In Bolton in 1851, only 27 per cent of
the population were regular churchgoers, though the wage books of the cotton
manufacturer John Ainsworth suggest that a further 35 per cent may have occasionally attended church, and, through spin-off institutions, religion will have
had some impact even on those who devoted Sundays to secular activities. This
lack of interest in organised religion appears to have been merely the continuation of a trend that extended into the third quarter of the century. In 1804,
the incumbent of St George's, Little Bolton, reported that 'members of the
public appear to disregard religion', and estimated that only 28.8 per cent of

inhabitants attended any place of worship. A religious census undertaken in 1881 by a local newspaper discovered a similar situation, with only 32.4 per cent of the town classified as regular churchgoers. Many commentators believe that attendances then fell even further, first among the dissenting communities and later in the Church of England. The rise of rationalism damaged faith, the greater availability of alternative leisure activities reduced the church's social role, and economic development and greater equity enabled people to obtain immediate material rewards, reducing the assumed value of salvation.[22]

The reasons for the low static attendance in the first half of the century are unclear. There is evidence that those who moved to the new industrial towns lost the habit of regular churchgoing, low church attendance correlating with population density, net migration and the presence of non-English migrants. The Anglican Church also failed to establish sufficient churches in the new urban areas, provided weak parochial supervision, and remained wedded to its trust relationship with the pre-industrial elite, a failing reflected in the social backgrounds, values and alliances of its clergy.[23] It thus had difficulty forming relationships with the new industrial aristocracy, and to its former parishioners appeared to be grossly out of touch. Its congregations thus dwindled, with only a small proportion moving to Nonconformism.

Church attendance and its associated impact on trust, furthermore, was restricted by gender and class. A large proportion of congregations was female. Women could devote more time to churchgoing than men, perhaps attended as family representatives, may have wished to strengthen their domestic moral reputations, from which they gained high returns, and were no doubt attracted by the relatively large number of positions of responsibility that were available to their sex. Men, meanwhile, had other meeting places, their business interests were often in contradiction to religious norms, and, in the case of the working class, their masculine trust reputations depended on 'immoral' activities, such as drinking and gambling. In many Anglican churches, women tended to favour evening services and men those that were held in the morning, a gender division that increased the value of networking, but again reduced inter-gender interaction.[24]

The social class of congregations was equally restricted. If the ability to rent a pew is seen as a reflection of middle-class or upper-working-class status, between 50 and 80 per cent of congregations belonged to these classes and the Anglicans had a socially more superior membership than the Nonconformists. In Bolton this social exclusivity is reflected in baptismal, marriage and burial registers and was clearly recognised by at least one Anglican Minister. Cotton operatives and artisans made up over 70 per cent of the congregations of Bolton Parish Church, the Dukes Alley Congregational Church, and the Fletcher Street Wesleyan Methodist Chapel and over half of the members of Bolton's Friends Meeting House and Deane Parish Church. Labourers, where listed, meanwhile, made up less than 10 per cent of congregations and it was generally accepted that 'of the labouring adults, especially the males, but a very small proportion attend any place of worship'. This high proportion of artisans and skilled workers, which is found elsewhere, further suggests that a large proportion of Bolton's churchgoers had resided in the town for a relatively long period and that few were migrants. In 1851, 72.1 per cent of Bolton's cotton operatives were born there and it seems likely that most of the artisans will have served their apprenticeships in the town.[25]

The trust benefits of church social interaction thus largely benefited the middle- and upper-working-class and long-term residents. The lower working class and immigrants were deprived of this trust, unless that is the latter constituted a particular ethnic group with a shared religion. Where this was the case, the migrants often brought their own church with them. Catholic churches in urban towns, for example, contained large numbers of Irish, and Presbyterian Churches many Scots. Immigrants and the labouring classes were rarely part of church groups for a number of reasons. Their long working hours and the more physical and tiring nature of their work no doubt made church attendance relatively difficult. They may have preferred to put their spiritual trust in the supernatural, lacked access to appropriate clothing, or found the service rituals so complex as to be incomprehensible or boring. Too often religion was 'presented to them in such a sombre and gloomy aspect' that it addressed 'neither the senses, the imagination, nor the heart'. As already discussed, they were also not always welcomed by middle-class congregations, who were fearful that their presence would damage their reputations and reduce networking returns.[26]

Of those who actually attended church, a small proportion were members of two denominations and thus established weak trust relationships with a wide variety of people. Many others remained members of congregations for relatively short periods, and an unknown number were non-believers. In Bolton, congregation turnover was high. In 1847, 53 per cent of the congregation of the Moor Lane Baptist Chapel had worshipped there for less than five years, and at the Mawdsley Street Chapel 15 per cent of worshippers in 1853 had been chapel members for less than one year and a further 15 per cent for just one to two years. Turnovers were even higher among those who rented pews. Only a third of those who paid for their seats at Chew Moor Chapel in 1856 did so five years later, and at St George's Road Congregational Chapel only 21 per cent of pew renters in 1866 continued to hire in 1870. Such high turnovers undermined trust formation and were related to a number of factors. Many worshippers will have left the church once they had made sufficient trust relationships or no longer required the critical life-situation gifts available or had found an alternative source of such gifts in their neighbourhoods or families. Some appear to have transferred their allegiance from one church to another in search of new or better trust relationships and gifts. Others appear to have moved churches in the belief that their trust contract with a minister had been breached. Movement from the Anglican to Nonconformist places of worship was often prompted by increases in Easter dues, failure to provide sufficient help in downturns and ministers' refusal to name babies privately, which enabled parents to avoid the cost of a public christening.[27] High levels of migration, both between and within towns, will also have contributed to turnover levels, though most intra-town movement involved very short distances.

What proportion of worshippers were true believers and followed religious norms is unknowable. Many, no doubt, refused to accept a lack of faith even to themselves, 'clinging all the more convulsively ... [to a] ... self deceiving belief in believing'. For such people, acknowledgement would have damaged their self-confidence, and, more importantly, for those who still retained a smidgen of belief, damaged their trust relationship with God, as by 'looking into the state of his soul ... [such a man would] ... reveal it to heaven'. Others, while accepting their lack of faith to themselves, kept their views secret, fearing that 'by speaking out ... [they] ... would tend to weaken existing beliefs and by consequence ... existing restraints', and thus contribute to a collapse in social trust.[28] Fellow sceptics probably had less worthy motives, pretending to believe in order to gain networking and reputation advantages or gifts.

Even faith did not guarantee moral behaviour. *The Nonconformist* in 1848 noted that some dissenting employers were 'grasping, selfish and niggardly' and treated their workers worse than those with no religious convictions. An explanation is that genuine believers used devout conduct on Sundays to expunge the guilt (and potential damage to their self-confidence) that had accumulated from less than ideal behaviour during the rest of week. 'The very classes which in all denominations make the loudest religious profession' were thus often 'the very classes among us who are most utterly given up to money making'. Other congregation members may simply have failed to see a connection between religious moral norms and their everyday lives. Whereas some ministers constantly pointed out their flock's sins, others preferred to concentrate on the intricacies of theological debate. As a religious author of the time commented, though the 'evils [of business] are almost universally admitted, it is feared that little attention is given to them by the pulpit'.[29]

The impact of religion on social capital was diminished further by both excess trust and active distrust. Intra-church trust could become so strong that it crowded out all other relationships. Congregations often socialised only with fellow worshippers and became wary of those outside the church. In many cases, this distrust was reciprocated. Abstinence from drinking and gambling caused the religious to be treated with suspicion, while particular denominations occasionally faced open hostility. There was much anti-Catholic feeling, and, in many towns, there was a deep Anglican revulsion towards Methodism, which some claimed actively promoted immorality.[30] Such animosity often appeared within churches. In Nonconformism, distrust based on religious disagreement was far from unknown and often led to secession, which damaged intra-congregation trust and caused deep fissures in family and neighbourhood relations.

In a static and highly competitive market for converts, denominations also distrusted each other; the mutual hatreds spilling over into the political sphere and adding to the already intense rivalry between Liberals, largely Nonconformists, and the mainly Anglican Conservatives. Such inter-denominational distrust only began to seriously weaken from the 1840s, when low working-class church attendance prompted the setting up of various non-sectarian bodies, such as the 1849 Young Men's Christian Association and the various temperance societies, which played down theological differences. At the same time, for both Anglicans and Nonconformists, their distrust of the Catholic church began to supersede their suspicion of each other, particularly after the restoration of the Catholic hierarchy in 1850. 'The church of England, so-called, Wesleyans, Independents and all the other various sects' put their own differences aside and came together 'to spit upon the "popish" poor'.[31]

Education networks

Education comprised schooling and adult education. School attendance in the early nineteenth century is not known, though, given the high levels of child employment and the small number of schools, it seems likely that it was low. By mid-century, the situation had improved. In Northern towns, day schools educated around a third and Sunday schools about half of children under the age of 15, though in both cases there was a significant difference between the numbers on school books and actual attendances.[32]

Education promoted trust in a variety of ways. It taught pupils social, language and communication skills, provided them with the knowledge and information necessary for daily social interaction, filled hours that would otherwise be spent in 'sloth' and 'dissipation', gave them an appreciation of the benefits of trust, made them more open minded and willing to accept 'otherness', and inculcated them with society's trust and moral norms. Whether all schools advanced trust in these ways, however, is open to question. Although government inspectors sought to ensure that they taught morality and divinity effectively, contemporaries claimed that teachers were frequently ignorant, that few day schools made any attempt to instil moral norms, and that pupils were often mistreated and had little respect for masters.[33]

Learning bestowed other trust benefits. Parents who ensured that their children attended school added to their respectable reputation, education was an important component of ascribed trust and the educated were regarded as relatively honest. Freedly in his *Treatise on Business* pronounced that 'a high degree of moral principle ... is usually associated with a cultivated and improved state of the intellectual faculties'. For some students, education widened their social and intellectual horizons, encouraging greater social interaction, and, for artisans, membership of self-improving and other networks. Others formed bonds of trust with their school, causing them to possesses a relatively high regard of all its students, both past and future, and may have gained by association the trust reputation attached to a particular place of learning or to Sunday schools in general. The latter could be valuable. According to a Sunday school minister, 'whenever steady men are wanted ... the master or over lookers apply to the superintendents of the local Sunday school to recommend them young men of ability and good character'.[34]

More importantly, many pupils formed strong relationships with their contemporaries, which often lasted a lifetime, and, in the case of businessmen, could pay high commercial dividends. The extent to which such inter-pupil bonds developed was highly dependent on the teaching methods adopted by an institution. The large classes of hundreds of students taught by single teachers in the early schools generated little inter-pupil trust. Monitorial teaching, whereby teachers trained child monitors, who, in turn, taught small groups of 8 to 36 students, again in a large room, led to the formation of deep trust links within the monitorial group and strong ascribed trust between the group and the monitor, but few relationships between the groups that shared the room. Conversely, the teaching methods promoted by Samuel Wilderspin, which became popular from the 1820s, generated both group and school trust. Single teachers taught small classes in classrooms, ensuring the development of strong group bonds; while corridors, the inevitable corollary of separate classrooms, and playgrounds provided spaces where wider school interaction could occur.[35] The two sexes, however, continued to be separated, leading to a gender distrust that continued into adult life.

Schools also had wider trust and power consequences. In the first half of the century, both the sons of the elite and middling classes attended the same place of learning leading to the generation of inter-class trust. Sunday schools, by permitting parents a few child-free leisure hours each week strengthened husband–wife bonds, the ability to write led to stronger ties with distant relatives, and it was hoped that pupils would pass the moral precepts they learned onto other family members. The elite, meanwhile, were convinced that education was a means of reducing the power of labour and the crowd. It was believed that learning caused men to be 'less swayed by mere passion and prejudice and much less likely to become the dupes of stump orators and imposters'. The educated, similarly, were less likely to be 'misled by any new and attractive doctrines' or influenced by radical literature, which 'preys upon the passions or ignorance of the uninstructed'. In reality, education may have had the opposite effect. Many believed that it raised expectations of what the employment and social contract should provide, giving 'many young men views and ideas not suited for their stations in life' and making them 'ambitious, envious and dissatisfied' and more redoubtable foes in labour struggles.[36]

The amount and strength of trust created varied from school to school. The period of teaching in Sunday schools was far shorter than in day schools and it therefore seems likely that the internalisation of trust and moral norms would have been correspondingly weaker. Such schools and therefore their class sizes were also far larger than their day counterparts, which would again have weakened norm internalisation. Conversely, Sunday schools provided their pupils with a wide range of gifts, including clothing, footwear, food, sick society benefits, apprenticeships, placements in superior day charity schools and leisure activities, such as picnics, outings, tea parties, field days, walks and later railway excursions. These will have created strong bonds of loyalty, and, in the case of the social events, increased pupil interaction, and, by involving the families of children, contributed to adult cordiality. Sunday schools and church schools also imparted stronger trust norms than their day and non-church counterparts; boosted future church/chapel attendance; enabled churches to monitor, and, if necessary, correct the morals of pupils' families; by promoting thrift, reduced the likelihood that students would later fall into morally degenerating poverty; and, in that parents 'confer[red] a favour [on their betters] by permitting [their children] to' attend, raised inter-class trust. However, as with religion, a large number of different denomination schools in a town may have created distrust, internalising in their pupils a deep suspicion of the followers of competing religions, though the tendency for children to attend the best schools rather than those operated by the church or denomination of their parents and to often move between institutions may have weakened this effect. It was also argued that by passing 'the parental duty . . . off to a stranger', Sunday schools damaged the parent–child relationship.[37]

The elite abandoned local places of education for public schools from the 1860s. The public school had a profound affect on trust. Attendance reduced inter-class attachments but raised regional and national class trust, as pupils mixed with other members of their class from other towns and regions, and led to the development of bonds between the urban elite and the aristocracy. For fathers, the presence of a son at a public school signalled to others his wealth and the associated trustworthiness and his belief in the morality taught by such schools. It also increased the likelihood that his son would possess self-confidence, develop masculine trustworthiness and be a gentleman, a key component of which was the adoption of an honourable code of behaviour.

To ensure that norms of honour and trust were internalised, many schools followed the educational strategies adopted by Thomas Arnold at Rugby. Masters were employed who had the personality to capture the boys' respect and loyalty and were able to overcome the moral influence of the pupils' peers. The schools themselves were split into houses, small student accommodation blocks, each under the control of one or more master. These ensured regular contact between teachers and students, and, through their collective organisation, taught pupils the skills required to live in a community and the advantages of co-operation. The teachers were supported by prefects, who acted as moral agents, and the main vehicle for the teaching of ethics was the Classics. Great emphasis was placed on the value of emulation (of teachers, prefects and other honourable individuals), chapel attendance and team sports. The latter taught players cooperation and prepared them 'the world they [were] soon to enter'. On the playing field, it was believed, 'conceit is humbled, mean tricks are scorned, unfair advantage taking is repelled, arrogant assumptions are brought down and a lad is made to feel that he must be frank and honourable among his fellows and respect their rights'. Such precepts were also learnt by spectators and were passed to other classes by old boys, who, as teachers, introduced these sports to provincial grammar schools or set up amateur or professional sports clubs.[38]

After leaving such schools, past attendance became a trust and wealth signal, creating ascribed and wealth trust and indicating that an individual had internalised moral norms. Attendance was signalled through the wearing of old school ties, accent and the use of a distinct public school vocabulary.[39] As with other places of education, pupils could free ride on the reputation of the school and formed strong trust relations with contemporaries, which were kept alive through old boys associations and sports events between past and current students.

Adult education was largely the preserve of the Mechanics Institute, mutual improvement societies, libraries and various voluntary associations. The former were initially financed and operated by local businessmen, who, through their involvement, polished their own reputations and gained valuable network connections. They may also have believed that the Institutes would impart technical skills and norms of trust and co-operation to their workforces and direct them away from leisure activities that encouraged immorality. If so, they were sorely disappointed. Memberships of Institutes remained low and a large proportion of students came from the upper working and middle classes. The unstable nature of their employment militated against committed working-class membership, even when only a modest subscription was charged. Most students also appear to have attended to make contacts and to generate ascribed trust, and the length of attendance was therefore short, generally just long enough for the establishment of viable trust relationships.[40]

The working class tended to gravitate towards mutual improvement societies, which became popular in the 1830s to 1850s as a result of the rise in literacy, the heightened profile of adult education brought about by the establishment of Mechanics Institutes, and the political excitement aroused by Owenism, Chartism and the new Poor Law. The societies were formed by a wide range of institutions, including the church, trade unions and temperance associations, and provided education either free of charge or for a small fee. The teaching offered took a variety of forms. Some societies provided elementary instruction; while others pursued more advanced studies, concentrated on one subject, or offered lectures and discussions on political and social issues. To prevent distrust among members and the development of views that could damage the reputation of the society, many discussion associations imposed rules on the subjects that could be debated, generally excluding political and religious topics. Attendance and socialisation were encouraged by the establishment of newsrooms or small libraries and the provision of recreational activities, such as outings.[41]

Libraries enabled members to educate themselves, acted as centres of sociability and kept 'artisans and operatives at their own firesides' away from the immorality of the 'alehouse [and] the public streets'. Most towns had subscription libraries, where middle-class members could read and talk quietly; commercial circulating libraries, usually attached to bookshops; factory libraries, the books of which were available to members of staff and their families; and libraries owned by churches, Sunday schools, political clubs and inns and so on, which supplied books to those who frequented these places. Public libraries appeared in the 1850s and quickly had large working-class memberships. As well as providing books, they also organised debates, discussions and lectures and rented rooms to voluntary associations, whose activities were advertised on notice boards.[42]

Middle-class adult education occurred in voluntary associations such as debating, scientific, literary and dramatic societies. Debating societies discussed a wide range of subjects, many directly impinging on trust. As with self-improvement discussion groups, the debates provided a release from the stresses of everyday life and raised self-confidence. Absalom Watkin, the Manchester cotton merchant, in his diary for 1830 reported that he had once found a fellow member of the Manchester Literary and Scientific club 'broiling over his study, forgetting everything else while engaged in calcining oyster shells for the purpose of producing phosphorescent light'. These and other educational groups also gave others the impression that members were logical and dispassionate and unlikely to act irrationally, and could generate geographic trust, with members often meeting their counterparts in other towns and attending conferences.[43]

Such groups, however, could equally be destructive of trust. Poor performance in a debate could cause a member to lose 'all confidence in himself', and disagreements could lead to division. A further member of the Manchester Literary and Scientific Club was forced to leave when he became 'very contemptuous . . . of the performances of others, which he was at no pains to conceal'. The associations also helped to spread and popularise the new ideas of individualism, which severely weakened trust norms, and for businessmen, involvement in certain societies could damage their reputations. Literary and dramatic societies, for instance, had few businessmen as members as there was 'a degree of notoriety' attached to membership, which rendered those who attended 'eccentric among his associates and ridiculous in the eyes of the world'.[44]

Conclusion

Charities, churches and schools produced great swathes of social capital. At the micro-level, the philanthropic, religious and educated reaped a variety of personal trust benefits from their association with the networks. They improved their trust reputations, learned and internalised moral and trust norms, formed close relationships with large numbers of like-minded people and gained in self-confidence. On a macro-level, the networks strengthened a wide variety of trusts, including kin, neighbourhood, geographic, spiritual and social trust. Care, however, should be taken not to become too carried away by their contribution. Religion was restricted to a demographically and socially small section of the community, many of whom were not true believers, and all the groups generated distrust. The religious were regarded with suspicion by the godless, moral hazard by charity trustees could poison the public's faith in the honesty of the elite and Sunday schools often internalised inter-denomination animosity. Overall, though, the networks appear to have had a positive effect on social capital, and, without them, nineteenth-century towns would have been less socially and economically successful.

5 Informal networks and miscellaneous trust determinants

Just as important as formal networks for the generation of trust were their informal counterparts. These comprised the neighbourhood, employment and leisure networks already discussed and a range of other casual associations. The first two sections of the chapter examine these networks and investigate the arenas in which they developed and were maintained – the pub, increasingly as the century progressed the habitat of the working class; the shop, an almost exclusively female space; and public pageants and funerals. The remainder of the chapter is devoted to a discussion of five miscellaneous determinants of trust, namely demographic change, the built environment, income, the media and happiness, which have been placed together largely for want of other suitable locations.

Informal networks

Access to informal networks was largely via relatives, membership of formal and other informal networks, apprenticeships, employment, partnerships and letters of introduction. The connections made were kept alive through constant face-to-face meetings, correspondence, attendance at formal networks and the reciprocal exchange of gifts.[1] Membership tended to peak during young adulthood, falling away as family and voluntary associations took up more time, but then rising again with retirement and widowhood. The working class tended to have shorter relationships than their middle-class counterparts, who were less prone to changes in employment and residence, and involvement sometimes led to invitations to join formal societies. Memberships of both types of network therefore often overlapped and there was much exchange of information between the two spheres, particularly regarding the trustworthiness of others. As with formal networks, there gradually emerged social leaders, who belonged to and thus linked a large number of social groupings and were often members of the elite and office holders or committee members of voluntary associations. The connections of social leaders to large numbers of potential members/subscribers made them attractive to formal networks; while heightened trust reputations and gift distribution powers, similarly, increased the allure of committee members/ officers to informal groupings.

As the nineteenth century progressed, male informal networking fell. The cult of domesticity forced middle-class men to spend much of their leisure time in their own homes and the creed of manliness stressed individualism and the importance of work. Mixed sex social interaction also became less popular. During the eighteenth century, women were thought to play an important role in the development of politeness, polishing and refining male manners. Much inter-gender informal socialising thus occurred in assembly rooms, public balls and theatres. From the 1830s, however, these arenas of sociability became less popular as the ethos of domesticity took hold and the networking aspect of social interaction increased in importance. There also developed a gender divide promoted by the single-sex public school and a greater understanding of gender sexual differences, which contributed to the rise of a curious sexism that depicted the female as passive, dependent and poor company.[2]

Important actors in informal two-person relationships were the trust and distrust intermediary. The former established a bridge of trust between those who possessed no previous connections, but could benefit economically or socially from a relationship. Each of the potential partners knew and trusted the intermediary and used this trust as a substitute for the absent trust relationship. By giving each the gift of the other person, the intermediary improved his own relationship with the couple and his wider reputation, and, in some cases, benefited from the association or charged a fee or commission for his work. The distrust intermediary, on the other hand, created animosity between individuals who had previously trusted each other. Such people again benefited from their actions; third-party manufacturers, for example, often sought to break up existing manufacturer–buyer partnerships in the hope that they would gain the rejected buyer's trade.

In the business world, a number of professionals took on the trust intermediary role, most obviously solicitors, bankers, accountants and agents. During the first half of the century, the number of professional intermediaries grew rapidly, the rate of growth then slowing as intermediary firms grew in size. Others who played the role on a more informal basis included multiple networkers, merchants, doctors, shopkeepers, moneylenders, pawnbrokers, publicans, carriers, postmasters, landlords and committee members, who could link ordinary members of their associations with counterparts in other societies by speaking to those on the committees of those groups.[3]

Arenas of informal networks

Pubs

Leon Faucher on his 1844 visit to Manchester observed that 'the public house is for the operative, what the public squares were for the ancients. It is where they meet one another and where they discuss the topics in which they are interested'. He may have added that it possessed business and employment roles and was a meeting place for voluntary associations. As regards general social interaction, the pub was a place where friends and neighbours could meet outside working hours and consume drink and food. To attract custom, landlords provided facilities for games, such as dominoes and skittles, organised street fairs and bowling, wrestling, running and other sporting competitions, arranged blood sport contests, such as cock, dog and bear fighting, held musical entertainments and dances, and played hosts to travelling magicians, menageries and freak shows. They also supplied customers with daily papers, would lend regular drinkers small sums of money, and, in some cases, provided them with sex, many beer houses being patronised by prostitutes. The pub, in addition, acted as a venue for a variety of neighbourhood and family social events, such as wakes, stag nights and parties, and usually contained people selling a range of domestic goods, though these disappeared with the rise of specialist shops, which, unlike pub traders, offered credit.[4]

Such interaction generated much trust. Robert Greenhalgh wrote that he had 'seen many fraternizations in public houses among people who were previously unacquainted with each other, and, which casually formed, have led to several years of friendship, occasionally indeed lasting the lifetime of one of the parties'. The rapid formation of relationships was facilitated by the common characteristic of a love of drinking and smoking and by pub norms, primarily that drinkers were free to converse with whomever they wished, but had a right not to be interrupted by a third party once they had begun to converse with a particular person or group. Feelings of loyalty and attachment, meanwhile, were generated by the norm of tolerance, the concept that no individual should take offence at minor irritations or insults; the consumption of alcohol, which reduces inhibitions; the bestowal of nicknames; the establishment of rituals; and the reciprocal exchange of gifts. The latter took the form of drinks bought for others, toasts, help and advice on domestic and work issues, presents to mark life-changing events, such as marriage, which were paid for by collections, and gifts in the form of sums of money, again collected from regulars and given to fellow drinkers who had fallen on hard times. Among the working class, pubs also generated masculine trust. Public houses were male bastions. Women who visited inns alone were regarded as disreputable at best and as prostitutes at worst. They therefore rarely entered such establishments, and, when they did venture forth, went as part of a group to known 'mixed sex' public houses, as members of a female friendly society, or at specific times with their husbands. Men who shunned inns were regarded with suspicion and subjected to sanctions, largely taunts that took the form of accusations that they were 'tight-fisted', 'hen-pecked', 'miserable' or 'not proper men'.[5]

Businessmen used inns and beer houses as temporary business addresses to be utilised on market days, as locations where deals could be made and goods sold either by individuals or by auction, and as places of companionship. According to the millwright John Galloway, tradesmen met 'in the bar parlour in the evening, smoking their long clay pipes, drinking ale and discussing matters, generally including business'. In some cases, businessmen also appear to have free rode on the trust reputations of particular innkeepers, naming a landlord rather than a hostelry in sales advertisements. Public houses thus played a part in the development of business trust, though their contribution gradually fell over time. As discussed below, from the 1830s it was no longer thought respectable for the middle class to frequent such dens of iniquity. Magistrates furthermore moved the old open markets into large specially built market halls or corn exchanges, where agreements could be finalised in comfort, and greater literacy meant that deals were written down and did not require the communal sanction furnished by fellow drinkers/witnesses.[6]

For labourers, alehouses were where they found employment, were paid and socialised. Until the 1830s, when it was claimed the practices encouraged drunkenness, employers recruited men in pubs and paid the salaries of existing employees there. Landlords could provide the float of small coin required for wages and the space needed to accommodate the pay table and the queue of workers. The employees of a specific firm would also socialise in the nearest adjacent hostelry, where, as industry was highly localised, they would mix and form trust relationships with other workers in the sector. Not infrequently, this alehouse was owned by a factory proprietor, who, by providing cheap beer, hoped to encourage workers to drink there and not to bring alcohol into the workplace.[7]

Pubs also played host to vestries and a wide variety of drinking clubs and voluntary associations. Drinking clubs appeared in the early eighteenth century and were formal societies whose members regularly met at a particular public house, after which the club was named. There were generally up to 30 members, who, to maximise networking returns and generate ascribed trust, were often in the same line of business and of the same generation. To ensure inter-club trust, memberships overlapped and often included men who belonged to clubs in other towns. Most met several times per week and compared 'notes on the rumours or news of the day' and deliberated 'upon . . . local and general politics, municipal management and almost everything else', and occasionally took practical action.

In the late eighteenth and early nineteenth centuries, most voluntary associations met in public houses. There were few other public places where they could convene and meeting in members' homes was not always possible, involving disruption and expense. Pubs also provided a regular supply of alcohol, sometimes at an especially low price or on credit, which ensured high attendances and facilitated sociability, and often accommodated similar associations, which facilitated the development of inter-society links. Landlords, furthermore, generally welcomed associations with open arms. Most licensees provided meeting rooms and storage space for the societies' papers, regalia or libraries, held their cash, particularly important before the spread of the Trustees Savings Bank in the 1820s, and supported their activities in the press. Others helped in the formation and running of the association, often acting as Treasurer, guaranteed the funds of Friendly Societies with a bond supplied by themselves or local brewers, and, in the case of Masonic lodges, covered the cost of getting a warrant from the Grand Lodge and buying the necessary ceremonial dress and objects.[8] In return, they gained trade, with many associations having to agree to spend a given amount on drink, a sum known as 'wet rent'; could free ride on the reputation of the club and thus attract further custom; form trust relationships with members, which they could use to further their own interests; and could be confident that members would be relatively trustworthy customers.

To maximise networking returns, the different social classes and groups congregated in separate pubs. The coaching inns, which additionally provided lodgings, catered for wealthy visitors and those plyers of wares and trades who toured districts. The taverns on the main thoroughfares met the needs of richer inhabitants and casual drinkers, the smaller, less elaborate alehouses located in side streets served local neighbourhoods, and the beer house was frequented by the poor. The very poor turned to the illicit beer house or hush shop, or, if they wished to buy spirits, the dram shop. There was also some ethnic and occupational stratification. Pubs in migrant residential areas naturally had largely migrant clienteles. Other pubs attracted particular occupational groups, which was signalled by their names, for example The Spinners' Arms or The Carpenters' Arms. Inside inns, there was further social division. The parlour was regarded the preserve of the more respectable customers, and the taproom, where drinks were cheaper, the domain of the less respectable.[9]

The trust generated by pub sociability was over time increasingly restricted to the lower classes and was offset by the distrust created by drunkenness. From 1800, those members of the upper and middle class who frequented public houses ran the risk of losing their reputation for respectability and trustworthiness. The pub was regarded as a source of immorality and the cult of domesticity ordained that those middle-class males who wished to be regarded as honourable should spend their leisure time at home. The elite and middle class therefore abandoned the inn, a trend encouraged by evangelical calls for them to set a good example to the poor, warnings by leading medical practitioners of the effect of inebriation on health and the appearance of new voluntary associations, which offered greater networking returns than the pub.[10]

From the 1830s, they were joined in their flight from the alehouse by trades people and skilled workmen, who again wished to retain respectable/trustworthy reputations, and, owing to the cost of maintaining their respectability, had little surplus income to spend on alcohol. Pub attendance was further damaged by the rise of the factory system, which stopped workers taking time or days off work in order to booze and prevented them arriving in the morning drunk, for which they could be fined or dismissed. Greater education had also widened the intellectual horizons of the skilled, who again could reap higher networking returns from voluntary associations. By mid-century, therefore, only labourers and the unskilled gained the trust benefits of pub sociability. Although, as the number of hostelries increased faster than population, it seems likely that the trust produced was far stronger and deeper than previously. The working class remained yoked to the pub, despite the efforts of the temperance movement for several reasons. As the elite were well aware, attendance generated neighbourhood and masculine trust, drink allowed them to 'forget troubles of every kind', took them out of the home, which 'held no charms for the operative', and filled the long days when they were cyclically or structurally unemployed.[11]

Against the trust generated by the public house must be set the distrust created by the consumption of alcohol. Pubs were believed to bring 'men and women, even children ... into contact ... with thieves, swindlers and prostitutes', and drink to lead to 'the ruin of the temper', the destruction of 'moral feeling' and the reduction of family income. The drunkard often committed acts of violence on family members, which affected kinship trust; unfairly blamed his low income on employers, weakening employer–employee trust; and damaged the reputation of himself, his family and his neighbourhood. Furthermore, he took no concern in the 'moral training and superintendence of his children', shunned 'all companions save the reckless profligates who are reduced to the same level as himself', and turned to 'little acts of knavery' before rushing 'headlong into crime' and 'innumerable other vices'. Drunkenness and its impact on trust, however, appears to have fallen from the 1840s and levels varied over time. Gattrell and Hadden, using national conviction figures, link drunkenness to prosperity, arguing that consumption of alcohol increased during periods of high wages and full employment. Conversely, Holding found, in times of distress, that drink-related and assault convictions rose, and, in periods of prosperity, assaults fell and the number of drink-related convictions remained the same.[12] Distrust arising from drunkenness would therefore have been high during downturns in the business cycle and low during upturns.

Shops

Shops were arenas of female sociability. During shopping expeditions, women signalled their trustworthiness through dress and deportment, and met fellow customers whilst making their purchases, or, in the case of the middle class, used the shop as a meeting place. *The Drapers Record* constantly bemoaned so-called 'tabbies', women who often spent hours in establishments talking. Shops tended to be geographically concentrated, increasing the intensity of interaction, and used price to ensure social exclusiveness and to maximise the value of networking. Many stores also had anterooms, where the elite could meet and take refreshment before making their purchases.[13]

To obtain and retain custom, shopkeepers had to build bonds of trust with their customers. This was achieved through involvement in networks, the generation of ascribed trust and gifts. To create the impression that they were of a similar social rank to customers and thus generate ascribed trust, those shopkeepers selling to the elite referred to shoppers as 'clients', spoke to them using the first-person plural pronoun, that is 'we', and, in the case of dressmakers, conducted their business in the clients' own homes. Gifts included physical presents and offerings of information and credit. To retain high-spending customers or those of high repute, shopkeepers offered these people refreshments when they visited their stores, a custom that helped to personalise the business relationship, and gave them large price discounts on the goods they purchased and gifts of their own products, generally at Christmas or to mark life-changing events. In return, they obtained custom, could free ride on a customer's reputation, and the shopkeeper or more usually his staff often obtained physical gifts in return, in the case of employees small amounts of money. Other customers received gifts of friendship, flattery, gossip, information and advice, and, most importantly, credit, which created binding relationships, but involved the risk of non-payment. For the regularly employed, the use of 'tick' was a sign of poor money management and led to neighbourhood distrust and thus was only resorted to in trade depressions. The poor, on the other hand, had no alternative but to use credit on a day-to-day basis, and for the very poor the ability to gain credit from a respected shopkeeper may actually have increased their community trust reputation.[14]

Over the period, the trust reputation of shopkeepers declined, owing to the fall in customer trust in the quality and utility of articles, which was related to the increase in the number of new products, changing selling and manufacturing methods, producer deception and the arrival of the duplicitous advert. Inevitably, this lack of trust in goods damaged societal trust. By mid-century, changes in the retail and production process had caused many articles sold in shops to be anonymous and distrusted. Customers' conception of goods was affected by their own experiences as producers. With the coming of the factory, workers had relatively little control over the production process and relatively weak trust relationships with their co-workers. They thus began to see manufactured objects as alienated commodities in which they had little confidence. As consumers, the development of the retail trade and urbanisation meant that they no longer knew or could obtain from others the reputations of producers and were unable to sanction those who proved dishonest. They were therefore forced to base their judgements of the quality of articles on careful scrutiny, which caused them to devote more time to shopping and thus reap additional trust benefits, and on the claims of shopkeepers or advertisements. Unfortunately, owners of shops generally had little control over the characteristics or utility of the products they sold. To retain customer confidence, they therefore had to devote even more time and energy in the establishment of customer trust relationships, invest their wares with their personal judgement or skill (wine and tea merchants, for example, began to blend their own wines and teas), or resort to duplicity themselves. Many kept their shops dark, which made the determination of quality difficult, claimed in advertisements and on trade cards to be manufacturers, and, in the case of high value goods, such as watches, engraved their own name on the article to give the impression that they were the maker.[15]

In the case of food, customers were right to be suspicious. Many foodstuffs had materials added to them, either to extend supply or to make them look or smell more attractive. A public outcry in 1851–4, arising from the publication of the results of Dr A. H. Hassall's analysis of a number of foods and drinks, served to stoke this distrust. Vested interests, however, ensured that effective legislation against adulteration was only introduced in 1875. In the meantime, the 'honest trader' came 'to be looked upon with the same suspicion as the adulterating merchant, manufacturer or tradesmen' and 'the status of that portion of the community that sells articles of consumption ' was 'looked upon with misgivings in all its transactions'.[16]

Advertisement became popular in the first few decades of the nineteenth century, and, by the 1860s, was directed at both the middle and working classes. Designed to persuade, it rapidly began to include elements of deception. Vendors, in particular those of patent medicines, began to use language that combined ambiguity, innuendo and sensationalism and encouraged consumer self-delusion. To pander to a customer's fantasy of social superiority, it was often suggested that a good was produced for upper-class use. Advertisements were addressed to the 'nobility, ladies and gentlemen and the public in general', used upper-class terms and falsely claimed that the retailer made home visits.[17]

The shops that generated the most trust were undoubtedly those operated by co-operative societies, which appeared in the 1850s and 1860s and ensured that customers obtained 'full weight and pure and unadulterated goods'. The stores also did much to promote social trust. Social interaction was facilitated through the shopping experience, monthly meeting of members, social events, and the establishment of reading rooms, newsrooms and libraries. Norms of trust and reciprocity were disseminated via use and example, the speeches of founders and society magazines, and co-operation between societies, particularly during their foundation, generated much geographic trust.[18]

Public pageants

Public pageants punctuated the urban year. They comprised parades and speeches, occasionally followed by communal meals, and were held to mark events such as national military victories, royal coronations and visits, the opening of public buildings, the election of mayors, the unveiling of statues and monuments, and commemorative points in the seasonal or Christian calendar, for example midsummer and Easter. They were in decline in the late eighteenth and early nineteenth centuries, regained their popularity from the 1830s, but then again waned in the last quarter of the century. Explanations for their later disappearance include the sheer number and scale of public spectacles, which may have satiated the appetite of observers, competition from political demonstrations and other leisure activities, the movement of the elite to the suburbs and beyond, and the general rise in social trust, which made them less necessary.[19]

The parades generally contained members of the elite, local voluntary associations and the workers of major employers, and signalled the competence trust of the organisers, added to the reputation of the town, raised the self-confidence of marchers, and increased intra-group and inter-group trust, though the latter was diluted by the strict segmentation of the processions which limited group interaction and weakened the sense of unity generated. As in the case of feast day processions, they also allowed groups to signal their trust power, members to display their association with a particular society, the elite to exhibit their status and wealth, and neighbourhoods to demonstrate their community feeling by draping their streets in bunting. By giving up their leisure time to parade, society members also advertised their lack of self-interest, the very inclusion of a working-class group in a column signalled that the middle-class organisers regarded it as a model of respectability, and, by marching, societies attracted new recruits, advertised their community involvement, and, if the pageant was to celebrate some national or royal achievement, their patriotism. Those parades to mark commemorative points in the seasonal and Christian calendar can even perhaps be seen as gifts designed to forge trust relationships, respectively, with nature, on which the success of the local economy so depended, and with the Almighty.

For the spectators, the processions generated community identity, which was aided by their dramatic nature, which lifted the senses of both marchers and spectators. Processions often included decorated floats, bands, and Morris and other dancers, and many participants wore special costumes and carried regalia, such as maces and swords They also involved intra-class and some inter-class sociability, though the latter was minimised by the tendency for the various classes to assemble in different places, generally those closest to their homes. Nonetheless, the excitement of the event no doubt caused many to lower their barriers of reserve and to interact. Afterwards, at a pre-arranged meeting place, notables made speeches lauding the town, which further generated community pride, identity and trust. During these addresses, the wives and daughters of the elite occupied an elevated and segregated position, generally a raised platform or a window or gallery. Their presence extended to the ceremony the virtuousness and morality associated with their sex, and, by acting as reminders of the organisers' family lives, added to their reputations. Such women, similarly, attended public meetings and hustings, where their presence played a similar role and was thought to promote peaceful debate by discouraging uncivil behaviour that could jeopardise their safety or virtue.[20]

Funerals

Both middle-class and working-class distant trust relationships were renewed at important rites of passage ceremonies, such as baptisms, weddings and funerals. The last bestowed trust upon both mourners and the deceased's relatives. Those who went to memorial services displayed their caring dispositions, could free ride on the reputation of the deceased and the other mourners, and, through their dress and carriage, could signal their wealth and affluence trust. A mourner's presence would be noted by fellow mourners and a wide section of the rest of the community; funeral processions attracted large crowds, and a list of those who attended was included in the local newspaper. By providing the gift of their attendance, a wreath and verbal commiserations, the bonding power of which was heightened by the context of the gifts, they also strengthened their trust relations with the deceased's relatives.

For the scion of the departed, the funeral could be used to signal the deceased's trust reputation, and ensure that this was inherited. This was achieved in a variety of ways. The route of the funeral procession could pass representative civic sites and locations specific to the life of the deceased and thus draw attention to his involvement in the local community. Heirs could maximise the number of mourners, particularly those with high status/trust reputations, with funeral attendance in some cases acting as a reciprocal gift, each partner in a trust relationship boosting the reputation of the other by attending the funerals of his relatives. The funeral address, again often published in the local press, could highlight the trustworthiness of the departed and its transference to his offspring. The minister conducting the funeral service of the Manchester cotton manufacturer and merchant Thomas Ashton, for example, reminded the congregation that 'his sons were becoming associated with the business [and that] they represented the third generation of Ashtons'. The funeral itself could be lavish, signalling affluence trust. This was particularly important for the working class, as a pauper burial would not only lead to the 'political and social degradation of a perfectly respectable family', but would damage the reputation of the neighbourhood. Neighbours therefore often gave the deceased's relatives burial clothes and money to be used to pay funeral expenses. To strengthen the trust of mourners, meanwhile, heirs could give them gifts. These included the invitation to attend the service, the meal eaten after interment, and funeral presents, usually gloves, scarves or hatbands, which were especially appreciated. On receiving a hatband and a scarf, the Somerset vicar William Holland wrote in his diary that it was 'not the value of either I regard so much as the intimation of respect it conveys'.[21]

Further trust could be generated through the choice of executors, the contents of wills and gravestones. Generally, executors were kin or friends of the deceased, and often possessed relative wealth, status or a trustworthy reputation. These people could be relied upon to carry out their duties honestly and not to divulge to others the financial viability of an inherited business, the testator and his heirs could free ride on their reputation and status and affluence trust, and the appointment could act as a gift, strengthening the relationship between the executor and the heirs. For many, such a gift possessed great trust value. The position publicly identified the individual as competent and trustworthy and as a confident of the deceased, which, if the testator had possessed wealth, status or had been greatly trusted, strengthened his own reputation. He was also able to determine the creditworthiness of the estate and its heirs, obtained introductions to those who received bequests and, was often himself a beneficiary.[22]

Wills produced trust in a number of ways. Leaving the bulk of an estate to kin advertised a family's strong kin trust, bequests to local charities signalled the deceased's and his heirs' benevolent natures, and gifts to non-family members, particularly if of a personal nature, strengthened the family's relationship with the recipients. Many people also left money to the poor on the provision that they attended their funerals, which ensured that mourners were aware of their benevolence, and others incorporated moral codicils in their wills, which required recipients to behave in an honourable manner, support other family members, and so on. As regards gravestones, owing to high levels of mortality, graveyards were much visited places and an expensive monument to the deceased generated for his dependants much affluence trust. Gravestones, in addition, often had inscriptions which specified that the departed (and therefore his offspring) was 'of this parish' and not a mistrusted incomer, assured visitors that he was a 'loving' or 'caring' father, thus highlighting the families' kin trust, listed any community positions held, and, to ensure that the memorial was linked to the living, named his children.[23]

Determinants of trust

Among the many miscellaneous factors that influenced the generation of trust the most important were the demography of a community, its built environment, the income and happiness levels of its residents, and the local and national media.

Demography

The size and rate of expansion of a town and the class, age, gender, civil condition and death rates of its inhabitants impacted on trust at the most basic level. Individuals in large urban areas are likely to interact with a greater number of people for shorter periods and thus form weaker trust relationships than the residents of small communities. Men are less trusting than women, and young adults and single people, with little personal investment in a community, are usually less involved in networks and generate less trust and are less trusting than their older or married neighbours. The gentry and middle class of a town, meanwhile, will generate greater amounts of trust than other classes; the trust created gradually permeating the various social strata. During the nineteenth century, the size of industrial towns grew at a relatively rapid rate, which slowed from the 1850s. All contained a large number of young adults and single people, though the proportion fell over time, and all initially had low gentry/resident ratios, which again rose over the period. Trust levels determined by these factors, consequently, will have been low at the start of the century, but will then have gradually risen.[24]

The demographic changes experienced by industrial towns were related to high birth and death rates and in-migration. Average lifespans were short. The average of age of death was 50 years, though those from the higher social classes could expect to live slightly longer. The high mortality rates were related to the poor urban environment, which was partly a consequence of low levels of social capital and a reluctance to take expensive collective decisions to invest in water and sewerage systems that would benefit the health of the whole community. The urban elites were divided by religion and politics, the middle classes distrusted both local government and the lower orders, and the poor were disenfranchised. Only from the 1870s, when social capital was on the rise did widespread investment in such public utilities begin to occur and mortalities start to fall. As already discussed, by this time, intra-middle-class and inter-class distrust had weakened, a larger part of the municipal electorate were enfranchised, and there was a growing realisation that a failure to act would damage the productivity of workers and the health of elite family members.[25]

Low levels of social capital had an impact on mortality in other ways. Weak neighbourhood gift networks increased the incidence of illness and recovery, and poor relationships between apothecaries, physicians and hospital officials and their clients will have reduced the quality of care given. The relative lack of social interaction, meanwhile, no doubt induced a negative psychological outlook and poor mental health, in particular anxiety and depression, which would have made people more likely to engage in health damaging behaviour and impaired those psychological triggering mechanisms that stimulate disease fighting immune systems. Ironically, the high mortalities, in turn, would have affected levels of trust and association. Poor health would have restricted social interaction and short average lifespans encouraged the adoption of a short-term outlook. People were thus less concerned with building long-term reputations or providing critical life-situation gifts, aware that the benefits of reputation and gift reciprocation could be limited.[26]

Migration involved people moving from the countryside to urban centres and from town to town, and was believed by followers of Adam Smith to counter dependence on poor relief and poverty and thus raise morality. The inflow of people reduced social, intra-firm and employer–employee trust, but raised migrant and geographic co-operation. Social trust was influenced by the age and norms of the immigrants. Many were single men and women in their late teens and early twenties, who, even in normal circumstances, tend to be relatively less involved in networks of social engagement. Easily identifiable by their accents, they held norms of morality that differed from those of natives, and, living in migrant communities, some would have retained their old norms for long periods. Indeed, the new environment may have caused an intensification of traditional behaviour patterns. Freed from the sanctions of their home towns, others may have abandoned their moral values altogether, and all would have possessed different reciprocity norms, leading to confusion over the meanings and timing of gifts.[27] Distrusted by natives, they would also have been less trusting. The young tend to be more suspicious of others than the old, and, as migrants, they were more likely to be victims of opportunism, owing to their naivety and the fact that those who exploited them suffered little or no reputation loss, their prey being regarded as socially beyond the pale.

The heads of migrant families and their wives obtained employment in a restricted number of industries. Any rise of distrust in these sectors, however, will have been offset by the tendency of migrants to undertake casual semi-skilled or unskilled jobs and to work for those who had migrated earlier.[28] Most incomers were unable to enter permanent, skilled employment, lacking the necessary skills, reputation and network connections and suffering from the aura of distrust that clung to immigrants. They were also too old for apprenticeships, even if they had been available, and often had work norms unacceptable to factory owners. Many, consequently, worked for previous migrants, who were less prejudicial towards them and possessed similar norms. Whether they will have had good relations with such employers, however, is questionable. The excess supply of immigrant workers will have given these masters power, enabling them to pay low wages and provide poor conditions. Employee turnover, furthermore, will have been high and the length of the employer–employee relationship short, as, wishing to better themselves and gradually gaining reputations and contacts, most migrants will have rapidly moved on to better jobs.

Few incomers will have escaped poverty. Not only were they badly paid and subject to periodic unemployment, but, given their age on arrival, most will have been encumbered in their first years of residence with the cost of raising children and deprived of their wife's income, most women giving up work on the birth of their first child. The resultant money shortages will have restricted social interaction, minimised their participation in neighbourhood gift exchange networks and damaged their self-confidence. Not surprisingly, most immigrants clustered together, settling in a street or neighbourhood that offered cheap housing and contained others from the same village or area. [29] Here, past migrants could provide them with critical life situation gifts – helping them to obtain housing and employment and to generally adjust to urban life. Sharing past histories, social norms and a religious faith, often related to and largely socialising with each other, past and new immigrants inevitably developed strong bonds of trust, which further crowded out social trust. Given the short distances most travelled, many migrants will also have kept in touch with those family and friends who continued to live in their villages of origin and thus generated geographic trust. Visits home and the emotional support provided during such return trips or in correspondence, however, will again have led to crowding out, reducing the time available for the creation of and the need for new relationships in the new home environment.

The immigrants with the greatest impact on trust were those who travelled long distances, whose norms and characteristics differed greatly from those of the indigenous population. The most distrusted group were undoubtedly the Irish, who largely came from rural areas, were Catholic and were often Gaelic speakers. Because of the lack of ascribed trust and the long tradition of anti-Irish prejudice, they had difficulty obtaining jobs and help from non-migrants. They thus tended to cluster together to a greater extent than other immigrant groups, to develop robust neighbourhood gift-exchange networks and to cultivate strong kinship trusts, which further reduced their involvement with the rest of the community. Lacking the skills and trust reputation to acquire skilled permanent jobs and accustomed to low standards of living, most became poorly paid labourers or took casual jobs as messengers or hawkers. They, consequently, lacked the funds to socialise outside their own communities, lived in 'dissoluteness and dirtiness', and were believed to make excessive use of poor relief, undermine wage rates and steal work from indigenous workers.[30]

The poverty and stresses of their lives, moreover, caused them to have 'a tendency to drunkenness and quarrels' and to become involved in petty crime. Their disruptiveness was also related to factional rivalry that existed between those migrants who came from different parts of Ireland and perhaps a greater tendency for professional criminals to emigrate. Their unruliness and involvement in subversive activities, in turn, caused the elite to view them as a threat to the social contract. Irish migrants were involved in radical causes such as Parliamentary reform, trade unionism and Chartism, campaigned for the revision of the terms of the Act of Union between Britain and Ireland, and, in the 1860s, Fenians were the perpetrators of a number of acts of terrorism.[31]

As discussed in Chapter 2, not only was there migration between towns, but also much movement within communities, which disrupted exchange and trust relationships. In addition, artisans routinely travelled around the country, a practice known as tramping. Examining the records of the Steam Engine Makers Society, Southall found that 13 per cent of the membership changed their town of residence each year and 7 per cent crossed a county boundary or went abroad. Trampers were more likely to be young than old and the numbers appear to have risen during trade downturns.[32] Inevitably, they will have had some influence on social capital, raising geographic trust, particularly among trade union members, and, like more permanent migrants, weakening neighbourhood networks and norms.

Built environment

The built environment influenced trust in a number of ways. The middle classes, particularly, perceived the city and large town as physically and morally dangerous, their fear intensifying with their withdrawal to the suburbs. In Manchester, 'at the very moment when the engines are stopped and the counting house closed' and gentlemen returned to their homes 'the moral order ... [flew] from the town and disappear[ed] in an instant'. Part of the problem was the condition of public places. The smoky atmosphere 'sadden[ed] the face of nature and prevent[ed] the possibility of any cheerful recreation out of doors'. 'The total absence of lamps in some places and ... there being put out too early in others' resulted in 'a great increase in vice and crime', which, with the dirty, unpaved and narrow streets and the lack of public buildings, further discouraged conviviality.[33]

Over time, as councils improved public environments, middle-class trepidation gradually disappeared. Streets were widened, paved, lighted, regularly cleansed and cleared of hawkers, town walls and gates demolished, regulations introduced to reduce atmospheric pollution, parks laid out and new public buildings erected, including assembly rooms and town halls.[34] The result was that town centres became arenas of sociability and many developed a cultural quarter. Here, the middle class could socialise together, thus ensuring high networking returns, and, at set times, promenade and display their wealth and class trustworthiness through their dress, accoutrements, posture and manner of walking.

The improvements raised trust in other ways. By providing a cleaner, airier and lighter environment, local authorities removed the associations with the poor and immorality that dark narrow and filthy streets conjured up in middle-class minds. The reduction of street noise, through the use of granite and asphalt as road surfaces and the removal of hawkers and ballad singers, minimised the nervousness and insomnia that had previously triggered 'indulgence in alcohol' and the downward decent into vice. Street lamps and wider roads, meanwhile, allowed the new police force, the local citizenry and members of temperance and decency associations to monitor public areas for disorderly or unacceptable behaviour, which residents and association members then brought to the attention of the authorities, either directly or through the correspondence columns of newspapers.[35]

The public buildings that were built were constructed in a monumental and ornate style in order to signal the power and the prosperity and therefore trust-worthiness of the town and the people they housed, and to transform the parochial loyalties of ordinary citizens into community pride and trust. Many incorporated friezes depicting female figures, and thus free rode on the supposed superior ethical nature of the fairer sex, and were built in the Gothic revival style of architecture. The latter became popular from the 1830s, popularised by W. N. Pugin, who argued that, not only were building styles expressions of society's morality, but that they played some part in determining its ethical nature. The Gothic style of the Middle Ages owed much to the strong religious belief of that period and its revival would thus 'remind us of our faith' and lead to moral recovery. This would be achieved partly by the structural honesty of the style, which incorporated 'nothing artificial – no deception – nothing built up to make a show – [for example] no sham doors and windows to keep equal numbers . . . [and no] high wall to hide a roof'. Prison, school, hospital, factory and barrack architecture, meanwhile, was greatly influenced by Jeremy Bentham's panopticon, an idealised prison, which, composed of an inspection tower from which cells fanned out in a circular pattern, allowed its inmates to be monitored day and night. The constant supervision, or at least its perception, supposedly not only resulted in the loss of 'the power to do evil [but] almost the thought of wanting to do it'. Such buildings also protected the value of male networking and reduced the likelihood of immorality by restricting female access to certain rooms, and possessed layouts that facilitated social intercourse.[36] Buildings had one entrance and rooms linked by single doors, which reduced the number of routes into and around the structures and thus enforced interaction.

Town-centre enhancements did little to calm the elite's suspicion of working-class districts, where they rarely ventured, and which, in Manchester, formed a 'cordon of beastliness and filth; enough to strike fear into the heart of every civilised inhabitant'. For the middle class and those who lived in these areas, the conditions were both a source of distrust and trust. Middle-class apprehensiveness towards the inner city was partly associated with disease, which the miasma theory proclaimed was largely caused and spread by gasses emanating from diseased bodies, waste products and decaying matter. The elite thus viewed their social inferiors as carriers of illness, though miasma theory led some to claim that the diseased air created a bond between the classes, being 'the fluid in which the rich and poor are equally immersed . . . (the) commonwealth in which we all are born, live and die equal'. It was also believed that poor living conditions corrupted residents. Contemporary sanitary reformers were convinced that overcrowding was 'destructive to the morality . . . of large classes of both sexes', and that 'dirty, dilapidated and unwholesome dwellings destroy orderly and decent habits, degrade the character and conduce to immorality'. The provision of an adequate water supply and good sanitation and the regulation of buildings were thus partly motivated by a desire to raise morals.[37]

Given the unavoidable social interaction of residents, however, it seems inevitable that overcrowding contributed to much household trust, though in lodging houses, which tended to house criminals and prostitutes, these loyalties may have increased crime and reduced social capital. Likewise, high housing densities, by forcing residents to mix in the street and in the pub, would have stimulated neighbourhood attachments. In Bolton in 1841, the population density was a high 21.9 residents per acre, and, although the average number of residents per house was only five, in working-class districts houses could contain up to 15 people, some of whom will have been lodgers.[38]

Income

Poverty reduced trust in a number of ways. The very poor withdrew from social activities, lacking the funds necessary to become involved and wishing to avoid the embarrassment of others' reaction to their hardships; were excluded from neighbourhood-exchange networks; moved house more frequently, preventing the establishment of strong neighbour relationships; and, in some cases, acted opportunistically or turned to crime. Poverty and the related resentment of the working class towards the elite also damaged inter-class trust relations. Income and trust were determined by the cost of living and wage levels and varied between towns and occupations, over time, and over workers' lifetimes. Geographical differences in occupational earnings and living costs were great. There were differences in wages between towns, and, in 1906, there were variations in rents and food prices and similar disparities will no doubt have existed in the nineteenth century. Wages also varied between occupations. Cotton industry salaries were relatively high. Women could earn 9s. to 16s. per week, male labourers and power loom operators up to 15s. per week, and male mule spinners, dressers, sizers and overlookers over 20s. per week. In comparison, in non-cotton industries labourers obtained up to 15s. per week and artisans 20s. to 30s. per week. Both, however, suffered much casual underemployment or unemployment and their average wages were far lower.[39]

During cyclical downturns, the wages and trust of all workers fell, and, in the first half of the nineteenth century, the regularity of recessions will have slowed the development of social capital. Income and trust further fluctuated over workers' lifetimes as their family size and the nature of their work changed. For families, poverty was greatest in stages two and three of Anderson's poverty life-cycle when the number of dependents exceeded the number of providers. Earnings, similarly, varied over the working life. As they aged, male cotton employees moved into less well-paid occupations, and the declining physical strength of labourers meant that they obtained work more infrequently and were paid less well as they got older.

The rate at which real wages grew over time is still somewhat controversial. Lindert and Williamson found that the average real wages of adult males rose by 84 per cent from 1820 to 1850, Crafts estimated a rise over the same period of 62 percent, and Crafts and Mills' calculations suggest that, though there was no increase from 1780 to 1813, from the latter year there was an annual average rise of 1.2 per cent p.a. until 1903. Such data thus implies that income-related social capital rose and inter-class relations improved from the 1820s rather than the mid-1850s. More recent research, however, suggests that advances in living standards were far more modest. Using more accurate price data, Feinstein again found that real wages began to rise from the end of the Napoleonic wars, but that progress was relatively slow, with levels in the 1850s only 30 per cent above those of the 1780s, and that substantial and sustained advances were only achieved from the late 1850s. Moreover, he argues that if other factors are taken into account, such as unemployment, short-time working, the increase in the number of dependents each worker had to support and the fall in poor relief expenditure, the living standard of the average family, in fact, improved by just 10–15 per cent from the 1780s to 1850s and rose at a faster rate only from the late 1850s. Research based on mortality and height data as measures of economic welfare has reached similar conclusions. Using infant-mortality data, Huck found no substantial increase in industrial living standards until mid-century and Johnson and Nicholas have shown that the height of habitual criminals born in Britain from 1812 to 1857 fell from the Napoleonic wars to the 1850s, with the most rapid decline occurring in the 1840s.[40] It therefore appears that income-related social capital strengthened and the anger and resentment that clouded inter-class relations began to dissipate only from mid-century.

For those with no income, a safety net was provided by the poor law. In normal times, however, labourers were reluctant to resort to parish relief, preferring to rely upon their local neighbourhood gift exchange networks and credit. Throwing themselves on the parish would damage their reputations by signalling to others that their assets were exhausted and suggesting that they lacked the trust necessary to obtain credit or to belong to a neighbourhood network. Relief for the long-term unemployed was also less than adequate. Poor law officials regarded those who had difficulty finding employment as undeserving of help and as generators of distrust. Their plight was believed to be the result of personal moral failings, such as idleness and drunkenness, and they were seen as a source of crime and social unrest.[41]

In trade downturns, alternatively, when neighbourhood and credit networks broke down under the sheer weight of poverty, the unemployed had no option but to turn to the parish for help. In these circumstances, requests for assistance had no affect on reputation, as poor relief was believed to be 'a right', an important component of the social contract, with a worker who received no or little help often making 'an angry appeal to a magistrate, not as a petitioner for charity, but as a claimant for justice'. Aware of their obligation and that operatives could not be held accountable for their distress, officials generally provided adequate aid.[42]

Proponents of the new poor law believed that its severity would limit both poverty and the related immorality of the poor by encouraging frugality, hard work and self-sufficiency. For the working class and propertied groups, however, the law threatened to disrupt the social contract, preventing the provision of outdoor relief during trade downturns, and it was believed that placing both the deserving and undeserving poor in the new 'bastiles' would cause the former to be infected by the morals of the latter. Such was the anger in the textile towns of Lancashire and the West Riding of Yorkshire that an Anti-Poor Law Movement emerged, which organised electoral boycotts, demonstrations and petitions and had both middle-class and working-class members and thus strengthened inter-class and intra-class trust. In the event, the movement had a short life, disappearing in 1838. Its loss of support was partly related to the rise of Chartism, but largely to the realisation by its supporters that little had changed under the new system and that the social contract was relatively undamaged. Although in some parts of the country, such as the North East, the new law was fully implemented, in Lancashire and Yorkshire, the arguments and activities of the Anti-Poor Law Movement had made the Poor Law Commission more conciliatory and more willing to permit local autonomy. The new Boards thus continued to provide outdoor relief and workhouses only began to appear in the 1850s and then possessed a relaxed regime – families were kept together and male and female inmates allowed to intermingle and enter and leave the premises at any time. The outdoor relief given, moreover, was relatively generous and in cash rather than in kind, recipients being trusted to spend the money received wisely. Only the undeserving poor were treated badly. Able-bodied males were made to perform work provided by the parish, and females forced to attend domestic training classes, which taught sewing and cooking skills. Both kept recipients occupied during the day, leaving them little time for social unrest and crime, acted against idleness and, in the case of the domestic classes, reduced wasteful domestic expenditure.[43]

The media

One of the gains of schooling is a high rate of literacy. It is generally accepted that between 1770 and 1815 literacy levels, as measured by the ability to sign a marriage register, fell, but that the efforts of Sunday schools and day schools then caused standards to rise, though great differences existed between towns. According to the Bolton bleachers R. Ainsworth and Son, in 1843 71 per cent of their workers were literate, and by 1868–9 in Blackburn, 85 per cent of cotton spinners and 95 per cent of cotton weavers sampled by the local factory inspector could read and write. The high and rising literacy rates fostered letter writing, which along with the development of the postal system increased geographic trust, and permitted a growth in local and national newspaper readership.[44]

There can be little doubt that the reading of newspapers boosted social capital. The concepts of trust and co-operation were actively promoted in editorials, essays written by local literati, readers' letters and poems. Papers also facilitated the growth of voluntary groups, publishing notices announcing their initial and later meetings, and, from the 1830s, nearly verbatim reports of speeches and interjections.[45] Potential members were thus alerted of the existence of societies and were assured that their association with a group, their involvement in public service or philanthropy and their altruistic views would be widely disseminated and their reputations strengthened. Similarly, the publication of annual accounts helped to signal the transparency and honesty of societies, reports of the activities of metropolitan associations inspired provincial emulation, and reporters and editors no doubt acted as intermediaries, increasing inter-network trust and providing useful channels of information. Inevitably, close trust relationships often formed between editors and groups. In return for the gift of publicity, editors were often given memberships, which could pay dividends in terms of information, news stories and, when sales fell, financial aid. They also obtained useful advertising income, increased circulations and, through their memberships and reporting of the societies' activities, improved their own and their papers' trust reputations.

Other types of trust were enhanced by the arrival of the newspaper. The publication of news and information, such as raw material and stock prices, minimised those collapses of business trust and credit recalls triggered by rumour and intrigue. The inclusion in correspondence columns of letters highlighting street disorder forced local authorities to take preventative action, warned others of dangerous areas, reducing the number of trust damaging assaults and crimes, and made perpetrators aware that their behaviour was subject to anonymous observation. By monitoring politicians, editors restrained 'the statesman who would abuse power' and, by increasing political awareness, ensured that breaches in the social contract were rapidly rectified, preventing later more serious breakdowns.[46] Moreover, coverage of local affairs and reminders of the history and progress of a town increased the sense of place identity so important in the development of community trust, reports of proceedings in local police courts acted as an additional deterrent against crime, and the recycling of information from other urban centres and the reporting of national events created geographic empathy.

Even the location where newspapers were read encouraged interaction and attachment. Until the repeal of stamp duty brought newspapers within the financial reach of all, most people read papers in the local inn or in local subscription newsrooms, where they met and socialised with colleagues. The diary of Captain Roger Dewhurst, for example, records in great detail the friends he met and the business he conducted in newsrooms. As with other networks, memberships of such establishments reflected the networking needs of members. The 1818 Bolton Exchange newsroom, for instance, was clearly one of the town's elite networks, including among its members the leading cotton manufacturers, bleachers and iron founders.[47]

Newspapers, however, did not always maximise social capital. Many claimed that they weakened trust. Most papers served the political interests of a particular party and produced highly biased versions of events; the vivid writing style adopted may have affected individuals' perception of the accuracy of stories; producing unsigned articles, reporters often expressed inconsistent views; and the extraneous noise in meetings, speakers' unclear articulation, the lack of a reliable shorthand system and the excisions and alterations forced by a lack of newspaper space often caused speeches to be inaccurately reported. The result was that readers had little faith in the veracity of what they read, a disbelief that did 'harm to the world in comparison with which robberies and treason are nothing'. Others were concerned that the emphasis placed by editors on crime stories increased the perception and fear of criminality and did nothing to discourage the lower classes from committing felonies. To increase circulations, editors described crimes in gruesome detail, in doing so turning 'into matters of sport the most painful and humiliating events of life'.[48]

These suspicions of newspapers extended to magazines and books. Penny dreadfuls were seen as glorifying crime and criminals, and radical publications as undermining 'the mind and morals of the poor', teaching them 'to regard the rich only in the light of their oppressors and . . . urging the exhibition of physical power'. So great was the alarm at the biased and inaccurate nature of serious periodicals that, from the mid-1850s, there was a campaign for articles to be signed, which it was believed would foster responsibility by writers. Penny dreadfuls, however, arguably provided a release from the burden of respectability, reinvigorating readers' ability to adopt respectable mores and manners in their day-to-day lives, and other street and periodical literature had a positive impact on trust. Street ballads and broadsides alerted newcomers to the dangers of opportunism and suggested ways in which it could be avoided. Periodicals, meanwhile, acted as signals of ascribed trust, the middle class openly perusing only those magazines read by other members of their caste, and pictorial journals, such as the *Penny Magazine*, actively promoted morality and social virtue. Most contained homilies on the merits of co-operation, scientific facts on the benefits of mildness of temper, essays on etiquette and politeness and numerous fictional stories, in which the depraved and untrustworthy invariably came to grief and, in the accompanying pictures, were depicted as ugly, badly dressed and often physically deformed.[49]

Some believed both the marketing and content of books to be corrupting. Most monographs were advertised through promotional devises known as 'puffs'. Supposedly impartial short essays or critical reviews, these were actually often written by authors and printed in literary journals owned by booksellers. As regards content, moralists claimed that 'it frequently happens that the worst character in a piece is the most engaging . . . and hence in the mind of the young reader especially all the distinction between virtue and vice are broken down'. In reality, major novelists such as Dickens and Gaskell stressed the importance of honesty and truth, and, in works such as *Hard Times* and *North and South*, strongly argued that the trust found in the family should be reproduced in all social relations. Through sympathetic character portrayals, they also promoted trust of the poor, though the accompanying descriptions of poverty ironically often had the opposite effect. National evangelical societies, nonetheless, began to publish their own monographs, often accounts of heroic lives that stressed the importance of honour and trust; while religious tract societies brought out books and pamphlets that urged readers to lead moral lives and warned of the dangers of immoral conduct.[50]

Happiness

Recent research suggests that trust is positively related to happiness, which causes people to be more trusting and co-operative and more likely to initiate and to be invited to take part in social interaction. Subjective happiness changes over time and is affected by the psychological processes of adaptation, people's adjustment of their subjective level of well-being to changes in their environment, and by aspiration and comparison, the evaluation of one's situation in relation to one's hopes and expectations, past attainments and the experiences of friends and relatives, and so on. Important determinants are personality; sociodemographic influences, such as age, gender, health and marital status; the economic environment, in particular income and employment levels; contextual and situational factors, for example interpersonal relations with friends and family; and institutional efficiency, that is opportunities for political participation, policing, and so on. Many of these determinants are, in turn, partly dictated by the amount of social capital present in a society. High social capital leads to rapid economic growth and therefore lower unemployment, higher incomes and less economic uncertainty, improves health, and has a significant affect on the quality and quantity of social relationships.[51] Social capital and happiness can thus be seen to be closely related, each generating the other. Life satisfaction levels in the nineteenth century are, of course, unknown and perhaps unknowable, and, not surprisingly, there has been little research on the topic. However, it may be surmised that the amount of happiness in existence varied over time and between classes, towns and individuals. Broadly speaking, the middle classes would appear to have been happier than their working-class counterparts and those with relatively good incomes and employment may have been more satisfied than the unemployed and the poor.

Conclusion

The impact on trust of informal networks is difficult to gauge. Most friendships leave little trace of their existence and what evidence remains, in the form of letters and the remarks of others, contains few direct references to trust and tends to represent the relationships of a small elite. Some measure of their impact on social capital, however, can be obtained by an investigation of the locations in which they were created and maintained. Given the size of their customer bases, pubs and shops were obviously important arenas for the generation of informal trust. But, as with religion, charity and education, care must be taken not to exaggerate their contribution. Over the period, shoppers' faith in the quality of their purchases fell, the social diversity of drinkers became narrower and inns produced much animosity, contributing, for example, to street violence and family breakdown. Because of their comparative rarity, pageants and funerals will have had less of an impact. Nevertheless, they respectively generated much town and kin social capital and were important regenerators of trust; occasions where neglected relationships could be renewed or reactivated.

The trust determinants discussed had a profound impact on social capital. The demographic changes of the early nineteenth century and low incomes depressed trust levels, while improvements in the built environment and the appearance of the new media increased them. As with other areas, though, tracking the influence of these factors is problematical. Many of the developments had both positive and negative impacts on trust. Newspapers facilitated the growth of voluntary groups, but, at the same time, their biases and inaccuracies weakened readers' faith in the veracity of 'facts'. In many cases, trust/distrust is both a cause and a result of change. Low levels of social capital contributed to the high mortality rates of towns, which, in turn, weakened social interaction and encouraged the adoption of a short-term trust-damaging outlook. Likewise, abundant social capital results in lower unemployment, higher incomes and better health, all of which generate even more social capital. In an historical context, therefore, social capital, like its counterparts' deference and solidarity, is an inexact concept, which, unfortunately, can provide few incontestable conclusions.

6   Governments and trust

This chapter and the one that follows examine the many ways in which governments can influence trust. This chapter concentrates on political trust and the
first section looks at political change from the perspective of social contract
theory. The theory, of course, is one of many hypotheses that seek to explain
political developments during the late eighteenth and nineteenth centuries and
has been adopted here because it accords most closely with the concept of social
capital.[1] It is argued that there existed between rulers and the ruled a strong trust
relationship. At the start of the century, this social contract encompassed the
community and the local elite, and, later, it additionally included the state and
the electorate. The macro then gives way to the micro and the second and third
parts of the chapter investigate how bonds of loyalty between the various political representatives and their electorates were established and identify the contribution made by local government networks to the production of personal, social
and various other types of trust.

The social contract

Breakdown of the social contract

A social contract is essentially a reciprocal trust relationship between the rulers
and the ruled in which each side agrees to fulfil certain obligations and trusts the
other party to deliver their side of the bargain. The ruled accept the authority of
rulers, but only provided that they fulfil their duties. Following John Locke, 'if
the prince or legislative act contrary' to their 'fiduciary trust' then the people
have every right to revolt and ultimately replace them.[2] In the eighteenth
century, the contract largely existed between the local community and the elite.
It was understood that, in return for social peace, the elite would treat the local
population benevolently, providing, among other things, help during economic
downturns, and ensuring that in normal times food was reasonably priced.

The latter obligation forms the basis of E. P. Thompson's moral economy,
which, though the subject of much criticism, continues to have many supporters.
When the cost of food increased because of unfair practices by producers or
retailers, the local population would raise their concern with the elite. If the

authorities failed to act, or, if for some reason, this stage was skipped, they would then riot; the resulting disorder initiating much social interaction and generating strong bonds of trust between those who took part, many of whom were women, who, as managers of household income, were directly affected by rises in food prices.[3] To distinguish these disturbances from collective action motivated by drunkenness, high spirits, and so on, the riots followed certain norms. They took place in broad daylight and in public places, and care was taken to avoid breaking the law. If grain was seized, for example, it was placed in full view of the authorities and later returned or the owner recompensed. Wishing to retrieve the crowd's trust and restore the contract, the elite, in response, would use their power or trust relations with local producers and retailers to ensure that prices fell. Farmers and traders would be persuaded to change their behaviour or prices fixed and laws against those who stored grain or sold short measures strictly enforced. To further restore trust, magistrates would adopt discretion as regards the number of rioters punished and the severity of the penalties meted out.

The strength of the social contract varied geographically, the bargain being stronger in the pastoral regions of the North, South West and South East than in the arable areas of Central England. Arable districts with their open fields were particularly subject to medieval manorial control.[4] By contrast, manorial power in the pastoral regions was far weaker, as villages were often under the jurisdiction of two or more manors. Inhabitants of pastoral regions thus developed a greater degree of political autonomy than their counterparts in the arable areas. This political self-sufficiency endured and was strengthened in the eighteenth century by the differing economies of the two regions. In arable areas, villagers largely worked the land under the direct supervision of their yeoman farmer employers and gentry landlords, who dominated local government and the judiciary and used their positions to assert their own private interests. In pastoral regions, on the other hand, many villagers were employed in the putting out system, producing work for merchant capitalists, who conducted their business through local middlemen and lived away from the village and thus rarely held any public office. Residents of pastoral districts consequently tended to have greater political self-confidence and leverage over the local gentry than people living in arable areas and were more successful in ensuring that the elite fulfilled their obligations. The social contact and concomitant trust between rulers and ruled was thus far stronger in these areas than in the arable regions.

The social contract began to disintegrate from the end of the eighteenth century. In the large industrial towns, the moral economy increasingly broke down. Riots became more numerous, with 240 occurring in the twenty years from 1790 to 1810, and were less orderly. Crowds often resorted to violence, food was seized without payment or damaged, and collective action often failed to have any effect on food prices. This collapse in the moral economy was the result of an absence of trust between its three main actors. Although urban industrial communities were more dependent on market supplies of grain, the urban elite had little power over producers, and, having few characteristics or networks in common, had non-existent or weak trust relations with them. Any attempts to force prices down were therefore doomed to failure. Similarly, as already discussed, they had relatively poor relationships with their communities.[5] When faced with riots, they therefore resorted to power, calling in the militia and severely punishing any rioters arrested. The fall of neighbourhood and other kinds of associational trust, meanwhile, weakened the social co-ordination and solidity that made collective action disciplined and effective.

The disintegration of the moral economy was accompanied by the abandonment by the elite of their paternalistic obligations. Explanations include the adoption of the tenets of laissez faire and self-interest; the French Revolution, which generated suspicion of subordinates; in the towns, inadequate resources, the urban elite lacking the wealth of the landed aristocracy; and, in rural areas, a decline in elite-community contacts. The gentry progressively became less involved in village activities, such as the beating of the bounds and the harvest supper, and adopted their own recreations, in particularly hunting, which led to clashes with farmers and poachers. They also had fewer personal dealings with employees and small traders, owing to the consolidation of estates through enclosure and economic rationalisation, which, along with the construction of large mansions, emphasised the distance between the rich and the poor.[6]

Re-invention of the contract

The breakdown of the old social contract and the resultant civil unrest and the threat of further disturbances caused the contract to be reinvented. In both rural and urban areas, the elite continued to fulfil some of their obligations to the community, but through their roles as poor law administrators, councillors, magistrates and leaders of charitable voluntary associations. Other duties were gradually taken over by the state, which sought to establish a new social contract between itself and the populace. State social contracts incorporate two important aspects – enfranchisement and the pursuit of collectivist policies. The 1832 extension of the vote was prompted by a fear of social disorder and the realisation that the old contract had collapsed. The Reform Act was preceded by the 1811–16 Luddite riots, the 1816 Spa Field riot, the 1819 Peterloo Massacre and the 1830 Swing riots, and, even the Prime Minister, Earl Grey, accepted that its purpose was 'to prevent the necessity of revolution'. The Act strengthened the social contract between the government and the middle classes. It granted the vote in all boroughs to those occupying a house worth £10 p.a. and thus increased size of the UK electorate from 492,700 to 806,000, and disenfranchised 86 of the smallest boroughs, distributing the freed seats to towns and cities, such as Manchester, which had large middle-class populations. It also provided for the registration of voters, which, along with the rise in real incomes, urbanisation and industrialisation, caused the English and Wales electorate from 1833 to 1866 to expand by 82 per cent. Drawbacks of the legislation were that, even after the redistribution of seats, the Northern industrial counties and London were still under-represented in terms of populations and wealth, and there still existed many proprietary or pocket boroughs, the seats of which were essentially the gift of a powerful individual.[7]

Although it gave the vote to the more affluent skilled workers, the 1832 Act actually reduced the size of the working-class electorate, eliminating the local customs and enactments that in some open boroughs had resulted in almost universal male suffrage. Most workers were therefore unable to fully participate in the political process, though they could petition Parliament and influence Parliamentary candidates and the voting intentions of middle-class voters. In Oldham in the 1830s, for example, the voting intentions of shopkeepers were influenced by the threat of the withdrawal of custom. Large numbers of the working class only received the vote with the passage of the 1867 Reform Act. What motivated this legislation is the subject of debate. Acemoglu and Robinson argue that it was prompted by a sharp downturn in the business cycle, which increased the likelihood of civil unrest unless the social contract was strengthened. Others contend that it was a gift to the new electors from the minority Conservative administration, which believed that the newly enfranchised would return the favour and retain them in office. Whatever the reason, the Act enlarged the franchise in the counties, and, in the boroughs, gave the vote to all householders, adding a further 250,000 to the UK electoral roll. As with the 1832 Act, voter registration and socio-economic change subsequently caused the size of the electorate to expand further, and the 1884 Reform Act, which gave householders in the counties the vote, increased the English and Welsh electorate by another 76 per cent.[8]

The adoption of collectivist policies was prompted the fear of further unrest, campaigns for greater state intervention and the need created by enfranchisement for individual governments to build trust relationships with the electorate and provide them with gifts of policy that would maximise their utility. The calls for the less individualistic laissez faire approach to government came from a group of intellectuals, which included William Cobbet, the Tory politician Michael Thomas Sadler, and the Romantic poets Southey, Coleridge and Wordsworth, and derived its ideas from the seventeenth-century social contract theorists Hugo Grotius, Samuel Von Pufendorf and John Locke and the eighteenth-century writers Montesquieu and Rousseau. The group stressed social and economic interdependence, that 'mankind are reciprocally producers and consumers and . . . under proper regulations . . . are necessary to each other' and believed that the interests of the individual were inseparable from those of the state. Governments thus had a duty to play a more active social and protective role, that is to take on some of the obligations of the gentry, and, if not to promote trust, then at least to restrain the use of power by the powerful, and to take 'care that one part of the people do not cause the other part to lead miserable lives'.[9]

Collectivist policies gradually began to emerge from the 1830s. The following decades witnessed gradual social reform, the extension of education to the masses, and, to pay for the changes, increased taxation, which, by 1867, accounted for 8.12 per cent of the national product, and, in 1927, 18.8 per cent. This rise in taxation, of course, itself posed a threat to the social contract. If taxpayers believed taxation was inequitable or revenues wasted, there was a danger of widespread non-compliance and perhaps social unrest. Over the period, the state consequently sought to develop a trust relationship with those on whom the tax burden fell. In 1842, the indirect taxes on trade and consumption that weighed heavily on trade and industry and working-class consumers were largely replaced by the more equitable income tax. Rather than adopting draconian policies to ensure payment, the government also allowed self-assessment, a gift of trust that was reciprocated by taxpayers. To overcome the suspicion that funds would be wasted through corruption, incompetence or their diversion to supporters of a particular government, from the second quarter of the century a clear set of accounting rules were introduced. These imposed strong controls on spending, ensuring that each item of expenditure was voted annually by Parliament. At the same time, wishing to regain the confidence lost during the Napoleonic wars when government expenditure rose to 23 per cent of gross national product, the state in the first few decades of the century adopted a policy of laissez faire, restricting as far as possible the size of the public sector.[10]

The collectivist policies adopted buttressed the social contract, generated trust between the electorate and individual administrations, and strengthened trust and reciprocity social norms by legitimising engagement with others and co-operation. They also increased inter-class trust by limiting the exploitation of the poor, and, in the last quarter of the century, reducing income inequality. Much of the early legislation, however, was limited, lacking effective enforcement machinery. It thus often failed to change the behaviour of those it intended to regulate. The various factory and mines acts, for example, were merely restrictive, and, even in 1880–1, the Alkali and Explosives Acts were enforced by a staff of just eight inspectors.[11] The state appears to have wished to preserve the electorate's faith in the social contract, but also desired to maintain the support of the capitalist elite and continued to be aware of the danger of losing the country's trust over the issue of taxation.

Other government initiatives sought to promote trust raising behaviour. For example, the establishment in 1861 of Post Office Savings Banks encouraged thrift and reduced the likelihood of moral hazard during downturns, the 1857 Obscene Publications Act increased police powers in the search for and confiscation of obscene material, and, in 1845, 1853 and 1854, legislation respectively made gambling credit debts legally unrecoverable, suppressed the operation of premises for cash betting, and strengthened the law against common gaming houses. Efforts were similarly made to create a moral urban environment, strengthen property rights and encourage arbitration, both in labour relations and in other areas. By mid-century, arbitration clauses were routinely appearing in legislation as disparate as the 1855 Coal Mines Inspection Act and the various public railway statutes.[12]

But, although the state took over certain services, it left many in the hands of voluntary associations, the growth of which it encouraged. Burial and sickness insurance, for example, was provided by a range of mutual societies, supported and regulated by the Register General of Friendly Societies. Other services were left with local government, and, even where they were provided centrally, their finance and administration were usually local. For instance, elementary and technical education was managed by local School Boards and Borough and County Councils. Such delegation enabled the central state to concentrate more effectively on a limited range of issues believed to be crucial to the well-being of the country, such as foreign policy and empire. More importantly, it permitted the survival of the rejuvenated elite–community social contract, which did so much to ensure social peace, and protected the community–state contract and individual administrations from distrust. Many services provided voluntarily or locally were controversial and divisive or vulnerable to moral hazard, and, by ceding control to others, the state avoided excessive taxation. Collective provision, meanwhile, unlike private sector supply, was free of the profit motive and thus less subject to moral hazard and could ensure universal provision and the fulfilment of the social contract.[13]

The most important service left in the hands of local administrators was poor relief. As already discussed, the new poor law of 1834 maintained local control through the retention of parish funding and local administration, albeit by elected guardians, and little effort was made to reign in those Boards of Guardians that failed to fully implement the Act. The state also left much poverty relief in the hands of voluntary philanthropic associations. In the late eighteenth and early nineteenth centuries, English poor law relief accounted for around 2 per cent of the national product, but this figure then fell considerably. Whereas between 1813 and 1833 cost per head ranged from 9s. 1d to 13s., from 1837 to 1900 it rose above 7s. on only six occasions. Conversely, charity receipts grew rapidly and probably exceeded the total national cost of state relief. In the 1860s, the annual income of the various London charities was around £5 million, 'twice that of the Swiss Confederation' and almost as much as the £7 million spent by all Boards of Guardians.[14] Only in 1948 did the state fully take on the provision of welfare, in the process strengthening its own social contract with the electorate, but weakening that between the local elite and the community.

Governments acquired further legitimacy and trust through the presence of the royal family and the adoption of a professed moral ideology and ethical administration. The royal family lent governments its continuity and own reputation for trustworthiness, and, by its actions, also influenced moral social norms. By 1867, Bagehot believed that the British people had 'come to regard the Crown as the head of [their] morality. The virtues of Queen Victoria and George iii [having] sunk deep into the popular heart'. Moral ideology and ethical administration promoted legitimacy, resulted in self-legitimisation, enabling rulers to justify their authority to themselves, and, in the case of ethical administration, ensured economy and therefore low taxation and again influenced moral norms. As Edwin Chadwick commented, officials 'by their intelligence and respectability' inevitably exercised 'a beneficial influence on the lower ranks'. To achieve an ethical public service, the 1854 Northcote–Trevelyan report, largely implemented by Gladstone in the 1870s, proposed the abolition of patronage and the establishment of an open competitive exam for civil service entry. The latter was designed to restrict public service to moral individuals, who would use their discretionary autonomy fairly and in the public's interest. It was based on Oxbridge final year examinations and therefore required a knowledge of Classics, a subject that was believed to imbue students with a liberal tolerance, and was itself regarded as a test of character. To pass involved long hours of study and 'habitual diligence', which 'brought other virtues in its train; for instance temperance and self-control . . . punctuality and accuracy [and] . . . truth and honesty'.[15]

Trust and the electoral process

The exercise of voting rights both indicates the presence of and generates social trust. Taking part in a ballot reflects and creates an interest in the problems of the local community and encourages an identification with its goals. Turnout in UK elections of the period was relatively high at around 70 per cent, though there were great variations between constituencies. Ballots were open, many believing that secret voting would inculcate habits of falsehood and deception and ultimately damage the nation's moral fibre. Electors generally voted for candidates rather than for parties, though from the 1830s there was an increasing tendency to support the latter. Party labels provided a cheap source of information about a prospective MP's political views and made the choice of a candidate who would maximise the voter's utility relatively easy.[16]

To gain or retain power, parliamentary candidates could make use of power or trust. The former involved obtaining votes through the use of influence. A landowner, for example, could enforce his tenants' 'compliance by menaces of expulsion from their farms or forfeiture of his favours' and a manufacturer by threatening to dismiss employers who refused to support him. Such behaviour, however, was not condoned by respectable society and would damage the culprit's trust reputation. Lord Moira wrote that forcing his tenants to support him would be counter-productive, as discovery would 'revolt those who on other occasions give me real weight by following my influence'. Candidates would also have found it difficult to pressure voters. Before 1832, the county voting qualification was ownership of freehold property worth 40s. per annum. In the boroughs, qualifications varied, but were of a similar size. Many voters were therefore men of independent means or successful retailers or craftsmen, who, though not immune to influence, were sufficiently prosperous to ignore it. After 1832, slightly more pliable constituents appeared, but the expansion of the electorate made it even more difficult for one individual to gain power through the exercise of influence. Also, where a landlord/manufacturer did force a tenant to support him, the custom was that he would only request one of his two votes, leaving him free to dispose of the other in any way he pleased.[17]

The majority of candidates depended on trust to garner their support. Trust was generated both between and during elections. Between polls, voters were given gifts of meals and picnics, to which their friends and family were invited, and, in the weeks before the annual electoral list was drawn up and the right to vote registered, each was visited by party representatives, who sought to build a trust relationship. If another party attempted to disenfranchise an elector by querying his right to vote, his own party would undertake his defence. This ensured his participation in the ballot and acted as a gift, the defence process, which involved proving one's qualification before a revising barrister, being expensive in both time and money. Candidates, meanwhile, signalled their trust-worthiness through their participation in voluntary charity associations, which suggested moral worth, compassion and duty to the community, and MPs indicated their competence trust by increasingly becoming more involved in Parliamentary business and ensuring that their conscientiousness was recorded in the local press. The average MP in 1836, for example, voted in only 22.8 divisions, but in 1899 took part in 38.6.[18]

During elections, trust was generated through canvassing and by candidates stressing their trustworthiness in speeches, which were reported in local newspapers, and in pamphlets and printed addresses. Nominees also gave voters gifts. This was a widespread custom and continued to be practised until the late nineteenth century when the introduction of secret voting, the rise of the national party electoral machine, and the passage of the 1883 Corrupt and Legal Practices Act led to its decline. The gifts were intended to strengthen ongoing trust relationships with both supporters, whose votes the candidates coveted, and non-supporters, whose reaction to policy initiatives could influence their success. Few were intended to induce a change in voting intention, which, in any case, was unlikely to take place, as most electors 'could not have been induced to vote against their own party, even if no money had been offered'.[19] Nonetheless, losing candidates regularly accused ballot winners of corruption, partly in the hope of getting the result overturned, but largely to damage their opponent's reputation.

The nature of the gifts bestowed was determined by local norms. Often they took the form of small sums of money or treats, such as the purchase of an alcoholic drink or a meal. Some candidates compensated voters for wages or business lost due to their attendance at electioneering rallies or the voting booth, paid their debts and fines, or, when buying their goods or services, paid a premium on the normal price. Others gave contributions to charities supported by constituents or employed their relatives to provide food and drink or to print and distribute pamphlets and other paraphernalia.[20] To increase the candidate's trust reputation, the gifts were openly bestowed and often advertised by word of mouth.

Gifts of food and ale were given to non-voters as well as to electors. Although they could not directly influence the poll result, displays of loyalty from the disenfranchised could raise an aspirant MP's general reputation, and reduced the likelihood that unpopular policies would be met by protest or fail to be implemented. Non-voters also participated in the various election processions and parades. At the start of campaigns, candidates ceremoniously entered constituencies, visits to electors were often accompanied by canvassing processions, and, on polling day, there was much competitive parading and the victor was marched or chaired around the streets. The involvement of the voteless in these rituals inevitably did much to raise community trust. Intra-party trust, meanwhile, was generated by the wearing of hat ribbons, sashes and armbands in the party colours, the singing of partisan songs, the display of banners and the burning of the effigies of political opponents. To avoid the associated partisan distrust remaining after the ballot, nominees and newspapers constantly stressed tolerance and post-poll celebrations involved the supporters of all parties.[21]

The growing importance of party in determining candidate trustworthiness, the ineffectiveness of influence, and the fact that voter gifts were intended to raise trust rather than change voting intentions can be demonstrated by an analysis of voting behaviour. Numerous such studies have been made and most show that the majority of electors over time remained loyal to one party and that few changed their political allegiance if placed under pressure to do so or presented with a 'bribe'. This stability of political allegiance contributed to the generation of ascribed trust, individuals being able to discover a colleague's political preferences by examining the poll books published after each election. It also played a part in the development of intra-sector and inter-sector business trust, there being a correlation between occupation and political party supported.[22]

Local government networks

Decision-making authorities

As in national politics, the local social contract was strengthened by the expansion of the electorate and the adoption of collectivist policies. Local representation and ethical administration was transformed by the 1835 Municipal Corporations Act, which replaced, with borough councils, 178 corporations, many of which had been unelected, incompetent and corrupt. The Act permitted other towns to petition for incorporation, and, within the new corporations, gave a vote to all occupiers of property who had resided and paid rates for three years and introduced annual elections for a third of all councillors and the public audit of accounts. Unfortunately, like the 1832 Reform Act, the legislation had drawbacks. The older undemocratic institutions, such as the Court Leets, were not obliged to concede power to the new corporations, many towns chose not to apply for incorporation, and a large proportion of the working class, who rented or regularly moved their homes, remained unenfranchised. Over time, however, the older institutions disappeared, boroughs began to incorporate, and more workers gained a vote. Economic stability reduced worker mobility, the 1850 Small Tenements Act, where adopted, gave suffrage to compounded rate payers, and the 1869 Municipal Franchise Act enfranchised all ratepayers, whether direct or indirect.[23] Residents used their new voting rights enthusiastically, and, electorally responsible, the new councils began to adopt collectivist policies, though progress was again slow.

Local government networks comprised the decision-making authorities themselves, around which there existed a hinterland of pressure groups and political parties. Local public offices were largely held by the elite, in particularly by businessmen and professionals. Such men possessed the spare time necessary for public office, manufacturers could use trust or power to encourage employee support during elections, and many government institutions were partly closed to other social classes. To join Boards of Trustees and Councils, candidates had to own property above a given rental value.[24]

Service on public bodies permitted the elite to fulfil the obligations required by the community–elite social contract and allowed them to neutralise government power. The local decision-making process could be restricted to topics that posed no threat to themselves and parliamentary initiatives could be diluted. Most manufacturers were deeply suspicious of government and were particularly wary of the state and its policy initiatives. There was a general belief that central governments were corrupt, incompetent and had little understanding or sympathy towards industry. Blame for these failings was laid on the aristocratic control of Parliament and manufacturing's lack of government influence, which arose from geographic isolation, the distrust that existed between the northern and southern elites, and poor representation in Parliament. From 1800 to 1831, only four of the 59 MPs returned for Lancashire had textile connections, and, even after the 1832 Reform Act, as many MPs had links with the land as with the cotton industry[25]

The holding of an office also offered the usual network trust benefits including networking opportunities, an improved reputation and the ability to free ride on the organisation's gift-giving role. The networking opportunities provided were highly cost-effective. As positions were open only to the elite/middle class, office holders could be assured that no time would be wasted socialising with those who could not advance their interests, and further networking value was gained by the social stratification of offices. Large employers tended to be councillors, whilst their smaller colleagues served in the less prestigious areas of government, such as local Boards of Health and Improvement Commissions. The reputation gains were also impressive. The very holding of a public position signalled unselfishness and trust, and suggested that the holder, wishing to retain the office, would not act opportunistically. Public officials could additionally free ride on the reputation of the institution served, and, in many towns, there was a norm of public service. Leading businessmen were expected to put themselves forward for office, and a refusal to stand would severely damage their reputation.[26]

As regards gifts, the very service of public officials was a symbolic offering to the community, for which they could expect reciprocity, and, through their organisations, they provided gifts in the form of libraries, parks, public baths and so on, which many hoped would inculcate morality and wean people away from neighbourhood networks and thus weaken the power of the crowd. Gifts were also given to those with whom they wished to form or maintain trust relations. In many towns, elite councillors curried favour with the general business community. The activities of large proprietors were less closely regulated than those of smaller men, rates were highly regressive and pollution rules were unenforced.[27]

As with philanthropy, from the 1880s, the elite began to withdraw from local government, their abandoned seats filled by the petit bourgeoisie, who thus began to reap the various trust benefits. The extent of the withdrawal varied from town to town and was dependent on a variety of factors, such as local social structure and the rate of industrialisation. In Norwich, for example, elite representation remained high even in the mid-1930s. The reasons for the withdrawal were the same as those behind the elite's departure from charitable associations. Additional explanations are that greater intra-elite trust caused many would-be councillors to be repulsed by the party conflict inherent in local politics, and that, from the 1880s, public service networking returns gradually declined. The expansion of the municipal electorate and the disappearance of candidate property requirements led to an influx of non-elite representatives, whose networking value was relatively low, whilst the bureaucratisation and the intrusion of national parties and issues into local politics constrained gift giving and increased councillor workloads.[28]

Political and pressure groups

Surrounding the decision-making authorities were a range of pressure groups and political clubs and parties. Pressure groups monitored political leaders for opportunism, alerted central and local government to policy areas where electoral dissatisfaction could threaten the social contract, and themselves generated much social capital. The most successful were generally those that were trusted by those in power, and groups therefore sought well-connected individuals as members and worked hard to establish a respectable reputation. Groups can be split into national, commercial, ratepayer and ad hoc associations. The most important national groups were the factory reform and anti-Poor Law movements and the Chartists and Owenites, all discussed elsewhere in the book, and the Anti-Corn Law League and political unions, which campaigned for parliamentary reform. The latter two movements were largely supported by middle-class liberals, though both included a working-class element. From 1830 to 1832 over 120 political unions were formed, largely in the industrial North and Midlands. The Anti-Corn Law League, meanwhile, comprised 223 associations, which supposedly contained 50,000 members, and, in England, were mostly to be found in the industrial towns and cities of Lancashire, Cheshire and Yorkshire.[29] Both campaigns generated intra-middle-class trust, some inter-class co-operation, and, through newsletters, national conferences and touring speakers, much geographic trust.

Commercial groups comprised those trading sectors that were poorly represented in local government, had few trust relationships with their supposed representatives and were often poorly treated. Over the years, in towns across the land, publicans, provision dealers, butchers, shopkeepers and market tenants formed themselves into a multitude of often temporary societies, frequently in response to negative local government action. Ratepayer groups waxed and waned in the same way and were generally established when rates reached what were considered unacceptable levels. Ad hoc groups, similarly, had short lives and were generally formed to campaign against specific council policies.

A major weapon of the pressure group was the petition, the use of which grew rapidly over the period. In the five years up to 1843 over 9,400 were laid on the table of the House of Commons, as compared to just 880 from 1784 to 1789. Petitions brought 'the people together' and thus generated much trust. The decision to create one was decided at public meetings, at which there was much social interaction. In the first half of the century, meetings were open to all. Later, some were restricted to the invited or the audience strictly segregated, both strategies increasing the networking returns of attendance. In segregated meetings, the front of the hall was reserved for ticket holders, mainly middle-class males, women sat in the gallery and the non-ticket holders stood at the back, with those who were ticketless but enfranchised occupying space closer to the stage than their unenfranchised counterparts, who were only allowed to enter just prior to the start of the meeting. Further social interaction occurred during the gathering of the signatures; many of the collectors were women and a good proportion of the signees were working class. By signing such a document an individual exhibited his concerned nature, gave a gift to the collector and thus strengthened their trust relationship, and demonstrated to the others who signed that he shared their views and could be granted ascribed trust. Once completed, the petition signalled to Parliament the community's solidarity and trust power. This was further emphasised by elaborate presentation rituals. The 1842 national petition, for instance, was carried to Westminster at the head of a procession of marchers who carried several hundred banners and flags and were accompanied by six bands.[30]

The attachments generated within political parties were offset by the distrust that developed between them. This mutual suspicion was intensified by the association of both political creeds with religious beliefs; Liberals tended to be Nonconformists and Conservatives to be Anglicans. In many towns, therefore, there emerged two political/religious groups that were utterly distrustful of each other. Inevitably, the mutual suspicions seeped into the business, social and philanthropic spheres, harming the development of social and business trust by restricting inter-party trading and social relations and inter-party philanthropic activities. The distrust also slowed public expenditure, which, where it involved the delay in the construction of places of social interaction and public works, again damaged the development of social capital.

As with religious distrust, from the 1850s the animosity gradually dissipated. Although allegiances remained intact, there was a gradual movement towards co-operation. The end of hostilities was related to the general increase in social and business trust and the desire of both Conservative and Liberal politicians to build social capital. During the 1860s and 1870s, the outlooks of both parties as regards working-class improvement also began to coalesce. Conservatives began to realise that sobriety, thrift and self-improvement were desirable and Liberals that moral exhortation alone was an inadequate solution.[31]

Conclusion

Over the period, the social contract, the trust relationship between rulers and the ruled, underwent major change. The elite began to fulfil their obligations to the local community through their roles as Poor Law administrators, councillors and leaders of charitable voluntary associations. At the same time, the state social contract grew in importance, and governments, faced with an enlarged electorate, were forced to retain the trust of both voters and non-voters through the adoption of collectivist policies, a moral ideology and ethical administration. Wishing to support the local elite–community contract and maintain its electoral trust, the state, however, continued to cede a large number of services, most significantly poor relief, to the local voluntary sector.

Players on the political stage included MPs and parliamentary candidates, those who served on a range of local public bodies, and members of local political parties and pressure groups. To win and maintain their constituents' trust, parliamentary candidates stressed their trustworthiness in speeches, joined numerous voluntary associations, and provided voters with a range of gifts, including food, drink, and money. Members of local government networks also sought the trust of voters, and, like their counterparts in religious and philanthropic networks, used their positions to increase their own and their communities' social capital. Local political parties and pressure groups, meanwhile, generated much network and extra-network trust and alerted central and local government to policy areas where electoral dissatisfaction could threaten the social contract.

7   The law and trust

One of the main generators of social distrust is actual and perceived crime. It is therefore important to determine whether crime rose or fell during the period and to examine the various government institutions that sought to sanction those who acted opportunistically. The chapter is broadly divided into two parts, which explore respectively crime and the civil legal system. The first section discusses the perceived rise in crime in the early part of the period under study and examines explanations for the phenomena – poor policing, an archaic legal system, private prosecution and an inadequate legal profession. The rejuvenation of the criminal system is then examined and the proposition put forward that the government sought to maximise social capital by deliberately depressing crime statistics. In the second part of the chapter, the spotlight turns to the civil legal system. The failings of the various courts and civil law are investigated, as are the ways in which, over time, the superior and local courts were reformed and civil law toughened.

Crime

Early inadequacies of the criminal system

The first part of the nineteenth century appears to have seen a rise in crime, which led to 'distrust, suspicion and watchful attention', discouraged people walking the streets and thus reduced sociability, and depressed capitalist endeavour. For 'a husbandman will not care to sow when he is apprehensive that the fruits will be reaped by another [and] the capitalist will not willingly risk his savings when he fears his production will not be secure'. The actual extent of the increase in crime is unknown. A 1826 select committee concluded that the number of misdemeanours in the country as a whole increased throughout the first 25 years of the century, and in Lancashire, Lancaster Gaol records show that the number of criminal prisoners rose from 563 in 1810 to 2,374 in 1826. Such statistics, of course, may simply indicate an increase in prosecutions rather than a rise in the number of offences committed. Yet, even if this is so, the figures, by leading to a perception of rising crime, will still have damaged trust. That such a perception existed is undeniable. Reminiscing about 1830s Bolton,

Thomas Bromley in a 1877 speech remembered that 'there was very little protection for persons or property. Even on a Sunday it was not safe for a cleanly dressed person to pass through the outskirts of the town without meeting with insult'.[1]

Assuming that crime did indeed increase, a number of factors can be highlighted to explain the rise. Firstly, inadequate primary internalisations of trust norms and the fall in social trust. The internalisation during childhood of norms, including the social rule that prohibits crime, may have declined in both quality and quantity during the first half of the period. Low social trust, meanwhile, will have reduced the cost of criminal activities, in that lawbreakers had few trust relationships or trust reputations to lose and were unlikely to suffer social sanctions. There was also more opportunity for criminal activity, less chance of being caught, and perhaps a greater need for the proceeds. The expansion of business and commerce led to more embezzlement, fraud and financial corruption, and the increase in the number of moveable and disposable goods of value in shops, warehouses and people's homes offered greater temptations for theft. Given the anonymity provided by the size of the new manufacturing towns, the constant movement of populations, the large number of houses inhabited by factory workers and empty during the day, and improvements in transportation, which facilitated the sale of stolen goods outside local communities, there was also less likelihood of apprehension. The destitute may even have been forced to turn to crime by unemployment and low wages. John Clay, the Chaplain of the Preston House of Correction, believed that there was a direct link between unemployment and wrongdoing. If so, the trust effects of crime will have shadowed the economic cycle. A study of Manchester and Salford crime figures, however, suggests that, here, at least, there was little connection between crime and poverty, with the number of arrests actually falling during periods of distress.[2]

Other important contributory factors were poor policing, an archaic legal system, private prosecution and an inadequate legal profession. Enforcement of the law was poor. Most towns were policed by constables, watches (that is, day and night patrols) and, at times of civil unrest, the military. Constables were appointed by the local civil authority. Local notables, they were respected by the community, with whom they had bonds of friendship and kinship. They therefore had little difficulty in gaining help in the solving crimes. Drawbacks were that constables were few in number, appointed only for 12 months, part time, received no training, obtained little remuneration and were expected to perform a range of duties in addition to policing, including the inspection and maintenance of roads, bridle paths and bridges and the collection of rates. Many, consequently, employed others to do the job, choosing the cheapest rather than the most efficient candidate. Constables and their employees also had a tendency to use their positions to strengthen their personal trust relationships, adopting a lenient attitude to those lawbreakers who happened to be friends, relatives, neighbours or fellow traders. Likewise, although the military could easily break up riots, they were unable to act with anything less than the maximum force. Commanders therefore often refused to become involved in local unrest, and, when they did intervene, the result could be the destruction of the local social contract.[3]

As in other areas, communities sought to overcome poor quality policing themselves. Victims offered rewards to those who detected a crime or gave evidence that led to a successful prosecution and placed advertisements in newspapers containing details of the offence, the goods stolen and the value of the reward tendered. Individuals and groups of traders or residents employed private watchmen to guard and protect their property, and watch societies were established.[4] These comprised groups of residents of all classes, who patrolled the streets, dealt with minor disturbances and, if necessary, made citizen arrests, and met socially, generating much inter-class trust. Such societies, however, were unable to tackle political unrest, and some argued that they merely displaced crime, causing thieves to move their operations to less vigilant communities.

In working-class areas, families and neighbourhoods policed themselves. To retain their own trust reputations, relatives monitored and applied sanctions on those members of the family who turned to crime, particularly if the offences were committed against those who lived in the same street and the risk of discovery was high. If this did not occur, their neighbours, fearing the loss of the community's reputation on which they free rode, would punish the entire family through gossip, insult and complete or partial exclusion from the reciprocal gift network. High neighbourhood trust was thus associated with low crime levels, which generated further social capital.[5]

Criminal offences were classified according to the method by which they were tried, that is into summary and indictable crimes. Indictable offences were subdivided into felonies, misdemeanours and treasons. Felonies were crimes punishable by death or transportation and Crown forfeiture of the felon's property. By 1800, there were over 200 felonies, including homicide, larceny, robbery, burglary, arson and rape, and, between 1810 and 1835, around a third of those convicted on indictment were either executed or transported. The advantage of both forms of punishment were that they acted as a deterrent to both actual and future criminals and they removed the immoral from the community, permanently in the case of capital punishment and for at least seven years and generally for life where the lawbreaker was transported. The felon was thus prevented from committing further crimes, contaminating others with his immorality, and procreating a new generation of criminals, many believing that criminal tendencies were hereditary. The drawback to the policy was that the severity of the punishments caused people to 'shut their eyes to crime and [make] difficulties about bearing witness' and led juries to become 'excessively indulgent' and prone to acquitting defendants, even in the face of incriminating and compelling evidence.[6]

Misdemeanours were for lesser offences, such as fraud and cheating, and were punished by whipping or other corporal punishment, such as the pillory or ducking school, imprisonment, a fine or a combination of these penalties. The effectiveness of corporal punishment arose from the humiliation involved if it was undertaken in public, and the pain inflicted, which forced those committed for violent crimes to empathise with their victims. It was also cheap, had little effect on the victim's long-term health and productivity, and left marks by which the immoral could be easily recognised. Those imprisoned were placed in local gaols or in hulks, old masterless ships of the line moored in the Thames at Chatham and Portsmouth. Confinement rarely lasted longer than 12 months and convicts undertook hard labour. The only form of instruction was the Sunday service, and, when not working, prisoners were generally confined together with no supervision. The prisons thus acted as schools of crime and immorality, and, to reduce the effectiveness of their lessons, in 1823 and 1824 the government passed the Gaol Acts, expressly designed to improve 'the morals of prisoners'. To this end, the various types of detainees were separated, for example the convicted from the unconvicted and vagrants from other offenders; gambling and the sale of liqueur was abolished; salaried governors appointed; the duties of Chaplains defined; and the importance of education stressed. Unfortunately, there was no enforcement of these provisions until the appointment of a prison inspectorate in 1835 and imprisonment thus continued to have a demoralising influence.[7]

Persons accused of felonies, misdemeanours or treasons were normally brought before a Magistrates Court, where a preliminary examination would be conducted. If necessary, they would then be committed for trial at the Old Bailey, an Assize Court or, for cases of petty larceny and misdemeanours, at a Court of Quarter Session. The inequities of these courts generated among the lower orders much distrust of the elite. Prisoners had to stand throughout trials; were denied copies of the deposition or indictment; in the case of felonies, their counsel were not permitted to address the jury on their behalf; and, in capital cases, juries often had to sit all night, the defence being presented when their power of concentration was at its weakest. The courts were also often ineffective in the conviction of the guilty. Juries were reluctant to 'send down' those accused of felonies, lay quarter session judges often had little knowledge of the law, the rules of criminal pleading were so strict that minor defects in indictments could lead to acquittal and prosecutions of paedophiles regularly collapsed as the victims were too young to be sworn.[8]

The second form of criminal offence was the summary crime. These were minor misdeeds that were punished by a fine, a very short prison sentence or time in the stocks. The cases were heard before local magistrates or Justices of the Peace, who had an impact on social capital far beyond their legal role. In 1830, there were approximately 31,000 such officials in the UK, and, in 1850, around 24,000. Of these, 20 per cent and 35 per cent respectively were active, that is had taken out the writ that empowered them to act.[9] They were appointed by the Lord Chancellor on the recommendation of the Lord Lieutenant of the county in the case of county magistrates, and on the advice of the local council in the case of borough magistrates. Unpaid and having to own or occupy land worth at least £100 p.a., county magistrates were from the landed classes, while their borough counterparts were usually members of the local commercial elite.

By becoming JPs, the gentry could ensure that the law was effectively applied. The industrialist James Scowcroft, when made a magistrate in 1846, for example, 'set himself the task of raising the moral and religious tone of the masses', declaring that 'that he would make the law so respected and induce the people to become so honest that he or anyone else might leave their watch in the market place on a Saturday night and it would be safe there on Sunday morning'. Others sought to promote trust by adopting the role of arbitrator, seeking to negotiate peace between disputants rather than secure prosecutions and convictions. Minor misdeed thus often failed to come to trial and punishments could be lenient.[10] For the ambitious, a place on the bench additionally afforded more selfish benefits. By associating themselves with the morality of the law and the ancient heritage of the position, they improved their own reputations. Furthermore, they gained the trust and information benefits that accrued from interaction with other elite businessmen and landowners who served as magistrates; came into contact with solicitors, who often acted as trust intermediaries; and acquired power, the existence of which discouraged employees and trading partners from acting opportunistically.

It was this power which caused many to distrust their local bench. A small minority of magistrates defrauded their courts, pocketing fees, and many acted in the interests of their class, particularly in the suppression of public unrest and employment cases. Further animosity arose from the manner in which justice was dispensed.[11] In some districts, the public and press were excluded from hearings and the accused refused legal representation. There were no set court procedures and both magistrates and their clerks often had little knowledge of the law. Defendants were thus often asked no questions and decisions were often contradictory and unfair. An appeal to a higher court, although possible in theory, in practice was generally infeasible.

Prosecution was essentially a private matter – the responsibility of the victim. At the beginning of the nineteenth century around 80 per cent of criminal actions were brought by injured parties, with the bulk of the remaining cases initiated by parish constables. Unfortunately, many victims were disinclined to take up the burden. The pursuit of the perpetrator of a crime through the courts took time, energy and money, and could carry a social cost, and, for businessmen, an economic charge in the form of a litigious reputation that could repel potential trading partners. Given the unpredictability of the court system and the difficulty of marshalling evidence, there was also no guarantee that a prosecution would be successful. To encourage prosecution, therefore, the government offered rewards. Those who took action against felons and obtained a conviction received a bounty, the value of which varied from £10 to £40 according to the crime committed. Boroughs, parishes and local magistrates, similarly, provided rewards, often raised by public subscription, for the conviction of the perpetuator of a particular crime, as did banks and insurance companies. As a result, there grew up a class of professional thief takers, who both investigated crimes and brought the culprits to justice.[12]

Wishing to limit crime further, in many towns prosecution societies were formed. These provided mutual assurance for members by sharing the cost of the investigation, detection and prosecution of crimes.[13] From the 1820s, they additionally began to organise local watches or patrols, and, in some cases, took on an insurance role, paying members some proportion of their loss if stolen goods were not recovered or no offender was prosecuted. The societies, again, generated intra-group and inter-class trust, and membership acted as a deterrent to thieves, names of members being widely broadcast in handbills and adverts. They also provided a public good, in that their activities reduced general crime, and, by mid-century, many societies had begun to form connections and links, which generated intra-community and geographic social capital.

To help them through the intricacies of the criminal and civil legal system, many turned to solicitors and barristers. Unfortunately, lawyers were in short supply and there was much distrust of their abilities and honesty. Most lawyers received poor quality training. Towards the end of his career, the solicitor Thomas H. Winder admitted that, as an articled clerk, he had 'read Blackstone's commentaries in a desultory way, but, as I had not to pass either a preliminary or intermediate examination, there was no inducement to study, and . . . I allowed the time to pass without gaining much knowledge of my profession'. Solicitor exams were introduced only in 1836, and, before this date, the clerk at the end of his training merely went before a judge 'who asked a few questions and granted his fiat for the applicant's admission [as] it was very unlikely that a judge with plenty of other work . . . would wish to prolong the interview or to ensure its repetition by holding the candidate unqualified'.[14]

The dishonesty of lawyers was renowned. A well-known business manual writer stated 'unhesitatingly that the man who has in any way to do with lawyers except in the most simple cases . . . must be a victim'. A view seconded by the Manchester clergyman Robert Lamb, who declared that solicitors had 'the insensibility of a cannibal'. Their duplicity was thought to partly to arise out of the nature of their work – one-sided advocacy comprising 'deception and avowedly so', their contact with the dishonest, the fact that their code of conduct developed in a less morally enlightened age and their possession of greater knowledge than their clients, which put them 'in a position no man ought to occupy towards another'. Clients were particularly suspicious of their fees. There was no fixed charge and payments for work could vary greatly from one solicitor to another. Those who wished to be charged reasonable amounts and avoid moral hazard thus tended to take great care in their choice of solicitor, often choosing fellow association members, and to have long relationships with them.[15]

Rejuvenation of the criminal system

By the 1870s, trust in the government as an agency of protection had risen – policing had improved, there had been changes in the operation of courts and punishments, and prosecutions had begun to be undertaken by the police. Modern policing began to arrive from the 1820s. In 1829, London obtained uniformed professional police; six years later the Municipal Corporations Act required all borough councils to establish watch committees and appoint paid constables and watchmen, and, in 1839, the counties were encouraged to set up forces. Regrettably, the 1835 legislation gave governments no powers of enforcement and incorporated no requirements as regards the number of policemen to be appointed, while the 1839 County Police Act left it to the discretion of magistrates as to whether a force should be established. In many areas, therefore, policing was slow to appear and was often inadequate; opposed by both ratepayers and vested interests. By 1842, 20 per cent of boroughs had failed to found forces, and, in 1853, only half of the 56 counties had put the 1839 statute into effect over the whole of their areas.[16] To rectify the situation, the government in 1856 passed further legislation, which required all counties to establish police forces, introduced regulations regarding pay, allowances and clothing, appointed four salaried government Inspectors of Constabulary, and gave each borough and county a grant that covered a quarter of the cost of paying and clothing its police, provided they were certified by the inspectorate as 'efficient'.

Welcomed by the propertied classes who had most to gain from their presence, the new police were distrusted by the poorer sections of the community. There were anti-police protests and riots in many towns and numerous convictions for police assault or obstruction. The animosity sprang from a number of sources. The police were the main enforcer of the poor and game laws and the vagrancy, juvenile and education acts. Some believed that they possessed a class bias, particularly in cases of drunkenness and assault, or that they were the tool of employers, vehemently opposed to trade unions and legitimate strike action. Others objected to their attempts to take over community self-policing and halt enjoyable recreational activities, and to their abuse of power. Low wages led to corruption and some officers appear to have taken a malicious delight in arresting (and eventually releasing) innocent people merely on the 'suspicion' that they had committed a misdemeanour.[17] The very nature of the police also stoked suspicion. To prevent partisanship, officers were often migrants and were encouraged by their superiors to isolate themselves from social contact with the local community, and many stayed in their jobs for only a few months. More importantly, communities rapidly became disillusioned about the effectiveness of forces. Owing to the poor quality of recruits and the heavy workloads, crime clear-up rates were initially poor, especially as regards offences against property.

Over time, this distrust dissipated, though never completely disappeared. Wages and the quality of recruits improved, and police forces learnt to exercise their powers with discretion, for example making use of cautions and avoiding involvement in family disputes. People also began to appreciate the security provided by the police. The greater number of officers and increasing professionalism caused crime clear-up rates to improve. It appears that in the second half of the century one person was apprehended for every three or four reported indictable offences and for every two or three felonies. The police were additionally believed to have had a deterrent affect on crime, their mere presence on the streets reducing offences such as pickpocketing and mugging.[18]

Both the higher and lower criminal courts underwent reform. In indictment trials, poor prisoners on capital charges began to be assigned counsel, the laws of criminal evidence were reshaped, from 1836 felony prisoners obtained a copy of the disposition and their counsel could address the jury and the 1851 Criminal Procedure Act relaxed the rules of criminal pleading. In summary proceedings, from 1836 the accused were given the right to be defended by counsel, the 1848 Jervis's Act obliged JPs to sit in open court and laid down a mandatory code of procedure, and other legislation improved the methods used for the recovery of fines and debts, created standard forms for warrants and summonses, and allowed the appointment of professional stipendiary magistrates. Over and above these changes, summary jurisdiction was extended to a mass of indictable offences hitherto tried in the Court of Assize and Quarter Session. The 1847 Juvenile Offenders Act empowered magistrates to try children under the age of 14 accused of simple larceny, and other statutes permitted various adult indictable cases to be heard summarily. The main benefit of the reform was that the guilty received lesser penalties and avoided imprisonment, which could corrupt the young and cause adults to lose their jobs and thus be forced a return to a life of crime on their release. The lower costs and less cumbersome procedures of magistrates courts also encouraged more people to prosecute and JPs were thought more likely than juries to convict in cases where there was an absence of strict legal proof.[19]

Punishment, similarly, underwent change. Capital and corporal punishment and transportation gave way to imprisonment, prison conditions improved, reformatory schools were opened and greater efforts were made to reduce recidivism. The disappearance of capital and corporal punishment and transportation was related to various campaigns for their abolition. Opponents of capital punishment were convinced that it 'weakened the moral taste or sensibility of the people'. The harshness of the penalty damaged the public's faith in the legal authorities and actual hangings caused spectators to 'become callous to the woes and torments of our fellow creatures' and thus promoted further crime and bloodshed. Likewise, flogging was said to degrade and demoralise its victims, a whipped man becoming either 'broken-hearted ... or a reckless criminal', and critics of transportation either claimed that it failed to act as a sufficient deterrent or that it was excessively severe. As a result of the anti-capital punishment campaign, the number of felonies punishable by death gradually fell, until by 1861 there were just three – murder, piracy with violence and arson of HMG ships. Transportation ceased in 1867, largely because the receiving colonies were concerned that it damaged their own levels of social capital, and whipping, again, slowly disappeared from the statute book, until it was used only for those convicted under the Vagrancy Acts. It then made a partial comeback, when an outbreak of street robberies in London led to the passage of the 1862 Security from Violence Act, which made flogging the penalty for robbery and garrotting.[20]

The replacement for these punishments was imprisonment, which campaigners believed, through 'religious instruction and moral precept', could inculcate in a wrongdoer 'a sense of shame and repentance for his past conduct' and restore 'the unhappy wretch' to society. For this to occur, prison conditions needed to be improved, and, after much campaigning, in the 1840s and 1850s new prisons were constructed and a more caring regime introduced. The new prisons were specifically designed to enhance the morals of inmates. Each prisoner had his own cell in which he spent most of the day. He was thus safeguarded from demoralising contact with other felons, forced to contemplate on his crimes and became more open to appeals to his own 'better self'. He received daily visits from the Governor and Chaplain, attended services in the prison chapel, where he was again allowed minimum contact with other prisoners and was treated with kindness, which 'tender[ed his] heart and [made him] more susceptible of [moral] impression'. If he responded well to this treatment, he was given gifts, which helped to build trust relationships with the prison authorities. In Dartmoor, those who behaved in a reasonable manner were allowed to wear 'liberty clothes' on Sundays, to grow their hair and beards, and to write more than one letter home per month, and in other jails they were rewarded with extra allowances of between 3d and 9d per week, which could be spent on luxuries such as tea, butter and cheese.[21]

This new philosophy of imprisonment, however, was short-lived. Critics argued that such prisons provided 'a sugar plum system of discipline', which failed to deter potential criminals, and the more humanitarian complained that separate confinement produced 'long suffering and deep mental affliction'. In 1863, a Royal Commission concluded that incarceration was not sufficiently dreaded, and, in the following year, the Penal Servitude Act introduced a new harsher regime that placed greater emphasis on punishment via hard labour and the treadmill. At the same time, Sir Joshua Jebb, the architect of the caring regime died and was replaced as Surveyor-General of Prisons by Edmund Henderson, who, along with his director Edmund du Cane, believed prisons should constitute a 'warning' to those tempted to turn to crime.[22] Inevitably, the new regime destroyed the trust relationship between prisoners and their guards and weakened working-class faith in the social contract. Whether it reduced crime, is debatable.

The harsher regime did not extend to juveniles, and, from the 1860s, greater emphasis was placed on the after-care of prisoners. Afraid that interaction with adult criminals would cause young offenders to imbibe their immoral norms, the government in 1854 set up reformatory schools to which magistrates could send any offender under 16 years of age for between two and five years. To encourage parents to restrain their offspring's criminal activities, it was also laid down that the fathers of inmates should contribute up to 5s. per week to their care and maintenance. Three years later, further legislation allowed JPs to send any child aged between seven and 14 whose parents could not give a surety for his/her good behaviour to an industrial school, where they would be free from the immoral influence of their peers and family. As with reformatories, fathers again had to make a contribution towards their children's maintenance. By 1860, there were 45 reformatories holding around 4,000 offenders, and, by 1871, 59 industrial schools had been founded. Both establishments were usually small, allowing the formation of strong trust relationships between teachers and residents, required inmates to perform physically hard work, 'the backbone of reformation', sought to equip them with skills that would enable them to later earn a living and become members of the respectable working class, and instilled in them such values as honesty, sobriety and godliness. On leaving the schools, students were found employment in environments where they would be unlikely to be recontaminated by immorality. Girls were usually placed in domestic service, boys were often sent to sea or enlisted in the army, and a number of children were found jobs in the colonies. In the event, relatively few appear to have turned to a life of crime. The 1884 Royal Commission on the work of the schools estimated that three-quarters of those discharged were 'doing well', and David Jones found that two-thirds of Welsh ex-pupils never had any further contact with the criminal courts.[23]

Unlike those hung or transported, all prisoners at the end of their sentences returned to the streets. To limit recidivism, the government in 1864 laid down that re-offenders would be given a minimum prison sentence of seven years, in 1875 established a register of former convicts, and, from the 1850s, required the police to monitor those prisoners who had served a portion of their sentence and had been released on licence. Convicts discovered associating with notoriously bad characters or leading an idle and dissolute life with no visible means of support would be rearrested and forced to undergo the remaining portion of their sentence, and those who reoffended would have this time added to their new prison term. To increase the effectiveness of the surveillance, from 1864 such men additionally had to report to the police once per month and to notify them of any change of address. Usually, the police lacked both the time and inclination to undertake such surveillance, and, from 1871, therefore only those former prisoners who the courts believed were particularly liable to reoffend were monitored. To prevent them joining the criminal underworld of the large cities, from 1823 convicts who had served their time were also given money to enable them to return to their place of settlement, and, particularly from mid-century, former prisoners could obtain financial and other help from a variety of specialised charities, such as the 1860 Discharged Prisoners Aid Society.[24]

From the mid-1840s, the rise in prosecution and indictable crime figures halted, and both then remained relatively constant until the mid-1920s, despite continued population expansion and the appearance of new crimes. From mid-century, moreover, people perceived that crime had fallen. In 1876, L. O. Pike declared that 'there never was in any nation . . . a time in which life and property were so secure as they are at present in England . . . any man of average stature and strength may wonder about on foot and alone at any hour of the day or night . . . and never have so much as the thought of danger thrust upon him'. It could be argued that this apparent fall in crime reflects the mid-century rise in social capital. Crime levels could also have been affected by the gradual rise in wages, the fall in cyclical unemployment and the improvements in policing, the criminal legal system and punishments described above. An alternative more controversial explanation is that the government wished the police to concentrate on non-indictable offences and sought to depress official indictable crime statistics. The primary role of the police was to halt violent leisure activities, such as dog fights and bull baiting, enforce local ordinances that made Sunday trading illegal, and to keep the central areas of towns free of disorder, clearing them of drunks, prostitutes, hawkers, sellers of indecent literature and users of profane language, and so on. By concentrating on these generally non-indictable offences, which were more visible than indictable crime, the police ensured high levels of social trust, maintained the electorate's faith in the social contract, strengthened their own trust relationship with rate payers, and helped to improve working-class morals.[25]

As regards indictable crime, such as robbery, Howard Taylor has claimed that the government and the police deliberately sought to depress official statistics.[26] Low crime and prosecution figures reduced prosecution and punishment costs and helped to maintain the legitimacy of the capitalist system, crime strengthening the arguments of and support for those who criticised capitalism. More importantly, they maximised social capital and all the benefits that accrued from such trust. From the 1820s, police forces began to prosecute indictable offences themselves, and, where this was not the case, reimbursed private prosecutors part of their costs. This new expenditure was met by central government and to a lesser extent by local authorities, both of which wished to keep the expense to a minimum, aware that increases in taxes and rates would damage their trust relationships with their electorates. Their reluctance to provide these funds was further strengthened by the belief that the replacement of transportation by prison as the normal penalty for indictable crime had reduced the cost-effectiveness of prosecution/punishment. Unlike transportation, prison failed to remove criminals permanently from society and was not in itself generally perceived as reformative; after serving their sentences, offenders usually rapidly returned to a life of crime. Prison was also expensive and relatively inelastic in terms of accommodation.

The government thus began to move away from a crime policy based on the prosecution of all wrongdoers towards one that sought to provide only a general deterrence through the punishment of a limited number of specimen crimes. Prosecution rates were kept low in a number of ways. Private prosecutions by the public were discouraged by requiring those taking action to continue to meet some of the costs themselves and by keeping the rate at which other costs were reimbursed by the government relatively low. Police prosecutions, on the other hand, were minimised by an appreciation by Inspectors of Constabulary that taking fewer people to court released more government funds for the police and that low prosecution/crime figures benefited their careers. There also developed a political climate in which police zeal in investigating and prosecuting crime became to be viewed with suspicion. Police constables, for example, were accused by politicians of manufacturing crime in order to profit from the fees and other perquisites they received when they brought cases to court. It was consequently in the interests of the police to keep prosecutions as low as possible and to ensure that figures of recorded crime matched prosecutions, a goal that was easily achieved since the government required them only to record crimes 'as in their judgement, from the circumstances attending them, would, if discovered, be sent for trial'. The result was that many indictable felonies went unreported, but the government could use the police's statistics to 'prove that [crime] is a decaying branch of business' and so calm the public's fears of criminality and increase levels of social trust.[27] Some indication of actual crime levels can be obtained from the Head Constable of Liverpool's admission in 1867 that the Liverpool police in the previous year had been aware of at least 16,000 robberies, but had recorded only 4,792.

The civil legal system

Failings of the system

At the start of the century, neither the civil courts nor the law succeeded in promoting high levels of trust. The court system comprised the superior courts and various local legal tribunals, the most important of which was the court of request. The superior courts of Common Pleas, Kings Bench, Equity and Exchequer in 1830 dealt with some 90,000 lawsuits, but generally provided an inadequate service. Their procedures were cumbersome and over-technical, forcing appellants to employ professional assistance, generally both an attorney and a barrister, which, along with the various court fees, caused any form of action to be expensive. Their complexity and the short periods during which they sat also meant that cases took a long time to settle and the jury's control over fact finding and the law of evidence could result in unexpected outcomes.[28]

Local and special courts suffered similar drawbacks. In 1830, there were over 300 such courts that dealt with 300,000 claims per annum. The least important were the Courts of the Principality of Wales and the Palatinates of Chester, Durham and Lancaster, the old County Courts and the municipal Courts of Record that were based in Bristol, Liverpool, London and Manchester, and those tribunals that applied special customary law, such as the Manor, Stannary and Mining courts. Of greater significance, were the courts of requests, which were concerned with the recovery of debts. These began to appear in the mid-eighteenth century, were established by civic authorities via statute and, by 1830, numbered around 250.[29]

Problems with the Courts of Request were that, created by separate Acts of Parliament, there was great variation in procedure, their geographic jurisdiction was confined to the area laid down by the statute and they generally oversaw cases involving sums of up to only 4 shillings, though later courts dealt with amounts of up to £5. There was therefore a range of actions involving debts of between £5 and £20 that were outside their jurisdiction, but could not be economically taken to the superior tribunals. The courts also followed the discretionary rules of 'equity and good conscience', as opposed to common law; their unpaid lay judges, drawn from the ranks of the social and commercial gentry, had little knowledge of jurisprudence; the legal representation of litigants was rare; and it was generally understood that decisions were not subject to appeal to a superior court. The decisions arrived at were thus often highly unsatisfactory and were often inconsistent.[30]

The other local courts had a similar bad press. The Palatinate courts were subject to complaints relating to their competence and independence and to judicial tenure. The Courts of Record were believed to have archaic procedures and to be costly, inefficient and corrupt, and the customary law of the Manor and Stannery Courts failed to keep pace with economic and social change and was often anachronistic and inoperable. The large number of different types of court also led to confusion, the newer industrial towns often possessed no tribunal of their own and all the courts had difficulty coping with ever-expanding caseloads.[31]

The most important civil laws were those that that applied to patents and debts. All left much to be desired. Patents could easily be circumvented through minor changes to inventions, and, 'as business became complex, it was found that ... [contract law was] too general'. Technological change and industrialisation created new situations that were not covered by statutes and led to uncertainty about legal rights and liabilities. As regards debt, given that the majority of business transactions were conducted on a credit basis, the ability of those owed money to obtain repayment via the legal process was a vital component of business trust. At the start of the century, debtors could either be declared insolvent or bankrupt. The insolvent could be arrested to ensure that they attended court, and, at the request of creditors, could remain in prison until they paid the amount owed, and, from 1826, until they surrendered their property. Alternatively, traders and those who owed at least £100 could declare themselves bankrupt, surrender their property for distribution among their creditors and absolve themselves of the liability to the sums unpaid.[32]

Over the period, the bankruptcy laws were in a constant state of flux, and, at times, acted against those who lent money.[33] In 1800, bankruptcies were dealt with by Commissioners, who, requiring no qualifications, were often incompetent and diverged in their decisions. On the other hand, creditors were allowed to appoint their own assignees to handle the assets of the bankrupt, who could only obtain discharge on the consent of four-fifths of those to whom he owed money. In 1831, a new more efficient bankruptcy court was established, but the creditors' assignees were replaced by officials appointed by the court, and, in 1842, creditors lost the power to veto a bankrupt's discharge. These changes greatly increased the cost of the legal process and led to much criticism, and, in 1849, the advantage again swung back in the favour of creditors. The statute of that year allowed defaulters to become bankrupt only if they could repay at least 5s. for every pound owed and created new discharge certificate classifications based on the degree of blame attached to a bankrupt's conduct, which it was hoped would help traders identify the fraudulent, prevent the deceitful re-entering commerce and discourage general business dishonesty. A first-class certificate was awarded to those who had fallen into debt through misfortune, a second-class discharge went to defaulters who had been careless and reckless and a third-class certificate to those who had acted dishonestly. Unfortunately, the courts found it difficult to define morality and failed to apply the law consistently, and it was discovered that a third-class discharge had no effect on an individual's ability to gain further credit.

In 1861, therefore, the classification system was abolished and the law was altered to favour the debtor. Although judges were given stronger powers to refuse to discharge or even imprison the fraudulent, the distinction between insolvency and bankruptcy was removed and it became easier to declare oneself bankrupt voluntarily. The Act, however, resulted in an eightfold increase in bankruptcies and a 50 per cent reduction in asset distributions, and, in 1869, the position of creditors was strengthened when they were again allowed to appoint their own assignees. Regrettably, as prior to 1831, those owed money had difficulty coming to agreements, and bankrupts and petitioning creditors conspired to defraud other lenders. The law thus underwent yet another change, and, in 1883, bankruptcy was brought under the jurisdiction of the Board of Trade and official receivers appointed to act as trustees and make recommendations as to discharge.

Inevitably, the confusion created by these constant changes, the occasional bias towards bankrupts and the cost and slow speed of the legal process caused many creditors to abandon the law and to negotiate private arrangements with debtors. In 1850, it is estimated that informal settlements exceeded bankruptcy cases by a ratio of seven to one. Private agreements were also less damaging to trust relationships than legal action and debtors were less able to 'conceal part of their effects for their future benefit in beginning in the world again'.[34] Depending on the degree of trust between the parties, the agreements were sanctioned by either the integrity of those involved, trade associations or the law; settlements could be registered with a civil court as a formal composition or deed of arrangement or assignment, and, from 1849, lodged with a Court of Bankruptcy.

Rejuvenation of the system

As with its criminal counterpart, the civil legal system underwent great change during the latter part of the period under review, which did much to raise trust. The law was toughened and the superior and local courts were reformed. In the middle decades of the nineteenth century, the procedures and pleas of the superior courts were simplified, their doctrines made more systematic, their relationship to other legal institutions more clearly defined, and, in 1873, they were merged into one High Court of Justice. As regards the local judiciary system, by the 1830s, most of the old County Courts had been assimilated into Courts of Record and many customary courts had fallen into disuse, the Courts of Wales and Chester had been abolished and many councils had enacted new statutes that increased the monetary or geographical jurisdictions of their Courts of Request. Courts of Record were also made more effective. In 1835, their jurisdictional boundaries were expanded to conform to the geographical area of the municipal corporation that administered them, and local councils were empowered to appoint to them legally trained judges. The most important change to the local court system, however, was the creation of new County Courts in 1846, which replaced their few remaining namesakes and the Courts of Requests. Almost five hundred of these tribunals were established in sixty districts, and each sat at least once per month. They employed paid professionals as judges, legal representation was permitted, the rules of common law were followed at all times, hearsay evidence was accepted, from 1850 there was a full right of appeal to a superior court and, over the following decades, the jurisdiction of the courts was expanded.[35] By 1870, therefore, they dealt with all civil matters with the exception of divorce.

Yet, although an improvement, the courts still left much to be desired. Critics complained that judges had 'a want of knowledge of the customs of trade' and made numerous errors of judgment and contradictory decisions. The requirement that a defendant be sued only in his local court led to much inconvenience, and the fees charged to suitors were regarded as excessive, often amounting to 50 per cent of the sum claimed. The recovery of debt could also be a lengthy process. Judges were said to be too lenient and to avail themselves too often of their new powers to order repayment by instalment. Bailiffs were poorly paid and lacked zeal in chasing up overdue instalments and levying warrants against goods, and were reluctant to seize articles, afraid of inter-pleader actions. There is even evidence that some businessmen began to use the courts to forestall the attentions of creditors, only paying a debt when a summons was registered with court officials. The result of these defects was that many traders abandoned the legal system, either accepting 'injustice or wrong', which 'injure[d] commercial morality by preventing the enforcement of contracts', or turning to private arbitration.[36]

Whether private prosecution statistics reflect changes in social capital is again questionable. Private litigation per head of population undertaken at the superior courts fell from the mid-seventeenth to the mid-eighteenth century. It then began to rise, reflecting the increase in economic transactions and perhaps a deterioration of trust. Whereas in 1750 the superior courts dealt with between 175 and 350 cases per 100,000 of total population, in 1830 they handled 653 actions per 100,000 people. At the same time, litigation in the provinces rose with the appearance of Courts of Request. The number of these courts rose rapidly from the late eighteenth century, and, by 1810, they were dealing with 2,767 suits per 100,000 residents. The subsequent rise in trust can perhaps be traced through an examination of County Court small debt litigation, which fell from an annual mean of 45 cases per 100 people in the 1860s to 33 per 100 at the start of the twentieth century. The fall has been solely attributed to the increase in real incomes, but must also have been related to the development of trust and co-operation, which facilitated private bargaining and the negotiation of debt repayment schedules and made recourse to the legal system less necessary. Not surprisingly, the figures broadly follow the peaks and troughs of trade union unemployment, demonstrating that moral hazard rose when economic conditions worsened. The number of cases also varies between towns, reflecting differences in incomes and divergent levels of trust.[37]

Conclusion

One of the main functions of the state was the delivery of law and order via the civil and criminal legal systems. At the turn of the century, the civil judicial system was far from adequate. There were too many courts that provided slow, costly and unreliable justice, and the bankruptcy laws often acted against creditors. Reform was slow and the new county courts less than perfect. Nevertheless, by the 1870s there had been great improvements and the knowledge that grievances would receive a fair hearing helped raise trust. As regards crime, the first part of the century saw an actual or perceived rise in criminal offences, which inevitably weakened trust. A number of factors explain the increase – poor policing, an archaic legal system, private prosecution and an inadequate legal profession. Well aware that crime could slow social and economic progress, local communities sought to overcome the lack of trust themselves. Various watch and prosecution societies were established, working-class neighbourhoods policed themselves, and the middle class became magistrates and campaigned against capital punishment and for improvements in prison conditions. Governments also began to take action, improving the operation of criminal courts and introducing modern policing and new punishments. Such initiatives no doubt contributed to the halt in the rise in prosecution and indictable crime figures that occurred from mid-century. This fall in crime, however, may also have been related to the general increase in social capital levels or been an attempt by governments to maintain the myth of a high-trust society.

8   Kin, geographic and masculine trust

Three other forms of social capital are kin, geographic and masculine trust. The first part of the chapter examines kinship trust, the loyalties that exist between family members, and is split into three sections. The first few pages seek to determine whether this form of social capital rose or fell during the period under study and attempts to determine its significance. This is followed by discussions on the importance of family trust reputations, the impact families had on community trust, in particular through the socialisation of moral social norms, and the benefits of and the changing nature of the trust generated within marriages. The chapter then looks at two other types of social capital – geographic trust, the loyalties that existed within towns, regions and countries, and masculine trust, the ties that bound men together – and traces how both were transformed by economic and social developments.

Kinship trust

Trust between family members

Kinship trust is generally stronger than that which exists between non-kin as it is underpinned by biology – the desire to ensure the survival of a family's genetic inheritance. The density of nineteenth-century kinship networks, the extent to which residents in a community were related to each other, is an area of dispute. Earlier historians claimed that networks were shallow and their conclusions have received support from recent micro-reconstructions of household relationships. Others, on the other hand, using similar techniques, but in different communities have found that networks were relatively dense. Reay, for example, discovered that in Hernhill, a rural village in the South East of England, 60 per cent of households were related. It seems likely that network density varied both geographically, socially and over time, and was influenced by the nature of the local economy, levels of out- and in-migration and mortality levels; a sudden outbreak of disease could decimate networks. In urban towns, in-migration will have initially led to shallow networks, though migrants from particular localities tended to cluster together. These, however, will have become more extended as immigrants married members of established families in the host community. It has also been suggested that as the century progressed longer life expectancy and marriages at a younger age and the birth of children early in the lifespan of parents increased the number of three-generation families.[1]

Whether kinship trust levels rose or fell during the period is open to question. To some extent, kinship trust was partly historically determined and dependent on past inheritance practices. Broadly speaking, in the arable regions of central England, families were compelled by manorial lords and gentry to adopt primogeniture, inheritance by the oldest male child. Alternatively, those living in the pastoral areas of the North, South West and South East, where there was an absence of manorial control, practised partible inheritance, the division of land and chattels among all the children of the deceased. The former custom led to small nuclear households, little familial and kin bonding, and high mobility and migration, all of which militated against the development of kinship trust. By contrast, the partible inheritance of pastoral areas caused extended or joint families to be more common and there to be less geographic mobility, as the expectation of inheritance discouraged migration. Moreover, the possibility of receiving a bequest gave children a strong motive to form trust relations with the older generation, aware that if they failed to do so they may not inherit.[2]

It seems likely that pre-industrial kinship trust was strong. Families worked together, lived close to each other and regularly socialised, and the close-knit community ensured that people adhered to family obligation norms. Apprentice-ships, which were generally obtained from kin or as a result of their influence, meanwhile, gave the young a reason to maintain trust relations with even distant relatives. Anderson's work suggests that industrialisation had little impact on such trust and indeed may even have strengthened it.[3] Kin continued to live close to each other, often in the same street or neighbourhood, and family members still worked together. Many employers had a policy of recruiting the relatives of existing members of staff, self-employed craftsmen usually sought to bring their children into their trade, and, in mule spinning and other indus-tries, sub-contractors generally employed family members as their assistants. Furthermore, the vicissitudes of life in the new urban areas and the greater intensity of industrial work, which shortened active careers and led to a lengthy period of dependence in old age, increased the reciprocal exchange of critical life-situation gifts between family members, thus strengthening their bonds of trust.

There was also a greater tendency to take in kin who had fallen on hard times. The rise in the standard of living allowed, particularly the middle classes, to subsidise an extra household member, and respectability norms ensured that a refusal to do so could be costly in terms of trust. The household head who 'over-looked this duty' was regarded as 'worse than an infidel', and it was feared that relatives who were allowed to fend for themselves would inevitably descend into immorality and thus damage their own, and, more importantly, their family's trust reputation. Further pressure to support extended kin came from the Poor Law authorities and other communal organisations. Overseers used a carrot and stick approach to encourage the maintenance of kin relationships. The availability of relief enabled families to take in the children of relatives and elderly kin. King, for example, found that in the Lancashire town of Garstang during the years 1801–11 12 per cent of the community's households gave a home to one or more child relative and were sponsored in some way by the parish for doing so. The stick took the form of legal sanctions. Individuals had a legal duty to support parents, grandparents, children and grandchildren, and many overseers enforced this requirement, bringing cases of neglect before magistrates. Similar pressures came from other institutions. The church, Sunday schools and secular schools strongly promoted the importance of family obligations, with the clergy intervening in family affairs where it was deemed necessary. Trade unions often couched wage demands in family terms, and one of the goals of relief funds set up during times of economic downturn was usually to keep families together, albeit those of respectable working men.[4]

This thesis, however, is only partly correct. In the cotton industry, the family work unit became less common as time passed. Sub-contractors began to disappear from the 1850s and many employed non-kin child assistants. As Anderson himself shows, not all children followed their father's profession, and at least a small proportion of women with children were in full-time employment. Most family members will therefore have worked alone, limiting family interaction during the day, and many will have formed non-kin trust relationships that partly crowded out kinship trust. Given the long working hours and the stresses of everyday life, the little family interaction that did occur was probably of poor quality, often involving 'parental cruelty and carelessness, filial disobedience ... (and an) absence of maternal love'. Earning high wages, young cotton operatives no doubt increasingly socialised away from kinfolk, in many cases moving out of the parental home to live with the families of friends or in lodgings. It has also been claimed that the Poor Law and the availability of poor relief actually lessened the need for kin trust and reciprocal exchange, and that the radical change in nineteenth-century household structure is little more than a myth, with even an arch proponent accepting that, at most, extended families made up only a fifth of all households.[5]

For much of the non-migrant working class, therefore, after the first stage of industrialisation, family and kinship trust declined. The fall will then have accelerated as residents became more prosperous and had less need for critical life situation gifts, or abandoned kinship trust for its neighbourhood counterpart, which offered a wider choice of potential partners and generated greater extra-trust benefits. Conversely, for migrants in areas of chain migration, where kin were present in the place of destination, bonds of kinship were crucial and will have strengthened, at least during the early years of settlement in a new town. Immigrants required help in finding housing and employment, and neighbourhood ties took time to develop. Indeed, the high levels of migrant kinship trust may initially have crowded out and slowed the growth of neighbourhood loyalties; socialisation and gift exchange occurring exclusively within the family group.[6]

For family members, the main benefit of kinship trust was that it facilitated the reciprocal exchange of critical life-situation gifts, which, along with lesser presents, further strengthened the bonds between kin. Inclusion in such exchanges also bolstered gift givers' extra-family reputations for trustworthiness, with those who neglected family duties suffering a loss of reputation. Other benefits of kinship networks included a greater chance of obtaining charity, and, in cases of sudden need, substantial short-term poor relief payments. Many overseers and vestries were willing to provide such support in the knowledge that the kin network would provide the longer-term help needed once they had marshalled their resources.[7]

Gifts took a variety of forms. Young people, for example, would receive help in finding a job and a suitable spouse. Newlyweds would be provided with temporary accommodation, and, later, fixtures for their new homes, new parents furnished with advice on and assistance in the rearing of children, parents offered financial and practical aid or even a home when they became incapacitated, and all kin helped if they became ill or were temporarily unemployed. As regards businessmen, relatives could provide cheap and reliable labour, subsidised premises, trading and reputation information, capital for business start-up and at times of financial difficulty, and access to formal and informal networks. The value and type of gift given was dependent on the nature of the network and the kin relationship and gender of the giver. Networks containing large numbers of male kin and blood links were more generous than those that mostly comprised female relatives and marriage connections. Parents tended to give children higher value gifts than extended kin, and more emotional support was forthcoming from female than from male family members.[8] As with neighbourhood gifts, a present to one relative was regarded as a gift to the family and would not necessarily be reciprocated by the recipient, who would be expected to give help in return to some other family member at some other time.

Exchanges between parents and children were rarely equal or symmetrical. Parents generally invested more in sons than in daughters, though the latter usually gave them a higher return in terms of help and care in old age. Women had more time for giving and were socialised into the role of gift giver, and, in some cases, daughters would forfeit their chances of work or marriage to care for an elderly mother or father.[9] Whatever the gender of their children, parents materially often gave more than they received. Many did not live to see their offspring come of age and there was no guarantee that their children would be willing or able to support them in later life, though reciprocation could be prompted through reminders of the debt owed and the generation of guilt, and, in the case of the middle classes, the threat of disinheritance. Any material losses were partially offset by genetic, emotional and trust gains. Giving children a good start in life increased the likelihood that the family gene line would continue, the beauty, intelligence or later success of progeny gave parents a sense of satisfaction, which increased self-esteem, and the possession of a family elevated the reputation of fathers and gave mothers access to networks of motherhood and anointed them with the maternal characteristics of kindness and tenderness.

Family trust reputations

The trust within families and the behaviour of kinsmen contributed to the development of family trust reputations, which, for better or worse, impacted on the personal reputations of all relatives. It was thus important to ensure that all members of the family behaved morally, and, to ensure that this was the case, there existed sanctions, such as gossip, insults and, in extreme cases, exclusion, that were imposed on those who let the family down. If these proved ineffective and some immorality occurred, family norms usually restricted members informing non-kin. The ability to free ride on family reputations led many sons to enter their father's trade, either joining and eventually taking over the patriarchal firm or initially or at a later date setting up on their own.[10] The practice facilitated access to networks and information regarding the sector, and, once their sons had become established, fathers gained from the developing reputations of their offspring and obtained access to the information exchanged in networks established by the younger generation. For much the same reasons, the sons of wage earners also followed in their fathers' footsteps.

Of those who did not trail in their father's wake, many entered sectors where kin were already employed or traded. They were thus able to free ride on the reputation of the relative, and, through them, gain network and information advantages, and, when the economic sector in which the family was primarily involved collapsed, if their own trade was more prosperous, they could provide their kin with critical life-situation gifts. In many towns, there was a tendency for siblings of the elite who failed to follow their father's trade to become lawyers and agents,[11] This is hardly surprising given the close network and other connections between business and the professions. It is also likely that some industrialists encouraged their offspring in such career choices. Professional occupations had a relatively high trust reputation on which the fathers could free ride, involved the acquisition of much useful information, and, in the case of the law, siblings could provide free and trustworthy legal advice. Needless to say, these generational links will have greatly strengthened the trust that existed between the business and professional worlds.

Kinship trust, however, was not wholly beneficial. The 'wilful and habitual blindness in near kindred to each other's defects' could cause trust to be misplaced. A request for help from one relative could generate distrust among others, for 'if the opinion of one relation be requested those who have not been consulted too frequently imagine this neglect as an insult and ... are offended'. Reciprocation could fail to occur, as sanctions, particularly that of exclusion, had high emotional costs and were relatively difficult to apply. And strong kin loyalties and attachments could crowd out trust and prevent families and family members from advancing economically or moving geographically. In the case of family businesses, for example, a fear of disrupting trust relations often led to the appointment of inefficient or ineffective kin to positions of power, the post-ponement of radical decisions crucial for future expansion and a reluctance to recruit outsiders as partners.[12]

Families and trust

The impact of families on trust was not only restricted to kinship trust and repu-tations. Families had an influence on general moral behaviour and on the primary socialisation of moral and trust social norms. Among the middle class, the family was regarded as a refuge from immorality, where men, under the influence of their wives, could recharge their ethical batteries. 'The world cor-rupts; home refines', and it was believed to be the responsibility of wives to 'call back the attention of man to those sunnier spots in his existence by which the growth of moral feelings have been encouraged and his heart improved'.[13] Women were well qualified for this role. At least in the domestic sphere, they were regarded as highly moral beings, largely owing to their 'natural' character-istic of gentleness, their exclusion from the dishonest worlds of business and politics, their apparent devotion to family life, their public teetotalism and non-participation in crime, and their strong support of the church and involvement in philanthropic associations.

From the 1820s, this belief developed into the cult of domesticity. The family was romanticised in every medium from novels to government reports, and the failure of middle-class males to spend their leisure time by their own fireside damaged their social and masculine trust reputations. As the conduct book writer J. A. James wrote, 'it is a sad reflection upon a man when he is fond of spending his evenings abroad. It implies something bad and it predicts something worse.' An exception to this norm was attendance at voluntary associations and societies that promoted self-improvement. Although even here advancement to the higher reaches of the networks, particularly political office, was dependent on the home lives of candidates, the moral qualities required in the domestic sphere being regarded as the same as those needed for public life.[14]

The romanticisation of the family extended to the family firm and particularly inter-generational businesses, which were regarded as more trustworthy than single-owner companies. Such was the strength of this belief that many firms falsely assumed a family name, for example Jones & Son.[15] The confidence arose from the conviction that these businesses were less likely to resort to fraud, which was related to the veneration of the family as the fount of morality, and the assurance that the firms could easily obtain help from kinsfolk if trading became difficult. In the case of inter-generational firms, the sheer longevity of the businesses meant that they had built up strong trust relationships with the local trading community, and it was thought unlikely that owners would risk the loss of their companies' reputations by acting immorally.

The primary socialisation of norms and rearing of children was increasingly undertaken by mothers, who spent much of their time in the home and were thought to possess superior morality. By the start of the nineteenth century, the belief that they, and, to a lesser extent, their husbands played an important role in norm socialisation was largely accepted. John Locke and the Scottish moral philosophers, in particular Frances Hutcheson, had forcefully advocated the premise, which had been popularised in innumerable parental guides, tracts and novels. It was thus generally acknowledged that 'the earlier years of mankind are the most important [as] ... the mind is then plastic as wax; impressions are easily received, but are maintained as rigid as marble'. Accordingly, even if someone committed an act contrary to the norms internalised and escaped 'without being punished or detected', they would 'nevertheless stand self condemned, be ashamed to trust [themselves] with [their] own thoughts, and wear in [their] very countenance both the consciousness of guilt and dread of a discovery'.[16]

Whether working-class primary socialisation became less effective in the early nineteenth century is debatable. The norms held by parents had certainly weakened and changed. Their strength had been lessened by competition from other social codes brought into towns by the new media (newspapers, periodicals and novels), migrants and professional authority figures, such as teachers and religious ministers, who had often been born or trained in other parts of the country. Weak neighbourhood networks meant that there was no certainty that the disregard of a norm would result in a social sanction, or that the penalty, if delivered, would be costly, and people had less contact with role models, such as local clergymen and members of the gentry.

More importantly, according to middle-class reformers, there was the fall in the quantity and quality of the contact that occurred between parents and their children. Lack of domestic space forced offspring to be 'driven into the street to play', making it unlikely that they would 'grow up with steady and domestic habits'. Larger families reduced the amount of time that could be devoted to each child, and the long factory working hours left parents unfit 'for much social enjoyment with ... (their) ... family' and caused the home to become 'a scene of physical exhaustion'. Many turned to drink, leaving 'the little ones [to] run about the streets barefoot and in rags', the parents' 'carelessness, selfishness and drunkenness and the bad example in other respects ... very soon impress[ing] themselves on the mind of ... offspring'. Fathers, raddled by drink, often acted in a violent and brutal manner towards both wives and children, weakening in the process their offspring's faith in their advice and views; a trust that was further diminished by their underemployment, low-status and low-paid jobs. Mothers, and, to a lesser extent, fathers also died young, leaving their children with just one or no parent to pass on norms, and migrants often lacked access to grandparents, the main source of parenting skills. Mothers were therefore 'little capable of training up ... children under a steady temperature and intelligent discipline', alternating instead between 'inordinate indulgence' and 'anger and violence'.[17]

The lack of parental contact was also related to the rise in child and female employment. According to the factory reformers, many children spent only 4.25 hours per week with their parents, resulting in a 'loss or absence of parental influence and filial attention'. Damage was at first limited. Handloom weavers continued to work as a family and mule-spinning sub-contractors employed their own children as assistants. From the 1820s, however, the family unit in both spheres began to disappear. In weaving, the arrival of the power loom forced parents to send their children into factories with greater frequency, and in spinning, the introduction of longer mules made the work more arduous, prompting the employment of more assistants, most of whom were the offspring of other workers. Child labour, furthermore, not only reduced the time children spent with their families. Because of their dependence on their offspring's income, parents had difficulty applying sanctions for non-application of norms. The children themselves were unable to benefit from the trust norms taught in the schoolroom and church/chapel, were more likely to drink excessive amounts of alcohol and engage in other immoral pursuits and often resented their parents' insistence that they accept the punishments meted out by overseers. Their financial independence also enabled them to make early, careless and trustless marriages and to have children before they possessed the maturity necessary for the inculcation of norms.[18]

Defenders of child labour, on the other hand, argued that there existed in factories a reciprocal exchange network of parental control and that 'even if none of their own children were working with them, [male workers had] ... a common interest, as fathers, in discountenancing indecencies of conduct and language'. It was further claimed that factory children learnt far more about the benefits of trust, co-operation and reciprocal exchange than those who worked at home. In factories 'not half an hour passes ... but what children are laying under obligations ... If one piercer finishes ... before another, he runs to his neighbour to help him, and this may save him a scolding or a blow and he may be immediately indebted to his neighbour in return. This creates feelings of kindness; and as spinners are continually changing their piecers ... the latter are constantly being brought into contact with strangers and so these feelings extend wider'. In comparison, those that 'work at home ... are shut up all day long with their parents and have scarcely any acquaintance with others ... [and] ... the whole of the feelings which they thus imbibe may be selfish'.[19]

Factory reformers argued that female employment similarly reduced primary socialisation and weakened trust in other ways. Millwork took mothers away from the home for the whole day, forcing them to leave their children with elder siblings or child minders. Once at the factory, they formed associations with female colleagues with whom they spent their leisure, which further reduced the time spent with their children and caused them to imbibe immoral norms. These were passed onto offspring and others in the neighbourhood and prevented them providing the 'honest and moralizing love of home'. Their employment also prevented them learning the domestic skills that encouraged husbands to spend their leisure time in the home rather than in the local inn, and led to deskilling, which affected the respectability and trust reputation of male artisans, and weakened their spouses' masculine trust reputations, which were partly based on an ability to be sole family breadwinner. Some even claimed that factory women were physically less feminine and therefore, by definition, less moral and maternal than their middle-class counterparts. Social scientists reported that physical labour caused many to gain a masculine physique and that most matured and menstruated earlier than other females and were less fertile.[20]

In reality, only around a quarter of female spinning and weaving factory operatives were married, most tending to drop out of employment as their families increased in size.[21] Other mothers took in work, either sewing or washing, and would thus have had day long contact with their children, and those who were employed outside the home generally left their offspring with adult kin, lodgers, neighbours, close friends or landladies, who possessed both the incentive and authority to inculcate norms.

Among the middle class, it was claimed that primary socialisation was weakened by the new political economy and the fashion for wet nursing. Writers such as Adam Smith and David Ricardo, who postulated that man was motivated by the competitive urge, supposedly weakened middle-class trust and moral norms. The failure to suckle one's child, meanwhile, was thought to impair the mother–child bond, and many believed that wet nurses, often unmarried mothers, imparted to their charges through their milk 'the germs of libertinism, criminality and alcoholism'. In reality, primary socialisation appears to have been undertaken as vigorously as previously, albeit in a different manner. In the eighteenth century, norms were internalised through the use of power. Parents were encouraged to break a child's will through intense psychological and physical pressure and to instill moral and other values through the creation of an awe and fear of authority. By the 1850s, these practices were increasingly being replaced by a new non-authoritarian style of child rearing widely promoted in popular manuals, which rejected physical force and stressed the establishment of consensual trust relationships. The new manuals argued that power was a poor means of inculcating morality and could itself lead to dishonesty, as children would avoid punishments 'by every heart of evasion and deceit in their power; until they became such proficients that it might have been said of them ... that "he could scarcely drink tea without a stratagem"'. Parents were therefore advised to avoid the imposition of rules, adopt methods of discipline that were suited to the character of the child and to make punishment as subtle as possible, with physical beatings reserved only for wilful disobedience. In lieu of rules and discipline, they were to furnish children with examples of morality and trustworthiness through their own behaviour and to form reciprocal emotional and psychological bonds with their offspring. Violations of norms by the child could then be punished through the withdrawal of love or expressions of parental disapproval that would evoke guilt and reduce the child's feelings of self-esteem.[22]

By the middle of the nineteenth century, the socialisation of trust norms by both the working and middle classes was more effective. Working hours were shorter, child employment had come to an end, the number of mothers working outside the home had fallen and there was better schooling. The elite had also begun to strengthen the secondary internalisation of norms through their philanthropic and public service activities, and norms had been influenced by the arrival of new political and economic theories that sought to increase trust and honesty and by the softening of the individualistic creed. Owenism argued that the implementation of a co-operative economy would eliminate the immorality of capitalism and unite the social classes. Chartists believed that political reform would lead to moral improvement, radicals campaigned for a Parliament that would establish a society based on 'the knowledge of morality and charity, the love of truth and virtue and social harmony' and Christian socialists preached that the fatherhood of God necessarily implied a brotherhood of mankind. At the same time, supporters of individualist theories became less dogmatic. Utilitarians stressed the importance of the 'love of truth' and abandoned Bentham's belief that falsehood was not inherently evil. Advocates of Scottish enlightenment writers highlighted the work of Adam Ferguson who believed that 'men [should] act in society from affections of kindness and friendship', and scientists attempted to connect their profession with the moral value of truth telling.[23]

Husband and wife trust

Perhaps the most important kinship bond was that between husbands and wives. For women, marriage brought with it both financial security and trust benefits. Spinsters were viewed with deep suspicion; seen as a sexual threat by the married, absent from motherhood networks and, owing to their inability to fulfil their biological destiny, believed to be embittered and vindictive. Men were advised to marry only when their businesses had been established, as marriage reduced the funds that could be invested in a firm and the time that could be devoted to the establishment of new trust relationships. Their choice of wife had important trust consequences. First, the personal reputation of the groom and the bride would be coloured by that of their partner and by their behaviour after marriage. Conduct books thus advised businessmen to marry women of good repute, warning that 'a vulgar, ostentatious woman [would] be ... [their] ruin'. Second, the husband and wife attained an immediate trust relationship with their partner's relatives. They were accordingly entitled to critical life-situation gifts, could free ride on the reputation of the family and gain access to a new collection of networks. Furthermore, relatives of the husband and wife also gained access to the resources, reputation and networks of the other family, albeit to a lesser extent than the groom and bride. Young men and women were therefore enjoined to chose partners from families with large resources and good reputations and, when married, to do nothing to damage their relationship with their in-laws.[24]

The trust benefits of marriage were particularly great if the suitor married someone whose father was in the same sector as himself. Such unions, of course, were only partly motivated by the perceived trust gains. They permitted the perpetuation of the socio-economic domination of the families involved, and sons and daughters will have naturally mixed in their parents' social circles and chosen mates from that coterie. Trustworthiness could be easily gauged from face-to-face interaction or discovered from others in the social circle and couples would possess similar characteristics, leading to ascribed trust.[25] Of those whose suitors followed a different occupation than that of their father, the daughters of the business elite generally married professionals, who, through marriage, gained access to business clients, and provided their father-in-laws with useful information and added to their trust reputation. Among the non-elite, there was a marked preference for textile workers, who were highly paid and numerous.

Other possible trust benefits of marriage were the use of wives as integrity signalling devices, greater self-esteem and access to female social networks. After a certain age, a married man was more trusted than a bachelor, as marriage established ascribed trust with fellow married men and it was believed that a male who had 'felt the joys, sorrows and strivings implied in the rearing of a family' was 'better able to understand and sympathise with the various characters and wants' of others. A good-looking wife would increase a man's masculine trust reputation, and, through the quality of her clothing and jewellery, could be used to indicate his wealth and affluence trust. Similarly, one who was supportive, urging her husband 'not to despair when the world seems too heavy a burden to be struggled against', would help maintain his self-confidence, as would a wife who was emotionally stable, healthy and provided a comfortable home life and children who were equally stable, healthy and successful. As regards a bride's friends, most had two, often overlapping, sets of aquaintances – her own made before and after marriage and the wives of her husbands' colleagues. Ideally, her own friends would have strong reputations, as her association with them would affect her own and her husband's reputation and could weaken her moral norms, causing 'the barrier between right and wrong [to be] broken down'. To prevent this, women were advised to avoid those whose 'characters and conduct stand impeached of anything dishonourable', and, wherever possible, to follow their husbands' advice 'as men mix more with the world and acquire a greater facility in discriminating character than women'. To maintain their trust relationships with their husbands, they were further counselled to shun male friendships, which 'duty and propriety both forbid', to take care not to 'communicate to others the failings of [their] husband[s] or the subjects of domestic disagreement' and to limit the time spent with female friends, as otherwise a husband could be tempted 'to seek society more agreeable to him than that which his home may present'.[26]

Within those female networks that comprised the wives of a spouse's colleagues, the ideal wife would possess a good reputation and strong relationships with all of her fellow members. She would thus be able to convince the other wives of her spouse's better qualities and learn much about the reputation of his colleagues and his colleagues' wives, and discover other information that would be of interest to him. The extent to which this occurred depended on a wife's personality, Emotional Intelligence Quotient and domestic commitments, a woman with few children or many servants having relatively more time to devote to networking.[27]

For both the middle and working classes, marriage was a form of social contract, albeit one in which the husband dominated. Each spouse agreed to fulfil certain obligations and trusted that their husband or wife would deliver their side of the bargain, trust breaking down when this failed to occur. The male role was to provide the money necessary for his family's survival, whilst women were expected to manage the household and to ensure that their husbands were well nourished and had a contented home life and were thus physically and psychologically able to earn a sufficient income. In order to ensure that their families survived on their spouses' wages, working-class wives depended greatly on trust, becoming part of neighbourhood and kinship networks and forming trust relationships with shopkeepers, pawnbrokers and moneylenders. They also took paid work inside and outside the home, and, to ensure that their husbands eat well, often deprived themselves and, to a lesser extent their children, of food, medical care and clothing, especially footwear.[28]

The marital contract broke down when either side did not fulfil their duties. Distrust arose when husbands failed to find or keep work or spent their wages on drink, betting or other women, and when wives managed their households poorly. Marital tension was therefore relatively more common amongst the very poor. Female sanctions included nagging and the withdrawal of sexual favours and the home comforts to which the spouse had become accustomed. The most common male sanction was physical violence, which also occurred as a reaction to the introduction of female sanctions. Domestic violence was regarded as an acceptable practice both by couples and the courts, though, to prevent its legitimacy being undermined, neighbours and kin often rescued battered wives or scolded violent husbands.[29]

Whether husband and wife trust rose or fell over the period is debatable. The fulfilment of marital obligations was made easier by the increase in incomes and middle-class attempts to educate women in household management and child raising and to reduce male gambling and drunkenness. As the century progressed, it also became increasingly accepted that middle-class husband–wife relationships should be based on sympathy or trust and patriarchal power exercised at the last resort. Reasons for this sea change were the continued replacement of arranged marriages with love matches, the growing ability of economically independent and educated young people to ignore the wishes of family and community in their choice of spouse, the greater range of marriage partners available in urban areas and the increased longevity of marriages. Equally significant was the growth of the polite and later respectable culture, which condemned and sanctioned unacceptable male behaviour in marriage, the rise of middle-class domesticity, a growing unwillingness by women to accept male cruelty (clearly reflected in the cases brought before the divorce courts) legal changes that reduced the inequity of marriage, and the influence of life manuals and novels. Female manuals advised readers to avoid conflict by humouring their husbands and becoming so in tune with their needs and desires that submission was accomplished before it was demanded. Manuals and other writings for a male audience enjoined husbands to take an interest in the domestic burdens of their wives and to be patient, tender, considerate and forbearing. Novels, similarly, heavily promoted companionability. Anthony

Trollope's 1869 *He Knew He Was Right*, for example, continued explicit criticism of husbands who unreasonably exercise their authority.[30]

On the other hand, the increasing age gap between brides and grooms and intellectual differences caused by women's inferior access to education lessened husband and wife ascribed trust, the exclusion of women from paid work increased the pecuniary power of male spouses, and the reduced transparency of reputations in towns and changes in courtship practice limited the extent to which suitors could discover and monitor the suitability of potential wives, who often resorted to deceit. As an anonymous London tradesman wrote in 1861, 'in olden times . . . a young man could get an insight into the actual character of his adored . . . but now our fair ones are so hedged about . . . that [he] has no chance of seeing [his] beloved . . . except when she is set out for the occasion'. Those who were considering engagement, consequently, were advised to look for a wife 'amongst those you know most of, so as to be likely to ascertain more easily what is the real disposition', to 'drop in unexpectedly and at various times and watch the exact effect of these visits', and to marry only if they had 'entire confidence . . . in every respect' in their partners.[31]

Couples also spent less time in each other's company. Before industrialisation, husbands and wives worked together, with even the wives of businessmen and professionals having some involvement in their husbands' working lives – keeping the accounts, supervising apprentices, and so on. Afterwards, they often spent much of the day apart. Working-class couples, likewise, spent much of their leisure hours in other people's company, each developing the trust relationships that ensured the availability of critical life-situation gifts. Males spent long hours at the local pub and wives invested much time in the creation and maintenance of neighbourhood and kin relationships and in the performance of reciprocal tasks. Middle-class men, meanwhile, devoted a large part of their leisure time to attending voluntary associations, 'a too prevalent cause of domestic discontent, jealousy, parental neglect misery and vice'.[32]

Geographic trust

Geographic trust comprises trust within towns, regions and countries. Generally, the working and middle classes belonged to spatially different networks. At the start of the nineteenth century, working-class network ties were largely restricted to the neighbourhood where they lived and worked. Most lacked the time and money to attend networks outside the immediate area and were highly dependent on the reciprocal exchange of gifts, which were more likely to be provided in close-knit high-trust communities. By comparison, elite and middle-class networks transcended the spatial constraints of neighbourhood. Both groups possessed the time and funds to visit inter-community networks and had no need for critical life-situation gifts. Instead, they required the trust and information gains that could only be obtained from social interaction with other members of their class, who, until the 1830s, were residentially relatively widely dispersed.

Over time, working-class networks and trust began to extend beyond the neighbourhood.[33] In most towns cheap and relatively frequent horse omnibus services were established, individuals had greater leisure time and disposable income and were less dependent on critical life-situation gifts, a class as opposed to an occupation consciousness began to develop, and, by the 1880s and in the cities, working-class suburbs had begun to grow up, leading to a separation of residence and workplace. The result was that the working classes spent less time in neighbourhood networks, and, instead, joined informal and newly established formal networks based outside their local communities. They began to patronise town-centre entertainments rather than the local pub, attend churches a distance from their residences, belong to voluntary associations that drew their members from the whole community and formed friendships with people who lived in other parts of the town. Such groupings possessed less dense ties and weaker norm sanctions than their older counterparts and thus generated less and weaker trust, but allowed members to meet a greater range of people and to obtain information, resources and socialisation benefits not available locally.

The appearance of inter-neighbourhood networks, along with inter-sector employer and employee contacts, led to the development of town trust, residents' identification with their town and their low-grade trust of fellow inhabitants. Town identity/trust was also generated through the idea of civil society, the belief that political participation was essential if the social and environmental problems that arose from industrialisation were to be solved, and the efforts of local authorities. Councils and councillors sought to engender a public spirit through the organisation of civic pageants, the publication of local histories, the commissioning of paintings of significant local events, the memoralisation of local heroes in statues, busts and tablets, the fostering of private clubs and organisations through the provision of donations and publicly funded prizes, and by helping the poor and those affected by natural disasters, such as fires or floods. Further loyalties were created via the performance of distinctive customs, mode of speech, pride in local technical or economic progress, the sharing of tacit knowledge regarding past events, and the belief that residents possessed similar characteristics, such as honesty, loyalty and conscientiousness. Such trust tended to be particularly high in urban centres with low inward and outward migration and one or more local newspapers, which promoted many of the above factors. It also derived much power from a concomitant distrust of the residents of nearby towns, which arose from differences in economic structures; where economies were similar, fear of competition; the poor relief settlement laws; long traditions of mutual insult and fighting; and, in rural villages, the need to protect common rights from interlopers.[34]

Town trust, in turn, influenced a town's trust reputation, the perception of its inhabitants' trustworthiness held by non-residents. This was of particular importance to local businessmen, who traded regionally or nationally or wished to set up businesses in other urban centres and whose reputation would be affected by that of their place of origin. Businessmen and councils thus 'worked to promote [their town's] interests and to advance its reputation'. Civic pageants and exhibitions were organised that were widely reported in the regional or national press, guides of the town were published, esteemed visitors given tours of the largest and most innovative factories, and campaigns organised for the improvement of factory conditions.[35]

Regional trust proliferated in the second half of the century and especially involved the elite, who increasingly joined district networks that could provide the regional information and trust that they now required. Many of the upper middle classes resided beyond town borders and had little loyalty to a particular urban area, had often themselves been migrants, and, in the case of manufacturers, supplied a regional or national market and had a regionally dispersed production base. Such trust was further promoted by the activities of local authorities, which forged links with national organisations and other councils, and by improvements in communications. The road system, postal service, telegraph and railway all reduced 'national antipathies . . . [binding] together more closely the great families of mankind'.[36] The 1865 Union Chargeability Act, which reduced Poor Law settlement disputes, migration, attendance at public schools and the development of district or national voluntary associations also played a part, as did district kin trust and new municipal needs, for instance for water or land, which could often only be satisfied beyond town boundaries.

Inevitably, regional trust was accompanied by inter-regional animosity, for example that between Yorkshire and Lancashire. Within the elite, perhaps the greatest suspicion existed between the manufacturers of the North and the financiers of the South. Both groups had very different backgrounds, characteristics and ways of life and therefore little ascribed trust. Many industrialists had petit bourgeois origins, were Nonconformist, lacked a public school/university education and did not possess the wealth, and, given the nature of their occupations, the time to indulge in a gentlemanly lifestyle. In comparison, the gentlemen of the City were usually Anglican, public-school-educated Oxbridge graduates who came from upper-middle-class families. The financiers of the South also believed manufacturing to be a dishonourable pursuit, a view encouraged by the comparative high levels of intra-City trust, their lack of knowledge of manufacturing for which they provided little finance and the adoption by many industrialists of a power labour relations strategy.[37] The Northern elite were thus often excluded from the capital's networks, which, in any case, they had difficulty attending owing to the length of the journey to London.

National identity and trust, rose during the period, fostered by transport developments, the proliferation of a national media, the French and later the Crimean wars, the various attempts to break up the UK, the state's pursuit of collectivist policies, imperial expansion, and the gradual disappearance of local dialects and customs. Within towns, national feeling was built via civic celebration of military victories and royal events, the organisation of volunteer forces and the collection of money for patriotic causes. Dissent, however, continued to exist between the various parts of the union, especially in the first half of the nineteenth century when a new wave of national consciousness appeared in

Scotland and relations with Ireland were threatened by the 1798 rebellions of the United Irishmen and the 1820s Catholic emancipation campaign.[38]

As regards national trust reputations, the British believed themselves to be morally superior to other nations. According to the artist Joseph Farrington, integrity was a word that 'the English may apply to their character . . . more universally than any other nation that exists in [the World]'. Surprisingly, this high opinion was held by other nationalities. Alessandro Verri, who spent time in both London and Paris, for example, thought the merchants of the former city to be infinitely more trustworthy than those of the latter. The origins of this moral superiority were contested. Many an Englishman believed it was a divine gift, or that it was inherited genetically. Foreigners, conversely, suspected that it originated from the oath-based justice system, the greater use of verbal or informal contracts, the relative absence of haggling and from industrialisation, with 'a strong industrial spirit' generating 'veracity'.[39]

As ever, the English considered foreigners to be inherently untrustworthy. Americans, for example, were thought to break their 'word with impunity and may without disgrace flagrantly violate those established customs, the infringement of which would in England irretrievably ruin . . . [their] character'. The scepticism as to the honesty of Europeans had a number of roots. Relatively few middle-class Victorians visited the continent, and those who did venture forth had as little contact as possible with the natives, travelling in groups, living in hotels and boarding houses managed by expatriates and only inspecting attractions recommended by their English tourist handbooks and guides. They and those who holidayed at home also regarded the continent as economically backward and illiberal; many transposed those qualities that were associated with Catholicism – secretiveness, servility and effeminacy – to the populations that practised the religion; and, at the start of the period, there was relatively little trade between nations, enabling competitors to 'gain more by one piece of fraud than [they] lose by having a bad character'. In the case of non-Westerners, distrust was further promoted by the Indian mutiny and the 1865 Jamaican rebellion, which caused non-white races to be seen as a threat, and the disciplines of ethno-climatology, which investigated the relationship between climate and morality, and anthropometric cartography, the mapping of cranial capacities. Practitioners of these 'sciences' believed that tropical climates led to 'a low state of morality' and a worrying sensuality, a conclusion supported by the skull sizes of the inhabitants of these regions.[40]

Masculine trust

Bourgeois masculine self-confidence and trust derived from the provision of a 'family wage', that would allow wives to remain in the home, the possession of a strong work ethic, the expenditure of leisure time in the domestic sphere and the abandonment of physical violence. Men were also required to adopt the polite code of manliness, which stressed physical vigour, energy and resolution and directness and sincerity in both action and speech. Such norms were followed by around 40 per cent of the adult population, largely the middle classes and the labour aristocracy, though younger members of both classes often adopted a laxer version of the code. Males in other classes followed other norms. Masculine trust among the working classes depended, among other factors, on the possession of a family, a sign of virility, the completion of physical work in a masculine environment, and a willingness to defend one's honour through physical aggression.[41]

Conforming to these norms proved difficult. The decline of the domestic system of production undermined men's ability to dominate and monitor family behaviour during the working day, and vicissitudes of the economic cycle meant that working men were often unable to provide for their families. Mechanisation led to an inflow into factories of female and juvenile labour, which destroyed the masculine work environment, caused work to take on a sedentary nature and weakened men's domestic pecuniary authority, and the associated deskilling impaired self-confidence and prevented fathers providing sons with a craft. Domesticity, meanwhile, minimised masculine interaction and competition, and, in business, ethical behaviour could result in bankruptcy.[42]

In the home, men's smaller role in the raising of children injured male self-esteem, but more importantly, damaged the masculine self-confidence of the next generation of men, which had an impact on other types of trust. All gender identities are unstable and are influenced by contact with each parent. Greater interaction with mothers from the early nineteenth century therefore caused the feminine traits in boys' natures to mature to a greater extent than the male features. The transition to an adult masculine identity was thus more difficult than previously and there came into being a new code of manliness that was more brittle and less tolerant of the feminine aspects of the male temperament, which weakened general trust. Young men began to associate tenderness and affection exclusively with women and came to abhor these feelings in themselves as unmanly. They thus became emotionally reticent, which made the formation of trust relationships more problematical. Their fear of their own femininity was projected onto those males with overly female actions or behaviour, who, along with genuine homosexuals, were increasingly stigmatised. To compensate for their feminine characteristics, they also had a desire to display their masculinity through acts of mastery in the workplace, reducing employer–employee co-operation, and, to a greater extent in the Empire, where the absence of native power removed the need to form trust relationships.[43]

The decline in masculine self-esteem and the need to gain the masculine trust of other males was yet another reason why men joined formal and informal networks. Within the male-dominated voluntary society, men could signal their manliness and the associated trustworthiness through such activities as smoking, gambling, drinking, sex talk and the competitive pursuit of dominance over others, and introduce younger members, in many cases their sons, to adult masculine norms. Perhaps the most important masculine network was the local yeomanry, in which one man in 12 had served by the 1870s. Membership of these volunteer regiments strengthened members' masculine reputation, and, by signalling their patriotism, improved their general reputation and gave officers status. The regiments also played some part in the generation of other trusts. Amateur soldiering was thought to engender self-discipline and self-reliance and to play a large role 'in the warfare of truth against error, of knowledge against ignorance and virtue against vice'. By keeping the size of the regular army small, it kept taxation low, maintaining the social contract, and, through the generation of ascribed trust, narrowed 'the gulf . . . between the [regular] soldier and the citizen'. The interaction between officers and men, meanwhile, engendered inter-class loyalties. Unlike the regular army, there was little military discipline. Volunteers were not subject to the Mutiny Act and could resign on giving 14 days notice. In most units therefore 'orders [were] inadmissible', officers made 'requests' and spoke to their men 'as gentlemen are accustomed to be addressed'.[44]

Another significant masculine network, at least for the lower orders, was the public house. The capacity to drink heavily was a working-class trait of masculinity, and, by heightening courage and dulling pain, facilitated violence. Fights between adult males outside public houses were regular features in working-class areas, and, attracting crowds of spectators, promoted sociability. Unable, because of their age, to signal their masculinity through the adoption of the status of breadwinner, the completion of physically demanding jobs or fights with adult males, working-class youths became members of street gangs. These mobs of juveniles aged between 14 and 19 reached their peak in Manchester in the third quarter of the century. The gangs, membership of which was dependent on place of residence rather than ethnic identity or religious affiliation, constantly fought each other. The fights provided an escape valve for youthful aggression and competitive urges, and fighting prowess and the ability to withstand pain gave members masculine self-esteem and a status, both among their peers and the general community.[45]

Conclusion

Kinship trust was one of the strongest forms of attachments in the nineteenth century, and, like the local community–elite social contract, was 'embedded' in the environment, partly determined by the economic and social history of a region.[46] The social capital generated took a number of forms. There was first the trust between nuclear and extended family members. Based largely on the exchange of gifts, this may or may not have declined during early industrialisation, but had almost certainly diminished from mid-century. Second, each family had a trust reputation on which its members could free ride. Sons thus entered their fathers' trade and great care was taken to protect a family's good name. With the arrival of the cult of domesticity, families per se became a source of trust. Time spent at the domestic fireside was believed to recharge moral batteries and the absence of a wife and children could damage reputations. Parents, in particular mothers, were also responsible for the primary socialisation of moral and trust norms, which determined future levels of social capital. Within the working classes, poverty and the employment of women and children may have weakened this process. In the middle classes, such internalisation increasingly involved the establishment of consensual trust relationships. Finally, the most important kinship bond was that between husband and wife. Matrimony brought a number of trust benefits, and, over the period, the nature of the relationship changed. Middle-class marriages began to be based on companionship and trust, and patriarchal power was exercised only on rare occasions.

Turning to the other trusts discussed, the spatial area linked by social capital grew over time. As the century progressed, more and more people began to acquire inter-neighbourhood, town, regional and even national trust. At the same time, geographic distrust intensified, and, in the case of the North–South divide, began to have serious social and economic consequences. As for masculine trust, this appears to have diminished over the period, damaged by changes in male work roles and norms of manliness and by the feminisation of child rearing.

9 Business trust

This chapter examines business trust in all its many guises. The first section investigates the reasons for the fall in economic social capital in the late eighteenth and early nineteenth centuries and seeks to explain why this decline was not as precipitous as one would assume. The various determinants of business trust are then discussed, specifically the economic environment in which trade was conducted, the personal characteristics and behaviour of businessmen, and the nature of their firms. The chapter concludes with a description of the formal and informal business networks that were in existence during the period, and, in particular, the activities of trading associations, professional societies and informal groupings based on trade, credit and shared directorships.

Levels of business trust

Fall in trust

For much of the nineteenth century, the general public believed that 'cheating and cozening' were normal practice in the business world. The writer Freedly admitted that, for many, 'sordid, low, base, selfish, grovelling are the mildest epithets ... used when speaking of industrial pursuits'. This pessimistic view of commerce arose from the negative representation of businessmen by novelists, such as Dickens and Eliot, and personal experience. Most people were more than familiar with traders charging excessive prices and 'adulterating a genuine production with a spurious one ... mixing old materials with new and ... substituting one commodity with another'. The middle class, meanwhile, had themselves been or seen others become the victims of white-collar crime. The insurance swindles of the 1830s and 1840s, the frauds committed during the 1840s railway boom, the banking collapses of the 1850s and the fraudulent company promotions of the 1850s and 1860s had all severely damaged trust in business.[1]

Businessmen were not equally condemned. The trust reputation of occupations depended on the past honesty of members and the role and cultural perceptions of the pursuit. Bankers and stockbrokers were less respected than manufacturers, who were thought less trustworthy than merchants and small craftsmen. Professionals were held in higher repute than all businessmen, but there were again great variations between occupations. Doctors, who held patients' lives in their hands, were more trusted than lawyers, whose profession awarded duplicity, as were scientists and engineers, who placed great weight on the accurate reporting of results.[2]

This distrust of businessmen was reciprocated. Many traders had 'no good feeling for any class but their own ... [were] distant, even hostile to all others', accusing 'whoever is not in trade ... of eating the bread of idleness'. Most, nonetheless, accepted society's criticism of their practices and were equally concerned about moral hazard, although what constituted duplicitous dealing was open to debate. Most commentators advised their readers to act morally in business, to 'use no deception ... take no advantage of ignorance and necessity and employ no improper means to enhance or diminish the market price of the commodity'. It was generally agreed, however, that businessmen possessed 'unquestionably a right to make as good a bargain' as possible and certain actions were regarded as permissible. The breaking of an agreement was acceptable when completion was impossible and the 'inability be necessary and unexpected', when a promise had been 'made involuntarily without the concurrence of will', where the other party 'had failed to comply with the acknowledged conditions', or when 'some sudden and remarkable event of providence' changed 'the nature or greatly affected the value of the property involved in the contract'. Likewise, it was 'not extortion to demand the current price, though the price may be enhanced far above its usual standard by scarcity', and it was thought admissible to withhold the truth or 'tell a falsehood to a person who has no right to know the truth'.[3]

More serious fraud often took on the identity of a gift or became a business norm. A businessman would accept minor impropriety from a partner on the understanding that the associate would not resort to costlier fraud, or if the partner, in his turn, reciprocally accepted the businessman's own minor dishonesty. Many fraudulent acts were within the moral norms of a particular sector. Some were permitted provided that they did not result in major losses and they promoted economic development. The forgery of bills of exchange by Norwich banks from 1829 to 1831, for example, was known about and accepted within the local community and only became a 'crime' when the practice was brought to the attention of the London Head Office. Other frauds were regarded as legitimate because they affected customers rather than fellow traders and were believed to be essential to business success. Even Daniel Defoe acknowledged that 'a talking, rattling mercer or draper or milliner behind his counter would be worth nothing if he should confine himself to that mean silly thing called truth'. The legitimacy of such frauds enabled perpetuators to commit them without psychological cost, with the result that men 'who, if the opportunity afforded, would shrink with abhorrence from purloining the property of their neighbour ... have no compunctions against robbing them in the way of business'.[4]

Yet, although certain types of fraud were thought acceptable, it was generally agreed that moral hazard was damaging to the individual trader. It was widely acknowledged that 'a purchaser upon whom an inferior article has been put off will seldom return'. Although 'some persons' believed 'that if they cannot get enough out of their customers the first time they would not wish to see them afterwards', most admitted that such behaviour was 'most unbusiness like and universally unsuccessful', as the customer would not only take his business else-where but would 'be certain to make [the duplicity] known to others'. The trader's reputation would thus be damaged and 'after his purse, nothing is more precious to a [businessman] than his mask – the reputation he has managed to acquire'. Indeed, so important was reputation regarded that by the 1850s on the sale of a business it was recognised as having a value and added to the cost of the concern. Dishonesty, furthermore, was believed to harm employer–employee relations and costs. Workers would have little faith in a master they knew to indulge in deceitful business practices, and could even be inclined to 'follow his example and when their opportunity arrives ... extract the highest wage their position will permit'.[5]

On a macro-level, moral hazard reduced business trust and economic growth. It was accepted that 'confidence in the honour, integrity and judgement of ... contracting parties' was 'the life and soul of commerce', and that opportunism in overseas markets, where purchasers were not 'always able to distinguish the false from the real' would severely damage exports. A poor reputation with the general public also affected businessmen, damaging their ability to build trust relationships with those not involved in commerce, and, in certain circum-stances, dishonesty could be self-generating. The duplicitous 'by being able to undersell the honest manufacturer and dealer ... often drive him out of the market', and their success encouraged emulation by their children and their social betters and inferiors, causing society to be 'extensively injured and demoralised'.[6]

The rise in dishonesty and distrust was related to economic growth. Some believed that duplicity was the inevitable outcome of industrialisation. Accord-ing to Robert Owen, 'all are sedulously trained to buy cheap and to sell dear, and, to succeed in this art, the parties must be taught to acquire strong powers of deception'. Others argued that it was the degree of competition rather than competition per se that was the main culprit. Low fixed capital requirements, the growth of the market, and the availability of second-hand plant, credit and, in some towns, property caused large numbers of people, many young and inexpe-rienced, to set up firms. Rate books for the Lancashire town of Bolton indicate that from 1787 to 1796 the number of owners of industrial properties doubled. Trade directories, meanwhile, show that over the period 1829 to 1861 9,251 people traded in the town, three times as many as during the years 1787 to 1821. The greater number of traders increased supply, which expanded further as a result of changes in technology and organisation, the coming of the railway and marketing, which allowed geographically distant manufacturers to enter local markets, and the tendency of new entrants to produce goods on a speculative basis without a known buyer. Generally, the increased supply exceeded demand and the lifespans of firms were therefore relatively short. During the period 1787 to 1861, 72 per cent of Bolton firms appeared in just one trade directory, and the average lifespan of firms, as measured by the time that elapsed between their first and last appearance in a directory, was just over four years (Table 9.1). Bleachers experienced the longest lifespans and textile manufacturers the shortest. Bolton, of course, was not unique. In Edinburgh, during the later period 1861 to 1891, 55 per cent of male-owned firms had a lifespan of three years or less, and in Ploughkeepsie, New York, 60 cent of the companies formed between 1843 and 1873 disappeared within four years.[7]

The growth in the number of traders and the short lifespans of firms had a devastating affect on trust. Businessmen were often strangers to one another; during their business's short lifes, they had insufficient time to establish reputations; and the limited number of trade interactions prevented the generation of strong bonds of trust with trading partners. The 'continual fluctuation' of tradesmen also took 'away all regard to character', as there was less of an economic incentive to invest in a reputation for honest behaviour since most businessmen did not expect to encounter trading partners repeatedly. Moreover, the knowledge that their colleagues, similarly, cared little about their own good names only intensified the atmosphere of distrust. The 'poor rising trader' thus found life to be 'a real struggle for existence' and 'deceit and fraud ... [became] great temptations to a man of easy conscience, especially when he finds that fair means fail'.[8]

The temptations were heightened by a fear of failure. In answer to the question 'what is it that the modern English soul does ... dread infinitely and contemplate with entire despair? What is his hell?', Thomas Carlyle responded 'the terror of not succeeding'. Failure was certainly far from pleasant. As discussed below, insolvency and bankruptcy usually condemned a trader to a lifetime of paid employment, led to the loss of his reputation, and often resulted in him

Table 9.1 Turnover of firms in Bolton, 1787–1861

	Average lifespan in years	*Percentage of firms that appear in just one directory*
Businesses established 1787–1861	4.2	72.3
Businesses established 1787–1821	N/A	62.1
Businesses established 1829–1861	N/A	75.6
Textiles	3.4	80.3
Engineering and metals	4.2	75.3
Retailers and service providers	3.9	71.6
Professionals	4.9	69.8
Bleachers	5.1	65.2
Other manufacturers	4.3	70.9

Source: Database.

Note
Sectors include firms that undertook occupations in each sector only.

becoming a social outcast. The insolvent could also be jailed until their debts were discharged; prisons being breeding grounds of disease, where the necessities of life were in short supply and, if procured from the outside world, expensive.[9]

Rapid economic growth, in turn, increased the use of credit, which further damaged trust. Credit took a variety of forms – loans, mortgages on a master's place of residence/business or tools, trade debt in the form of deferment of payment for goods, promissory notes and bills of exchange. Such indebtness was essential to economic development, facilitating business formation and expansion, and enabling businessmen to overcome the shortage of ready money, the undeveloped financial sector and the problems encountered in moving cash around the country. Credit, consequently, was endemic, and, according to d'Archenholtz, 'ready money [was] never employed but in regard to trifling demands'.[10]

Many blamed the wide availability of credit for the rise in dishonesty. Creditors often had little option but to continue to trade with fraudsters, particularly if they owed them large amounts of money. 'The cheapness of credit' permitted 'a host of needy adventurers and violators of open honest dealing' to set up businesses, and encouraged traders to enter sectors and expand more rapidly than the state of the market would justify, contributing to the excessive competition that was one of the causes of dishonesty. To obtain money, some were tempted to act deceitfully. Claims as to their skills, business competence and past and present trading success were often lies. Securities for loans sometimes did not belong to the borrower, and letters of reference were often forgeries or provided by dishonest friends or existing creditors, who, fearing that the person was about to become insolvent, gave 'a false character that he may be enabled for a while longer to carry on business'.[11]

Inevitably, many failed to repay their debts. Borrowers were often incompetent businessmen, obtained 'credit to an amount beyond what they have any possible means of paying for', frittered away the money lent 'in dissipation and amusements', or got into spirals of debt, repaying creditors by taking out further loans. When this occurred, creditors lost their money and were less willing to trust others, and, in many cases, were left with damaged trust reputations. Fellow traders were aware that they had misjudged the character and means of the borrower, who to salvage his own reputation often sought to blacken the name of the creditor. Freedly in his treatise on business remarked that he had 'never known a debtor who was not in his own estimation an injured man' and had unfortunately 'generally found that those who had not suffered by them were disposed to side with them'.[12]

To limit the danger of non-repayment, a trader sought creditworthy customers, whose reputations would, in turn, strengthen his own creditworthiness. Creditors also often required debts to be at least partly paid in kind, demanded goods as security, charged interest on unpaid accounts, asked borrowers of capital to fund at least a third of their total capital outlay out of their own pockets, during downturns placed limitations on the period of credit, offered price discounts to those who paid their bills promptly, or transferred the debt to others. In Manchester, for example, cotton manufacturers bought yarn through agents who accepted responsibility for the whole or part of the risk of non-payment, their rate of commission being determined by the amount of debt they took on and the length of the repayment period. If a debtor was unable to repay what he owed, in good times his creditors would occasionally agree among themselves not to call in their debts, aware that the collapse of the firm would damage the entire community's creditworthiness.[13]

Credit also increased the destructive effect of the failure of a single company and more significantly trade downturns on both the economy and trust. Firms extended short-term credit to customers and were themselves granted credit by suppliers. The clients and suppliers, in turn, permitted and accepted credit. The result was that a network of debt was established, which would collapse if a large business became insolvent, there were rumours that this was about to occur, or the trade became depressed. Asked to repay their debts, each owner would demand the payment of his own outstanding bills, fearing bankruptcy or the loss of his trust reputation if he failed to pay his own creditors. Eventually, large swathes of the businesses that made up the network would fail and trust would be decimated. The distrust could even spread to money. Fearing the collapse of country banks, businessmen often developed a preference for Bank of England notes, and, in extreme crises, would convert these into gold and silver, which possessed 'an intrinsic value'.[14]

Other explanations put forward for the rise of dishonesty include the withdrawal of women and their civilising influence from trade; the disappearance of Guilds, which sustained shared norms, and punished norm violators; the individualism promulgated by Smith, Ricardo and Malthus; the decline in apprenticeships and the bonds generated between apprentices and apprentices/masters; and the popularity of the verbal contract. From the 1750s, the greater rapidity of commercial transactions and the high cost of arriving at legal agreements caused the sealed document to give way to the informal written contract or the verbal promise. By the 1860s, it was claimed that 'ninety nine out of a hundred contracts are given verbally', despite the fact that many believed that such agreements created more opportunity for deceit and fraud.[15]

In London, the expansion of the securities market and the changes in company organisation brought about by the Limited Liability Act of 1855 and the various Companies Acts, again, opened up new opportunities for fraud.[16] Little was done, however, to curtail the resultant dishonesty. Shareholders lacked the knowledge to determine whether losses were the result of incompetence, negligence or downright dishonesty, accountancy was in its infancy and commercial law was weak. Both the 1844 Company Act and Joint Stock Bank Act were ineffective and were gradually diluted by free traders. As regards self-regulation, moral norms developed that permitted certain forms of dishonest behaviour. Balance sheet manipulation, insider trading and the bribery of journalists for favourable articles on company performance were all regarded as acceptable. The large-scale and complex structure of business, meanwhile, allowed fraudsters to avoid questions of conscience. Most had little or no contact with their victims and could transfer personal responsibility and guilt to the company that employed them, or, if they were directors, to their board colleagues.

Maintenance of an effective level of trust

If interest rates are taken as a broad indicator of business confidence, commercial trust fell from the 1780s to the 1820s (Figure 9.1). Given the 'historically unique and internationally remarkable' rate of economic growth during the period 1750–1850, however, the fall in trust cannot have been great, though it perhaps elucidates why economic progress was not even more rapid. One explanation for the limited nature of the fall in trust is that there was a rise in the perception of business dishonesty, rather than of dishonesty itself. People were made more aware of commercial chicanery by the evangelical movement, social campaigners, newspapers, legislation that created 'new crimes . . . [and] offences . . . which would have been simply meaningless' to previous generations, and the work of novelists and non-fiction writers. Moreover, much of what was written

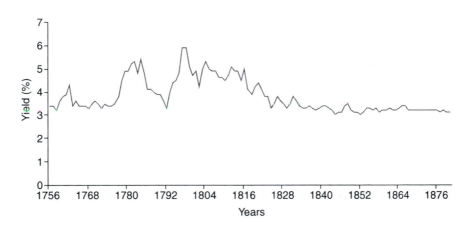

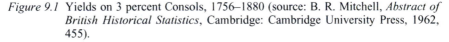

Figure 9.1 Yields on 3 percent Consols, 1756–1880 (source: B. R. Mitchell, *Abstract of British Historical Statistics*, Cambridge: Cambridge University Press, 1962, 455).

Note

As country bank data is not available, the yield on 3 per cent Consols is used as a measurement of private-sector borrowing rates. Consols were the largest component of British-government-funded debt, and, though they paid a fixed nominal interest rate of 3 per cent, their price fluctuated. Although there is every reason to assume that private-sector borrowing was more expensive than that of the government, it seems likely that Consol yields accurately reflect private-sector rate trends over time (P. Antras and H. J. Voth, 'Factor prices and productivity growth during the British industrial revolution', *Explorations in Economic History*, 40 (1), 2003, 61). The belief that the Consol and private-sector rates diverged during the Napoleonic wars, due to the high government borrowing crowding out private investment, has now been discounted (G. Clark, 'Debts, deficits and crowding out: England 1727–1840', *European Review of Economic History*, 5 (3), 2001, 1–35).

on commercial integrity was far from a true reflection of reality. Many aristo-cratic writers, jealous and resentful of the urban elite, exaggerated business mal-practice and fictional condemnations of traders' honesty were founded, not on first-hand experience of commerce, but on the writings of Ricardo and Smith and the Benthamites and Utilitarians, whose theories, in turn, ironically were often based on abstract thought rather than on personal knowledge.[17]

A further explanation is that industrial growth and credit both reduced and promoted trust. The view that economic growth raised both business and social trust was widely held in the late eighteenth and early nineteenth centuries. The religious writer Edward Miall argued that 'trade multiplies our relations with our fellow man ... creates countless grades of mutual dependence and necessitates mutual trust in all its stages'. Adam Smith declared that 'whenever commerce is introduced into any country, probity and punctuality always accompany it', pointing out that the Dutch were 'the most commercial [and] are the most faith-ful to their word'. The radical Thomas Hodgskin, meanwhile, asserted that labour prevented a descent into 'avarice, vanity, indulgence and extravagance', and *The Economist* avowed that trade carried with it 'a rigid morality ... [which] naturally inculcates punctual and rigid honesty'. Some even claimed that business fraud, rather than reflecting commercial distrust, was an indicator of high levels of integrity, as 'it is the confidence reposed and deserved by the many which affords facilities for the bad faith of the few'.[18]

Credit raised trust in a number of ways. Creditors had to trust that borrow-ers would repay their debts and borrowers that lenders would not call in loans with little notice; both had to develop good reputations in order to encourage individuals to borrow to or lend from them; and, once given, a debt discour-aged both parties from indulging in dishonest behaviour for fear that the other party would refuse or be unable to repay the debt or would call it in. Indebt-ness between individuals, social groups and regions, furthermore, generated intra-class trust, inter-class trust and geographic trust, and, in economic down-turns, acted against the collapse of social capital, with the knowledge that pulling in a loan could cause the whole network of borrowing to collapse and ultimately damage their own businesses and trust reputations, encouraging creditors to keep their lines of lending open. Credit also acted as a gift, in the form of a signal that an individual had faith in his trading partner, and rein-forced reputation. The ability to gain credit added to the debtor's good name, particularly if the terms were good or the loan was provided by someone regarded as trustworthy or by kin, which suggested that further support would be forthcoming if the individual got into difficulties.[19] Likewise, creditors who refrained from calling in the debts of those unable to pay because of family problems, for example illness or death, greatly augmented their reputations for benevolence. Unpaid debt, meanwhile, promoted repeat trading and long busi-ness relationships, which generated trust, and reduced the impact of the trust crises suffered by family firms when the founder retired or died, encouraging those who traded with the former owner to continue to do business with the less trusted heirs.

Another reason for the high levels of trust was that businessmen wasted little time in seeking to reverse the perceived fall in honesty. Unlike, for example, in the field of labour relations, the advantages of integrity were well understood and there was little ingrained hostility between traders. Trust was raised through the use of the various signals discussed in Chapter 1, the membership of the voluntary associations and societies examined in Chapters 3 and 4, and the formation of informal and formal commercial networks and the adoption of business practices that tended to raise confidence, both of which are considered below.

Post-1850 business trust

From mid-century, commercial trust rose. Greater prosperity, the arrival of recognised raw material and product standards, the weakening of individualism, the introduction by banks of paper currency, which reduced the use of credit, the gradual improvement in commercial law and better education, all increased business social capital.[20] Trust was further strengthened by changes in criminal law, the spread of limited liability via the 1856 Companies Act, and the transference of trust and network connections from the market to the firm. Legal sanctions against fraud gradually became more stringent as the century progressed, culminating in the 1906 Prevention of Corruption Act. Prosecution under this legislation, however, was difficult, penalties were relatively light, and the Act was largely used in extreme cases or where other offences with equivalent penalties had been committed.[21] As with ordinary crime, it appears that the government passed the statute in order to lay down general boundaries of acceptable business behaviour and to maintain the electorate's faith in the social contract, but deliberately ensured that prosecutions would be low. High levels of litigation would have damaged the public's belief in the honesty of the commercial world and the legitimacy of the capitalist system, and would have excessively constrained business moral hazard and reduced economic growth.

Many of those who campaigned for the 1856 Companies Act, which made limited liability easier to adopt, were motivated by a wish to raise social trust. It was maintained that a change in the law would facilitate the finance of large urban infrastructure schemes, encourage working-class investment in their employers' firms, and raise business trust. Infrastructure schemes, such as parks and model housing, would improve the living conditions and morality of poorer city dwellers, who would 'feel [that] the richer classes really had their welfare at heart' and could even become shareholders themselves and thus acquire ascribed trust relationships with their wealthier neighbours. Worker shareholding would redraw the 'trenchant line of demarcation between capitalists and labourers that is ... the root of conflict', and, if the companies failed, would reveal to employees the skills and qualities required for business success and thus legitimise entrepreneurial profits. In the business world, it was thought that the new law, by causing men to 'associate with one another' and placing them 'in relations of mutual dependence and reciprocal benefit', would generate 'feelings of goodwill, sympathy and friendship' and give 'strength ... beyond estimation' 'to the social fabric'. Others, however, were more pessimistic arguing that it would rather reduce business trust, inducing 'parties to advance their money, without due caution, for speculative schemes and speculative ventures', a tendency that would be 'detrimental to the fair trader and to men who conduct their business with prudence and discretion'.[22]

In practice, limited liability appears to have reduced the cost of business failure and thus weakened the temptation to resort to moral hazard, and, through the constituents and by-laws of joint-stock companies, made white-collar crime more difficult, though the separation of ownership from control arguably increased the opportunities for deception. In the decades immediately following its conception, the act also seems to have generated strong local shareholding networks and social capital.[23] In Sheffield and Oldham, the two manufacturing centres that most enthusiastically took up the legislation, the new equity was largely sold to local businessmen and professionals, who knew the vendors, the company promoters and their fellow shareholders either socially or through their business dealings or kin and met them at annual shareholder meetings. Local purchase discouraged dishonest company promotion, and the resulting networks facilitated commercial trust, businessmen having a direct financial interest in the success of local industry; minimised opportunism, shareholders continuously monitoring firms; and promoted company growth. Many investors provided managements with information and access to resources and were reluctant to withdraw their funds during periods of poor trade, afraid of damaging their relations with boards of directors/fellow shareholders and their wider reputations.

Trust and network connections were transferred from the market to the firm when companies vertically integrated, that is took over businesses involved in other parts of the production process, which caused the possibility of supplier/customer moral hazard to be replaced with that of employee duplicity, a form of dishonesty that was easier to monitor and control. In many sectors, this form of integration became commonplace, though, in the cotton industry, such was the strength of formal and informal vertical networks that the practice was comparatively rare. Later, horizontal integration occurred with the formation of holding companies that linked a large proportion of firms in a particular industry. In 1898, 30 cotton manufacturers banded together to form the Fine Cotton Spinners and Doublers Association, and, in 1900, 52 bleaching companies, primarily located around Bolton and Bury, came together to create the Bleachers Association.[24] These organisations, again, facilitated the generation of trust and the establishment of networks.

Such integration, however, inevitably led to the enlargement of firms, which could damage attachments. Large-scale companies formed relatively weak relationships with their many suppliers/buyers, sometimes operating through agents and wholesalers; occasionally exploited their dominance of the market by resorting to the use of power; and reduced trust between their trading partners, which inter-traded less. To operate effectively, they also required managers, who possessed less power than owners to give and reciprocate gifts, were reluctant to participate in local networks, and, relatively less dedicated to the success of the firm, engendered less commitment and invested less energy in the development of relationships.

All in all, whether the high-levels of business trust were advantageous to the British economy during this period of growing foreign competition is debatable. It can be argued that greater co-operation dulled competitive instincts and resulted in the export of high priced and poor quality goods, trust based labour relations raised costs and served as barriers to innovation, and governments attempts to strengthen the social contract led to excessive and unproductive public expenditure. The strong business networks, meanwhile, may have actively impeded economic development. Formal and informal associations were reluctant to alter those norms and routines that had served them so well for so long, and were equally unwilling to accept as members new business entrants, representatives of the new commercial sectors, and, in the 1920s and 1930s, the financiers and politicians who were so crucial to change. Instead of promoting innovation and economic transition, therefore, they rather protected the status quo, and, in the process, stifled entrepreneurship. When eventually the inevitable occurred and the traditional industries went into steep decline, vertical networks found that they could not even work towards a common purpose. Facing uncertainty, each industry thus protected its own interests, which were often incompatible with those of related sectors.[25]

Determinants of business trust

Industry trust

Business trust can be split into a number of types – that within and between whole business communities, that within and between industries, and that between individual businessmen. All were interrelated, community and industry trust partly determining inter-firm trust and vice versa, and were shaped by the local social, cultural, political, economic and institutional environment, the amount of social and kinship trust in existence, and the history of a firm, industry or town, especially its past decisions and leaders. Of the environmental factors, the most significant was the structure of the local economy. Industry trust was partly determined by the number and size of firms in the sector, the size of other industries, and the sector's capital requirements and its susceptibility to downturns. The number of firms influenced the amount of trust created by company interaction. An industry that contained comparatively few businesses would have had relatively high trust levels, as all or a large proportion of its entrepreneurs would have socialised with each other and formed relatively strong bonds of trust. For the same reason, towns with a small number of sectors would have developed relatively robust business community trust. In nineteenth-century Lancashire, the average number of firms per sector and number of sectors per town were relatively small, though they increased over time, and trust would therefore have been high.[26]

The size of the companies and other economic sectors affected the trust norms of an industry. The norms of a sector that contained a few dominant firms or shared a town with a much larger and more pre-eminent industry were inevitably influenced by the mores of the dominant company or industry. So, for example, a sector that contained a relatively large firm that had norms that discouraged trust formation or was in a town that contained a pre-eminent industry that held such norms would inevitably itself acquire this outlook.[27] In Lancashire, the dominance of sectors and individual companies differed between towns and sectors. Oldham, for instance, was dominated by cotton manufacture, whereas Bolton had a far more mixed economy. In engineering, there were few pre-eminent firms until the 1850s, but in many towns cotton was dominated by just two or three companies.

A sector's capital requirements affected its trust levels in a number of ways. Industries with high fixed capital costs would have generated relatively large amounts of trust. The high entry costs would have restricted firm numbers and may have reduced company turnover, that is the rate at which companies entered and left the sector, and would therefore have increased the longevity and strength of trust relationships. The heavy cost of bankruptcy would have created a greater need for trust, and new entrants would have been men of moderate wealth, in many cases with a commercial background. They would therefore have benefited from the various class-trust advantages discussed below and elsewhere and already possessed network connections plus experience of effective networking. Using this measure, trust in the cotton-spinning sector would have been relatively high and would have risen over time. In the 1780s, an Arkwright mill of 1,000 spindles required a capital expenditure of £3,000 to £5,000; the cost doubling to £10,000 with the coming of steam. In engineering, on the other hand, trust would have been low in the first part of the period when machine-shop equipment was relatively rudimentary, but, with the coming of machine tools and steam power, would have risen considerably.[28]

An industry and a town's susceptibility to economic downturns was pertinent in that, during recessions, competitive forces revived, reducing trust, the damage inflicted depending on the length, severity and regularity of the depression and the initial strength of sector trust. During the 1830s and 1840s, the cotton industry experienced a roller-coaster series of booms and slumps, which no doubt greatly damaged trust both in this sector and, to a lesser extent, in engineering, which largely produced textile machinery. The downturns then became less regular and their impact on the sector varied from town to town. Bolton, for instance, was far less affected by the cotton-trade cycle than its counterparts. The town specialised in fine spinning, which was relatively immune to foreign competition, its engineering sector had diversified its output away from textile machinery and it contained a large number of industries, the prosperity of which was only partly connected to that of cotton.[29]

Inter-businessman trust

The trust between traders took three forms: competence trust, that the other party would perform his work adequately; contractual trust, that he would fulfil his written or verbal contract; and goodwill trust, that he would not act in his own narrow interests if unanticipated events arose.[30] Those traders who were successful in the formation of trust relationships tended to share certain personal characteristics, adopted particular modes of behaviour and action that signalled trustworthiness and facilitated the creation of network linkages, and managed specific kinds of businesses.

Personal characteristics

Features that have already been discussed include the possession of strong kin relationships, a trustworthy extrovert personality, a high Emotional Intelligence Quotient, physical attributes that conformed to the trustworthy traits laid down by the 'sciences' of physiognomy and phrenology, and a local place of birth. Other important personal characteristics were entrepreneurial ability, class, age, gender and self-confidence. An individual with entrepreneurial ability would have been able to use these skills to gain more from networking. Proactive, he would have anticipated the need for new contacts; positive towards risk, he would have accepted the possibility that the pay-off from making ties would not necessarily cover the costs; and his innovativeness would have enabled him to discover new ways of using networks and contacts. Likewise, an entrepreneur from a middle/upper-class, well-established business family would have obtained more in the way of information, finance and secure transactions from his kin than someone who had a more humble background. He would have been able to free ride on a more widely recognised family reputation and on the trust connected to his class, been well-endowed with the characteristics that generated middle-class ascribed trust, and, through his kin, would have had access to higher value networks and have possessed the social and etiquette skills and the knowledge of socialisation norms necessary for successful networking. His very wealth would also have generated trust and he would have been untainted by the distrust of the self-made entrepreneur. Misgivings about the self-made are particularly reflected in the nineteenth-century novel, which, from the 1840s to 1870s, depicted such people as villains who preyed on the naivety of others and operated on the edge of respectable society.[31]

A middle-class businessman would have been even more trusted if he was middle aged. In the nineteenth century, young entrepreneurs were thought to be prime candidates for bankruptcy and were thus distrusted. They were highly dependent on credit, lacked sufficient experience to effectively evaluate risk, possessed relatively few network connections, and were unskilled in the trust building arts of etiquette. They were also thought to be too trusting, possessing 'an unguarded openness ... that makes them the ready prey of the artful and designing ... [and] easily led away by the feigned friendship of a knave or a fool'. Although more trusted than the young, the elderly, similarly, possessed less trust and network connections than other age groups. They were less able to attend and become involved in networks, had difficulty in interacting with younger colleagues, possessed diminished mental and physical capacities, and were more easily duped.[32]

Women were a rarity in business. In Bolton, they accounted for around 10 per cent of traders listed in the town's directories (Table 9.2). As in other localities, they were largely found in teaching, many running their own schools, the garment industries and retailing, particularly operating shops that sold food and drink.[33] These occupations had a largely female clientele, which led to the generation of ascribed trust and were an extension of their domestic role. Businesswomen were largely distrusted, males believing that their true place was in the home. They also lacked access to male-dominated networks, and, having to complete household tasks, could devote little time to socialising. Not surprisingly, therefore, they were far less successful than their male counterparts. In Bolton, the average lifespan of the female-operated firms listed in the trade directories was just three years, as compared with male businesses' 4.4 years, a figure that rises to 5.2 years for those few women who can be identified as having taken over a deceased husband's trade and inherited his trust reputation.

Self-confidence, or the trust people have in their own capabilities, is determined by genetic inheritance, early parent–child socialisation, the memory of the success or otherwise of past actions, information received from others, and the comparison of one's attainments with those of peers. Successful businessmen and those who socialised a great deal would thus have had greater confidence than the unsuccessful and unsociable. As today, self-assurance enabled people to act and persevere with their actions. Low self-esteem was acknowledged to 'destroy energy . . . wither hope . . . repress ambition . . . make the will to vacillate and the judgement to falter; it terrifies and alarms or crushes and annihilates; it makes a man timid, dastardly, uncertain, useless!' Faith in oneself also led others to have confidence in one's capabilities, facilitated social interaction and, via 'the pleasure of self-approbation', encouraged benevolent actions. Excessive self-confidence, on the other hand, could be debilitating. There is 'a strong tendency in the human mind to flatter itself with secret hopes' or 'to exaggerate or extenuate' its 'excellences'. If carried to an excessive

Table 9.2 Women listed in Bolton trade directories, 1787–1861

	Percentage of women listed	Percentage of women who appear in just one directory	Average lifespan of female-controlled firms
1787–1861	9.7	78.3	3.0
1787–1821	7.1	72.2	N/A
1829–61	10.6	79.6	N/A
Textiles	2.7	–	2.0
Engineering and metals	1.4	–	2.7
Retailers and service providers	14.6	–	3.3
Professionals	19.3	–	2.4
Bleachers	3.0	–	7.1
Other manufacturers	11.4	–	2.5

Source: Database.

length, such delusion inevitably led to distrust. The arrogant failed to fulfil expectations, and, as 'their sense of their own rights and merits' was 'perpetually infringed', they were 'in constant collision with their friends and with society'.[34]

Methods of doing business

Other factors that had an impact on trust/success include business behaviour, the adoption of negotiating routines and norms, the place of domestic/business residence, the advertisement of services and the maintenance of relationships with geographically distant business partners. Behaviour that promoted trust was voluminously recorded in the business etiquette books that became popular in the early part of the century. These manuals sought to raise trust by recommending that their readers follow 'the laws of honour', cajoling them with various promises. It was claimed that 'the more elevated the business character, the more easy it will be to get money', that the honourable 'act with more simplicity and therefore with less chance of error', and that moral behaviour 'conduces to the highest intellectual development' and wisdom. To help them become 'knights of righteousness', the books provided readers with long lists of 'dos and don'ts'. They were advised, for example, not to 'use information confidentially entrusted ... to anticipate the informer', 'sell below the market price to get away ... neighbours' customers', take advantage 'of another's unskilfullness or inexperience', to be 'unmindful of favours' and to 'always tell the truth to and insist on it being told by' their employees. Care, however, had to be taken not to declare one's honourable nature too openly, as the trader 'holding himself up as the only honest fellow in the neighbourhood' was generally the most distrusted.[35]

Further trust-generating behaviour recommended by such books included punctuality and abstemiousness. Punctuality 'in reference to time engagements, money engagements and engagements for work' was regarded as a sure sign of trustworthiness. 'An unpunctual man' caused 'uneasy feelings', as his failure to complete actions at the agreed time suggested 'a want of system, defective calculation and imprudence in making promises'. To signal their punctiliousness, many businessmen carried large and prominently displayed watches. Luxury and extravagance were similarly suspected. It was believed that the pursuit of extravagant pleasures caused businessmen to disregard their affairs; 'business neglected ... [being] business lost'. Furthermore, it stretched their financial resources and they were thus more inclined to 'grasp ... at riches by the most unjustifiable means', including outright dishonesty, and became less risk averse, plunging 'headlong into engagements immense, distant and dangerous'. Traders were also advised to keep careful accounts and to 'take care that every transaction is in writing' so as to 'prevent litigation or mistake'; to make sure that others 'see that you know your business' by giving an outward show of competence; and to avoid the use of paper currency. Until mid-century, banknotes were mistrusted owing to their unfamiliarity, a fear of forgery, their flimsy nature as compared to the 'noble' metals, and the printing of paper currency by the perpetrators of the French Revolution and the American War of Independence, which gave them subversive connotations.[36]

During business negotiations, trust was generated by conforming to negotiating routines and norms, which varied between industries and trading networks. Routines dictated the number of meetings that had to be held, the participants, where the discussions should occur, the language to be used (both verbally and in correspondence) and the topics to be discussed. In the case of negotiations between large firms, a preliminary meeting of owners was generally held at which technical specifications, price, method of payment and date of delivery were agreed. There was then a further meeting(s) attended by middle managers, technicians and legal advisors at which the details of the contract would be decided and specialised technical and legal language used.[37] Important norms included honesty or transparency as regards capabilities, and that each side would attempt to drive a hard bargain, though its toughness was tempered by market conditions and by fairness norms, which reflected customary conceptions of normal and reasonable profit margins. To prevent time consuming haggling and one side making excessive demands and generating animosity, specific signals were adopted to indicate that a final offer had been made. These were usually linguistic phrases that were personnel to the trading network or the sector.

Place of domestic/business residence affected social capital in a number of ways – creating inter-sector trust, adding to reputation and, through relocation, increasing network connections. In most towns, the business community lived and worked in a small geographical area, leading to the development of much inter-sector co-operation. Moreover, those who undertook particular trades tended to cluster together, facilitating intra-sector trust. In 1829, almost 20 per cent of Bolton's traders had premises in one of five streets, and 63 per cent of its hatters were to be found in Taylor Brow, half of its fishmongers and druggists had premises in Clarks Court and Deansgate respectively, and over 80 per cent of the listed residents of Back Rothwell Street and Clayton Ford Bridge were weavers. In many cases, those in the same sector and sometimes in different trades shared premises, which further promoted inter-sector and intra-sector trust. The middle class, similarly, lived close to each other and there was again much occupational clustering. Twenty-one per cent of those who voted in Bolton's 1841 election gave one of just four streets as their place of residence, and a third of middle-class mechanics and cabinet makers who voted in the 1832 election had houses in Black Horse Street and Newport Street respectively, 37 per cent of tailors and drapers resided in Deansgate, and half the saddlers lived on Manor Street.[38]

As already discussed, 'a good address' and a large and well-furnished house signalled wealth and trustworthiness. The same applied to work premises, and factory owners thus began to occupy specialised properties built on a monumental scale, with many architectural flourishes and intricate decorations that clearly signalled prosperity and competence, and, to signal their wealth over a large area, high and ornate chimneys. Within was to be found the most up-to-date equipment, which again often incorporated much superfluous decoration.[39] To ensure that these signals were broadcast as widely as possible, many owners regularly took suppliers, customers and local notables on tours of their realms and often used the premises for the paternalistic dinners that they laid on for their staff, to which local dignitaries and others were invited.

Business relocation increased a trader's vocational network connections. An entrepreneur who moved his business premises retained the links formed with previous neighbours, though these inevitably weakened, and created fresh connections with traders in his new locality. He may also have been able to free ride on the reputation of the previous occupier of the property. In Bolton, 11 per cent of traders listed in the town's directories had more than one address over the lifetimes of their firms, movement being more common during the period 1787 to 1821 than from 1829 to 1861 (Table 9.3). Those involved in the engineering and metal trades appear to have been the most mobile, and retailers and service providers to have moved the least, probably because a shop's site and its continuity of location were important aspects of trading success. The effect of changes in address and the related increase in network connections on business lifespans was dramatic, though mobility may have been a consequence rather than a cause of commercial success. Those who relocated had three times the survival rate of those who occupied the same premises, with bleachers and professionals particularly benefiting. The gains, again, were greater in the first than in the second part of the period, perhaps because there were fewer traders and the extra relationships formed were thus stronger.

A tradesman's locational network connections, similarly, rose when he owned multiple premises. In Bolton, 2 per cent of businessmen listed in the town's directories had more than one address in any one year, with those involved in textiles being most likely to possess multiple premises (Table 9.3). As with relocation, this factor lengthened business lifespans, though this may have been as much a consequence as a cause of commercial success. In the period 1787 to 1861, those with more than one place of work had double the lifespan of other firms. Bleachers and other manufacturers were the main beneficiaries, and the factor was again more influential in the first than in the second part of the period.

Trust in products could be maintained and raised through advertisement and a range of other marketing strategies. Advertisements, whether in the form of newspaper adverts or trade cards, signalled trust in a number of ways.[40] Some simply stated that the manufacturer or retailer was honest. Others allowed the trader to free ride on other people's reputations. Adverts often mentioned that the individual was trained or formerly employed by a local and revered master, or that the business had been bought from and previously operated by such a person, or included endorsements from 'experts' or 'ordinary users'. National insurance companies and banks listed their directors, all of whom usually held important political or business positions or were members of the aristocracy. Traders with relatives in the same trade occasionally name checked them,

Table 9.3 Relocation of Bolton traders, 1787–1861

	Percentage of traders with more than one address over lifetime	Percentage of traders with more than one address in any one year	Lifespan of traders with more than one address over lifetime	Lifespan of traders with more than one address in any one year
1787–1861	11.1	2.1	14.0 (66.7)	8.6 (58.8)
1787–1821	16.7	2.0	N/A (81.2)	N/A (62.3)
1829–1861	9.3	2.1	N/A (58.3)	N/A (34.5)
Textiles	10.7	3.6	13.1	7.2
Engineering and metals	13.6	2.0	14.0	5.5
Retailers and service providers	9.9	2.1	13.3	8.3
Professionals	12.4	0.4	16.8	5.7
Bleachers	10.0	1.3	17.8	17.3
Other manufacturers	12.4	1.5	13.7	9.6

Source: Database.

Note
Brackets contain the percentage of those firms with more than one address over a lifetime/in any one year that had lifespans of ten years or more.

declaring that they were the son or brother of a particular individual, even if the person was deceased. If they had a prized long-term customer, this information too would be included, particularly if the client was royal, an aristocrat, a well-known company, or a government department and thus had a good reputation.

The success and prosperity of a firm was flagged by listing in the advert all the products produced or sold and the addresses of more than one place of business, and by noting that the advertiser was the inventor of a particular device or held certain patents, which additionally suggested innovativeness. Prosperity and competence could further be signalled via the form of the advertisement. Many had complex and costly typological arrangements, using, for example, a different font and type style for every line of text, or contained highly detailed illustrations. Trade cards were printed on thick good quality card, and occasionally copied the design of other successful and trusted advertisers so as to give a conscious or unconscious impression that the firms had much in common. As time progressed, many adverts also began to free ride on kinship trust through the depiction of family groups and children.

Publishers, meanwhile, claimed that the books they produced were moral and would make buyers more honest and decent citizens, shops, inns and ordinary businesses were often named after trusted royal figures, national or local notables or saints or had names with religious connotations, and apprentices setting up on their own often incorporated into their new firm's name that of their more respected master. Many also had good-quality signs, often three-dimensional or painted in deep relief and containing a picture of a related historical figure, on whose reputation the owner could free ride.[41] The signboards of instrument makers, for instance, sometimes included a bust of Sir Isaac Newton. By mid-century, urban stores additionally had glass windows, which heightened the appeal to the eye of the goods they framed.

Other ways of raising product trust included the development of brands, which could be stretched to encompass new products, offering customers free shipping, compensation for damage that occurred in transport or a satisfaction-or-money-back guarantee, initially targeting trustworthy customers and giving products trust engendering names. Josiah Wedgwood, for example, ensured that new merchandise was sold to elite customers and often named pieces of crockery after female members of the aristocracy. Further reassurance could be provided by displaying goods at exhibitions and entering exhibition best product competitions, employing teams of salesmen, who could form strong trust relationship with retailers and by setting relatively high prices. Wedgwood, for one, was convinced that 'low prices ... beget a low quality in manufacture, which will beget contempt'.[42]

To maintain trust relationships with geographically distant customers and suppliers, businessmen regularly visited and wrote to them. To signal their prosperity and generate wealth trust, they travelled first class, stayed at the best hotels, wore the attire of a gentleman, and often met people in banks and solicitors offices, which, if the bank/solicitor had a good reputation, further raised trust. Correspondence peaked in the winter months, when travel was difficult.

Generally, each action was accompanied by a letter, which, in addition to containing information, acted as a gift of regard. The receipt of goods was acknowledged, correspondents thanked and praise liberally dispensed. Enquiries were made about the health or welfare of the individual and his family, and the letters generally begin and end with terms of endearment – 'my dearest', 'best wishes', 'yours forever'.[43]

Nature of business

Of equal importance to the personal characteristics and behaviour of tradesmen was the nature of their business, in particularly the age and size of their firms and their choice of partners. Diversification and the failure of companies also inevitably involved issues of trust. As has already been noted, the majority of firms were in business for a relatively short period. Survival in the first few years of trading was difficult. New entrants lacked both a reputation and access to business and other networks and therefore had to operate in a trustless environment. Comprising newcomers and opportunistic companies that had failed to gain access to or had been expelled from networks, this market was replete with opportunism. Some entrepreneurs, of course, had the advantage of family reputation and kin who operated in the same economic sector, and others partly circumvented the trust problem through the purchase of existing businesses that already possessed reputations, though these were weakened by the arrival of the new owners. The chances of success were also highly dependent on the point in the trade cycle at which a firm was established. Companies that were set up at the start of the cycle had a better chance of survival than those that appeared towards the end, as they had greater time to build network connections and trust relationships before the downturn and concomitant rise in competition and opportunism. Unfortunately, given people's tendency towards risk aversion, most business start-ups appear to have occurred late in the cycle, when the prospects of success were perceived to be high.

The longer a firm traded, the more it built up trust and network connections and the more likely it was to survive. Those Bolton firms that appeared in more than one trade directory during the period 1787 to 1861 had an average lifespan of 12.4 years, three times that of all directory firms (Table 9.4). Relatively few firms, though, had long business lives. In Bolton from 1787 to 1861, only 17 per cent of traders appeared in the town's directories for ten or more years, 28 per cent in 1787 to 1821 and 13 per cent in 1829 to 1861 (Table 9.4). In both periods, professionals appear to have had longer lifespans than any other group, and lifespans varied between towns. For those firms that did survive, their sheer longevity generated trust. The past success of the firm indicated its competence and suggested that it would continue to trade and that those with which it formed trust relationships would fully reap the rewards of their connections.[44]

The majority of companies were either small or of middling size, even in the cotton industry. Of the two, the medium-sized firms were more trusted, as it was believed that they had a greater chance of survival, a supposition confirmed by

Table 9.4 Lifespans of Bolton firms, 1787–1861

	Average lifespan of firms that appeared in more than one trade directory	*Percentage of firms that appeared in directories for ten or more years*
All 1787–1861	12.5	16.8
Textiles	13.3	13.5
Engineering and metals	13.9	17.3
Retailers and service providers	11.3	15.2
Professionals	14.0	19.4
Bleachers	12.9	20.4
Other manufacturers	12.3	17.4

Source: Database.

studies of the cotton and other industries.[45] The owners also had less need to act opportunistically, more time and energy to devote to networking, and, possessing information and trading opportunities of value to others, had better access to networks.

Large firms were few and far between. Expansion demanded a consuming and penalising dedication to business, which most owners did not possess, and increased the risk of insolvency and bankruptcy. Many owners, furthermore, retired early, or, for reasons discussed later in the chapter, ensured that their firms were sold on their death. Large and rapidly growing businesses were also distrusted. One explanation is that in pre-industrial times the goal of most traders was to earn the customary income with the least exertion and the most comfort. Another reason was the suspicion of those who sought riches, particularly from industry, that pervaded the Victorian novel and inevitably influenced its middle-class readership. The plots of such fictions clearly demonstrated that a craving for money corrupted and that wealth destroyed fellow feeling, humanity, family and loving relations and led to alienation and madness. A further explanation is that not everyone was convinced that the economies of scale, at least of large-scale cotton firms, enhanced their chances of survival. Big concerns were supposedly better able to consume their own waste, develop and exploit labour saving technology and achieve managerial economies. But in the cotton industry, there was an external market for waste; by the 1830s, many innovations in cotton machinery were made by the engineering sector; and, despite patents, new designs were rapidly diffused into the industry, greatly reducing the period of time an innovator could enjoy the benefits. There are also doubts, given the effect of a large workforce on employer–employee trust relations, that sizeable firms were better able to exploit labour saving technology and many proprietors were reluctant to appoint professional managers or were unwilling to delegate to them.[46]

Indeed, many believed that rapidly growing firms were relatively more vulnerable to insolvency than their smaller counterparts and that their collapse was a major cause of trade depressions. In the second quarter of the century, the economic environment did not appear to favour rapid expansion. The tightening of profits, the introduction of restrictive tariffs and Malthusian fears caused many to be sceptical about the continued growth of the market. Such companies were also thought to be particularly susceptible to moral hazard and over-trading. Extending a business generally involved dealing 'with new men ... and in opening accounts with new customers', 'men whom you do not trust' and who were more likely to be fraudulent than long-term associates. Large firms, furthermore, were forced to depend on a large number of suppliers, 'whose accounts cannot by any means be subject to effective scrutiny' and whose activities were 'beyond ... control'. Despite the greater likelihood of opportunism, however, owners supposedly did little to ensure the honesty, competence and trading status of customers and suppliers, 'trusting with providence for coming through safe'. The desire for growth caused them to 'rush' into alliances, many lacked the time and energy to undertake such checks, and 'great profit ... has a tendency to produce a relaxation of exertion'. At the same time, there was a fear that rapid expansion led to over-trading, that firms would extend their business activities to a point where they were unable to synchronise transactions and revenues. When an economic downturn or the bankruptcy of a major concern caused others to call in its debts, therefore, the company would lack the necessary funds to pay them, leading to its collapse. So great was this danger that Defoe proclaimed that there were 'more tradesmen undone by having too much trade than for want of trade'.[47]

Business partners added to the economic viability and therefore trustworthiness of a firm. Many contributed capital and managerial or technical skills not possessed by the other owner, reduced the need for outside labour, and, in some cases, enabled a trader to maintain outside wage-earning activities, thereby reducing risk. They also brought their 'good character', access to networks and networking abilities, which greatly facilitated the generation of trust relationships, and, in some cases, individuals with few social skills chose as their associates people who found networking relatively easy. Given unlimited liability and the financial precariousness of business in the early nineteenth century, it was important that owners trusted collaborators. A dishonest partner could defraud the firm, and, more importantly, taint the trust reputation of the owner. They thus chose as associates close friends and relatives, whose personal morality and reputation was already known to them, with whom they already had a trust relationship and for whom opportunism would carry a high social cost. Once a partnership had been formed, a good trust relationship could be maintained through the provision of gifts of regard; when dealing with partners, owners were advised to 'give no offence, talk sweetly, [and] be ready to oblige when you can do it without inconvenience'.[48]

Diversification into related areas suggests the existence of high intra-sector trust, and, for the diversifying firms, will have increased their network connections and extended their trust reputations. According to the trade directories, from 1787 to 1861, 16 per cent of Bolton's businessmen had more than one same sector occupation, the proportion being slightly higher in the first part of the period when the smaller number of firms in existence made such diversification easier (Table 9.5). The practice almost doubled average lifespans, and was most popular among those involved in engineering/metals and retailers and service providers, probably because these sectors offered more opportunities for diversification.

Expansion into unrelated spheres, for example from the textile to the engineering sector, was more difficult, as firms lacked network connections and reputations in the new trading area. It thus suggests the existence of a great deal of inter-sector trust, and, at the same time, helped to generate such attachments. In Bolton, 4.5 per cent of traders moved into other economic areas, which reduced their exposure to sector downturns and increased others' confidence of their survival, and raised their average business lifespans to 11 years (Table 9.6). Many of those who diversified were relatively large traders that in the course of their business careers had established inter-sector links and whose reputations went before them. In other cases, diversification involved a master moving into a less strenuous occupation, leaving his children to manage his original business, or resulted from creditors taking over the firms of traders who were unable to repay loans.[49]

The sector most involved in diversification was retailing and service provision, more specifically shop keeping and innkeeping (Table 9.7). Operating a shop increased network connections, extended reputations and strengthened social skills. Many shopkeepers thus moved into other areas and traders moved into retailing. Innkeepers had an even closer relationship with business. They gained information and network connections from the voluntary associations that met on their premises, often provided repositories and collection points for letters and parcels, supplied loans and change to customers, and acted as bill discounters, exchanging bills for money at a slight discount.[50] Not surprisingly,

Table 9.5 Diversification of Bolton traders into related areas, 1787–1861

	Percentage of traders with multiple occupations	*Average number of occupations held*	*Average lifespan*	*Percentage of traders with lifespans of ten years or over*
1787–1861	15.8	2.3	7.2	32.9
1787–1821	17.9	2.2	–	47.2
1829–61	15.2	2.2	–	27.5
Textiles	9.6	2.1	10.3	–
Engineering and metals	23.0	2.4	8.3	–
Retailers and service providers	21.0	2.4	6.4	–
Professionals	0.8	2.8	9.8	–
Bleachers	6.08	2.1	9.6	–
Other manufacturers	20.5	2.2	7.3	–

Source: Database.

Table 9.6 Diversification of Bolton traders into unrelated areas, 1787–1861

	Percentage of traders with multiple occupations	Average number of occupations held	Average lifespan	Percentage with lifespans of ten years or over
1787–1861	4.6	2.5	11.0	52.1
1787–1821	6.2	2.5	–	65.6
1829–61	4.0	2.5	–	45.4

Source: Database.

therefore, many landlords turned to manufacturing and vice versa. In Bolton, those traders who owned an inn as well as undertaking other occupations had an average business lifespan of ten years, as compared with the 6.5 years of those who additionally owned a store (Table 9.8).

The disappearance of a business, either through its failure or the death of the owner, inevitably had trust implications. Generally, 'when a man … [had] once been down it … [was] next to impossible for him to rise'. Failure ruined the trader's reputation and was a 'stain or tarnish [that] may never be wiped off'. He lost his competence trustworthiness and was regarded as dishonest, even if insolvency was due to factors beyond his means, many being convinced that 'prima facie, a judgement debtor is not an honest man'. He also found continued membership of networks difficult and lost much of his self-confidence. Network members placed social sanctions on failed colleagues designed to discourage attendance. The insolvent could contribute little to the network, and their presence could damage the association's reputation, and, by extension, that of the other members. Self-confidence evaporated because social norms deemed business failure to be 'the most dreadful of all human conditions'. Describing his

Table 9.7 Most common inter-sector combinations

Sectors	Number of firms in which the sectors are represented
Retailers and service providers/other manufacturers	160
Retailers and service providers/textiles	111
Retailers and service providers/professionals	74
Retailers and service providers/engineering and metals	55
Retailers and service providers/white-collar employees	47
Retailers and service providers/farmers	19
Textiles/other manufacturers	19
Engineering and metals/other manufacturers	16
Textiles/bleachers	16
Textiles/white-collar employees	15

Source: Database.

Table 9.8 Diversified owners who operated shops or inns or acted as agents

	Average number of occupations held			Average lifespan			Percentage of firms with lifespans of ten years or over		
	Inns	Shops	Agents	Inns	Shops	Agents	Inns	Shops	Agents
1787–1861	2.5	2.2	2.8	10.3	6.5	12.1	51.8	29.6	50.2
1787–1821	2.7	2.3	3.0	–	–	–	84.2	45.6	78.8
1829–61	2.5	2.1	2.5	–	–	–	46.5	24.3	40.1

Source: Database.

father's bankruptcy, Gibbon wrote 'the pangs of shame, tenderness and self-reproach preyed on his vitals, his constitution was broken, [and] he lost his strengths'.[51] Those few traders who did return to the business world often established new firms in a new economic sector or in a different town where they had no negative trust reputation.

The death of the owner of a business had trust ramifications for his heirs. A study of wills and trade directories in Stockport over the period 1800–57 suggests that over two thirds of businesses had stopped trading five years after their founder's death. The primary reason was that well over half of the deceased owners had directed in their wills that their firms were to be sold off, either immediately or when disposal would generate a sufficient amount of funds. In the latter case, the business was usually operated by trustees until the sale occurred. Such directions were given because owners died childless, lacked offspring willing to take over the firm or wished their estates to be distributed equally among their descendants, which necessitated the disposal of their businesses.[52]

A further explanation is that the death of a founder inevitably sparked a trust crisis that often led to the collapse of a business. Indeed, the likelihood that this would occur may have prompted many owners to instruct that their firms should be sold. After an owner's death, a business would be run either by the heir, or, if the beneficiary was still a child, by trustees until he reached the age of majority. The heir and trustees, however, would lack the reputation and network connections of the founder, and, if the company was left to a number of family members, kin animosity could lead to management problems. The tendency for founders to direct firms to be sold on their death and the high probability that an inherited company would fail also caused both suppliers and customers to suspect that this would occur in every case. On or even before the death of the founder, they would thus begin to establish new trust relationships with other buyers and sellers and act in a less trustworthy manner. It was unlikely that they would gain any long-term returns from the continuation of their trust relationship with the company, and, if the owner had directed the firm's eventual disposal, it was possible that trustees would be less scrupulous in their dealings with buyers/sellers. These problems could be lessened by founders, long before their deaths, bringing heirs into the business and allowing them to build up their own trust reputations and network connections, and descendants retaining the original name of the firm to disguise the change of ownership. Masters could also invest time and thought in the selection of trustees. Ideally, these would be loyal friends or relatives of the deceased, who were in the same line of business and thus possessed strong reputations and network connections of their own and would suffer a reputation loss if they acted immorally.

Business networks

Business networks comprised formal trading associations and professional societies, and informal networks based on trade, credit and shared directorships. In the early part of the nineteenth century, most employers' associations were horizontal networks, and were generally established during times of industrial unrest and other crisis, when action was needed that could not be provided by social and informal networks and it was important that as many employers as possible acted in concert. The associations grew out of existing networks, generated intra-sector and geographic trust and were generally short lived, disappearing after the dispute or crisis was over, though most left behind a residue of new network connections and trust relationships. Ironically, they were most likely to be established in towns with low employer–employee trust and poor labour relationships.[53]

The Combination Acts made the establishment of employer associations illegal and thus may have discouraged their formation and the concomitant generation of trust. Nevertheless, in the late eighteenth and early nineteenth centuries, employers combinations appeared in, among other sectors, the cotton, coal, printing, shipbuilding, cutlery and paper industries, and it seems likely that more clandestine bodies were established in other sectors. They generally had one of three purposes. Some had purely commercial goals, largely the fixing of prices, the arrangement of production quotas or the elimination of fraud. Others sought to put pressure on Parliament or to combat trade union activity. To break intra-union trust, multi-firm lockouts were organised. During strikes, blacklegs were recruited and funds to finance the prosecution of strikers collected. In the aftermath of the disputes, lists of blacklists were circulated and the completion of the non-unionist pledge, agreements signed by workers that they were not and would not become trade union members, was organised.[54]

A major drawback of the associations was their lack of inter-member trust. To increase their power, combinations had little option but to recruit the inherently untrustworthy, and many of their members had previously competed with their new associates, with whom they had had little or no contact, and, owning firms of differing types and sizes, had few common interests other than those created by the labour unrest or crisis. In the case of price-fixing cartels, members' trust relationships with their customers were also often stronger and more valuable than their bonds of trust with the association. To combat the danger of opportunism, associations usually introduced strategies that increased the cost of defection. Financial penalties were introduced for disloyalty, and labour unrest associations used membership levies to build up a central fund, from which firms hit by a strike could draw payments. Nonetheless, many employers' agreements proved ineffective, after the labour unrest/crisis was over most associations disappeared, and, even where prolonged price or output control was achieved, non-price competition persisted.[55]

Employers' associations experienced their most rapid growth from the 1850s. At the same time, they became more permanent bodies, had a regional or even national membership, and often became vertical networks, incorporating related sectors. A number of factors were responsible for the changed situation. The consolidation of industry into large firms led to more unified trades and instilled a greater feeling of equality amongst large capitalists, who had sufficient capital to endure periods of non-productivity and were more able to come to agreements to support each other in labour lock-outs. Stronger general business trust reduced the likelihood of member defection and created a stronger unity of interest, and there was a greater need for such associations in the political, industrial relations and networking spheres. During the 1850s and 1860s, the government, seeking to strengthen the social contract, pushed through Parliament much legislation that favoured workers. In response, numerous political employers associations were formed, including the 1854 Factory Law Amendment Association, and, a year later, the National Association of Factory Occupiers. Fear of economic depression and foreign competition in the 1870s then prompted the establishment of many other societies, including the United Railway Companies Association and the National Federation of Associated Employers of Labour. Gradually withdrawing from local public service, elite manufacturers, also used these and more local bodies to monitor and control local authorities.[56]

In industrial relations, the growth of union power forced employers to establish equally powerful and permanent employer bodies, which, after the adoption of a trust-relations strategy, proved useful in the negotiation of wage and other agreements. As regards networking, local informal and social networks could no longer provide the ever-expanding amount of information required by business, and, with the replacement of the entrepreneur by management, firms had less connection with these networks. Managers were less willing to participate in after-hours local social networks, to which, in any case, they had difficulty gaining access because of their socially more humble backgrounds. Employer association networks, conversely, were open to all firms of a given size, permitted cost-effective acquisition of information, and, in the case of national and regional bodies, enabled companies with regional/national markets to network.

Closely related to the employers associations were the trade protection societies and the various accountancy, legal and engineering professional associations. Trade protection societies developed from the 1840s, were town based and had a multiple trade membership. The societies promoted sociability and also raised business trust by publishing weekly or monthly circulars, which contained much local commercial information; by providing a credit-referencing service, which gave members information on the creditworthiness of potential customers/suppliers; and by offering debt-collection facilities. The various professional associations sought to reduce member incompetence and fraud and thus raise the reputation of the professions concerned and expand their customer base. This was achieved through the introduction of uniform educational requirements, lengthy periods of apprenticeship during which character traits could be evaluated, strict ethical codes, a range of sanctions, culminating in expulsion from the society and qualifying exams, which, as with the Civil Service open entry examination, were tests of both learning and moral character. The societies also strove to divorce themselves from the perceived immorality of the commercial world. The academic nature of the work performed was emphasised, objectivity stressed, a concern for public welfare highlighted and a rhetoric of service devised that cloaked member self-interest. Fees were referred to as 'honorariums', payments often received indirectly, for instance through clerks, and advertising discouraged or forbidden.[57] In the case of accountancy, the formation of such associations additionally helped to raise business trust. Aware that fraud by a company or its collapse would damage their own reputations and could even lead to expulsion from the society, accountants ensured that businesses were operated honestly and efficiently reducing both fraud and bankruptcies.

Informal networks included those based on trade, credit and shared director-ships. Trading networks comprised firms and businessmen who regularly did business with each other, and were in a constant state of flux. Although often propagated in and supported by other groupings, they could also be free-standing, originating from and being sustained by economic exchange alone. Many were spatially extensive and thus generated much geographic trust. Horizontal networks contained same industry companies that traded excess raw materials, goods in various stages of production and so on, and, in the early part of the period, colluded in the fixing of prices.[58] Vertical networks, by compari-son, consisted of firms operating in the various sectors that made up a produc-tion process and primarily involved the trading of raw materials, part and finished goods and waste products.

The strength of trust that existed between trading partners depended on the nature of the relationship. Businessmen put relatively little effort into develop-ing bonds of attachment and loyalty with collaborators whose activities or goods could be easily monitored or whose trade was small or intermittent, as any loss from moral hazard would have been minor. Likewise, the axis between power and trust between two firms generally swung towards the former where partner *a* was highly dependent on partner *b*, and particularly where firm *a* had made transaction specific investments, that is bought machinery or tools or set up pro-cedures that were idiosyncratic to the requirements of company *b*. In such cir-cumstances, moral hazard was tolerated by firm *a*, as, if it had objected, it would have gone out of business or lost the capital that it had invested in its unique machinery/procedures. Where firm *a* could reciprocate the deceit and the recip-rocated duplicity was costly and difficult to detect, however, firm *b* usually made limited use of its power. Monopolistic merchants, for example, rarely paid sup-pliers excessively low prices, since they were well aware that the contractors, in retaliation, could reduce the quality of the goods produced.

The most important credit relationship was that between a bank and its cus-tomers. Given that approximately 30 per cent of credit extended by provincial banks was unsecured or extended on the basis of personal guarantees, banks made very sure that they could trust borrowers to repay loans. In the early nine-teenth century, decisions to provide credit were based on information picked up by bank directors. These tended to be businessmen, who had trading relation-ships with or were partners, directors or shareholders of local firms, and were often pillars of the local community, holding high positions in a range of reli-gious, philanthropic, government and other formal associations. They therefore had access to information regarding the honesty and abilities of borrowers. With the arrival of the joint-stock bank, the involvement of directors in the day-to-day operation of banking business declined and decisions to extend credit were made by managers, who recorded their reasons for giving loans in 'opinion' books. These indicate that they related trustworthiness to both subjective and objective factors. Subjective indicators included a reputation for industriousness, frugality and reliability, social standing and the presence of wealthy partners or relatives. Objective factors were the client's personal wealth, the length of his relationship with the bank, and the profitability, turnover, tangible assets and debt burden of his business. To obtain the necessary information, managers normally interviewed the borrower, asked to see his balance sheet, sometimes visited his business premises, if he was an existing customer examined his bank account and if he had been granted a loan in the past, determined whether the repayments had been made on the given dates.[59]

Director networks were found in those organisations formed by local business leaders to promote economic growth, that is insurance, canal, railway and water companies, banks and turnpike trusts. The directors were elite businessmen, with intermediate tradesmen acting as shareholders or subscribers; in the case of railway and canal companies, were based in the towns the railways/canals connected, which increased geographic trust; and either came from a variety of sectors, which strengthened inter-sector trust, or from just one sector.[60] Participation allowed them to free ride on the reputation of the institution, and, as regards banks, gave them access to much useful information on the solvency and trustworthiness of trading partners and permitted them to provide such people with gifts or punishments.

Conclusion

Business social capital can be split into industry trust, that within and between sectors, and the mutuality that exists between individual traders. The former was dependent on the number and size of firms in a sector, its capital requirements and susceptibility to downturns, and the size of other industries present. An individual businessman's trustworthiness, meanwhile, arose from, among other things, his personal characteristics, particularly his age, class and sex, and the way in which he conducted his business. The most trusted and therefore the more successful entrepreneurs were those who behaved in an honest manner, conformed to negotiating routines and norms, possessed architecturally impressive premises, which they occasionally relocated, and made extensive use of advertising and marketing practices to raise their reputations. The nature of a trader's business also played a part. Generally speaking, those with long established and mid-sized companies were more trusted than colleagues with newly established or very small or extremely large firms. Acquiring a partner or diversifying into another sector could also pay high dividends, but could equally lead to disaster, and the death of an owner inevitably sparked a trust crisis.

As in other areas, social capital was most easily acquired by the elite, who found it relatively easy to form close relationships with others with economic resources. Trust thus tended to support the status quo. Elite businessmen possessed ascribed trust, could free ride on widely known family reputations and afford to live at good addresses, had access to high value informal and formal associations, including business networks, operated mid-sized firms that had strong reputations and could easily diversify into other economic sectors.

Over time, levels of business trust rose and fell. In the late eighteenth and early nineteenth centuries, people's faith in the integrity of business and traders' belief in the honesty of their colleagues declined, though it should be noted that the public did not equally condemn all businessmen and the integrity of each sector was determined by honesty norms, which made some double-dealing permissible. The fall was largely an outcome of the expansion of the market economy. Greater competition forced many to become less scrupulous in their dealings, and the explosion of credit again fuelled dishonesty and led to the formation of networks of debt, which during economic downturns collapsed and decimated social capital. The decline in trust levels, however, was not as great as in other spheres and recovery was rapid. The fall owed much to perception, economic growth and the expansion of credit strengthened as well as weakened social capital, and businessmen successfully increased trust through the adoption of middle-class honesty signals and new business methods and membership of formal and informal business and other networks. In some sectors, their efforts were too successful, and, by the fourth quarter of the century, had led to the generation of a surfeit of trust, which ultimately contributed to relative economic decline.

10 Employer–employee trust

Employer–employee reciprocal trust relationships were akin to and a component of the social contract. In return for a 'fair' amount of effort, workers expected their masters to provide 'fair' wages and working conditions. If these were unforthcoming and the trust contract was unilaterally broken, employees, in retaliation, would restrict effort, withdraw their labour and, in extreme cases, riot. Before industrialisation, there supposedly existed a 'community feeling between' workers and their masters, which arose 'from long connection and the remembrance of kind offices received and faithful services performed' and that took the form of 'an inheritance transmitted from parent to son'. Certainly, the state and some employers tried to ensure the establishment of a virtuous relationship with workers. The Statute of Artificers of 1563 sought the enforcement of apprenticeship regulations and thus the survival of the guilds, which limited competition and upheld ethical behaviour through rules, fines and even imprisonment. It also attempted to secure 'unto the hired person, both in time of scarcity and plenty, a convenient proportion of wages' by requiring local magistrates, after taking the advice of 'discrete and grave persons', considering the level of prices and 'conferring together', to set appropriate wage rates, which were enforced by local constables through fines. Other legislation sought to dampen economic change that threatened the employer–employee reciprocal contract. Statutes, for example, sought to limit the number of looms owned by individuals outside the corporate towns and to prohibit the gig mill, which was thought to lead to unemployment.[1]

In reality, masters often retained the upper hand over employees. Legislation to limit economic change was generally ineffective, many guild members '[thought] up all sorts of tricks and dodges . . . for exploiting the poor', and, by the mid-sixteenth century, cloth making and other trades had moved to the country away from the control of the urban-based guilds. As regards the Statute of Artificers, its wage regulation provisions only required the setting of maximum wages, and, given that the assessors were landowners and employers, it was often used to keep earnings low. The Statute also made labour compulsory when employment was offered, and enabled local justices to imprison craftsmen who left work unfinished, a ruling that acted against strikers and was not applied equally throughout the country.[2]

Workers in the pastoral areas of the North, South West and South East benefited from its existence to a far greater extent than their counterparts in the arable regions of central England, largely because of differences in the way the legislation was implemented. As already discussed, arable areas were largely under the control of a powerful gentry, who dominated the local magistracy, which failed to consult the local community prior to deciding wage rates. Constables were generally yeomen farmers, highly dependent on the gentry for their livelihood and isolated from the labouring community, which was relatively quiescent, rarely engaging in outbursts of crowd violence. On the other hand, pastoral areas were marked by a weak gentry. Magistrates, though members of the elite, had less community power and consulted the local population before setting rates. Constables were husbandmen, weavers and artisans, who were independent of the magistracy and had many network linkages and trust relationships with the local community and were thus aware of and more willing to act on its views, fearing sanctions if they acted autonomously. The local populace, meanwhile, were more politically confident, willing to organise petitions to bring employers who violated regulations to court, and to use crowd action to exert pressure on the magistracy. Consequently, in arable areas the law was applied in the interests of the elite and in pastoral regions it was articulated in a way that ensured the setting of wages that were fair to both employers and workers. Employer–employee trust relationships were therefore relatively stronger in the pastoral areas and the resulting norms continued to influence labour relations long after industrialisation.[3]

The reorganisation of industrial production and the coming of the putting-out system and later factory manufacture caused employer–employee trust relationships to become even weaker. The putting-out system involved the employment by merchants of spinners or weavers who worked in their own homes. The merchant or his agent distributed raw cotton or linen to the outworkers, and after this had been worked upon, collected the finished products and paid the workers for their labour. Most merchants had long-term relationships with their staff, and provided them with gifts in the form of loans and equipment that could be paid for in small instalments. This would suggest that trust was strong in the sector. This assumption, though, seems to be undermined by the high levels of moral hazard present. Outworkers often delivered goods later and to a standard lower than agreed and engaged in minor embezzlement. Common practices included spinners returning reels of yarn shorter than demanded or containing a number of short threads, and weavers increasing the weight of fabrics by steaming yarn or coating it with butter or grease.[4]

Instead of stoking distrust of workers, as one would expect, these practises were for many years tolerated by employers, who were in a weak position vis-à-vis their employees. Given the restricted labour supply, an employer was 'as much dependent upon (the) good opinion (of workers) as they (were) upon him for employment', especially during periods of high demand. The physical distance between the merchant and the outworker also made the monitoring of work difficult if not impossible, and recourse to law, if major embezzlement was discovered, was expensive and, because of the excessive amounts of evidence required, often failed to result in a conviction. Furthermore, there was always a danger that employees would resort to major fraud, stealing raw materials, loans or the equipment bought off merchants in weekly instalments. By providing workers with the gift of acceptance of visible opportunism, therefore, employers created trust that increased the likelihood that outworkers would be available in times of high demand. In addition, the gift by increasing the cost of dismissal (dismissed workers would lose their income plus the returns from minor embezzlement) reduced the likelihood that workers would engage in less visible embezzlement or in major fraud.[5]

This tolerance began to wane from the mid-eighteenth century as a result of market changes. The rise in the demand for goods, and the greater importance of quality, uniformity and punctual delivery increased the cost of the gifts. Master complaints about opportunism thus rose and attempts were made to limit the practices formerly accepted, particularly the late delivery of poor quality goods, which could be achieved relatively easily through the introduction of fines and deductions.[6] Such action, however, reduced both employees' faith in their masters and their incomes, prompting them to increasingly turn to visible/less visible embezzlement and even fraud in order to offset the fall in their earnings and to punish employers for the breach of the former relationship. This, in turn, reduced masters' trust of their employees, causing a vicious circle of animosity to develop.

With the arrival of water and later steam power, many masters sought to reduce worker opportunism by turning to factory production, which, among other advantages, permitted them to monitor closely both the work and output of employees. Unfortunately, in the putting-out sector, this merely caused the vicious circle of distrust to spiral ever further downwards. Masters faced with a large pool of under-employed workers resorted to the use of power. Incapable of competing with factories, they cut wages and resorted to opportunism themselves. Of 200 cases brought by weavers against masters by Thomas Thorpe of Bolton, 25–30 per cent were settled out of court, and, of the remainder, the arbitrators found in favour of the weaver in 75 per cent of the cases. Outworker incomes and distrust of employers thus fell further. Unable, because of the large quantities of surplus labour, to use the power of the strike against their masters, workers turned to their only other source of strength, embezzlement. This reduced returns and fuelled employers' distrust of their workers, causing them to intensify their own opportunism and to cut wages further. It also appears likely that the reduction in agent wages prompted agents to act opportunistically against masters and to blame the losses on outworkers. Agents gave weavers inadequate amounts of yarn, replaced the employer's high-quality thread with low-quality substitutes and charged those outworkers who bought equipment from masters an extra fee. Few outworkers complained to employers about such activities, as agents allocated work, and, perhaps correctly, they believed that masters would take the word of an agent over that of an employee.[7]

The mutually destructive use of power eventually lessened in the 1830s to be replaced by a more trusting relationship. In 1834, masters and men came together to lobby Parliament for the introduction of local boards of trade. These would comprise both outworkers and employers, who together would determine minimum wage rates. Workers would be shown the profit figures of employers, who were 'trusted and trustworthy', and masters would ensure that there were no 'unnecessary reductions in wages at the caprice or from the folly of one manufacturer'.[8] Unfortunately, the rapprochement was unable to save the industry from the onslaught of the factory system and it gradually disappeared.

Factory labour relations

Power relations

In the factory industries, mechanisation reduced worker skill requirements and permitted the substitution of male with female and child labour. Masters were thus able to use power in their dealings with workers in the knowledge that there would always exist an adequate supply of new recruits. Moreover, women and children were more compliant than men and less likely to object to poor treatment. By 1818, 60 per cent of those working in cotton factories were under the age of 19, and, in Preston, 11 per cent were under the age of nine years. A combination of public pressure, parochial concern, and ultimately legislation then reduced the number of children available for mill work and forced owners to employ in their place women, who particularly dominated throstle spinning and power weaving; men being restricted to mule spinning.[9]

The employers used their new-found power to introduce more machinery, which led to the disappearance of apprenticeships and the bonds of trust that developed during these periods of training, and to reduce working conditions and wages. Employee resistance in the form of Luddism merely reflected their own weakness and further stoked employer distrust. The reduction in working conditions primarily involved the introduction of long working hours and the dismissal of staff during economic downturns, which, in addition to creating much resentment, shortened the average length of employer–employee relationships and the period in which trust could develop. Wage cuts led to further bitterness, as did the tendency of those employers who owned their workers' homes and operated local shops to claw back wages through rent increases and the sale of expensive goods and to punish recalcitrant employees through eviction.[10]

Having seen the response of outworkers to wage cuts, factory owners were well aware of the danger posed by employees' power of opportunism. Able to monitor the work process in addition to the product, factory masters, however, had less to fear from moral hazard than their putting out counterparts. They, nevertheless, used power, in the form of dismissals, fines and prosecutions, to neutralise any opportunism, and in the process further stoked worker animosity. Fines were imposed for lateness, talking with fellow workers, and unnecessary waste. If the offence was repeated, the worker was simply dismissed. The

Manchester firm A. and G. Murray had an annual labour turnover of almost 42 per cent, and, in 1815, the common practice of Manchester spinners was to engage work people on a week by week basis and to renew the contracts of only those who had been productive during the previous six days. For theft and to combat strikes, prosecutions under the Master and Servant Act were begun. If found guilty of breaking their contracts, strikers could either be forced to serve the requisite notice, giving employers sufficient time to recruit blacklegs, or imprisoned and thus act as a deterrent to those tempted to follow their lead. The Act was biased in the favour of masters, in that breach by the employer was only a civil wrong for which an employee could sue for damages, whereas a violation by a worker was a criminal offence punishable by a fine or imprisonment, and, unlike his employees, a master sued by a worker could act as a witness in his own defence. Since most magistrates were themselves employers, the likelihood of an operative actually winning a case was slim.[11]

Within the factory, employers surrendered a degree of worker control to others – in throstle and power spinning to overseers, who were paid according to the quantity of work they could force employees to produce; in weaving to out-workers, who employed their own staff; and in mule spinning to sub-contractors. The practice relieved masters of the costs of maintaining discipline, ensured that at least some worker distrust would be directed at people other than themselves, and, by creating shared interests, on occasion, led to the generation of trust between the employer and the overseer, sub-contractor or outworker. Sub-con-tractors were paid a set sum for the completion of a particular job or order, employed and paid their own team of assistants, and, within the rules of the factory, determined the manner by which they controlled their staff. Many used power and acted opportunistically, resorting to 'nibbling', refusing on some pretext to pay the agreed rate for a job on its completion, or 'chasing', employ-ing an assistant who set an excessive work rate that the others were forced to follow.[12] A minority, on the other hand, formed bonds of trust with their workers. Work groups were small and the sub-contractor had constant face-to face interaction with his employees, with whom he shared characteristics, having himself usually begun his career as an assistant. He also generally lived alongside his workers, who in some cases were members of his own family.

The extent to which employers resorted to power varied between sectors. In non-factory industries, firms were small. 71.5 per cent of masters in England and Wales in 1851 employed between one and four workers, and 87 per cent had less than ten employees. They thus had close personal relationships with their staff, who often lived in and were perceived as quasi-kin and taught moral norms, and they regularly moved in and out of the ranks of the self-employed and therefore had many characteristics in common with their workers. Even in these sectors, however, trust fell over time. Staff increasingly lived out and many industries adopted outwork systems of production, replacing skilled arti-sans with unskilled or semi-skilled females and adolescents.[13]

In the cotton and other factory industries, the use of power was influenced by the size and nature of a sector's labour force, its ownership profile, general prosperity and the seriousness of its downturns, and by the morality of individual masters. A sector with a large labour supply could treat its workers poorly, as they were less likely to object to mistreatment, and, if they did, replacements could easily be obtained. Preston, located on the edge of Lancashire's main agricultural district, possessed a large reserve of workers. The 'cotton lords' of the town could thus use their power indiscriminately, and, by 1842, according to one commentator had gained a reputation as 'the greatest tyrants in the country'.[14] Bolton's labour supply, on the other hand, was more restricted. With its bleach works, engineering shops and mines, the town had far more alternative employment. Cotton masters, here, were thus forced to be more constrained in their use of power.

Of equal significance were the incomes and sex of the labour force. High wages made a variety of collective and private worker actions possible. Women employees, conversely, were less likely to organise than their male counterparts, owing to their more submissive temperaments and the tendency for those who were married to work on an intermittent basis. They also possessed less power, as they earned relatively low wages, lacked alternative employments and could easily be replaced, undertaking relatively unskilled work.[15]

As regards ownership, where a few firms dominated a sector, employer trust was strong and the implementation of power relatively easy and successful. At the same time, worker trust, the feelings of loyalty and attachment that existed between employees of a company, was weak. The sheer size of large factories and the greater specialisation and differentiation of the workforce reduced the density and multiplicity of social relations and made organisation more difficult. In Preston, the spinning industry was dominated by relatively large mills, the five largest in 1841 employing 40 per cent of the town's spinning hands. Employers thus exhibited a high degree of trust that facilitated the successful use of power over their relatively weak employees. By comparison, in Bolton, where in 1841 the five largest mills housed 30 per cent of the spinning labour force, the slightly weaker employer trust and stronger worker co-operation made uniform implementation of employer power more difficult. Large mills also prevented employers forming trust relationships with their workers, there often being 'less personal communication between [a] master cotton spinner and his workman than between the Duke of Wellington and the humblest labourer on his estate'. As for who owned the companies, family proprietors had relatively close relationships with their staff, particularly if they lived near to their factories. In the early nineteenth century, most masters resided close or even next door to their premises, but then began to move away, the distance varying between towns. By the 1850s, although the homes of Bolton masters were mostly within walking distances of plants, albeit in exclusive suburbs, those based in Oldham lived outside the town.[16]

The adoption of power could also be influenced by miscellaneous factors, such as a tradition of militant radicalism or poor elite relations, and by the prosperity of a town and the seriousness of its downturns. Bolton's cotton industry was always profitable, the town in the 1880s possessing 'a prosperity not excelled by any (other community) in the kingdom'. Mill owners were therefore subject to relatively weak competitive pressures and had no need to resort to the more aggressive implementations of power. The town's balanced economy also meant that during downturns in the cotton industry, other sectors were relatively buoyant, and overall employer–employee trust remained relatively high. The town particularly escaped lightly from the cotton famine, which elsewhere badly damaged trust relations. As a centre of fine spinning, Bolton consumed less cotton than the other towns and was less dependent on American supplies. Furthermore, it benefited from the increased availability of Egyptian long stapled cotton and a treaty with France, which expanded the French fine yarns and mixed fabrics market. Consequently, while expenditure on poor relief rose between ten- and twelve-fold in Preston, in Bolton it grew less than three-fold.[17]

Within sectors, the extent to which individual employers used power and trust was partly dependent on their personal trust and moral norms. Factory legislation prosecutions show that, whereas most manufacturers never broke the law, a small number were regularly prosecuted and that prosecutions between towns varied greatly. From 1837 to 1870, Bolton had 68 prosecutions as compared with Preston's 16, and 15 per cent of the culprits were prosecuted at least twice. Contemporaries associated systematic infringement with small technically backward companies, forced by their poor financial positions to act illegally. Research by Gray, however, has shown that prosecutions during 1834–55 involved a cross-section of employers in each locality, including leading firms.[18] It was also found that those firms that broke the law had a slightly greater than average chance of survival, suggesting that manufacturers with weak personal trust norms were more likely to reap business success than those with more socially acceptable norms.

Trust relations

Cotton masters began to reject the use of power as a means of conducting labour relations from the 1840s. It is generally, though not universally, agreed that in the third quarter of the nineteenth century industrial relations entered a long sustained calm; strikes were more infrequent and those that occurred were less violent. The abandonment of force was the result of a number of factors, in particular a rise in employee power. Workers growing distrust of employers and their iniquitous treatment prompted greater efforts to be made in the generation of worker trust, which was aided by the rise of neighbourhood networks. In the changing economic environment, such trust constituted power. Having heavily invested in capital equipment, such as the mule, employers were particularly susceptible to strike action, which could greatly damage the viability of their businesses. Employees also had discretion over the effort that they put into their work, which could affect productivity and more significantly quality, which, as consumers' expectations rose, was of increasing importance. The manufacture of goods that were below par would damage both profit margins and trust relationships with purchasers, ultimately resulting in 'a second rate price and set of customers'. Such moral hazard, moreover, was difficult to overcome. Monitoring was expensive; quality was difficult to quantify, work being subject to 'many grades of imperfection without becoming so obviously defective as to [be] . . . liable to a fine'; and, according to Huberman, employers had little knowledge of the productive capabilities of new machines.[19]

For some, there was additionally a danger that workers would act fraudulently. Embezzlement by those in clerical or retail work was relatively common, legal retribution uncertain and the possible management solutions again ineffective. Staff could be asked provide securities and their work carefully monitored. Employers of clerks, for example, were advised to request receipts for all goods their employees purchased. However, as with effort, a master could exercise 'the most irksome vigilance', only to find it failed 'to prevent him being overreached by his operatives – the whole of whom . . . conspire' against him.[20]

There were other economic reasons for the improved treatment of workers. The more prosperous state of trade from mid-century, along with the general rise in business trust, weakened the competitive pressures that had demanded the mistreatment of workers, slowed the pace of technological change and reorganisation, and widened the margin for bargaining. There was growing concern about competition from 'rival nations', which some claimed could only be met 'by the hearty co-operation among us of head and hand, of employer and employed'. There had also been a change in labour requirements. To realise adequate returns from new technologies, a supply of reliable and skilled workers was required. Margins were narrow and an increase in wastage caused by bad workmanship or a rise in inventory costs due to slow turnaround times could lead to losses. Unfortunately, such employees were in comparatively short supply, and mill owners could therefore no longer afford the high labour turnovers that resulted from the use of power.[21]

A further contributory factor was that manufacturers were becoming increasingly aware of the benefits of enlightened capitalism, which were promoted in newspapers, novels, sermons and Factory Inspector reports. The Mining Commissioner H. S. Tremenheere, for example, directly linked the pursuit of benevolence with profit, claiming that 'enlightened management' resulted in 'a moral, sober, industrious and intelligent' workforce. Many employers were also convinced that 'the useful bond of mutual confidence' with their workers would crowd out the latters' faith in trade unions, which increased the power of labour and militated against employer–employee co-operation. There was a general belief that to maintain and increase memberships, trade unions and purveyors of radical literature seized 'upon every topic by which feelings of envy and jealousy against the classes above them can be encouraged and embittered'. It was further accepted by some that the 'harsh and cruel treatment' of workers could have wider trust ramifications, driving the 'young and ardent . . . down the declivity of vice and crime', affecting the owner's relationship with trustworthy traders, who treated their employees well, and, in the case of the religious, damaging their spiritual bond with the Almighty.[22]

By mid-century, therefore, employers had begun to accept that they and their workers were 'mutually obliged', and that, although employees were 'sometimes entirely dependent upon [their] master for work and subsistence', the factory owner was 'equally dependent upon [his workers] for the necessary service they perform'. This view was echoed by trade unionists, who were well aware that employer acceptance of mutuality would be beneficial to their members, and, contrary to the accusations of the elite, had never wished to overturn the capitalist system of production. Most Unionists blamed bad working conditions on the action of individual employers or subscribed to the radical world-view that poverty and distress were the result of the aristocratic domination of Parliament. Both employers and unions thus entered into a reciprocal trust relationship on the lines of the social contract. In return for a fair amount of effort, workers expected 'a sufficiency out of the produce of the earth to maintain' themselves and their families. They would strike only if 'unjust and oppressive employers' broke the unwritten agreement, and, for instance, 'attempted to make an arbitrary and uncalled for reduction of wages'.[23] Masters, in turn, would resort to lockouts or other action only if their workers breached the bounds of the relationship, for example by demanding an unreasonable rise in salaries.

To ensure the payment of fair wages in the cotton industry, employers and employees began to consult with each other and to set wage lists that fixed the incomes of all classes of workers and were implemented by all the firms involved in the negotiations. The consultations increased employer–employee trust, and, at the same time, promoted employer trust and worker trust, increasing interaction within the two groups, and, by contributing to the disappearance of unviable smaller firms, made the generation of intra-sector employer trust easier. Each town had its own list, and the timing of their introduction and the wage levels they contained clearly reflects the level of employer–employee trust present in each community. In Bolton, the standard list appeared in 1827, and remained relatively unchanged despite the introduction of new technology. Preston mill owners, on the other hand, turned to lists only after the 1853–4 strike, the damaging consequences of which clearly demonstrated the drawbacks of the use of power. Although the owners had emerged victorious from the dispute, their triumph had taken seven months to achieve, during which time they had lost market share. Oldham lists appeared even later – in 1872. Surprisingly, the lists failed to alter the wage differentials that had always existed between the towns and which could have been expected to converge as heavy capital investments in coarse spinning increased productivity and the introduction of self-actors in fine spinning reduced differences in skill. Bolton, with the longest and strongest trust relations, paid the highest wages, followed by Oldham and then Preston.[24]

There was a similar movement towards fair wages in other sectors, no doubt prompted by pleas to that end by newspapers, the business manuals of the day and other publications. These also urged employers to go beyond fairness. 'Faithfulness' and trust was earned not 'in the mere doing of things which we are obliged to do, but in the performance of acts and in the extremes of care, which we are not obliged to do and for which we receive no direct remuneration'. There were thus calls for greater transparency and the adoption of 'a course of open and straight forward dealing ... on the subject of wages', which would have 'the effect of gradually establishing a very satisfactory degree of confidence' between employers and employees. Some went further and called for the payment of a wage premium during booms and even profit sharing, which would cause an employer's output to 'increase in quantity and improve in quality ... [and] would establish between himself and his workmen an intimate and permanent union'.[25]

The rate at which trust appeared varied between sectors and towns and depended on the extent to which power had formerly been used in labour relations and existing levels of business, social and kinship trust. Generally, its generation was initially slow and difficult, and involved countless mistaken assumptions and setbacks. Neither capital nor labour had social norms of trust to guide their actions nor statutory rules and codes. Workers, bitter at the way that they had been treated in the past, remained suspicious of benevolent employers, rejecting or exploiting their trust-based behaviour. Manufacturers, in turn, were loath to abandon their previous practices and many thus continued to make use of fines and the Master and Servant Act, refuse to recognise trade unions and punish active participation in radical politics. Not surprisingly, therefore, strikes and lockouts did not disappear, though they occurred with less frequency and intensity than previously. In Bolton, there were industry wide conflicts in 1861, 1869 (when 5,000 operatives struck over a 5 per cent reduction in wages) 1874 (a lockout which involved 13,000 operatives) and 1877. There were also various small-scale disputes at local mills.[26]

Problems especially arose during downturns. For employers, the trust relationship incorporated the laws of political economy, that supply and demand regulated wage levels. Many workers, on the other hand, rejected these natural laws, believing that employers should maintain wages in recessions, given the 'monuments in large profits in the past and the visions of probable profits in the future'. During downturns, therefore, when a cut in wages or hours was met by a strike action, both sides genuinely believed the other had broken the trust relationship and that their resort to power was explicable. Gradually, however, workers accepted the futility of striking at such times and the trust relationship was extended to cover recessions. A speaker at an operative tea party in 1845, recalling the 1841 downturn, remembered that employees 'did not...as in former times ... come rashly onto the street and leave [their] employment', as they 'had more sense', realising 'that to go into opposition to [their] masters would be useless and no good'. Their demands would probably not have been met and the strike would have damaged employer and employee trust, and, 'in place of a friendly feeling, ... hatred and ill feeling would have ruled'. Labour unrest would also have had a 'bad and injurious effect ... on the whole community', reducing social trust and causing 'public opinion to rally against [both] masters and men'.[27]

In return for this acceptance of economic reality, workers expected to be

treated fairly by employers. Any wage cuts were to be reinstated when conditions improved. More importantly, to minimise the impact of unemployment
during downturns, it was expected that short-time working would be introduced,
and, where lay-offs were unavoidable, younger workers, who could more easily
obtain alternative employment, would be dismissed. If this did not occur and
workers were laid off and the reciprocal trust broken, they would turn to protest,
and, even if they accepted the employers' action, 'a sense of deep injustice
would rankle in [their] breast', and, during recovery, they would reap their
revenge by demanding excessive wage rises. Conversely, if 'patient endurance'
was 'met by universal sympathy', recession could actually cause 'a closer union
and more friendly relations' to exist both between the employers and employees
involved and 'among the several classes of society'. In the cotton industry,
employers increasingly adopted a sympathetic policy. When the 1841 recession
hit, many introduced short-time working, and, during the 1861 cotton famine,
some went even further, postponing the payment of rents, running soup kitchens
and making loans to those employees most in need.[28]

To build trust in normal times, many employers abandoned the sub-contractor
system, which generated much animosity amongst those who worked for opportunistic sub-contractors and impeded the development of master–worker relations. They also established workplace friendly societies, supported factory
reform, adopted new recruitment practices, turned a 'blind eye' to minor pilfering and increasingly socialised with workers. As has already been discussed, the
campaigns to end child employment and to reduce female working hours were
partly motivated by a desire to improve the primary socialisation of moral norms
and to raise social trust. Those manufacturers who campaigned for the Ten Hour
Bill, similarly, believed that a shorter working day would allow workers to
devote more time to education and religious study, promote temperance and
improve employer–employee relations. There was also a wish to eliminate those
smaller speculative manufacturers who adopted a power employer–employee
labour strategy and would be driven out of business by the legislation. When the
Bill finally passed into law in 1847, most cotton masters adopted it, though a
few initially sought to circumvent its requirements through the use of relays of
children.[29]

In the recruitment of staff, masters avoided candidates with poor reputations,
as 'what a man has done once, he may and probably will do again', and often
gave preference to those of the same religious denomination as themselves and
to the friends, neighbours and relatives of existing workers. The wage books of
the Bolton bleacher R. Ainsworth contain numerous employees with the same
surname, and, during 1838–41, the skilled foundry work at the Oldham engineering company Hibbert and Platts was virtually the preserve of a mere ten
families. The strategy raised trust in a number of ways. The gift of employment
strengthened the feelings of attachment between the employer and the referrer,
and those recruited were likely to possess the same characteristics as the person
who recommended them. People tend to refer those most like themselves, and,
in the case of offspring, there was a high chance that 'virtuous parents [had]

given their children a . . . virtuous education'. Even if this was not the case, new recruits were unlikely to act exploitatively, as the costs of opportunism would be high – a damaged company reputation to those who had referred them, and, for the newcomer, a lost relationship and an impaired social or kin status. Recommended employees also obtained a more accurate understanding of the informal rules that governed work performance at a firm, reducing the likelihood of unrest, and the manufacturer acquired accurate information about the recruit's skills and personality, improving the worker/employer 'fit'.[30]

If possible, those recruited were retained for long periods. In 1845, 53 per cent of the employees of the Bolton spinning firm Knowles and Son had worked for the company for more than five years, 35 per cent for over ten years, and 16 per cent for over 20 years, and at the Halliwell bleachworks in 1857 the average age of male workers was 38 years and the average length of service was 25 years. Long periods of employment led to the development of strong bonds of loyalty and attachment between master and worker and older people tend to be more trustworthy than younger colleagues. To demonstrate their caring attitude, many employers even kept on the elderly, whose productivity was low. The Halliwell bleachworks, for example, employed eight workers aged between 60 and 69 and eight who were over 70 years of age.[31]

To build even stronger bonds of trust, many employers tolerated minor pilfering. 'The purloining of raw material [was] universally practiced', and, in his 1867 journals, Thomas Wright, a journeyman engineer, describes men ' skulking or having a sly read or smoke or . . . engaged on corporation work – that is work of their own'. The acceptance of such practices increased employer–employee trust, though many believed it damaged social trust leading to the development of 'bad propensities'. Other employers developed 'a more friendly feeling' towards their workers, regularly touring factories, visiting evening schools, 'saying a kind word as opportunity may offer', and circulating amongst the guests at Work's dinners, teas and outings. Their wives and daughters, meanwhile, often visited employees or members of workers' families who were sick, such 'manifestation of kindness' eliciting 'a reciprocity of esteem and the spirit of truth and honesty'.[32]

These efforts to increase trust were matched by the trade unions. From mid-century, unions were more moderate. The newfound restraint was related to the disappearance of depressed outworkers, the increasingly dominant position of the skilled within the movement, and the bureaucratisation and centralisation of union affairs and the emergence of a more moderate trade union leadership who wished to achieve a stake in society. In order to generate trust, unions sought to improve their members' day-to-day behaviour, discouraging drunkenness, insolence and dishonesty. They also became active supporters of arbitration and conciliation. Leaders, from the 1860s, increasingly saw their role as facilitators for the 'establishment of a solid and substantial ground of intercourse and confidence between masters and men'. They thus sought to resolve disputes through negotiation, and did all they could to prevent unofficial 'wild cat' strikes, though sometimes with little success. As already discussed, there was often little trust between union leaders and their members, and, on occasion, the will of the latter prevailed. In the 1861 cotton dispute, for example, a proposal by the committee of Bolton Spinners Union for workers to accept a 2.5 per cent as opposed to the original 5 per cent reduction in wages was roundly rejected by the rank and file.[33]

Paternalism

An important method of building employer–employee trust was paternalism, the reciprocal exchange of gifts. As has been discussed in Chapter 2, Joyce inter- prets paternalism as a Lukian power relationship, arguing that it was used by employers to alter the norms, values and beliefs of society to the extent that the working class accepted the elite's position of dominance and thus adopted a def- erential attitude. It seems more likely, however, that paternalism was just another way in which masters sought to create trust relationships with their workers. The initial gifts were designed to signal to employees the master's trustworthiness and his desire to form an association. Subsequent gifts then strengthened the ties formed, and, through their regular provision, stabilised the relationship. Where employers wished only to obtain the loyalty of skilled workers, the gifts were restricted to this group. Other masters focused their gift giving on younger members of the workforce, confident that kind treatment would pay dividends in the future, as 'when you once know a man thoroughly and he you . . . a kindly word or look when you happen to be thrown together, quite keeps up the cordiality of feeling'.[34]

Paternalism first appeared in rural factory communities, the potential work- force of which was dispersed and reluctant to move to the new mills, possessing a general distrust of factory work, and, because of the Acts of Settlement, fearing destitution if they subsequently became unemployed.[35] Many factory owners thus used gifts to build pre-employment bonds of trust that would encourage prospective workers to relocate, offering new recruits housing, schools, recreational facilities, livestock, and so on. To prevent them leaving and to ensure high productivity, they sought to raise post-employment trust through the provision of further, often more ephemeral gifts. Other rural owners, con- versely, preferred to rely on power, obtaining their labour from parochial author- ities in distressed areas, and using fines to ensure good work performance.

In towns, where there was a ready supply of labour, all employers used power. Urban masters turned to paternalism only from the 1840s for the reasons discussed above. The gifts presented to workers took two forms. The first and less common type of offering involved lasting monuments, such as reading and dining rooms and educational facilities, the opening of which was often accompanied by a ceremony and a communal meal. Most, however, were more ephemeral – meals, outings to the seaside and such like – to which employees were generally allowed to invite guests, which increased the value of the gift, as they could use the guest invitations to strengthen their own friendships and kin relationships. Meals were often held to celebrate some milestone in the employer's life, the birth of a child, a marriage, attainment of the age of consent, a political success, and thus indicated that the master wished to form a personal almost familial relationship with his workers, or to celebrate some national success or anniversary. The employer in such cases no doubt hoped that the trust generated by the national celebration would augment the employer–employee attachments created. To ensure that everyone present understood the meaning of a gift, the master usually made a speech after its presentation in which he made clear his wish to form a reciprocal relationship or the importance he attached to an existing association, and the room in which the speech was made was often decorated with banners bearing messages such as 'May good feelings continue' and 'Let brotherly love live'.[36]

Employer gifts were reciprocated by workers. Following the social norms of giving, the gift often took the form of an object, such as silver cups, clocks or self-portraits, or a meal. If not, the present would incorporate some value for the employer. When the master was involved in politics, workers could give him their political support, where he was devoutly religious, they could regularly attend church, and, if he was acting opportunistically against other traders, they could decide not to divulge his fraudulent activities to others. The gift was often a public verbal acknowledgement of his trustworthiness, which burnished his reputation in the community and among future business partners and workers. Following a tea party provided by the Bolton spinning company Knowles & Sons in 1845, for example, the workers' representative declared that 'he believed Mr Knowles ... to be an honest and upright man, [and] a better charac-ter he could not give him'. Similarly, workers often touched their caps when passing an employer or his family, receiving the verbal gift of ' "a good day" in return'. Such an exchange involved 'neither servility on the one side nor assumption on the other', but was merely 'becoming in itself and mutually agreeable'. Like employer presents, the gifts were sometimes presented to mark some milestone in the master's life or a national event, and were accompanied by a speech from a worker representative or a written address that clearly indi-cated their wish for a trust relationship to commence or continue.[37]

Paternalism did not just improve employer–employee relations. It increased the human capital of workers, causing productivity to rise, and had other impacts on trust. The meals and excursions promoted social interaction and trust among employees, an outcome particularly welcomed by masters whose staff worked in teams. In many cases, other members of the town were invited to these events and allowed to use the mill's facilities, which aided the generation of commun-ity social capital. Through the provision of educational and rational recreational facilities, many employers hoped that workers would gain the trust advantages discussed in Chapter 4 and that they would be weaned away from 'immoral' recreations, such as drinking and gambling, and that neighbourhood trust and the power of the crowd would be weakened. Others used the speeches that they made at the presentation of gifts to influence the moral norms of their audience. The gifts also checked public criticism of the factory system and thus improved relations with the Southern gentlemanly elite; increased the self-esteem of employers, both individually and as a class, allowing them to see themselves as providers rather than exploiters; and acted as signals of an employer's trustworthiness to prospective employees, potential trading partners and to the general community. Masters often invited the friends and families of workers, fellow traders and other members of the local gentry to presentations and made sure that their generosity was well recorded in the local press.[38]

In discussing paternalism, however, care must be taken not to exaggerate the phenomena or its effect. Even by 1870, it was not the everyday practice of the ordinary employer. Since the provision of gifts was expensive and small masters could form trust relationships with their workers through face-to-face interaction, such benevolent behaviour was mainly embraced by larger firms in the more profitable sectors. Likewise, many paternalistic firms merely provided ephemeral treats. The construction of libraries and so on was costly and workers were reluctant to make use of such facilities, lacking the energy and inclination after a long working day to become involved in activities from which they gained little utility. Permanent paternalism thus probably generated less trust than communal meals and excursions and had relatively little influence on trust norms. Inevitably, it also seems clear that some paternalists continued to exploit their employees. In Bolton, for example, the paternalistic mill owners Henry and Edmund Ashworth paid their workers excessively low wages and a counterpart, Peter Ormrod, illegally forced staff to live in unhygienic cellars.[39]

Equally, there is little evidence that paternalism created a deferential workforce or guaranteed industrial peace. Employees who believed that a paternalistic employer had broken a trust relationship took strike action, even though they had previously been treated well. Those who worked for the paternalistic Bolton mine owners William Hulton and Francis Egerton, for example, withdrew their labour on a number of occasions in protest over the relatively low wages both men paid. Similarly, paternalistic employers who believed that their workers had acted dishonourably had no hesitation in resorting to power, for example using the Master and Servants Act to force strikers back to work.[40]

Master–servant trust

In that they had servants, all members of the middle class were employers and thus faced the principal–agent dilemma. The master–servant relationship was generally one of suspicion. Servants were seen as 'domestic enemies ' who 'watched every opportunity to injure' their employers. The distrust partly arose from the high turnover of domestic staff, which prevented the development of long-term trust relationships, the growing professionalism of the occupation, and, in the urban North, the fact that most servants were migrants, often from Ireland. Young women born in these towns preferred to enter the cotton factories, which paid higher wages and offered better working conditions and were reluctant to employ immigrants. Mutual animosity was further generated by the use of power. Some masters forced their staff to work long hours for little pay or sexually harassed them, and, in response, servants often left their positions at short notice.[41] Their employers thus had to obtain a replacement, which could prove difficult, and, if this became a regular occurrence, could gain them a reputation for ill-treating their staff.

To overcome this distrust, the middle class sought to form trust relations with their retainers. They thus presented them with gifts of cast-off clothing, Christmas boxes and sometimes sums of money, paid them in arrears, and, following the advise of conduct books, addressed them with 'mildness and affability', gave 'orders with decency', and avoided the use of punishment. At the same time, masters reduced the number of live-in servants employed.[42] To ensure that their houses were clean, a signal of respectability and trust, they instead engaged casual staff, who were older and more likely to be locally born than live-in servants, less likely to discover the family's secrets, and had a less disruptive affect on family interaction and therefore kin trust.

At a macro-level, the master–servant relationship acted to raise social trust. Servants monitored their employers, reporting any immoral behaviour to their friends and relatives and to colleagues in other households, who in turn related the information 'to other gossips in the neighbourhood with appropriate exaggerations'. Aware that they lived 'in a glass house' or the possibility that this was the case, masters and their families, consequently, took care to act at all times in a respectable manner.[43] Servants, similarly, monitored visitors to their masters' households. Acting literally as doorkeepers, they sent away undesirables, and, by their presence, discouraged genuine guests from behaving in an inappropriate manner. Just as servants monitored their employers, however, so their masters monitored them. Dishonest or dissolute servants were dismissed without a reference, and, to prevent such behaviour, many mistresses took it upon themselves to morally educate their staff.

Conclusion

As with business trust, employer–employee relations changed over time. When the putting-out system was profitable, it was in the interests of employers to retain the trust of workers. There was a restricted labour supply and the monitoring of work was difficult. They thus gave their staff gifts of loans and equipment and accepted minor opportunism. With the arrival of the factory, however, trading conditions worsened and withdrawals from the sector resulted in a large pool of under-employed workers. Masters thus began to resort to the use of power, cutting wages, acting opportunistically towards employees and taking legal action against even minor acts of embezzlement.

Factory employers adopted power-based labour relations from the start. Mechanisation permitted the substitution of male workers with women and children, who were more passive and could easily be replaced, and the ability to monitor the work process reduced the danger of employee moral hazard. Taking advantage of the situation, masters introduced long working hours, reduced wages, used fines and prosecutions to neutralise opportunism, and dismissed staff during downturns – actions that caused employer–employee trust to plummet. The extent to which they resorted to such power strategies depended on the state of the local labour market, the ownership pattern of the industry, the prosperity of the local economy, and their own personal moral norms.

By mid-century, power had begun to be displaced by trust. Having heavily invested in new technologies, employers were more susceptible to strike action and required a supply of reliable and skilled workers to operate the new machines. At the same time, the more prosperous state of trade weakened the competitive pressures that had demanded the mistreatment of employees, and masters gradually became more aware of the benefits of enlightened capitalism. Many manufacturers therefore began to develop trust relationships with their workers, introducing wage lists, employing the friends and relatives of existing staff, adopting a tolerant attitude to minor pilfering, and, in some cases, providing employees with paternalistic gifts of meals, outings, libraries and educational facilities. Their workers, increasingly represented by moderate trade union leaderships, responded in kind, supporting arbitration and conciliation and presenting their employers with small gifts. Given the bitterness of the past, progress was sometimes slow. Many manufacturers were reluctant to abandon their power strategies and the hands of moderate union leaders were often tied by their more militant members. Nonetheless, by the fourth quarter of the century employer–employee bonds were relatively strong.

Conclusion

The importance of trust is evident to everyone. We are all aware that people are self-interested, an important evolutionary trait, and that they may act opportunistically. Those of us who are wise, consequently, only enter relationships if we are certain that the other party will honour his or her obligations. If this is not the case, the collaboration does not occur and the benefits, both to ourselves and the wider society and economy, are lost. Since self-interest is partly genetic, opportunism will have been as prevalent in earlier periods as it is today and trust equally as important. Moreover, as social capital is an environmental construct, its reserves will have changed over time, rising and falling in response to socio-economic change. From the mid-eighteenth to the mid-nineteenth century there appears to have been an overall decline in trust levels. As today, the fall was noted by numerous social commentators, many of whom warned that it threatened social stability and economic growth. In 1795, for example, John Holland noted that 'in social and civil life, among the different professions and employments of mankind, [and] from the cottage to the court, duplicity and dissimulation are found greatly prevalent and abounding'. The *Illustrated London News* in 1843, meanwhile, expressed worries that if the dishonesty were to 'sweep on unchecked', there was a danger that it would 'destroy the very fabric of society by shaking every confidence between man and man'.[1]

The fall in confidence was caused by the social and economic upheavals of the period, in particular urbanisation and industrialisation. The expansion of towns caused many urban dwellers to live in a world of strangers, or, at least, casual acquaintances, in which it was more difficult to determine trustworthiness, but easier to act opportunistically.[2] In the rural village, residents interacted in both formal and informal networks with a limited number of people. They therefore had a great deal of personal experience of the intrinsic merit of fellow residents and could easily discover their reputations from others. If a person acted unscrupulously, his reputation and chances of entering advantageous relationships in the future would be badly damaged and he would be subject to sanctions, such as gossip or exclusion. Having broken the strong moral social norms, and, probably having had a bond of friendship with his victim, he could even suffer psychological costs.

Conversely, in the industrial town, the larger population, high levels of residential and occupational mobility and the relative absence of formal net-works meant that most residents came into contact with a relatively large number of people with whom they had fleeting, superficial relationships. They therefore often lacked the personal knowledge necessary for judging moral char-acter and had no access to reputational information. Duplicitous behaviour was therefore likely to be more successful and would involve lower costs. The lack of fellowship meant that an opportunist would suffer little damage to his good name and be subject to few and weak social sanctions. There would also be a smaller psychological downside. It was unlikely that the opportunist had a close relationship with his victim, 'men in cities . . . contract[ing] a contempt for their species', and urban moral social norms were far less powerful than their rural counterparts.[3] The result was that individuals increasingly acted unscrupulously in their personal, economic and social relationships and crime soared, fanned by an inadequate legal system and inefficient policing. The poor relations between the urban elite and both growers of grain and local communities, meanwhile, led to a breakdown of the social contract.

Residents of towns could not even depend on the signals of ascribed, afflu-ence or status trust that in the village had served them so well. People began to dress in a more uniform manner, and, aware of their new anonymity, to wear clothes that suggested that they belonged to a higher social class than was actu-ally the case. 'The nobleman [began] to emulate the grandeur of a prince, . . . the gentleman . . . aspire to the proper state of the nobleman [and] the tradesman step[ped] from behind the counter into the vacant place of the gentleman'. These changes in dress were related to the greater availability of cheap mass-produced standardised clothing made possible by mechanisation and the use of patterns, the rise of the shop, the decline in occupational garb, the increase in middle class disposable incomes, and the increasing importance of fashion. London styles were carried to provincial towns by national newspapers and the gentry, who, along with their servants, constantly shuttled between the capital and their country estates. The new fashions then percolated down the social scale, via the provincial press and social interaction in formal and informal networks, eventu-ally reaching the lower classes, who bought such clothing second-hand, and, if migrants, were often ignorant or disdainful of urban dress codes.[4]

Industrialisation damaged business trust, industrial relations and kinship ties. Economic growth greatly increased opportunities for dishonesty. There were more traders, whose businesses often had short lifespans, commercial relations were more complex, credit was endemic and businessmen were increasingly reliant on others to perform tasks that had previously been undertaken by them-selves or a third party under their direct supervision. For the small trader produc-ing goods on a speculative basis, there was also a greater temptation to turn to opportunism, as such was 'the pressure of competition' that many could only stay in business by acquiring 'strong powers of deception'.[5] In the factory industries, one way of meeting this increased business rivalry and maximising profits was mechanisation, deskilling, the substitution of male with female and child labour, the payment of low wages, long working hours and the dismissal of staff during trade downturns. Such actions, however, severely damaged employer–employee trust relations, which were further weakened by the sheer size of factories and high staff turnovers. The harsh factory regime also arguably impaired kinship bonds, the socialisation of moral norms and masculine self-confidence, and, along with the poor living conditions of the new towns, led to working class immorality.

Aware of the importance of and fall in trust, people sought to strengthen their own and their community's reserves of social capital. Formal and informal networks were established, in particular voluntary associations and neighbourhood networks, which brought individuals, the various middle-class sub-groups, and the middle and working classes together. Commonly accepted indicators of trust and trustworthiness, such as dress, etiquette and respectability were adopted. Care was taken to act in a honourable manner at all times and thus build a reputation for honesty. Gifts were given to friends, neighbours and employees, by the elite to the community and by the state to the electorate. To foster morality, people were monitored by others and social sanctions were applied against those who broke trust and moral norms, harsher and more wide-ranging legal sanctions and more effective policing were introduced, and the middle-class male spent more of his leisure time in the bosom of his family, where it was believed he could best recharge his ethical batteries. The elite sought to raise working-class morals through campaigns to outlaw pursuits that fostered depravity, the espousal of rational recreation, the provision of educational facilities, where pupils could learn trust and moral norms, the improvement of the urban environment, the direction of charity and poor relief to the deserving poor, and the promotion of factory reform. Central government, meanwhile, acted to improve its trust relationship with the electorate and depended on local voluntary associations for the delivery of many of its services.

At the same time, trust levels were raised by socio-economic change. New political and economic theories softened the creed of individualism, newspapers and the improved postal service lowered the barriers to friendly and social intercourse, there were fewer distrusted migrants, and technological advances created a need for reliable and skilled workers and forced many employers in the cotton and other industries to adopt a trust-based labour-relations policy. More importantly, the sustained economic upswing from the 1850s reduced the need to adopt power strategies and promoted trust in other ways. Commercial competition was moderated, credit network collapse less likely, businessmen could spend more time establishing formal and informal networks and provide better working conditions, middle-class attitudes became more liberal, philanthropic and general gift giving increased, the trust associated with income was strengthened, and radicals were forced to accept the permanency of the capitalist system.

The result of these initiatives and environmental change was that by the third quarter of the century social capital reserves had recovered and the perceived danger that a lack of trust would slow economic growth and disrupt social relations had passed. As today, however, the aggregate fall and rise in trust does not tell the whole story. Over the period, the nature of trust changed. Kinship and other highly personalised trusts became less important, overshadowed by weaker loyalties based on everyday contact and supported by institutions such as the police force, the legal system and trading associations. Factors that weakened trust could also strengthen it. Economic growth and credit, for example, were generators of both trust and distrust and industrialisation was itself the product of high levels of social capital.[6] The rate and timing of the decline and upturn in trust, meanwhile, varied from sphere to sphere. The fall in business trust, for instance, was not as great as the collapse in inter-class and employer–employee trust and the recovery was far more rapid. Likewise, neighbourhood and kinship trust appear to have weakened from mid-century, whereas the trust generated by the legal system and policing and regional and national trust strengthened. This should not be taken to imply that the various spheres were impervious. Trust and distrust could and did seep from one sector to another. The trust norms learnt in church, for example, inevitably influenced how a manufacturer conducted his affairs in the wider world.

The amount of trust produced and the timing of its generation, likewise, varied between towns and regions. Determinants of town/regional social capital included the quantity of kinship trust, business trust, and so on, in existence; the social, cultural, political, economic and institutional environment in which the community was embedded; its history, which partly influenced its trust and ethical norms; and the manner of urban expansion. Those towns that absorbed established villages and their associated trust cultures will have had greater social capital than those that sprawled over land devoid of hamlets. Among the mill communities of Lancashire there was much variation in trust levels; some urban areas were 'marked by a . . . moral order; others [were] notorious only for turbulence'. Bolton, for example, was a high-trust town, renowned for its friend-liness and good industrial relations. Oldham, on the other hand, had a poor repu-tation as regards its labour relations and community spirit, and its low level of social capital is clearly reflected in its rankings in various social and economic lists. In the first half of the century, the town had a lower church attendance than Bolton, fewer charities, schools and newspapers, a lower ratio of tradesmen to lawyers, a relatively low poor rate, experienced faster population growth and had a greater number of non-Lancastrian migrants.[7]

The trust generated, furthermore, was not wholly benign. Some trusts were closely related to power; high social capital increased the solidarity and there-fore strength of trade unions and the crowd. Networks often crowded out community mutuality or generated animosity. Involvement in religious activ-ities, for example, left little time or inclination for community pursuits, and, in many towns, anti-Catholicism was rife. The rich and powerful, meanwhile, pos-sessed privileged access to the advantages of trust. Members of the elite found it far easier to form trust relationships with fellow members of the gentry and the middle class than their more lowly born counterparts. They thus had greater access to the resources owned by this caste and had little difficulty in achieving economic success. A gentleman, for example, had characteristics in common with his fellow class members, possessed the social and etiquette skills necessary for successful networking, could easily afford to lavish gifts on social and business acquaintances, and could probably free ride on a widely recognised family reputation. Likewise, he would find it easier to join middle-class formal networks. He would have friends or relatives who were existing members and would add to an association's trust reputation, increase its attractiveness to others by strengthening the networking value of membership and could provide some of its funds. Once ensconced in a voluntary association, he could then ensure that it continued to restrict access to the non-elite, who would dilute networking returns, and, through the benefits of membership, could eventually pose a challenge to his economic position. He could also use his authority to set self-serving network trust and moral norms and influence the actions of the less powerful in ways that again benefited himself. Established traders, for example, could discourage innovation and diversification.

The elite, similarly, used trust and morality to tackle threats to their dominance that arose from crime, trade unions and the crowd. In the industrial sphere, employers created trust relationships with their workers, giving them paternalistic gifts, introducing wage lists and improving working conditions. To prevent social unrest, the state strengthened the social contract, and, at a local level, the elite fulfilled their communal obligations and sought to weaken neighbourhood social capital and to establish in its place a less socially divisive form of trust. They thus tried to reduce the influence of the pub, the main arena of working-class association; in order to minimise reliance on exchange networks, provided generous charitable/poor law relief and promoted the respectable norms of frugality and foresight; and established or encouraged attendance at formal networks, such as the church and rational recreation associations, where socially positive mutuality would be generated.

Finally, neither the elite nor the individual wanted moral hazard to be completely eliminated. Both were aware that opportunism was unavoidable, given the genetically based self-interested nature of man and the ethos of the capitalist system. They thus sought to support their society's trust myth, its moral norms and ethical values, which ensured that there was sufficient trust to allow action, but ignored opportunism that posed no threat to the myth. Governments gradually introduced improved criminal legislation and policing, which, if prosecution figures are to be believed, reduced both ordinary and white-collar crime. Such initiatives strengthened the social contract, gave individuals the confidence to enter into new relationships and prevented criticism of the capitalist system. In reality, the legislation was arguably designed to keep prosecution figures artificially low. Any serious attempt to tackle ordinary and business indictable crime would have been unacceptably costly and the resultant large numbers of prosecutions would have lowered social and business trust and caused many to question capitalism's legitimacy. Likewise, provided that it was not known to others outside their social circle, individuals turned a 'blind eye' to hypocritical or unrespectable behaviour committed by colleagues, fearful that punishment would attract others' attention to the actions and damage the group's and their own trust reputations.

Trust cycles

Trust changes over time and it seems likely that there exists a trust equilibrium, a level of social capital that facilitates economic growth and social stability. Any movement away from this equipoise will prompt a countervailing response that eventually causes a return to the equilibrium. Exogenous changes that lower trust will therefore be followed by actions that return it to its former levels, and oversupply will reduce its value and elicit an increase in self-interested behaviour (Figure C.1). There may even exist a trust cycle, which both follows and influences the Kondratieff cycle of economic performance. When business is depressed, reserves of trust will be low, but will then rise as the economy begins to expand. Growth and the accompanying prosperity will calm inter-class conflicts caused by the unequal distribution of income, increase government trust, prosperity being a criteria of political success, and make it easier for people to attain their personal goals, weakening individual frustrations. At the same time, it will diminish political competition, encourage employers to treat their workers in a fair manner, and enable the state to improve policing and shower the public with gifts and thus strengthen the social contract. Exceptions to this rosy scenario will occur where growth is uneven, takes place in a landscape with few trust-generating institutions, or arises from major technological change. In these circumstances, as in the late eighteenth/early nineteenth centuries, social capital may in the short term fall further and could even slow economic progress.[8]

As the economy accelerates, trust will continue to rise, but will eventually overshoot the equilibrium level and give rise to structural impediments that damage growth. Business co-operation will dull competitive instincts and lead to inefficiencies; high employer–employee trust will cause wage increases to

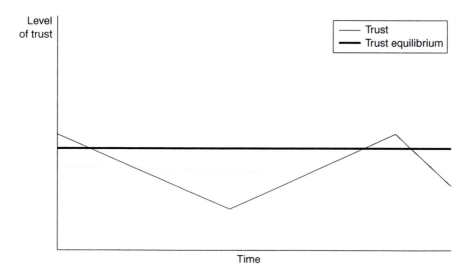

Figure C.1 Trust over time.

exceed productivity growth; long-established business networks will stifle innovation, entrepreneurship and change; intensive networking will lead to the promotion of individuals with high levels of social capital but few skills; and, to strengthen the social contract, governments will engage in excessive and unproductive public expenditure. Economic performance will thus weaken and trust will fall to levels well below the equipoise, further debilitating economic progress; a process that can be seen to have occurred at the end of the nineteenth century.[9] Aware of the collapse of trust and its social and other costs, communities will then seek to restock their reserves of social capital, which will lay the foundations for the eventual economic upturn that will itself raise trust (which will further strengthen growth).

Victorian and present day trust

Turning to present-day trust levels. These appear to be low and falling, and the social capital problems of the Victorians are therefore arguably as relevant today as then. Surveys indicate that the percentage of Britons who trust others has declined from 56 per cent in 1959 to 44 per cent in 1990, with the collapse being most marked among the working class and the young. The likely explanations for the fall are reminiscent of those that operated in the early 1800s. The movement of women into the workforce, longer working hours and the practice of commuting to work has reduced participation in voluntary associations and neighbourhood networks, weakened the primary socialisation of trust and moral norms, and loosened kinship ties. Firms have become larger and more impersonal, employment less secure and often short term, and trade unions less powerful, with the result that there is now less employer–employee trust. There is greater residential mobility, which has damaged formal and informal networks and community co-operation. New media, television and the Internet rather than newspapers and periodicals, have caused local norms to be challenged by national and even international social codes and have again reduced interaction.[10] Crime is perceived to be high, though, as ever, prosecution figures often suggest the opposite, immigration is on the increase and the migrant viewed with suspicion, and church attendance is in free fall.

Other contributory factors include the changing nature of voluntary associations, which are now often mass organisations whose members rarely interact; political correctness and the devaluation of the honesty of language; rising affluence, which reduces co-operation and self-control and encourages selfishness and individuals to gratify their baser instincts; and the weakening of the social contract. Electoral turnouts are low, memberships of political parties and pressure groups are on a downward trend, and trust of politicians is virtually nonexistent, largely due to corruption and 'spin'. As in the early nineteenth century, governments, like their electorates, have also been influenced by individualism, in the form of Thatcherism, and, to some extent, 'Blairism'. Oddly, though, this creed sits alongside a liberal ethos. Admittedly, this has reduced much former distrust, for instance of racial and sexual minorities. Conversely, some argue that its insistence that acts detrimental to social capital can be blamed on environmental factors has injured individual responsibility and self-control and diluted sanctions and punishments.

The solutions to the present trust downturn, like the causes, can perhaps be found in the nineteenth century. As in the early 1800s, there needs to be greater involvement in voluntary associations. Membership could be increased by the government adding community service to the national curriculum, enabling schools to offer a greater number of extra-curricular activities, limiting working hours and encouraging employers to give those workers involved in community affairs time off work. Association would be further stimulated if the church adopted a more evangelistic role and raised attendances, political parties and charities requested time rather than money participation, and the media promoted the benefits of community involvement. A shorter working day and larger church congregations would also improve the primary and secondary socialisation of trust and moral norms, as would a more responsible media, the introduction of school civic courses and government policies that promoted the two-parent family and enabled those mothers with young children who wished to devote their days to their upbringing to do so. Social and other trust, meanwhile, could be raised through government initiatives that increased the use of public transport, reduced crime, provided more public space, created a welfare state less susceptible to moral hazard and encouraged philanthropy, employer 'paternalism' and the construction of community friendly housing. If some or all of these changes were instituted, as in the third quarter of the nineteenth century, social capital would again rise, benefiting the economy, strengthening democracy and improving the quality of life. For, as John Holland concluded in 1795, if 'men [can]not in general depend on one another ... without doubt, there [will] be an end to the whole intercourse of society'.[11]

Notes

Introduction

1 J. Fedderke, R. de Kadt and J. Luiz, 'Economic growth and social capital', *Theory and Society*, 28, 1999, 710; R. D. Putnam, 'Democracy in America at century's end', in A. Hadenius (ed.) *Democracy's Victory and Crisis*, Cambridge: Cambridge University Press, 1997, 31; S. Knack and P. Keefer, 'Does social capital have an economic payoff?', *Quarterly Journal of Economics*, 112, 1997, 1251–88; R. Rose, 'How much does social capital add to individual health', *Social Science and Medicine*, 51, 2000, 1421–35; L. W. Pye, 'Civility, social capital and civil society', *Journal of Interdisciplinary History*, 29 (4), 1999, 764; E. L. Glaeser *et al.*, 'What is social capital', *NBER Working Paper Series*, 7216, 1999, 2.

2 P. Milgrom and J. Roberts, *Economic Organisation and Management*, New Jersey: Prentice Hall, 1992, chapters 5 and 6.

3 Ferguson, *An Essay on the History of Civil Society*, Cambridge: Cambridge University Press, 1996 (originally published 1795); C. de Secondat Montesquieu, *The Spirit of the Laws*, Cambridge: Cambridge University Press, 1989 (originally published 1748); A. de Tocqueville, *Democracy in America*, New York: Knopf, 1945 (originally published 1840); M. Woolcock, 'Social capital and economic development', *Theory and Society*, 27 (2), 1998, 151–208; P. Bourdieu, 'Forms of capital', in J. G. Richardson (ed.), *Handbook of Theory and Research for the Sociology of Education*, Westport: Greenwood, 1983; J. S. Coleman, *Foundations of Social Theory*, Cambridge, Mass.: Harvard 1990; R. D. Putnam, *Making Democracy Work. Civil Traditions in Modern Italy*, Princeton: Princeton University Press, 1993; R. D. Putnam, *Bowling Alone. The Collapse and Revival of American Community*, New York: Simon & Schuster, 2000; F. Fukuyama, *Trust. The Social Virtues and Creation of Prosperity*, London: Penguin, 1996.

4 P. Joyce, *Work Society and Politics: The Culture of the Factory in Later Victorian England*, Brighton: Harvester, 1980; N. Kirk, *The Growth of Working Class Reformism in Mid-Victorian Britain*, London: Croom Helm, 1985; B. Harrison, 'Religion and recreation in nineteenth century England', *Past and Present*, 38, 1967, 98–125; W. B. Stephens, *Regional Variations in Education During the Industrial Revolution 1780–1870*, Leeds: University of Leeds, 1973.

5 R. I. Rotberg (ed.), *Patterns of Social Capital. Stability and Change in Historical Perspective*, Cambridge: Cambridge University Press, 2001; C. Muldrew, *The Economy of Obligation. The Culture of Credit and Social Relations in Early Modern England*, Basingstoke: Macmillan, 1998; L. Newton, 'Trust and virtue in English banking. The assessment of borrowers by bank managements at the turn of the nineteenth century', *Financial History Review*, 7 (2), 2000, 177–99; A. Popp, 'Trust in an industrial district. The Potteries 1850–1900', *Journal of Industrial History*, 3 (1), 2000, 28–53; E. P. Thompson, 'The moral economy of the English crowd in the eighteenth

century', *Past and Present*, 50, 1971, 76–136; G. G. Holden, *Respectable Militants. The Lancashire Textile Machinery Makers*, Salford: University of Salford, 1987; T. Griffiths, *The Lancashire Working Classes, c.1880–1930*, Oxford: Oxford University Press, 2001; M. Huberman, *Escape from the Market. Negotiating Work in Lancashire*, Cambridge: Cambridge University Press, 1996; M. B. Rose, *Firms, Networks and Business Values. The British and American Cotton Industries since 1750*, Cambridge: Cambridge University Press, 2000; R. Pearson and D. Richardson, 'Business networking in the industrial revolution', *Economic History Review*, 54 (4), 2001, 657–79; J. F. Wilson and A. Popp (eds), *Industrial Clusters and Regional Business Networks in England, 1750–1970*, London: Ashgate, 2003; S. Barrett, 'Kinship, poor relief and the welfare process in early modern England', in S. King and A. Tomkins (eds), *The Poor in England, 1700–1850. An Economy of Makeshifts*, Manchester: Manchester University Press, 2003; N. Tadmor, *Family and Friends in Eighteenth Century England*, Cambridge: Cambridge University Press, 2001; J. C. Doherty, 'Short distance migration in mid-Victorian Lancashire', University of Lancashire, PhD thesis, 1985; A. Offer, 'Between the gift and the market. The economy of regard', *Economic History Review*, 50 (3), 1997, 450–76; L. Davidoff, *The Best Circles. Society, Etiquette and the Season*, London: Croom Helm, 1973; T. Laqueur, *Religion and Respectability. Sunday Schools and Working Class Culture*, New Haven: Yale University Press, 1976.

  6 T. R. Tholfsen, 'The intellectual origins of mid-Victorian stability', *Political Science Quarterly*, 86, 1971, 75; J. Holland, *Thoughts on Truth on Prejudice and on Sincerity*, London, 1795, 11; Anon., *The Young Man's Own Book. A Manual of Politeness, Intellectual Improvement and Moral Deportment*, London, 1838, 325.

  7 M. Lessnoff (ed.), *Social Contract Theory*, Oxford: Blackwell, 1990, 4.

  8 H. Schmitz, 'From ascribed to earned trust in exporting clusters', *Journal of International Economics*, 48, 1999, 143.

  9 W. W. Powell, 'Trust based forms of governance', in R. M. Kramer and T. R. Tyler (eds), *Trust in Organisations*, London: Sage, 1996, 55.

 10 M. Freitag, 'Beyond Tocqueville', *European Sociological Review*, 19 (2), 2003, 226; T. W. Smith, 'Factors relating to misanthropy in contemporary American society', *Social Science Research*, 26, 1997, 170–96; Boyd Hilton, *The Age of Atonement. The Influence of Evangelicalism on Social and Economic Thought, 1795–1865*, Oxford: Clarendon, 1988, 256.

 11 G. Dei Ottati, 'Trust, interlinking transactions and credit in the industrial district', *Cambridge Journal of Economics*, 18, 1994, 533; I. Nonaka, 'The knowledge creating company', *Harvard Business Review*, 104, 1991, 52.

 12 Burchill and F. Wilkinson, 'Trust business relationships and the contractual environment', *ESRC Centre for Business Research, University of Cambridge, Working Paper*, No. 35, 4; L. D. Molm, N. Takahashi and G. Peterson, 'Risk and trust in social exchange', *American Journal of Sociology*, 105 (5), 2000, 1405; E. Lawler and J. Yoon, 'Commitment in exchange relations', *American Sociological Review*, 61 (1), 1996, 89; J. H. Turner, 'The formation of social capital', in P. Dasgupta and I. Serageldin (eds), *Social Capital. A Multifaceted Perspective*, Washington: World Bank, 2000, 135; A. R. Anderson and C. J. Miller, 'Class matters. Human and social capital in the entrepreneurial process', *Journal of Socio-Economics*, 32 (1), 2003, 19.

 13 Offer, 'Between', 451; A. Smith, *Theory of Moral Sentiments*, Oxford: Clarendon, 1982 (originally published 1767), 50; Lawler, 'Commitment', 91; A. E. Komter, 'Reciprocity as a principle of exclusion', *Sociology*, 30 (2), 1996, 299, 301.

 14 M. Anderson, *Family Structure in Nineteenth Century Lancashire*, Cambridge: Cambridge University Press, 12; O. Leimar and P. Hammerstein, 'Evolution of co-operation through indirect reciprocity', *Proceedings of the Royal Society of London*, series b, 1468, 2001, 745.

 15 H. Peyton Young, 'Social norms and economic welfare', *European Economic Review*, 42, 1998, 829.

16 J. Wieselquist and C. Agnew, 'Commitment, pro-relationship behaviour and trust in close relationships', *Journal of Personality and Social Psychology*, 77 (5), 1999, 944; G. S. Becker, 'Altruism, egoism and genetic fitness', *Journal of Economic Literature*, 14 (3), 1976, 817–26; M. Zuckerman, 'Attribution of success and failure revisited', *Journal of Personality*, 47, 1979, 245–87; C. Snyder, R. L. Higgins and R. J. Stucky, *Excuses. Masquerades in Search of Grace*, New York: Wiley, 1983; Pye, 'Civility', 766. It is possible that the genetic attributes of co-operating and expecting others to co-operate have a fitness advantage over genes supporting other qualities (J. M. Orbell and R. M. Dawes, 'Social welfare, co-operators advantage and the option of not playing the game', *American Sociological Review*, 58 (6), 1993, 798).

17 D. C. North, *Institutions, Institutional Change and Economic Performance*, Cambridge: Cambridge University Press, 1990, 3, 23; G. Boyce, 'Network knowledge and network routines. Negotiating activities between ship owners and shipbuilders', *Business History*, 45 (2), 2003, 52–76; R. R. Nelson and S. G. Winter, *An Evolutionary Theory of Economic Change*, London: Belknap, 1982, 14, 99, 134, 400.

18 Putnam, *Bowling*, 21–3; S. Szreter, 'The state of social capital', *Theory and Society*, 31 (5), 2002, 578.

19 F. Fukuyama, 'Social capital, civil society and development', *Third World Quarterly*, 22 (1), 2001, 8–14; *Bolton Chronicle*, 23 April 1853.

20 P. Blau, 'A macro-sociological theory of social structure', *Journal of Sociology*, 83, 1982, 26–54.

21 George Moyser and Geraint Parry, 'Voluntary associations and democratic participation in Britain', in Jan W. Van Deth, *Private Groups and Public Life. Social Participation, Voluntary Associations and Political Involvement in Representative Democracies*, London: Routledge, 1997, 27; Putnam, *Bowling*, 94; J. L Pierce, D. G. Gardner, L. L. Cummings and R. B. Dunham, 'Organization based self-esteem. Construct definition, operationalization and validation', *Academy of Management Journal*, 32, 1989, 622–48; F. Heider, *The Psychology of Interpersonal Relations*, New York: John Wiley & Sons, 1958; Casson, 'An economic', 34.

22 G. Ainslie, 'Beyond microeconomics', in J. Elster, *The Multiple Self*, Cambridge: Cambridge University Press, 1986; Smith, *The Theory*, 10.

23 Janis and L. Mann, *Decision Making. A Psychological Analysis of Conflict, Choice and Commitment*, New York: Macmillan, 1977; M. Rabin, 'Psychology and economics', *Journal of Economic Literature*, 36 (1), 1998, 11–46; G. R. Searle, *Morality and the Market in Victorian Britain*, Oxford: Clarendon, 1998, 79; Weinstein, 'Unrealistic'; S. Oskamp, 'Overconfidence in case study judgments', *Journal of Consulting Psychology*, 29, 1965, 261–5; A. D. Baddeley and G. Hitch, 'The recency effect. Implicit learning with explicit retrieval?', *Memory and Cognition*, 21 (2), 1993, 146–55; S. Pressman, 'On financial frauds and their causes', *American Journal of Economics and Sociology*, 57 (4), 1998, 416; A. Tversky and D. Kahneman, 'Judgement under uncertainty', *Science*, 185 (4157), 1974, 1124–31.

24 R. A. Dahl, 'The concept of power' in R. Bell *et al.* (eds), *Political Power. A Reader in Theory and Research*, London: Macmillan, 1969, 82; R. M. Emerson, 'Power-dependence relations', *American Sociological Review*, 27, 1962, 32.

25 Bolton Archive, FZ 18/2/20, Bolton Hesperus Literary and Christian Association 1853–66, Minute Book, President's address, 1863, 13.

1 Middle-class trust

1 S. Smiles, *Self Help*, London: Penguin, 1986 (originally published 1859), 236. For practitioners, the costs involved in following the code were relatively low and the savings, in terms of reduced information search costs and lower levels of moral hazard, were high, especially in dealings with strangers.

2 Ibid., 352, 366; S. S. Ellis, *The Women of England. Their Social Duties and Domestic Habits*, London, 1839, 109; Anon., *The Young*, 256.

3 Revd J. B. Owen, *Business without Christianity*, Manchester, 1855, 29–43; T. L. Nichols, *How to Behave. A Manual of Manners and Morals*, London, 1873, 68; Anon., *The Young*, 180, 240.

4 Anon., *The Young*, 150, 218, 221; M. Morgan, *Manners, Morals and Class in England, 1774–1858*, Basingstoke: Macmillan, 1994, 73–4; P. Perrot, *Fashioning the Bourgeoise. The History of Clothing in the Nineteenth Century*, Princeton: Princeton University Press, 1994, 90–1, 113.

5 Anon., *The Young*, 258; Smiles, *Self*, 237; *The Illustrated Guide to London*, Leipzig 1851, quoted in W. L. Arnstein, 'A German view of English society, 1851', *Victorian Studies*, 16 (2), 1972, 186; T. Bobbin, *The Lancashire Dialect by Way of Dialogue*, Middlewich, 1757.

6 K. C. Phillipps, *Language and Class in Victorian England*, Oxford: Blackwell, 1984, 49–53; Bates, *A Discourse*, 112; Anon., *The Young*, 151, 222.

7 W. Cobbett, *Cobbett's Sermons*, London, 1822, 1; Bates, *A Discourse*, 112; P. Langford, *Englishness Identified. Manners and Character, 1650–1850*, Oxford: Oxford University Press, 2000, 129; R. Lamb, *Free Thoughts on Many Subjects*, London, 1866, vol. i, 173.

8 J. Harris, *An Essay on Politeness*, London, 1820, 33; P. Carter, 'Polite persons. Character, biography and the gentleman', *Transactions of the Royal Historical Society*, 12, 2002, 333–54.

9 Carter, 'Polite', 344; Morgan, *Manners*, 59–63, 119; J. Tosh, 'Gentlemanly politeness and manly simplicity in Victorian England', *Transactions of the Royal Historical Society*, 12, 2002, 460–8.

10 Cobbett, *Cobbett's*, 2; J. Dymond, *Essays on the Principles of Morality*, London, 1829, 286; Lamb, *Free*, vol. i, 182, 193; W. Bagehot, 'The character of Sir Robert Peel', in F. Morgan (ed.), *Works*, vol. iii, Hartford, 1891, 4–5. Inevitably, not everyone agreed that minor duplicity should be tolerated. It was argued that hypocrisy weakened the personal moral norms of the culprit and, more importantly, degraded the morality of children, servants and the lower orders, who were set a bad example (Bates, *A Discourse*, 56).

11 Morgan, *Manners*, 119; Anon., *The Young*, 174, 241; quoted in M. Rabin, 'Cognitive dissonance and social change', *Journal of Economic Behaviour and Organization*, 23, 1994, 187; T. Binney, *Is it Possible to Make the Best of Both Worlds? A Book for Young Men*, London, 1853, 71; Mrs W. Parkes, *Domestic Duties or Instructions to Young Married Ladies on the Management of their Households*, London, 1825, 416.

12 Parkes, *Domestic*, 416; J. Stone et al., 'When exemplification falls. Hypocrisy and the motive for self-integrity', *Journal of Personality and Social Psychology*, 72 (1), 1997, 54; R. L. Trivers, *Social Evolution*, Menlo Park: Benjamin/Cummings, 1985, 415–20.

13 M. J. Huggins, 'More sinful pleasures. Leisure, respectability and the male middle classes in Victorian England', *Journal of Social History*, 33 (3), 2000, 589–92. See also S. Koven, *Slumming. Sexual and Social Politics in Victorian London*, Oxford: Clarendon, 2004.

14 J. Graham, 'Lavater's physiognomy in England', *Journal of the History of Ideas*, 22 (4), 1961, 561; M. C. Cowling, 'The artist as anthropologist in mid-Victorian England', *Art History*, 6 (4), 1983, 69–70; J. Fahnestock, 'The heroine of irregular features. Physiognomy and conventions of heroine description', *Victorian Studies*, 24 (3), 1981, 335–9.

15 *The Gentleman's Magazine*, 71, February, 1801, 124; 'A visit to Newgate' in C. Dickens, *Sketches by Boz: Our Parish*, London, 1836–7, 147; Lamb, *Free*, vol. i, 107. Facial features that indicated honesty may have been added to portraits to ensure that they signalled these qualities to viewers. Through the dress and posture of the sitter,

portraits also indicated affluence and status trust (J. Mulvihill, '"True portrait and true history" William Hazlitt's art criticism', *Prose Studies*, 21 (3), 1998, 35).

16 S. Nenadic, 'Middle rank consumers and domestic culture in Edinburgh and Glasgow, 1720–1840', *Past and Present*, 145, 1994, 141–5.

17 M. Hellman, 'Furniture, sociability and the work of leisure in eighteenth century France', *Eighteenth Century Studies*, 32 (4), 1999, 415–45.

18 E. C. Kirkland, *Dream and Thought in the Business Community, 1860–1900*, New York: Cornell University Press, 1956, 34; W. Hazlitt sen., *Table Talk or Original Essays on Men and Manners*, vol. i, London, 1824, 323; D. Garrioch, 'House names, shop signs and social organization in Western European cities, 1500–1900', *Urban History*, 21 (1), 1994, 28; J. Seed, 'Commerce and the liberal arts. The political economy of art in Manchester, 1775–1860' in J. Wolff and J. Seed (eds), *The Culture of Capital. Art, Power and the Nineteenth Century Middle Class*, Manchester: Manchester University Press, 1988, 45; 'Banting on corpulence', *Blackwoods Magazine*, 96, 1864, 608. To aid intra-gender networking and trust, houses had separate male and female domains, e.g. the billiard room and the drawing room (J. Lewis (ed.), *Labour and Love. Women's Experience of Home and Family, 1850–1940*, Oxford: Blackwell, 1986, 29).

19 Bates, *A Discourse*, 63; S. Hoffmann, 'Civility, male friendship and Masonic sociability in nineteenth century Germany', *Gender and History*, 13 (2), 2001, 235; Phillipps, *Language*, 57–9; B. Bernstein, *Class Codes and Control, vol. i. Theoretical Studies Towards a Sociology of a Language*, London: Routledge, 1971, 125–77.

20 Parkes, *Domestic*, 17; Binney, *Is It*, 37. Speaking style includes such things as choice of words, accent and use of nuance. Communication accommodation theory proposes that individuals who adopt this stratagem are regarded by listeners as more credible, competent, intelligent and friendly (R. L. Street and H. Giles, 'Speech accommodation theory. A social cognitive approach to language and speech behaviour' in M. E. Roloff and C. R. Berger (eds), *Social Cognition and Communication*, Beverly Hills, Calif. 1982, 193–226).

21 P. Clark, *British Clubs and Societies, 1580–1800*, Oxford: Clarendon, 2000, 160; Nenadic, 'Middle', 135, 136; M. C. Finn, 'Men's things. Masculine possession in the consumer revolution', *Social History*, 25 (2), 2000, 143.

22 H. L. Carmichael and W. B. Macleod, 'Gift giving and the evolution of co-operation', *International Economic Review*, 38 (3), 1997, 487; C. Camerer, 'Gifts as economic signals and social symbols', *American Journal of Sociology*, 94, supplement, 1988, s193, s195; D. Vaisey (ed.), *The Diary of Thomas Turner, 1754–1765*, Oxford: Oxford University Press, 1984, 214.

23 Vaisey, *The Diary*, 10.

24 N. Z. Davis, *The Gift in Sixteenth Century France*, Oxford: Oxford University Press, 2000, 8, 14, 42; J. Beresford (ed.), *Woodforde. Passages from the Five Volumes of the Diary of a Country Parson, 1758–1802*, Oxford: Oxford University Press, 1935, 142; Anon., *The Young*, 254; *The Bolton Reflector*, 8, 1823, 60. Finn argues that as the century progressed such 'special occasion gifts' increasingly replaced ad hoc giving (M. C. Finn, *The Character of Credit. Personal Debt in English Culture, 1740–1914*, Cambridge: Cambridge University Press, 2003, 87).

25 Binney, *Is It*, 36, 73; M. S. Servian, 'The fair swindler of Blackheath. A case study on the importance of reputation in late eighteenth century legal and commercial affairs', *Journal of Legal History*, 8 (1), 1987, 78; Anon, *The Young*, 145; D. Defoe, *The Complete English Tradesman*, Oxford, 1841 (originally published 1726), 153.

26 Anon., *The Young*, 163; Anon., *Business Life. The Experiences of a London Tradesman*, London, 1861, 39; Hazlitt, *Table*, 308, 323; Bates, *A Discourse*, 63.

27 Bates, *A Discourse*, 54; D. T. Andrew, 'The code of honour and its critics. The opposition to dueling in England, 1700–1850', *Social History*, 5 (3), 1980, 411–34; R. Shoemaker, 'Male honour and the decline of public violence in eighteenth century

London', *Social History*, 26 (2), 2001, 200–6. There was also a decline in the habit among gentlemen of carrying a sword. Duelling eventually disappeared in the 1840s.

28 T. Freedley, *A Practical Treatise on Business*, London, 1853, 56; Langford, *English-ness*, 126; Robert Greenhalgh, *Sixty Years of Local Records and Reminiscences*, Bolton, 1908, 23.

29 Anon, *Beeton's Complete Etiquette for Gentlemen*, London, 1876, 1; Prince Puckler-Muskau, *Tour in England*, vol. iii, London, 1832, 381; M. J. Curtin, 'Etiquette and society in Victorian England', University of California, DPhil thesis, 1981, 146–203; Anon., *Routledge's Manuel of Etiquette*, London, 1875, 1.

30 Y. C. Draznin, *Victorian London's Middle Class Housewife. What She Did All Day*, London: Greenwood, 2001, 153; Lewis, *Labour*, 38. In the early nineteenth century, the religious boycotted balls, in the belief that dancing, and, in particular the waltz (which required dancers to hold each other), encouraged immorality (Davidoff and Hall, *Family*, 436). To further ensure high value networking, many middle-class associations were patrolled by stewards, who were usually members of the elite and acted as gatekeepers, deciding who was to be admitted to the get-together and who gained access to inner circles.

31 Nenadic, 'Middle', 148; J. Cleland, *Statistical Facts of Glasgow*, vol. ii, Glasgow, 1837, 38–9.

32 Parkes, *Domestic*, 48–50, 52, 53; Morgan, *Manners*, 102; Bates, *A Discourse*, 111; *The Illustrated* quoted in Arnstein, 'A German', 199.

33 N. B. Ferris, 'An American Diplomatist Confronts Victorian Society', *History Today*, 15 (8), 1965, 558.

34 Davidoff and Hall, *Family*, 437; J. Tosh, *A Man's Place. Masculinity and the Middle Class Home in Victorian England*, New Haven: Yale University Press, 1999, 124; N. Auerbach, *Private Theatricals. The Lives of the Victorians*, Cambridge: Cambridge University Press, 1990, 114.

35 *Frasier's Magazine*, February 1859, 252 and H. Irving, *All the Year Round*, 22 April 1876, quoted in S. Phillips, 'Rational entertainment, music hall and the nineteenth century British periodical press', *Theatre Studies*, 22, 2002, 199, 200; M. Vicinus, 'Helpful and unfriended. Nineteenth century domestic melodrama', *New Literary History*, 13 (1), 1981, 139; R. Peel, Parliamentary debates, 1832, 14.645 quoted in S. H. Hurtado, 'The promotion of the visual arts in Britain, 1835–1860', *Canadian Journal of History*, 28 (1), 1993, 60; Viscount Palmerston, 1856, quoted in G. P. Nuding, 'Portraits for the nation', *History Today*, 39, June 1989, 31; H. Cole quoted in S. Tait, *Palaces of Discovery. The Changing World of Britain's Museums*, London: Quiller, 1989, 9. Playbills usually advertised the morality of plays, and, to increase their trust reputations, individuals and voluntary associations often sponsored such dramas (R. Poole, 'Popular leisure and the music hall in nineteenth century Bolton', *Centre for North West Regional Studies, University of Lancaster, Occasional Paper*, 12, 1982, 46). To reap the trust benefits for their workers, some industrialists dis-played their art collections in mills and mechanics institutes (Hurtado, 'The promo-tion', 75).

36 S. Gunn, *The Public Culture of the Victorian Middle Class Ritual and Authority and the English Industrial City, 1840–1914*, Manchester: Manchester University Press, 2000, 136–7, 145. Until 1896, galleries and museums were closed on Sundays, which was the only day most workers were available to make visits.

37 J. K. Walton, *Lancashire. A Social History, 1558–1939*, Manchester: Manchester University Press, 1987, 235; P. Taylor, 'A divided middle class', *Manchester Region History Review*, 6, 1992, 4; J. Smith, 'Urban elites 1830–1930 and urban history', *Urban History*, 27 (2), 2000, 259, 267; M. J. Daunton, 'Public place and private space' in D. Fraser and A. Sutcliffe (eds), *The Pursuit of Urban History*, London: Edward Arnold, 1983, 217.

38 Lamb, *Free*, vol. ii, 257; A. Young, 'Virtue domesticated. Dickens and the lower

middle class', *Victorian Studies*, 39 (4), 1996, 484–91; R. A. Soloway, 'Reform or ruin. English moral thought during the first French republic', *Review of Politics*, 25 (1), 1963, 110–28; J. Garrard, 'Urban elites, 1850–1914. The rule and decline of a new squirearchy', *Albion*, 27 (3), 1995, 595–9. Public protest led by groups, such as the 1787 Society for the Reformation of Manners, evangelicals, Anglican churchmen and Utilitarians prompted the aristocracy in the first half of the century to behave in a more restrained manner or, at least, to practice their vices in secret.

39 B. Doyle, 'The structure of elite power in the early twentieth century city', *Urban History*, 24, 1997, 179–99; M. Savage, 'Urban history and social class', *Urban History*, 20, 1993, 61–77; Garrard, 'Urban', 598; M. L. Bush, *The English Aristocracy*, Manchester: Manchester University Press, 1984, 77; R. J. Morris, *Class, Sect and Party. The Making of the British Middle Class,* Manchester: Manchester University Press, 1990; J. Barry, 'Bourgeois collectivism? Urban association and the middling sort', in J. Barry and C. Brooks (eds), *The Middling Sort of People. Culture, Society and Politics in England, 1550–1800*, Basingstoke: Macmillan, 1994. Rubinstein's insistence that few businessmen bought estates has been challenged by Eileen Spring (W. D. Rubinstein, 'Businessmen into landowners. The question revisited' in N. Harte and R. Quinault (eds), *Land and Society in Britain, 1700–1914*, Manchester: Manchester University Press, 1996; E. Spring, 'Businessmen and landowners re-engaged', *Historical Research*, 72 (177), 1999, 77–91).

2 Working-class and inter-class trust

1 J. Davis, 'Jennings buildings and the Royal borough', in D. Feldman and G. Stedman Jones (eds), *Metropolis. London Histories and Representations since 1800,* London: Routledge, 1989, 21, 30; S. Cordery, 'Friendly societies and the discourse of respectability in Britain, 1825–1875', *Journal of British Studies*, 34 (1), 1995, 38; C. Lis and H. Soly, 'Neighbourhood social change in west European cities', *International Review of Social History*, 38, 1993, 16, 23.

2 P. Bailey, 'Will the real Bill Banks please stand up. Towards a role analysis of mid-Victorian working class respectability', *Journal of Social History*, 12 (3), 1979, 338; E. Ross, '"Not the sort that would sit on the doorstep." Respectability in pre-World War One London neighbourhoods', *International Labour and Working Class History*, 27, 1985, 51–2.

3 P. Johnson, 'Conspicuous consumption and working class culture in late Victorian and Edwardian Britain', *Transactions of the Royal Historical Society*, 38, 1988, 35–9; J. B. Lamb, 'Turning the inside out. Morals, modes of living and the condition of the working class', *Victorian Literature and Culture*, 1997, 40–6; E. Chadwick, *Report on the Sanitary Condition of the Labouring Population of Great Britain*, Edinburgh: Edinburgh University Press, 1965 (originally published 1842), 323; 'The manufacturing poor', *Fraser's Magazine*, 37, 1848, 3; *Occasional Papers of the Working Men's Club and Institute Union*, no. 20, January 1872. Virtuous dress both signalled and promoted morality. The cost of finery could result in debt and moral hazard, and, for women, decorative clothes could lead to trust endangering sexual degeneracy.

4 Kirk, *The Growth*, 189, 220–1, 222; G. Crossick, 'The labour aristocracy and its values. A study in mid-Victorian Kentish London', *Victorian Studies*, 19 (3), 1976, 303; B. Bramwell, 'Public space and local communities', in G. Kearns and C. W. J. Whithers (eds), *Urbanizing Britain. Essays on Class and Community in the Nineteenth Century*, Cambridge: Cambridge University Press, 1991, 39–40, 54; Bailey, 'Will'.

5 R. M. Feldman, 'Settlement identity. Psychological bonds with home places in a mobile society', *Environment and Behaviour*, 22, 1990, 188; C. Tilly, 'Citizenship, identity and social history', *International Review of Social History*, 40, 1995, supplement 3, 5; R. Parkinson, *On the Present Condition of the Labouring Poor*, London,

1841, 10–11. The middle class, having less need of such gifts, possessed weaker neighbourhood links.

6 King and Tomkins, *The Poor*, 265; E. Ross, 'Survival networks. Women's neighbourhood sharing in London', *History Workshop*, 15, 1985, 14.

7 Ross, 'Survival', 14; S. D'Cruze, 'Women and the family', in J. Purvis (ed.), *Women's History. Britain 1850–1945*, London, 2002, 64; Lamb, *Free*, vol. i, 18; Lis and Soly, 'Neighbourhood', 21; A. J. Hammerton, 'The targets of "rough music." Respectability and domestic violence in Victorian England', *Gender and History*, 3 (1), 1991, 25–6; M. Tebbutt, *Women's Talk? A Social History of 'Gossip' in Working Class Neighbourhoods, 1880–1960*, Aldershot: Scolar, 1995, 176, 178, 183; C. M. Parratt, *'More than Mere Amusement' Working Class Women's Leisure in England, 1750–1914*, Boston: Northeastern University Press, 2001, 139. Where neighbourhood trust was low, the cost of sanction delivery will have been relatively high (Szreter, 'The state', 577). Nevertheless, most communities possessed individuals who were more than willing to engage in the punishment of others, gaining a high psychological return from their actions.

8 J. Winter, 'Widowed mothers and mutual aid in early Victorian Britain', *Journal of Social History*, 17 (1), 1983, 115–25.

9 Anderson, *Family*, 41–2; J. M. Field, 'From Salt Pie Yard to Ridgway Gates. The development of a Bolton slum', Manchester Metropolitan University, MA thesis, 1997, 45–60; D. Garrioch, *Neighbourhood and Community in Paris, 1740–1790*, Cambridge: Cambridge University Press, 1986, 227–8.

10 Ross, '"Not the"', 51–2.

11 Lis and Soly, 'Neighbourhood', 10; Daunton, 'Public', 214–26.

12 Lis and Soly, 'Neighbourhood', 27–8.

13 Poole, 'Popular', 6, 24.

14 H. Voth, *Time and Work in England, 1750–1830*, Oxford: Clarendon, 2000, 120, 175; A. Worthington, 'The people's institution or an instrument for middle class hegemony? A case study of the Bolton and district Sunday school movement, 1780–1850', Manchester Polytechnic, MA thesis, 1992, 7; L. Faucher, *Manchester in 1844*, London, 1844, 55; *Bolton Chronicle*, 22 June 1850. Strangers in a neighbourhood were often verbally or physically abused.

15 H. Spencer, *The Principles of Ethics*, vol. i, London, 1892–6, 530; H. A. Boardman, *The Bible in the Counting House*, London, 1854, 240; Searle, *Morality*, 238; R. McGowen, 'Civilizing punishment. The end of the public execution in England', *Journal of British Studies*, 33 (3), 1994, 261. The 1802 Vice Society, which theoretically sought to restrict blasphemy and obscenity, additionally targeted radicals and radical texts (H. Rimke and A. Hunt, 'From sinners to degenerates. The medicalisation of morality in the nineteenth century', *History of the Human Sciences*, 15 (1), 2002, 67–8).

16 P. N. Dale, *Many Mansions. The Growth of Religion in Bolton, 1750–1850*, Bolton: Dale, 1985, 81, 83, 87; J. Black, *A Medico-topographical, Geological and Statistical Sketch of Bolton and its Neighbourhood*, Bolton, 1836, 52–3; T. Tholfsen, *Working Class Radicalism in Mid-Victorian England*, London: Croom Helm, 1976, 68–72; Harrison, 'Religion', 98–125; Parratt, *'More'*, 58–9.

17 Rimke and Hunt, 'From', 63, 70–8; J. C. Pritchard, *A Treatise on Insanity*, London, 1835, 6.

18 *Transactions of the National Association for the Promotion of Social Science*, 1858, 64 quoted in M. S. Gaskell, 'Gardens for the working class', *Victorian Studies*, 23 (4), 1980, 488; *The Gooseberry Growers' Register*, Manchester, 1843, 30.

19 *Bolton Chronicle*, 21 September 1833; ibid., 22 July 1850; ibid., 12 October 1850.

20 J. K. Walton, *Lancashire. A Social History, 1558–1939*, Manchester: Manchester University Press, 1987, 295.

21 Harrison, 'Religion', 112, 109; *Bolton Chronicle*, May 1827.

22 Parratt, *'More'*, 110–11.
23 M. W. Steinberg, *Fighting Words. Working Class Formation, Collective Action and Discourse in Nineteenth Century England*, London: Cornell University Press, 1999, 154; A. Walker, 'Feasting in a South Yorkshire colliery district, 1860–1900', *Family and Community History*, 4 (1), 2001, 15; Poole, *Popular*, 12; R. B. Shoemaker, *Gender in English Society, 1650–1850*, London: Longman, 1998, 276.
24 Parratt, *'More'*, 124, 126; Baptist Minister quoted in Poole, *Popular*, 56; *Bolton Chronicle*, 22 October 1842. To limit prostitution, the better halls barred unaccompanied women, though others would allow them to enter if they were respectably dressed (Parratt, *'More'*, 124).
25 T. Wright, *Our New Masters*, New York: Garland, 1984 (originally published 1873), 100; T. Wright, *Some Habits and Customs of the Working Classes*, London, 1867, 101, 104; *The Poor Man's Advocate*, 21 January 1831.
26 Wright, *Some*, 87–8, 102, 104; W. Marcroft, *Ups and Downs. Life in a Machine Making Works*, Oldham, 1889, 10.
27 Marcroft, *Ups*, 5.
28 Wright, *Our*, 5, 6, 12, 15. See also P. Thompson, *The Edwardians. The Remaking of British Society*, London: Weidenfeld and Nicolson, 1975, 132.
29 F. W. Peoples, *History of the Great and Little Bolton Co-operative Society*, Bolton, 1909, 29; M. Gorsky, 'Mutual aid and civil society. Friendly societies in nineteenth century Bristol', *Urban History*, 25, (3), 1998, 307–8, 310; P. Bailey, *Leisure and Class in Victorian England*, London: Routledge, 1978, 10; M. Gorsky, 'The growth and distribution of English friendly societies in the early nineteenth century', *Economic History Review*, 51 (3), 1998, 499–500, 507. See also P. H. Gosden, *The Friendly Societies of England, 1815–75*, Manchester: Manchester University Press, 1961.
30 *Laws for the Government of the Independent Order of Oddfellows*, Manchester, 1841, rule 1; Cordery, 'Friendly', 42–50.
31 S. d'Cruze and J. Turnbull, 'Fellowship and family. Oddfellows lodges in Preston and Lancaster, *c.*1830–*c.*1890', *Urban History*, 22 (1), 1995, 28, 43; Gorsky, 'Mutual', 316.
32 D. Lord, ' "Weighed in the balance and found wanting." Female friendly societies, self-help and economic virtue in the East Midlands in the eighteenth and nineteenth centuries', *Midland History*, 22, 1997, 101, 103; Gorsky, 'Mutual', 316.
33 Holden, *Respectable*, 42, ref. 43, 64; P. Taylor, 'The new paternalism and labour capital relations in the Bolton cotton industry 1848–77', Manchester Polytechnic, BA thesis, 1986, 44.
34 W. Thompson, *Report Adopted at a General Meeting . . .*, London, 1828 quoted in J. A. Jaffe, 'Commerce, character and civil society. Critiques of capitalism during the early industrial period', *The European Legacy*, 6 (2), 2001, 259, 256.
35 G. Perusek, 'The internal politics of trade unions. The neglected view of Sidney and Beatrice Webb', *Labour Studies Journal*, 18 (1), 1993, 32–42; S. O. Rose, 'Respectable men, disorderly others. The language of gender and the Lancashire weavers strike of 1878', *Gender and History*, 5 (3), 1993, 382–97; S. Webb and B. Webb, *The History of Trade Unionism*, London: Longman, 1920 (originally published 1894), 340–1.
36 M. I. Thomis, *The Town Labourer and the Industrial Revolution*, London: Batsford, 1974, chapter 10; Joyce, *Work*; M. Taylor, 'Rethinking the Chartists. Searching for synthesis in the historiography of Chartism', *The Historical Journal*, 39 (2), 1996, 487; D. Thompson, 'The language of class', *Society for the Study of Labour History Bulletin*, 52, 1987, 54–7; G. Stedman Jones, *Languages of Class. Studies in Working Class History, 1832–1982*, Cambridge, 1983, chapter 3. See also Neville Kirk, 'In defence of class: A critique of recent revisionist writing upon the nineteenth century English working class', *International Review of Social History*, 32, 1987, 2–47.

37 W. H. Fraser, 'Owenism in Scotland', *Scottish Economic and Social History*, 16, 1996, 60; M. Hewitt, *The Emergence of Stability in the Industrial City. Manchester, 1832–67*, Aldershot: Scolar, 1996, 208; B. Taylor, *Eve and the New Jerusalem. Socialism and Feminism in the Nineteenth Century*, London: Virago, 1983, xiii; *New Moral World*, 30 July, 1844 quoted in Tholfsen, 'The intellectual', 77.

38 J. P. Kay, *The Moral and Physical Condition of the Working Classes Employed in the Cotton Manufacture in Manchester*, London, 1832, 49; Bates, *A Discourse*, 65; D. Philipps, 'Crime, law and punishment in the industrial revolution', in P. K. O'Brien and R. Quinault (eds), *The Industrial Revolution and British Society*, Cambridge: Cambridge University Press, 1993, 157, 161; A. D. Gilbert, *Religion and Society in Industrial England*, London: Longman, 1976, 77; E. Gauldie, *Cruel Habitations. A History of Working Class Housing, 1780–1918*, London: Allen & Unwin, 1974, chapter 1.

39 The existence of the discontinuity has been primarily rejected by Musson (A. E. Musson, 'Class struggle and the labour aristocracy, 1830–60', *Social History*, 3 (2), 1976, 2). P. Taylor, *Popular Politics in Early Industrial Britain*, Staffordshire: Ryburn, 1995, 11; Kirk, *The Growth*, 3, chapter 5; E. J. Hobsbawm, 'The labour aristocracy. Twenty five years after', *Society for the Study of Labour History Bulletin*, 40, 1980; J. Foster, *Class Struggle and the Industrial Revolution. Early Industrial Capitalism in Three English Towns*, London: Weidenfeld & Nicolson, 1974, 206–38; G. Stedman Jones, 'Class struggle and the industrial revolution', *New Left Review*, 90, 1975; Joyce, *Work*, 51–2.

40 Joyce, *Work*, chapters 2–3; A. Russell, 'Local elites and the working class response in the North West, 1870–1895. Paternalism and deference reconsidered', *Northern History*, 23, 1987, 167; Kirk, *The Growth*; H. I. Dutton and J. E. King, 'The limits of paternalism. The cotton tyrants of North Lancashire, 1836–54', *Social History*, 7, 1982, 59–74; L. H. Lees, 'Work society and politics', *Social History*, 8 (2), 1983, 242–4.

41 Jones, 'Class', 65–7; Kirk, *The Growth*, 12–13. Railways lessened the impact of cyclical crisis and stimulated coal, iron, steel and machinery production. Later, industry benefited from the capital cheapening effects of new technology, cheap coal and food, and increasing foreign profits. Craft and Harley's index of industrial production rises from 5.07 in 1800 to 21.2 in 1850 to 44.2 in 1875, and 76.4 in 1900 (N. F. R. Crafts and C. K. Harley, 'Output growth and the British industrial revolution. A restatement of the Crafts–Harley view', *Economic History Review*, 45 (4), 1992, 726–7).

42 Taylor, *Popular*, 48, 107–19, 218; Jones, *Languages*, chapter 3; J. Garrard, *Democratization in Britain. Elites, Civil Society and Reform since 1800*, Basingstoke: Palgrave, 2002, 53; Anne Digby, *The Poor Law in Nineteenth Century England and Wales*, London: Historical Association, 1982, 19.

43 *Monthly Repository*, 6, 1832, 1888 quoted in McGowen, 'A powerful'. 321; C. D. Kaufmann and R. A. Pape, 'Explaining costly international moral action', *International Organization*, 53 (4), 1999, 647–8.

3 Formal networks

1 J. Stephen (ed.), *Essays in Ecclesiastical Biography*, vol. ii, London, 1907, 248; *Bolton Chronicle*, 9 October 1861; R. J. Morris, 'Voluntary societies and British urban elites, 1780–1850' in P. Borsay (ed.), *The Eighteenth Century Town. A Reader in English Urban History, 1688–1820*, London: Longman, 1990, 338; Davidoff and Hall, *Family*, 1. It seems likely that the Bolton newspaper figures grossly underestimate the actual number of groups.

2 Morris, 'Voluntary', 341; R. J. Morris, 'Civil society and the nature of urbanism', *Urban History*, 25 (3), 1998, 294; Clark, *British*, 166, 171.

3 J. Taylor, *Autobiography of a Lancashire Lawyer*, Bolton, 1883, 124.

4 Bolton Archive, FZ 30/1; *Bolton Chronicle*, 26 November 1831.

5 G. L. Anderson, 'Victorian clerks and voluntary associations in Liverpool and Manchester', *Northern History*, 12, 1976, 203.

6 Anon., *Business*, 5; Anon., *The Young*, 168.

7 A. E. Watkin (ed.), *Absalom Watkin. Extracts from his Journal, 1814–1856*, London: T. F. Unwin, 1920, 130–1.

8 B. H. Burbidge Hambly, *Competition or Co-operation*, London, 1874, 16; Bolton Archive, ZHE 9/20.

9 Anon., *The Young*, 163; PP 1852–3, xxii.1 q. 390; E. Shepherd, *A Series of Lay Sermons*, London, 1834, 77; W. E. Channing, *Self Culture*, London, 1838, 13.

10 J. Wild, *An Essay on Co-operation*, London, 1862, 7; R. Benabou and J. Tirole, 'Self-confidence and interpersonal strategies', *Centre for Economic Policy Research, London, Discussion Paper*, no. 2580, 2000, 19–22. The self-esteem gains will have especially benefited women, who appear to have had little self-confidence. Any self-esteem they possessed derived from their husbands or fathers and was partly related to their physical appearance, which deteriorated as they aged.

11 K. Waddington, 'Subscribing to a democracy. Management and the voluntary ideology of the London hospitals, 1850–1900', *English Historical Review*, 118 (476), 2003, 375; Hazlitt, *Table*, vol. i, 309.

12 G. W. Wood, *A Proposal for Establishing in Manchester an Institution for the Fine Arts*, Manchester, 1823; Richard Rodger, 'The "common good" and civic promotion. Edinburgh 1860–1914', in R. Colls and R. Rodger, *Cities of Ideas. Civil Society and Urban Governance in Britain, 1800–2000*, London: Ashgate, 2004, 10.

13 C. E. Harrison, *The Bourgeois Citizen in Nineteenth Century France*, Oxford: Oxford University Press, 1999, 222. The members of the 1885 Bolton Walt Whitman Fellowship, for example, developed an intense interest in the homo-erotic aspects of Whitman's poetry and in sexual inversion in general, and formed passionate friendships. On meeting a new recruit, Dr John Johnston, a local GP and a founder of the society, recorded in his diary 'I felt a curious and irresistible attraction for this gentle mannered beautiful–souled man, who seemed dowered with the grace of a women and yet was possessed with the masculinity of a young man' (BA, ZJO/1, Johnston Diaries, 28, 21 July 1894; H. Cocks, 'Calamus in Bolton. Spirituality and homosexual desire in late Victorian England', *Gender and History*, 13 (2), 2001, 191–223).

14 Olson has argued that entrenched special interest groups accelerated Britain's post-war economic decline, distorting public policy and causing planning deadlock (M. Olson, *The Rise and Decline of Nations*, New Haven: Yale University Press, 1986).

15 Hazlitt, *Table*, vol. i., 242.

16 Anon., *Rules and Regulations of the Bolton District Widow and Orphans Fund*, Bolton, 1843; Clark, *British*, 195; BA, FP 1.2; G. P. Brockbank, *St John's Lodge 221*, Bolton, 1880, 16; Taylor, *Autobiography*, 123; Bolton Archive, ZHE 9/20; R. W. Moffrey, *A Century of Oddfellows*, Manchester, 1910, 22, 28, 39; C. Smith, *Centenary History of the Ancient Noble Order of United Oddfellows*, Manchester, 1932, 11.

17 Brockbank, *St John's*, 15; Clark, *British*, 223; N. McKendrick, J. Brewer and J. H. Plumb, *The Birth of a Consumer Society. The Commercialisation of Eighteenth Century England*, London: Europa, 1982, 222.

18 Smith, *Centenary*, 12; Clark, *British*, 163, 227, 268. A Popular Oddfellows hymn was 'Friendship, Love and Trust'. Another Oddfellow song included the line 'the bonds of society, friendship and unity, honour and secrecy doth us unite' (Smith, *Centenary*, 23).

19 McKendrick *et al.*, *The Birth*, 222–3; Clark, *British*, 225.

20 D. B. Reeves and R. Bylund, 'Social density and public ritual in non-industrialized communities', *Sociological Quarterly*, 30 (2), 1989, 227. The level, the compass, the plumb line and the pillars of the temple were evocative of 'solidarity, rectitude,

directness and good craftsmanship', all of which were representative of masculinity (Davidoff and Hall, *Family*, 426).

21 Secord, 'Science in the pub. Artisan botanists in early nineteenth century Lancashire', *History of Science*, 32 (3), 1994, 284.

22 Those groups that required facilities for shared use required a relatively large number of members in order to spread the cost of the amenities.

23 Casson, 'An economic', 31.

24 Anon., *Rules and Regulations of the Union Library*, Bolton, 1817; Anon., *Rules of the Society for the Prosecution of Felons, 1836*, Bolton, 1836; Anon., *Bolton Billiard Club, Rules, 1847*, Bolton, 1847.

25 Morris, 'Civil', 299; Brockbank, *St John's*, 15; Anon., *Byelaws and Regulations of the Provincial Grand Lodge of East Lancashire*, Bolton, 1872, rule 49; Clark, *British*, 218, 224.

26 P. Clark, *The English Alehouse. A Social History, 1200–1830*, London: Longman, 1983, 319; Anderson, 'Victorian', 203; Bolton Archive, E. Greenhalgh, 'Scrapbook of News Cuttings', unknown date; Anon., *Bolton from the Foresters Miscellany 1866*, Bolton, 1866.

27 A. Tyrrell, 'Woman's mission and pressure group politics in Britain, 1825–60', *Bulletin of the John Rylands University Library*, 63, 1980–1, 194–230; A. Digby, 'Victorian values and women in public and private', *Proceedings of the British Academy*, 78, 1992, 199, 200. During the Napoleonic war, women were additionally heavily involved in patriotic groups, which collected money and clothing for soldiers (L. Colley, *Britons. Forging the Nation, 1707–1837*, Yale: Yale University Press, 1992, 281). Women took a particular interest in the organisation of public bazaars, their involvement distancing such fund-raising events from the perceived immorality of the masculine business world.

28 Shoemaker, *Gender*, 245; Clark, *British*, 200.

29 Digby, 'Victorian', 199; Shoemaker, *Gender*, 244; Clark, *British*, 202; Gunn, *The Public*, 65; P. Hudson, 'Women and industrialization' in Purvis, *Women's*, 38; M. Poovey, *Uneven Developments. The Ideological Work of Gender in Mid-Victorian England*, Chicago: University of Chicago, 1988, 37, 46; Parkes, *Domestic*, 415; R. Southey, *Letters from England*, London, 1814, vol. ii, 47; T. Laqueur, *Making Sex: Body and Gender from the Greeks to Freud*, Cambridge: Cambridge University Press, 1990; Tosh, 'Masculinities in an industrializing society. Britain 1800–1914', *Journal of British Studies*, 44 (2), 2005, 330–43. Women, for instance, could not sign documents in their own right or be held responsible for financial accounts.

30 Defoe, *The Complete*, 66; B. Braidley, *Memoir of Benjamin Braidley*, Manchester, 1845, 39–40; T. L. Rushton, *Memoirs of Thomas Lever Rushton*, Bolton, 1885, 25. Belonging to a number of networks also increased the chances of obtaining accurate reputational information. In dense networks, when passing on gossip about a common acquaintance, people are relatively less likely to offer the unvarnished truth. They may fear that their interlocutor may divulge to the acquaintance the provision of the gossip and thus damage the relationship between the gossip spreader and his victim. On the other hand, if the relationship between the interlocutor and the acquaintance is strong, by spreading negative information, the gossip spreader may hurt his relationship with his interlocutor (James G. Rauch and Alessandra Casella, *Networks and Markets*, New York: Russell Sage, 2001, 559–600).

There is a possibility that entrance to sectors in which information was valuable and members required good networking skills was self-selective; new entrants were those who possessed high levels of social capital. If sociability skills are inherited, either genetically or through the child socialisation process, this mechanism may also partly explain the tendency for sons to enter their fathers' occupations.

31 J. F. Wilson and J. Singleton, 'The Manchester industrial district, 1750–1939' in Wilson and Popp, *Industrial*, 52; D. O'Connor, *Barrow Bridge. A Victorian Model of*

Achievement, Bolton: O'Connor, 1972, 6; P. W. Pelling, 'Hick Hargeaves and Co. The history of an engineering firm', University of Liverpool, PhD thesis, 1985, 83; Casson, 'An economic', 33, 35, 41. The best entrepreneurs were attracted to cities by the relatively large profit opportunities they offered.

32 Anon., *Bolton Ladies Auxiliary Society in Aid of Promoting Christianity, fifth report 1817,* Bolton, 1817; Anon., *Bolton Clothing Charity, 1816–17 Report,* Bolton, 1817; T. H. Winder, *A Life's Adventure,* London, 1921, 19; Anon., *Rules.* Votes were often gifts intended to improve the trust relationship between the voter and the recipient of his vote.

33 E. A. Farnie, 'An index of commercial activity. The membership of the Manchester Royal Exchange, 1809–1948', *Business History,* 21, 1979, 97–106; Secord, 'Science'.

34 Bolton Archive, FZ 18/2/20; Secord, 'Science', 279.

4 Philanthropic, religious and education networks

1 For example, in 1800, Bolton had 52 registered charity trusts, Oldham ten, Blackburn 29 and Preston 37. In 1824/8, Bolton's charity trusts had a gross income of £2,141, Oldham's had an income of £145, Blackburn's an income of £212 and Preston's one of £717 (Anon., *Return Comprising the Reports Made by the Charity Commissioners . . . 1818–37, Volume iv,* February 1910).

2 P. Shapely, *Charity and Power in Victorian Manchester,* Manchester: Manchester University Press, 2000, 66. To ensure exclusiveness, new committee members were often required to make a substantial contribution to the coffers of the society they were to manage (R. Trainer, 'Urban elites in Victorian Britain', *Urban History Yearbook,* 1985, 3).

3 P. C. Parker, 'Fictional philanthropy in Elizabeth Gaskell's *Mary Barton* and *North and South*', *Victorian Literature and Culture,* 25, 1997, 323.

4 A less material reciprocal gift was the expression by recipients of the 'pleasure of being gratefully loved' (Sarah Scott, *Millennium Hall,* New York: Bookman Associates, 1955 (originally published in 1762), 530).

5 P. Shapely, 'Charity status and parliamentary candidates in Manchester. A consideration of electoral and charity fields and the social basis of power, 1832–1910', *International Review of Social History,* 44, 1999, 13; Freedley, *A Practical,* 223. The names of charity donors were published in local newspapers and in annual reports. Subscriber names were published alphabetically rather than by size of contribution, strengthening the association between the poorer and wealthier subscribers. Women took particular care in the choice of charities they publicly supported. Those who subscribed to foundling hospitals, for example, often did so anonymously afraid that public association with an organisation connected with sexual immorality would damage their trust reputations.

6 I. Bradley, *The Call to Seriousness. The Evangelical Impact on the Victorians,* London: Cape, 1976, 119; P. Halfpenny, 'Trust, charity and civil society', in F. Tonkiss, A. Passey, N. Fenton and L. C. Hems, *Trust and Civil Society,* Basingstoke: Macmillan, 2000, 143.

7 M. Baker and M. Collins, 'The governance of charitable trusts in the nineteenth century. The West Riding of Yorkshire', *Social History,* 27 (2), 2002, 164–7.

8 Thorp, 'One phase of the recent distress', in Odds and Ends, Manchester, 1886, 120; P. Shapely, 'Urban charity, class relations and social cohesion. Charitable responses to the cotton famine', Urban History, 28 (1), 2001, 61. Some also believed that the example of charity would encourage recipients and others to adopt a philosophy of 'moderation, benevolence and kindness' (C. Cappe, Observation on Charity Schools, York, 1805, 96, 111). It was thus important that philanthropy be visible.

9 Bates, *A Discourse,* 133–4, 135; J. S. Mill, *The Subjection of Women,* Bristol: Thoemmes Press, 1980 (originally published 1869), 88–9; M. Hennell, *An Outline of*

the Various Social Systems and Communities which have been Founded, London, 1844, 28; from the 1836 founding meeting of the Liverpool Mission, quoted in J. Seed, 'Unitarianism, political economy and the antinomies of liberal culture in Manchester, 1830–50', *Social History*, 7, 1982, 14.

10 J. Carre, *The Crisis of Courtesy. Studies in the Conduct Book in Britain, 1600–1900*, Leiden: Brill, 1994, 157; Anon., *The Duty of Workhouse Visitation and How To Do It*, London, 1857, 1; E. Fry, *Observations on the Visiting, Superintending and Government of Female Prisoners*, London, 1827, 21–2; S. Trimmer, *The Economy of Charity*, London, 1787, 40; Perrot, *Fashioning*, 94. Many believed that 'the art of giving so as to render gifts readily acceptable … [continued to be] but little understood and … seldom thought of' (Anon., *Hints for Improving the Condition of the Poorer Classes*, London 1838, 19).

11 Shapely, 'Urban', 53; R. Cobden MP, *Speech on the Cotton Famine*, 29 April 1862, Manchester, 1862; Lamb, *Free*, vol. ii, 296; J. Garrard, *Leadership and Power in Victorian Industrial Towns, 1830–80*, Manchester: Manchester University Press, 1983, 50.

12 Garrard, 'Urban', 603; Shapely, 'Charity', 15; Trainer, 'Urban', 3, 5.

13 M. R. Watts, *The Dissenters. Vol. ii, The Expansion of Evangelical Non-Conformity*, Oxford: Clarendon, 1995, 629. Believers' relationship with the Lord was founded on the reciprocal exchange of gifts. In return for observation of a particular religion's norms, followers expected the eventual reward of eternal salvation. Belief in a higher being and prayer also made the world appear a more stable and safer place and thus reduced the psychic costs that arose from insecurity.

14 Bolton Archive, NP 1/6/1; Bolton and District Family History Society, *Christenings at St John's Church, 1849–54*, Bolton, 1983; Bolton and District Family History Society, *Index of Christenings. Walmsley Old Chapel, 1789–1840*, Bolton, 1983.

15 Bolton Archive, NMWB 1/7/1; Lancashire Record Office, frm16/14, frp/16/14; G. R. Searle, *Morality and the Market in Victorian Britain*, Oxford: Clarendon, 1998, 259, 260.

16 H. O. Fielding, *James Slade*, Bolton, 1853, 17, 30, 32; Barton, *Historical*, vol. ii; F. Baker, *The Rise and Progress of Nonconformity in Bolton*, London, 1854, 59, 63.

17 Fielding, *James*, 1, 3, 4, 15; Gunn, 'The ministry', 27; *Bolton Chronicle*, 3 March 1832; P. N. Dale, *Many Mansions. The Growth of Religion in Bolton, 1750–1850*, Bolton: Dale, 1985, 5.

18 Gunn, 'The ministry', 25; H. M. Wach, 'A "still, small voice" from the pulpit. Religion and the creation of social morality in Manchester, 1820–1850', *Journal of Modern History*, 63 (3), 1991, 448.

19 Kirkland, *Dream*; R. Pearson and D. Richardson, 'Business networking in the Industrial Revolution', *Economic History Review*, 54 (4), 2001, 657–79; Gunn, *The Public*, 125; *The Bolton Literary Journal and Weekly Miscellany*, 28 August 1886; Bolton Archive, 'Internments in the Friends Burial Ground, Bolton'.

20 Dale, *Many*, 21; Pearson and Richardson, 'Business', 103; Gunn, *The Public*, 110. Of the parents of infants receiving baptism from 1800 to 1805 at the Bolton Presbyterian Unitarian church, Ainsworth, only 42 per cent lived in the district, the remainder coming from surrounding villages and towns. Over time, as worshippers moved residence, the geographic spread of the congregation members of such churches widened. From 1835 to 1840, only 28 per cent of those who attended this church lived in the area, and, from 1860 to 1865, a mere 7 per cent (W. Howarth, *Presbyterian Unitarian Chapel, Ainsworth, Lancashire. Baptism records*, Bolton, unknown date).

21 J. J. Taylor, *Christian Faith and Worship*, Manchester, 1839, 7–8. Christians were further encouraged to form trust relations with other members of society by the belief that they would face reunion in the life everlasting.

22 PP 1852–5, lxxxix, 94–7; Dale, *Many*, 4; *Bolton Evening News*, 5 December 1881; A. Crockett, 'Variations in churchgoing rates in England in 1851. Supply side deficiency

or demand led decline?', *Oxford Discussion Papers in Economic and Social History*, 36, 2000, 3, 5, 6.

23 Crockett, 'Variations', 3, 10, 15, 16; Gilbert, *Religion,* 129–30; A. D. Gilbert, *The Making of Post-Christian Britain*, London: Longman, 1980, 71, 86.

24 B. Deacon, 'Religion and community. Frameworks and issues', Family and Community History, 5 (1), 2002, 33–44. Sixty-eight per cent of the worshippers at Mawdsley Street Chapel, Bolton during the period 1808–53 were women, and, of those who attended the Moor Lane Baptist Chapel in 1847, 74 per cent were female (J. Johnston, Mawdsley Street Congregational Chapel, 1808–1909, London, 1908). Women could become Sunday school teachers, sit on various committees and, until the 1840s, in the primitive Methodist and Bible Christian churches, could preach.

25 Worthington, 'The people's', 13; W. J. Else, 'Industrialisation and the religious life of Bolton', Salford University, MPhil thesis, 1992, 32–4; Mark Smith, *Religion in Industrial Society, Oldham and Saddleworth, 1740–1865*, Oxford: Clarendon, 1994, 126–31; M. R. Watts, *The Dissenters. Vol. i. From the Reformation to the French Revolution*, Oxford: Clarendon, 1986, 741–2; M. Huberman, 'The economic origins of paternalism. Lancashire cotton spinning in the first half of the nineteenth century', *Social History*, 12, 1987, 184.

26 Dale, *Many*, 1985, 58, 16, 105; Gunn, 'The ministry', 22–36; Smith, *Religion*, 260; Faucher, *Manchester*, 54.

27 Bolton Archive, ZZ 257/4/1, NMWB 5/3/1, NC 10/13/2; Johnston, *Mawdsley*, 58, 120–1; Winder, *A Life's*, 72; J. A. Phillips, 'The social calculus. Deference and defiance in later Georgian England', *Albion*, 21 (3), 1989, 434. The boundary between Anglicanism and Wesleyan Methodism was particularly porous. The practice of attending two denominations gradually declined as the century progressed. Dissenting denominations were professionalised and developed a stronger identity, and, by the 1850s, most Anglican Bishops demanded 'double duty', attendance at both morning and evening services (Deacon, 'Religion', 38).

28 C. Kingsley, 'Yeast. A Problem', in C. Kingsley, Works, vol. ii, London, 1851, xxii; W. Hazlitt quoted in W. Houghton, The Victorian Frame of Mind, 1830–1870, New Haven: Yale University Press, 1957, 413; J. S. Mill, Autobiography, Oxford: Oxford University Press, 1924 (originally published 1873), 38.

29 *The Nonconformist*, 20 December 1848, 967; ibid., 27 December 1848, 991; C. Kingsley, 'Sermon 26', in C. Kingsley, *Works*, vol. 28, London, 1852, 293–4; Wach, 'A "still"', 447; A. J. Morris, *Religion and Business*, London, 1853, preface.

30 Dale, *Many*, 60; A. Clark, *The Struggle for the Breeches. Gender and the Making of the British Working Class*, London: Rivers Oram, 1995, 94. In some cases, the courage and independence of spirit demonstrated by secessionists may have strengthened their trust reputations.

31 Taylor, *Popular*, 59; *Bolton Chronicle*, 23 April 1853; J. Watts, 'On cooperation as an economic element in society', *Transactions of the Manchester Statistical Society*, session 1872–3, 47.

32 PP 1852–3, lxxxviii, part 2, 611–12; PP 1852–3, xc, 262–5. In 1851, 27 per cent of children under 15 years living in Bolton attended day schools and 60 per cent Sunday schools (ibid.).

33 P. Gaskell, *Artisans and Machinery*, London, 1836, 240; J. Tooley, 'Education in a voluntary city' in D. T. Beito, P. Gordon and A. Tabarrok (eds), *The Voluntary City. Choice, Community and Civil Society*, Ann Arbor: University of Michigan, 2002, 231; PP 1837–8, vii, 2–3, 120. The statistician Joseph Fletcher claimed that improvements in literacy correlated with falling crime figures (J. Fletcher, 'Moral and educational statistics of England and Wales', *Quarterly Journal of the Statistical Society of London*, 10, 1847, 193–233).

34 Freedley, *A Practical*, 86; J. Griffin, *Memories of the Past. Recollections of a Ministerial Life*, Bolton, 1883, 231. Modern research indicates that the educated tend to be

far more involved in community affairs and to have more trust relationships than the uneducated (C. Wetherall, 'Historical social networks', *International Review of Social History*, 43, 1998, supplement 6, 435).

35 One Stockport Sunday school comprised a room that could accommodate up to 3,000 pupils. Elaborate room layouts were devised to prevent children in one group making eye contact with those in another (T. A. Markus, 'Early nineteenth century school space and ideology', *Paedagogica Historica*, 32 (1), 1996, 30, 33). In the case of playgrounds, a teacher was (and is) always present to prevent the socialisation of bullying and other trust damaging behaviour.

36 Laqueur, *Religion*, 19; Bolton Archive, FZ 18/2/20, Inaugural address 1873, 14 and ZHE 42/49; PP 1849, xxii, 395, 23, 24; A. Ure, *The Philosophy of Manufactures*, London, 1835, 427.

37 Markus, 'Early', 30; R. J. Hind, 'Working people and Sunday schools. England 1780–1850', *Journal of Religious History*, 15 (2) (1988), 211; P. Dale, 'A study of the growth of churches in Bolton during the industrial revolution', University College of North Wales, PhD thesis, 1984, 105; *Christian Observer*, 31 (1831), 738 quoted in Hind, 'Working', 209. It was further hoped that Sunday school gifts would encourage attendance and that early experience of rational recreation would encourage pupils to adopt such morally enhancing pursuits later in life. Not everyone was convinced of the moral improvement offered by such schools. Joseph Fletcher believed that they taught few morals, concentrating on 'little more than the bare task work of teaching ... the mechanical arts of reading and spelling' (Fletcher, 'Moral', 199). Dale, 'A study', 105.

38 J. Pedersen, 'The Victorian public school', *History of Education Quarterly*, 19 (4), 1979, 467–71; A. Wells, *An Address ...*, London, 1845 quoted in T. L. Chandler, 'Games at Oxbridge and the public schools, 1830–80', *International Journal of the History of Sport*, 8 (2), 1991, 187. Sport equally acted as an escape valve for the players' violent and competitive tendencies, which would otherwise damage social harmony. In Lancashire, Harrow educated John and Robert Kay in 1871 established Turton football club and the sons of the mill owner Nathaniel Walsh, again Harrow alumni, formed Darwen FC (R. W. Lewis, 'The genesis of professional football. Bolton, Blackburn, Darwen. The centre of innovation, 1878–85', *International Journal of the History of Sport*, 4 (1), 1997, 26, 28)

39 Phillipps, *Language*, 44.

40 B. Price, 'Bolton Mechanics' Institution: economic, social, political and religious factors in its formation and development to 1868', University of Manchester, PhD thesis, 1978.

41 M. Watson, 'Mutual improvement societies in nineteenth century Lancashire', *Journal of Educational Administration and History*, 21 (2), 1989, 9–14.

42 *Bolton Chronicle*, 15 October 1853; PP 1854, xiv.33, q. 2402; M. Hewitt, 'Confronting the modern city. The Manchester free public library, 1850–80', *Urban History*, 27 (1), 2000, 65–73.

43 Watkin, *Absalom*, 34–7; Second, 'Science', 281.

44 Watkin, *Absalom*, 37, 39; *The Bolton Literary Journal and Weekly Miscellany*, 4 December 1830, 63; ibid., 5 February 1831, 133.

5 Informal networks and miscellaneous trust determinants

1 J. Stobart, 'Information, trust and reputation shaping a merchant elite in early 18th century England', *Scandinavian Journal of History*, 30 (3–4), 2005, 300–400.

2 Tosh, 'Gentlemanly', 463, 465; Laqueur, *Making*.

3 In Bolton, the ratio of tradesmen to intermediaries fell from 37:1 in 1828/9 to 22:1 in 1851 and 21:1 in 1869. Similar trends are found in Oldham, Burnley, Blackburn and Preston (Pigot and Co., *National Commercial Directory for 1828–9*, London, 1830;

Slater's Royal National Commercial Directory of Lancashire, 1852, London, 1853; *Slater's Royal National Commercial Directory of Lancashire, 1869*, London, 1870).

4 Faucher, *Manchester*, 52; Clark, *British*, 163; Lis and Soly, 'Neighbourhood', 17; Poole, 'Popular', 12; PP 1854, xiv.33, q. 2390; PP 1852–3, xxxvii.1, q. 6178, 6275.

5 R. Greenhalgh, *Sixty Years of Local Records and Reminiscences*, Bolton, 1908; Parratt, *More*, 120; J. Kneale, 'A problem of supervision. Moral geographies of the nineteenth century British public house', *Journal of Historical Geography*, 25 (3), 1999, 334.

6 W. H. Chaloner, 'John Galloway', *Transactions of the Lancashire and Cheshire Antiquarian Society*, 64, 1954, 116; Clark, *The English*, 315; McKendrick *et al.*, *The Birth*, 223. Some businessmen appear to have free rode on the trust reputations of particular innkeepers. In some sales advertisements, the name of the landlord rather than that of the inn is given.

7 Clark, *The English*, 280, 316–17. Employees who were paid on work premises often still had to enter pubs to change their wages into small coin.

8 Clark, *The English*, 221; Gorsky, 'Mutual', 311; Clark, *British*, 164; L. L. Shiman, *Crusade Against Drink in Victorian England*, Basingstoke: Macmillan, 1988, 32.

9 Clark, *The English*, 279, 308; M. Smith, 'Social usages of the public drinking house. Changing aspects of class and leisure', *British Journal of Sociology*, 34 (3), 1983, 367–9. To permit the police to monitor customers, from the 1830s the compartments that had previously been found in parlours and taprooms were removed, an innovation that encouraged greater interaction (Kneale, 'A problem', 337).

10 Clark, *The English*, 307.

11 Ibid., 308–9; Anon., *Organization*, 58; Faucher, *Manchester*, 27. The number of residents per pub in Bolton fell from 641 in 1828/9 to 376 in 1851 and to 234 in 1869. A similar trend was found in Oldham, Burnley, Blackburn and Preston (Pigot, *National ... 1828/9*; *Slater's ... 1853*; *Slater's ... 1869*).

12 F. Engels, *The Condition of the Working Class in England*, Oxford: Blackwell, 1969 (originally published 1845), 156–7; W. T., *Evils of Intemperance*, Bolton, 1850; *Bolton Chronicle*, 26 October 1833, 2; D. Holding, 'A profile of criminality in Victorian Bolton, 1839–70', Manchester Metropolitan University, MA thesis, 1996, 50, 53, 54; V. A. C. Gatrell and T. B. Hadden, 'Criminal statistics and their interpretation' in E. A. Wrigley (ed.), *Nineteenth Century Society*, Cambridge: Cambridge University Press, 1972, 370–1. In Bolton, the percentage of the population taken into custody for drunkenness fell from 0.91 per cent in 1841 to 0.73 per cent in 1871. A similar trend was seen in Blackburn, Oldham and Preston (PP 1852–3, lxxxi, 295; PP 1877, lxix. 291).

13 P. D. Glennie and N. J. Thrift, 'Consumers, identities and consumption spaces in early modern England', *Environment and Planning A*, 28, 1996, 35; 427, p. 386; J. Stobart, 'Shopping streets as social space. Leisure, consumerism and improvement in an eighteenth century town', *Urban History*, 25 (1), 1998, 13.

14 Phillipps, *Language*, 93, 95; Finn, 'Men's', 149; H. Berry, 'Polite consumption. Shopping in eighteenth century England', *Transactions of the Royal Historical Society*, 12, 2000, 386–9; P. Johnson, *Saving and Spending. The Working Class Economy in Britain, 1870–1939*, Oxford: Clarendon, 1985, 149.

15 A. Offer, *The Challenge of Affluence. Self-Control and Well-being in the United States and Britain Since 1950*, Oxford: Oxford University Press, 2006; J. G. Carrier, *Gifts and Commodities Exchange and Western Capitalism Since 1700*, London: Routledge, 1995, 11, 66; Berry, 'Polite', 387; M. A. Crawforth, 'Evidence from trade cards for the scientific instrument industry', *Annals of Science*, 42, 1985, 477. The greater time spent browsing, likewise, enabled shopkeepers to more effectively evaluate an unknown customer's creditworthiness.

16 P. J. Atkins, 'Sophistication detected or the adulteration of the milk supply,

1850–1914', *Social History*, 1991, 16 (3), 1991, 317–19; Searle, *Morality*, 91; A. H. Hassall, *Food and its Adulteration*, London, 1855, xxxv.

17 R. Church, 'Advertising consumer goods in nineteenth century Britain. Reinterpretations', *Economic History Review*, 53 (4), 2000, 632, 636; *Manchester Mercury*, 8 October 1782 quoted in N. Cox, *The Complete Tradesman. A Study of Retailing, 1550–1820*, Aldershot: Ashgate, 2000, 130. To distance themselves from duplicitous language, the honest adopted a minimalist approach, often including in their adverts only the product's and their own name and address.

18 Wild, *An Essay*, 7; Peoples, *History*, 30, 31, 35–6, 49, 72.

19 P. Borsay, '"All the town's a stage"', in P. Clark (ed.), *The Transformation of English Provincial Towns, 1600–1800*, London: Hutchinson, 1984, 230–7; Gunn, *The Public*, 164–78.

20 S. J. Morgan, 'Middle class women, civic virtue and identity. Leeds and the West Riding of Yorkshire c.1830–60', York University, DPhil thesis, 2000, 228–37; Borsay, 'All', 237–8. The wives and daughters of the elite, in turn, free rode on the trust generated by the ceremony and their segregation increased the networking value of their interaction.

21 Mrs P. Reeves, *Round About a Pound a Week*, London, 1913, 17–19; J. Ayers (ed.), *Paupers and Pig Killers. The Diary of William Holland. A Somerset Parson, 1799–1818*, Gloucester: Allan Sutton, 1984, 18; Finn, 'Men's', 147–8.

22 A study of Cheshire and South Lancashire probate records for the period 1701–60 found that a third of executors were members of the deceased nuclear family, 13 per cent were non-nuclear kin and 57 per cent were non-kin. Surprisingly, a quarter of executors lived, on average, over 25 miles from the residence of the deceased, which suggests that middle-class informal networks were spatially extensive (J. Stobart, 'Social and geographical contexts of property transmission in the eighteenth century' in J. Stobart and A. Owens, *Urban Fortunes. Property and Inheritance in the Town, 1700–1900*, Aldershot: Ashgate, 2000, 112, 114). If a family business was viable, executors could be depended upon to advertise the fact. Bequests to executors further ensured their honesty.

23 J. M. Smith, 'Philanthropic community in *Millennium Hall* and the York Ladies Committee', *The Eighteenth Century*, 36 (3), 1995, 269; K. D. M. Snell, 'Gravestones, belonging and local attachment in England, 1700–2000', *Past and Present*, 179, 2003, 101, 120. Legacies to non-family members also advertised the recipient's connection with the deceased, which, if the latter had possessed wealth, status or had been greatly trusted, would again strengthen the beneficiary's own reputation. To ensure that fellow mourners did not assume that the deceased aided the disrespectable poor, the charity mourners often received a set of funeral clothes.

24 Freitag, 'Beyond', 226; Smith, 'Factors', 170–96; Wetherall, 'Historical', 438. In Bolton, in 1851, 20 per cent of the population was between the ages of 15 and 25 years, and, in 1871, 19 per cent; 28 per cent in 1851 were bachelors and spinsters, and, in 1871, 9.7 per cent; and 25 per cent in 1851 were widows and widowers, and, in 1871, 9.9 per cent (PP 1852–3, lxxxviii, part 2, 611–12; PP 1873, lxxi, part 1, 407–8; PP 1852–3, lxxxviii, part 2, 621; PP 1873, lxxi, part 1, 416–17). The Bolton gentry comprised 0.08 per cent of the population in 1828/9, 0.13 per cent in 1851 and 0.51 per cent in 1869 (Pigot, *National ... 1828/9*; *Slater's ... 1852*; *Slater's ... 1869*).

The amount of intra-elite trust produced was related to the size of the elite group. If there was a large elite, cliques developed. Malthus argued that population growth in excess of the rise in food supplies would not only result in poverty, famine, wars and plagues, but also in immorality. Together, these consequences would act as a positive check on overpopulation (E. N. Santurri, 'Theodicy and social policy in Malthus' thought', *Journal of the History of Ideas,* 43 (2), 1982, 318).

25 S. Szreter and M. Woolcock, 'Health by association? Social capital, social theory and

the political economy of public health', *International Journal of Epidemiology*, 33, 2004, 657–61. Large-scale investment in public utilities first began in Birmingham, where there was a united elite.

26 S. Szreter, *Health and Wealth. Studies in History and Policy*, Rochester: Rochester University Press, 2005; L. Berkman and T. Glass, 'Social integration, social networks, social support and health', in L. F. Berkman and L. Kawachi (eds), *Social Epidemiology*, Oxford: Oxford University Press, 2000, 137–74; Putnam, *Bowling*, 326–7.

27 Doherty, 'Short', 68–9, 359; Anderson, *Family*, 37, 39; Black, *A Medico*, 67. Migrants may also have possessed higher than average trust-building skills, successful migration partly depending on the ability to forge links with others.

28 Doherty, 'Short', 357.

29 Anderson, *Family*, 101; Field, 'From', 77. Participation in neighbourhood networks was made even more difficult by their greater tendency to move residences.

30 M. A. Busted and R. I. Hodgson, 'Irish migrant responses to urban life in early nineteenth century Manchester', *The Geographical Journal*, 162 (2), 1996, 5; Holding, 'A profile', 15; Black, *A Medico*, 66.

31 Motte, 'The dark', 376; Busted and Hodgson, 'Irish', 144; E. Baines, *History, Directory and Gazetteer of the County Palatine of Lancashire*, London, 1825, 571.

32 H. R. Southall, 'The tramping artisan revisited. Labour mobility and economic distress in early Victorian England', *Economic History Review*, 44 (2), 1991, 290, 294. See also E. J. Hobsbawm, 'The tramping artisan', *Economic History Review*, 3, 1951, 299–320.

33 Faucher, *Manchester*, 26; PP 1850 xxiii.571, 14; Bolton Archive, ZHE 36/10; *Bolton Express*, 27 September 1823.

34 Street vendors and hawkers were believed to be petty criminals and pimps and their presence acted as a visual affront to urban respectability/morality (A. B. May, 'A charitable indulgence. Street stalls and the transformation of public space in Melbourne, 1850–1920', *Urban History*, 23 (1), 1996, 52, 69).

35 *The Sanitary Record*, 6 February 1875, 98–9 quoted in C. Otter, 'Making liberalism durable. Vision and civility in the late Victorian city', *Social History*, 27 (1), 2002, 12; A. Croll, 'Street disorder, surveillance and shame Regulating behaviour in the public spaces of the late Victorian British town', *Social History*, 24 (3), 1999, 264. To prevent such monitoring, vandals smashed street lights and made threats of physical violence.

36 Gunn, *The Public*, 40; W. N. Pugin, *An Apology for the Revival of Christian Architecture in England*, Oxford: St Barnabas, 1969 (originally published 1843), 6; W. N. Pugin, *Present State of Ecclesiastical Architecture in England*, Oxford: St Barnabas, 1969 (originally published 1843), 18; M. H. Bright, 'A reconsideration of W. N. Pugin's architectural theories', *Victorian Studies*, 22 (2), 1979, 151–71; J. Bentham quoted in D. Lyon, 'Bentham's Panopticon. From moral architecture to electronic surveillance', *Queen's Quarterly*, 98 (3), 1991, 598; Davidoff and Hall, *Family*, 428; W. R. G. Hillier and J. Hanson, *The Social Logic of Space*, Cambridge: Cambridge University Press, 1984. In some cases, public buildings directly promoted trust. The interior dome of the Manchester Royal Exchange had painted on its interior 'a good name is rather to be chosen than great riches and loving favour rather than silver and gold' (Gunn, *The Public*, 40).

37 *Freelance*, 12 March 1870 quoted in Gunn, *The Public*, 62; F. B. Head, 'Report on the sanitary condition of the labouring classes', *Quarterly Review*, 71, 1843, 421; Chadwick, *Report*, 423; G. Goodwin, *London Shadows. A Glance at the Homes of the Thousands*, New York: Garland, 1985 (originally published 1854), 45. Overcrowding also drove children into the street, which reduced the likelihood that they would 'grow up with steady and domestic habits' (J. Entwisle, *A Report on the Sanitary Condition of the Borough of Bolton*, Bolton, 1848, 90).

38 Anderson, *Family*, 47; Holding, 'A profile', 6; PP 1852/3, lxxxvi.

39 P. Hall, 'Social capital in Britain', *British Journal of Political Science*, 29, 1999, 443, 445; N. J. Smelser, *Social Change in the Industrial Revolution*, Chicago: University of Chicago, 1959, 253; Lis and Soly, *Neighbourhood*, 22; Anderson, *Family*, 29, 31; PP 1908 cvii.319, xliv. Adam Smith believed that the tendency for English 'manufacturers [to] give the poorer sort better wages than any master can afford' was one of the reasons why 'the common people of England ... are the honestest of their rank anywhere to be met with' (Adam Smith, *Lectures on Jurisprudence*, Oxford, 1978, vol. vi, 6–7).

40 P. H. Lindert and J. G. Williamson, 'English workers' living standards during the industrial revolution. A new look', *Economic History Review*, 36 (1), 1983, 1–25; N. F. R. Crafts, 'English workers' living standards during the industrial revolution', *Journal of Economic History*, 45 (1), 1985, 139–44; N. F. R. Crafts and T. C. Mills, 'Trends in real wages in Britain, 1750–1913', *Explorations in Economic History*, 31 (2), 1994, 176–94; C. Feinstein, '"Pessimism perpetuated". Real wages and standards of living in Britain during and after the industrial revolution', *Journal of Economic History*, 58 (3), 1998, 642, 645–9; P. Huck, 'Infant mortality and living standards of English workers during the industrial revolution', *Journal of Economic History*, 55 (3), 1995, 528–50; P. Johnson and S. Nicholas, 'Male and female living standards in England and Wales, 1812–57', *Economic History Review*, 48 (3), 1995, 470–81. See also J. Komlos, 'Shrinking in a growing economy? The mystery of physical stature during the industrial revolution', *Journal of Economic History*, 58 (3), 1998, 780, 793.

41 G. Boyer, 'Poor relief, informal assistance and short time during the Lancashire cotton famine', *Explorations in Economic History*, 34, 1997, 58; R. Hall, 'A poor cotton weyver. Poverty and the cotton famine in Clitheroe', *Social History*, 28 (2), 2003, 235.

42 PP 1824, vi, 7; Boyer, 'Poor', 68; P. Dunkley, 'Paternalism, the magistracy and poor relief in England, 1795–1834', *International Review of Social History*, 24 (3), 1979, 395; D. Stack, 'The secret concatenation in the mid-nineteenth century. The case of George Poulett Scrope, a still neglected political economist', *History of Political Economy*, 32 (3), 2000, 555.

43 J. Townsend, *A Dissertation on the Poor Laws*, London, 1786; Taylor, *Popular*, 121, 122; M. E. Rose, 'The anti-poor law movement in the North of England', *Northern History*, 1, 1966, 70; Digby, *The Poor*, 20; S. King, *Poverty and Welfare in England, 1700–1850. A Regional Perspective*, Manchester: Manchester University Press, 2000, 244–7; Walton, *Lancashire*, 194; Taylor, *Progress*, 122; R. Boyson, 'The new poor law in north east Lancashire, 1834–71', *Transactions of the Lancashire and Cheshire Antiquarian Society*, 70, 1960, 126–54; Hall, 'A poor', 237–8.

44 M. Sanderson, 'Literacy and social mobility in the industrial revolution in England', *Past and Present*, 56, 1972, 76; Stephens, *Regional*; D. Vincent, *Literacy and Popular Culture. England 1750–1914*, Cambridge: Cambridge University Press, 1989; Bolton Archive, ZZ 109/3; PP 1868–9, xiv, p. 66.

45 J. Dwyer, 'The Caledonian Mercury and Scottish national culture, 1763–1801', *Journal of History and Politics*, 7, 1989, 147–69; Morris, 'Civil', 297. In addition, newspapers advertised books and pamphlets on moral questions.

46 Dymond, *Essays*, 389. To avoid reprisals from the disorderly elements, most letter writers used pseudonyms.

47 R. Dewhurst, *Diary of Roger ... Dewhurst*, Bolton, 1881; Price, 'Bolton', 50.

48 D. L. Gump, 'The role of vivid language in the perception of fairness and other story attributes by readers and reporters', PhD thesis, University of North Carolina, 2002; Dymond, *Essays*, 388; Channing, *Self*, 29.

49 A. Davies, 'Youth gangs, masculinity and violence in late Victorian Manchester and Salford', *Journal of Social History*, 32 (2), 1998, 353; D. Liddle, 'Salesmen, sportsmen, mentors. Anonymity and mid-Victorian theories of journalism', *Victorian Studies*, 41 (1), 1997, 38, 43; M. Vicinus, *The Industrial Muse*, London: Croom

Helm, 1974, 30; J. Klancher, 'Reading the social text. Power, signs and audience in early nineteenth century prose', *Studies in Romanticism*, 23 (2), 1984, 183–204; P. J. Anderson, 'A revolution in popular art. Pictorial magazines and the making of mass culture in England, 1832–60', *Journal of Newspaper and Periodical History*, 6 (1), 1990, 24.

50 Morgan, *Manners*, 38; Shepherd, *A Series*, 50; T. L. Alborn, 'The moral of the failed bank. Professional plots in the Victorian money market', *Victorian Studies*, 38 (2), 1995, 204; C. Gallagher, *The Industrial Reformation of English Fiction, 1832–67*, Chicago: University of Chicago, 1980, 147; Bradley, *The Call*, 146–7. Dicken's moral viewpoint is summed up by the philosophy of the character Joe Gargery in *Great Expectations* – 'there's one thing you may be sure of, Pip . . . namely that lies is lies' (C. Dickens, *Great Expectations*, Harmondsworth: Penguin, 1965, 100). His description of London's Field Lane in *Oliver Twist*, will, if anything, have heightened his readers' distrust of the poor. The street comprised 'covered ways and yards, which here and there diverged from the main street, [and] disclosed little houses where drunken men and women were positively wallowing in filth; and from several of the doorways great ill looking fellows were cautiously emerging, bound, to all appearance, on no very well-disposed or harmless errands' (C. Dickens, *Oliver Twist or the Parish Boy's Progress*, London, 1843, Chapter 8).

51 B. S. Frey and A. Stutzer, *Happiness and Economics*, Princeton: Princeton University Press, 2002, 3, 10, 53, 57; R. H. Frank, 'The frame of reference as a public good', *Economic Journal*, 107 (445), 1997, 1832–47; J. Fernandez-Dols and M. Ruiz-belda, 'Are signs a sign of happiness?', *Journal of Personality and Social Psychology*, 69 (6), 1990, 1113–19; C. Bjornskov, 'The happy few. Cross country evidence on social capital and life satisfaction', *Kyklos*, 56 (1), 2003, 10, 14. John Stuart Mill additionally believed that virtue and the enjoyable experience of being virtuous led to happiness (R. Crisp, 'Mill on virtue as a part of happiness', *British Journal for the History of Philosophy*, 4 (2), 1996, 367–80).

6 Governments and trust

1 Other hypotheses include those based on rational choice theory, Marxism and the writings of L. Namier. See, for example, D. C. Moore, *The Politics of Deference*, Hassocks: Harvester, 1976; S. D. Krasner, 'State power and the structure of international trade', *World Politics*, 28, 1976, 125–37; I. Mclean, 'Rational choice and the Victorian voter', *Political Studies*, 40, 1992, 496–515.

2 M. Lessnoff (ed.), *Social Contract Theory*, Oxford: Blackwell, 1990, 4; J. Locke, *Two Treatises of Government*, second treatise, Cambridge: Cambridge University Press, 1960, 149, 156, 240.

3 Thompson, 'The moral'; Digby, 'Victorian', 199. Critics of Thompson include J. Stevenson, 'The moral economy of the English crowd', in A. Fletcher and J. Stevenson (eds), *Order and Disorder in Early Modern England*, Cambridge: Cambridge University Press, 1985; D. E. Williams, 'Morals, markets and the English crowd in 1766', *Past and Present*, 104, 1984, 56–73; A. M. Urdank, 'The consumption of rental property. Gloucestershire plebeians and the market economy, 1750–1860', *Journal of Interdisciplinary History*, 21 (2), 1990, 261–82. Support most recently came from A. Randall and A. Charlesworth, 'The moral economy: riots, markets and social conflict', in A. Randall and A. Charlesworth, *Moral Economy and Popular Protest. Crowds, Conflict and Authority*, Basingstoke: Macmillan, 2000.

4 M. R. Somers, 'Citizenship and the place of the public sphere. Law community and political culture in the transition to democracy', *American Sociological Review*, 58, 1993, 601–5; J. Thirsk, 'Seventeenth century agriculture and social change', in P. S. Seaver (ed.), *Seventeenth Century England*, New York: Garland, 1976, 151; K. Wrightson, *English Society, 1580–1680*, London: Hutchinson, 1982, 172.

5 J. Bohstedt, 'The moral economy and the discipline of historical context', *Journal of Social History*, 26 (2), 1992, 275–6. Community distrust was raised by the fact that some of the elite were themselves corn dealers and engrossers (C. A. Horner, '"Proper persons to deal with." Identification and attitudes of middling society in Manchester, *c*.1730–*c*.1760', Manchester Metropolitan University, PhD thesis, 2001, 251–3).

6 Dunkley, 'Paternalism', 372–3; E. P. Thompson, 'Patrician society, plebeian culture', *Journal of Social History*, 8, 1973–4, 383; H. Perkin, *The Origins of Modern English Society, 1780–1880*, London: Routledge, 1972, 182–3; Garrard, 'Urban', 590–1.

7 D. Acemoglu and J. A. Robinson, 'Why did the West extend the franchise? Democracy, inequality and growth in historical perspective', *Quarterly Journal of Economics*, 115 (4), 2000, 1167–99; A. Briggs, *The Age of Improvement, 1783–1867*, London: Longman, 1959; S. J. Lee, *Aspects of British Political History, 1815–1914*, London: Routledge, 1994; quoted by E. J. Evans, *The Forging of the Modern State. Early Industrial Britain, 1783–1870*, London: Longman 1983, 24; Garrard, *Democratization*, 43, 45, 51; G. W. Cox, *The Efficient Secret. The Cabinet and the Development of Political Parties in Victorian England*, Cambridge: Cambridge University Press, 1987, 10. Under-representation continued until 1885.

8 Acemoglu and Robinson, 'Why', 1187; G. Himmelfarb, 'The politics of democracy. The English Reform Act of 1867', *Journal of British Studies*, 6, 1966, 97–138; R. B. Collier, *Paths Towards Democracy. The Working Class and Elites in Western Europe and South America*, Cambridge: Cambridge University Press, 1999; Garrard, *Democratization*, 45, 53, 59; Cox, *The Efficient*, 10, 11. In fact, the Conservatives lost the 1868 election. In 1885, the English and Welsh electorate topped 4 million.

9 K. Lawes, *Paternalism and Politics. The Revival of Paternalism in Early Nineteenth Century Britain*, Basingstoke: Macmillan, 2000, 5–19, 48–52; W. Cobbett, *The Poor Man's Friend*, London, 1829, iv.

10 Lawes, *Paternalism*, 190–1; C. J. Holmes, 'Laissez faire in theory and practice. Britain 1800–1875', *Journal of European Economic History*, 5, 1976, 671, 683; W. C. Lubenow, *The Politics of Government Growth. Early Victorian Attitudes to State Intervention*, Newton Abbot: David & Charles, 1971; Acemoglu and Robinson, 'Why', 1167; M. Daunton, *Trusting Leviathan. The Politics of Taxation in Britain, 1799–1914*, Cambridge: Cambridge University Press, 2001. The imposition of higher taxes was also helped by rapid economic growth and economic changes that facilitated collection, for example waged employment and the enlargement of trading units.

11 P. W. J. Bartrip, 'State intervention in mid-nineteenth century Britain. Fact or fiction', *Journal of British Studies*, 23 (1), 1983, 63–83. The gini coefficient for income inequality in England and Wales rose from 0.4 in 1823 to 0.627 in 1871, but then fell to 0.443 in 1901 (J. G. Williamson, *Did British Capitalism Breed Inequality*, London: Allen & Unwin, 1985, Table 4.2. See also N. F. R. Crafts, 'Real wages, inequality and economic growth in Britain, 1750–1850. A review of recent research' in P. Scholliers (ed.), *Real Wages in Nineteenth and Twentieth Century Europe*, Oxford: Berg, 1989; P. Lindert, 'Unequal English wealth since 1670', *Journal of Political Economy*, 94, 1986, 1127–1162). Part of the decline was no doubt related to the increase in the proportion of skilled workers in the economy, but a large portion was due to state redistribution of income to the poorer sectors of society.

12 Rimke and Hunt, 'From', 67–8; R. Munting, 'Social opposition to gambling in Britain. An historical overview', *The International Journal for the History of Sport*, 10 (3), 1993, 300; J. A. Jaffe, 'Industrial arbitration, equity and authority in England, 1800–50', *Law and History Review*, 18 (3), 2000, 20. Environmental legislation included the 1847 Town Clauses Act and the 1848 Public Health Act. Property rights were protected through the creation of the land registry, patent and design registries, and so on. State encouragement of arbitration in labour relations had a long history. The Combination Act of 1800 and the Cotton Arbitration Acts of 1800 and 1804 all

contained procedures for the arbitration of disputes. In 1820, seamen and their masters were given the opportunity of seeking redress through arbitrators, and a 1824 act sought to extend the relevant clauses in the 1804 Cotton Arbitration Act to all trades. Unfortunately, neither employers nor workers made much use of any of this legislation (Jaffe, 'Industrial arbitration').

13 M. J. Daunton, 'Payment and participation. Welfare and state formation in Britain, 1900–1951', *Past and Present*, 150, 1996, 113, 170; A. Offer, 'Why has the public sector grown so large in market societies?', *University of Oxford, Discussion Paper in Economic and Social History*, 44, 2002, 6, 8. Likewise, doctors were regulated and registered by the General Medical Council, the activities of accountants were controlled by the Institute of Chartered Accountants, non-profit housing was largely provided by charitable trusts, and hospital care supplied by local voluntary societies.

Where private-sector supply was used, local governments sought to ensure universal provision by ensuring that voters paid a low and fair price for the services. They thus restricted the companies' rates of returns and imposed price caps and service standards. Moral hazard was prevented through the close monitoring of their affairs (see D. Sunderland, '"Disgusting to the imagination and destructive of health"? The Metropolitan Supply of Water, 1820–52', *Urban History*, 30 (3), 2003, 359–80).

14 Kidd, 'The liberal state. Civil society and social welfare in nineteenth century England', *Journal of Historical Sociology*, 15 (1), 2002, 116–18; M. Ball and D. Sunderland, *An Economic History of London, 1800–1914*, London: Routledge, 2001, 371.

15 W. Bagehot, *The English Constitution*, London: Watts, 1964 (originally published 1867), 96; PP 1854–5, xx, 28, 177; T. Osborne, 'Bureaucracy as a vocation. Governmentality and administration in nineteenth century Britain', *Journal of Historical Sociology*, 7 (3), 1994, 305.

16 L. Kinzer, 'The unenglishness of the secret ballot', *Albion*, 10 (3), 1978, 243; McLean, 'Rational', 510. In the 1837 Parliamentary election, turnout in Preston was 86 per cent, in Bolton 76 per cent, in Blackburn 70 per cent and in Oldham 62 per cent (PP 1837–8, xliv.553).

17 T. Gisborne, *An Enquiry into the Duties of Men*, vol. ii, London, 1798, 400–1; Dutton and King, 'The limits', 64; quoted in F. O. Gorman, 'Electoral interference in 'unreformed' England, 1760–1832', *Journal of Modern History*, 56, 1984, 402. Joyce claims that deference influenced voting behaviour, quoting as evidence voting patters in Blackburn and Bury in 1868 (P. Joyce, 'The factory politics of Lancashire in the later nineteenth century', *The Historical Journal*, 18 (3), 1975, 525–53). The conclusions he drew from his analysis of the poll books have been questioned by Lees (Lees, 'Work', 242–4).

18 P. Salmon, 'Local politics and partnership. The electoral impact of municipal reform 1835', *Parliamentary History*, 19 (3), 2000, 364–6; Garrard, 'Urban', 593; Shapely, 'Charity', 5; Cox, *The Efficient*, 53–4.

19 M. A. Mania, 'Influence, corruption and electoral behaviour in the mid-nineteenth century. A case study of Lancaster, 1847–1865', *Northern History*, 29, 1993, 154; *Lancaster Guardian*, 27 October 1866. See also Gorman, 'Electoral', 401; Mania, 'Influence', 159. In the 1865 election, two-thirds of the Lancaster electorate obtained gifts (K. T. Hoppen, 'Roads to democracy. Electioneering and corruption in nineteenth century England and Ireland', *History*, 81 (264) (1996), 560).

20 Gorman, 'Electoral', 411; F. O. Gorman, 'Campaign rituals and ceremonies. The social meaning of elections in England, 1780–1860', *Past and Present*, 135, 1992, 101.

21 Gorman, 'Campaign'.

22 Mania, 'Influence', 29; McLean, 'Rational choice', 496–515; J. C. Mitchell and J. Cornford, 'The political demography of Cambridge, 1832–1868', *Albion*, 9, 1977, 242–72. Of those who participated in Bolton's 1832 parliamentary election, for instance, over 40 per cent of businessmen involved in textiles, other manufactures and retailing and service provision supported Liberal candidates.

23 Garrard, *Democratization*, xi, 48, 54; D. Fraser, *Power and Authority in the Victorian City*, Oxford: Blackwell, 1979, 11.

24 Garrard, *Leadership*, 16–18, 166. In Bolton, from 1830–49 manufacturers constituted between 50 and 72 per cent of the Little Bolton trustees, and, from 1843/5 to 1866/7, between 42 and 53 per cent of the town's councillors (ibid. 18).

25 G. R. Searle, *Corruption in British Politics, 1895–1930*, Oxford: Clarendon, 1987, 44; A. C. Howe, *The Cotton Masters, 1830–1860*, Oxford: Clarendon, 1984, 96. The distrust of central government varied over time and was partly dependent on the strength of the national economy (A. W. Ryley, *The Itinerant or Memoirs of an Actor*, London, 1817). Pitt's income tax, for example, was widely regarded to be the result of financial mismanagement.

26 Trainer, 'Urban', 4; Garrard, *Leadership*, 24. Other benefits of holding office included greater self-esteem from the attainment of social status, a chance to advance trust norms through speeches and the example of the sacrifice of personal interest for the greater good, and, for the religious, spiritual trust derived from the provision of service to others.

27 Garrard, *Leadership*, 43–4.

28 Doyle, 'The structure'; Trainer, 'Urban', 3; Garrard, 'Urban', 603. The growth of employers associations, which closely scrutinised central and local government, also reduced the need for individual manufacturers to use public service as a way of monitoring council activities (Arthur J. McIvor, *Organised Capital Employers Associations and Industrial Relations in Northern England, 1880–1939*, Cambridge: Cambridge University Press, 1996, 50).

29 Eastwood, 'Men, morals and the machinery of social legislation, 1790–1840', *Parliamentary History*, 13 (2), 1994, 194; N. D. Lopatin, *Political Unions. Popular Politics and the Great Reform Act of 1832*, Basingstoke: Macmillan, 1999, 160–1; P. A. Pickering and A. Tyrrell, *The People's Bread. A History of the Anti-Corn Law League*, Leicester: Leicester University Press, 2000, 41, 44, 250.

30 *Northern Star*, 19 October 1839; J. Belchem and J. Epstein, 'The Nineteenth century gentleman leader revisited', *Social History*, 22 (2), 1997, 188; P. A. Pickering, '"And your petitioners." Chartist petitioning in popular politics 1838–48', *English Historical Review*, 116 (466), 2001, 368–88. After the fiasco of the 1848 petition, which contained many false names, the trust reputation of this form of protest fell.

31 Garrard, *Leadership*, 162; P. Hills, 'Division and cohesion in the nineteenth century middle class. The case of Ipswich, 1830–70', *Urban History Yearbook*, 1987, 46; Poole, 'Popular', 22.

7 The law and trust

1 Bates, *A Discourse*, 47–9; PP 1826–7, vi, 62–8; Philipps, 'Crime', 158: *Bolton Chronicle*, 10 November 1877. More directly, crime also forced 'upwards of two millions annually' to be spent on 'protection and security', 'to which amount must be added the loss of production that might otherwise be realized by those who are now employed in checking … the evil' (Bates, *A Discourse*, 47–9).

2 R. Loeber and M. Stouthamer-Loeber, 'Family factors as correlates and predictors of juvenile crime conduct problems and delinquency' in M. Tonry and N. Morris, *Crime and Justice, Volume 7*, Chicago: University of Chicago, 1986; Lancashire Record Office, ms f 310.6, m5–146; C. M. de Motte, 'The dark side of town. Crime in Manchester and Salford, 1815–1875', University of Kansas, PhD thesis, 1977, 378. Basil Montague, a Commissioner of Bankruptcy, believed that crime was 'prevented by three modes; first by the fear of punishment awarded by the law … secondly by the fear of the disapprobation of the community; and, thirdly … by the fear of the disapprobation of the Almighty' (PP 1818, vi.23, 19).

3 S. H. Palmer, *Police and Protest in England and Ireland, 1780–1850*, Cambridge:

Cambridge University Press, 1988, 74; R. D. Storch, 'The plague of blue locusts. Police reform and popular resistance in northern England', 1850–57, *International Review of Social History*, 20 (1), 1975, 64.

4 S. Davies, 'The private provision of police during the eighteenth and nineteenth centuries', in Beito *et al.*, *The Voluntary*, 158, 162. Some also protected their property with booby traps (M. Weaver, 'The new science of policing. Crime and the Birmingham police force 1839–42', *Albion*, 26 (2), 1994, 293).

5 Lis and Soly, 'Neighbourhood', 21.

6 D. Bentley, *English Criminal Justice in the Nineteenth Century*, London: Hambledon, 1998, 2, 11; J. Bentham quoted in K. J. M. Smith, *Lawyers, Legislators and Theorists. Developments in English Criminal Jurisprudence, 1800–1957*, Oxford: Clarendon, 1998, 45.

7 Bentley, *English*, 11, 46; L. Radzinowicz and R. Hood, *The Emergence of Penal Policy in Victorian and Edwardian England*, London: Sweet & Maxwell, 1990, 142, 145, 701–2. The barrister J. Fitzjames Stephen considered pain 'the greatest natural check by which man is governed ... [it] exercises perhaps stronger moral influences than any power in the World; ... the lessons which are taught by discomfort and suffering are wonderfully valuable' (J. F. Stephen, *Essays By a Barrister*, London 1862, 147 quoted in Radzinowicz and R. Hood, *The Emergence*, 702).

8 Bentley, *English*, 8, 297–8.

9 Ibid., 11; R. S. Tompson, 'The Justices of the Peace and the United Kingdom in the age of reform', *Journal of Legal History*, 7 (3), 1986, 274, 284.

10 Greenhalgh, *Sixty Years*, 145; G. Morgan and P. Rushton, 'The magistrate, the community and the maintenance of an orderly society', *Historical Research*, 76 (1), 2003, 57, 75. See also D. Hay, 'Property, authority and the criminal law', in D. Hay, J. G. Rule, E. P. Thompson and C. Winslow (eds), *Albinon's Fatal Tree. Crime and Society in Eighteenth Century England*, New York: Pantheon, 1975, 17.

11 Bentley, *English*, 22, 276, 297.

12 Philipps, 'Crime', 156; Smith, *Lawyers*, 42; Bentley, *English*, 7.

13 Davies, 'The private', 160–9; C. B. Little and C. P. Sheffield, 'Frontiers and criminal justice. English private prosecution societies and American vigilantism in the eighteenth and nineteenth centuries', *American Sociological Review*, 48 (6), 1983, 796–808. In some societies, members also agreed to share any information they received concerning any offence against a colleague and promised not to receive stolen goods.

14 Winder, *A Life's*, 14, 68. In Bolton, there were 662 tradesmen to each lawyer in 1828/9, 88 in 1851 and 175 in 1869 (Pigot, *National ... 1828–9*; *Slater's ... 1852*; *Slater's ... 1869*).

15 Anon., *Business*, 132–3; Lamb, *Free Thoughts*, vol. i, 190; J. M. Robson (ed.), *Collected Works of John Stuart Mill*, Toronto: University of Toronto, 1965–91, xxvi, 389; Searle, *Morality*, 97; C. W. Brooks, 'Interpersonal Conflict and Social Tension. Civil Litigation in England, 1640–1830', in A. L. Beier, D. Cannadine and J. M. Rosenheim, *The First Modern Society*, Cambridge: Cambridge University Press, 1989, 382.

16 Palmer, *Police*, 400; J. J. Tobias, *Crime and Police in England, 1700–1900*, Dublin: Gill & Macmillan, 1979, 98. An earlier 1833 Lighting and Watching Act had permitted vestries to levy a police tax and appoint paid inspectors and watchmen, and, fearful of Chartist agitation, in 1839 the government established centrally controlled police forces in Birmingham, Bolton and Manchester, which three years later reverted to local control (Weaver, 'The new science', 289).

17 D. J. V. Jones, 'The new police, crime and people in England and Wales', *Transactions of the Royal Historical Society*, 33, 1983, 165–6; Holding, 'A profile', 43; D. Jones, *Crime, Protest, Community and Police in Nineteenth Century Britain*, London: Routledge, 1982, 22, 175–6; Storch, 'The plague', 66; PP 1840, xxxix.253.

18 Weaver, 'The new science', 290. New stations were built, patrols became more regular, officers were better trained, and new methods of identification and communication were introduced (Jones, *Crime*, 175–6; Jones, 'The new ', 162).

19 Bentley, *English*, 23, 28, 298; Tompson, 'The Justices', 280, 282, 283; Smith, *Lawyers*, 364; Radzinowicz and Hood, *The Emergence*, 618–20.

20 Parl. Debates, 1920, vol. i, col. 236 and J. J. Gurney quoted in R. McGowen, 'A powerful sympathy. Terror the prison and humanitarian reform in early nineteenth century Britain', *Journal of British Studies*, 15 (3), 1986, 312, 319; Radzinowicz and Hood, *The Emergence*, 474–82, 692; Bentley, *English*, 3.

21 Parl. Debates, 1810, vol. xvii, col. 359 and E. Fry, quoted in McGowen, 'A powerful', 326; M. H. Tomlinson, 'Prison palaces. A reappraisal of early Victorian prisons, 1835–77', *Bulletin of the Institute of Historical Research*, 51 (123), 1978, 61–3; Radzinowicz and Hood, *The Emergence*, 493, 506.

22 *The Times*, 26 December 1862, H. Mayhew, J. Binney and E. F. du Cane quoted in Radzinowicz and Hood, *The Emergence*, 509, 506, 528.

23 Radzinowicz and Hood, *The Emergence*, 180, 181; S. Turner quoted in Radzinowicz and Hood, *The Emergence*, 190; R. Grigg, 'Educating criminal and destitute children. Reformatory and industrial schools in Wales, 1858–1914', *Welsh History Review*, 21 (2), 2002, 307, 321; Jones, *Crime*, 237. Pupils started the day with prayers and a bible reading and on Sundays attended church or chapel.

24 Jones, *Crime*, 245–62, 603, 615.

25 H. Taylor, 'Rationing crime. The political economy of criminal statistics since the 1850s', *Economic History Review*, 51 (3), 1998, 569–70; L. O. Pike, *A History of Crime in England*, London, 1876, 480–1; M. Ogborn, 'Ordering the city. Surveillance, public space and the reform of urban policing, 1835–56', *Political Geography*, 12 (6), 1993, 505–21. See also C. A. Williams, 'Counting crimes or counting people. Some implications of mid-nineteenth century British police returns', *Crime Histoire and Societes*, 4 (2), 2000, 77–93. New crimes included ones relating to fraud, embezzlement, bribery and corruption, and offences against good morals (Radzinowicz and Hood, *The Emergence*, 118). Prostitutes were only allowed to ply their trade in particular areas, where their activities could be controlled and they were unlikely to tempt the unwary (P. Howell, 'A private Contagious Diseases Act. Prostitution and public space in Victorian Cambridge', *Journal of Historical Geography*, 26 (3), 2000, 377).

26 Taylor, 'Rationing', 569–90. Taylor's thesis has been criticized by Morris, who believes that it fails to take account of the decentalised and disaggregated character of the nineteenth-century criminal justice system and policing, and exaggerates the significance of criminal statistics (R. M. Morris, '"Lies, damned lies and criminal statistics." Reinterpreting the criminal statistics in England and Wales', *Crime Histoire and Societes*, 5 (1), 2001, 111–27).

27 J. T. Hammick and H. B. Simpson, Assistant Secretary, Home Office, 1892 quoted in Taylor, 'Rationing', 580, 573.

28 H. W. Arthurs, *'Without the Law.' Administrative Justice and Legal Pluralism in Nineteenth Century England*, Toronto: University of Toronto, 1985, 16, 17; P. Polden, *A History of the County Court, 1846–1971*, Cambridge: Cambridge University Press, 1999, 8, 9. Distrust of the civil and criminal courts may have also affected people's attitude towards the state and the social contract.

29 W. H. D. Winder 'The courts of request', *Law Quarterly Review*, 52, 1936, 369–74; Arthurs, *Without*, 26.

30 Arthurs, *Without*, 26, 28, 45; Polden, *A History*, 11, 12. Some critics even claimed that the courts induced working-class debt, and thus contributed to 'the debauchery' of the poor (witness to the 1933 Commission on Provincial Courts quoted in Arthurs, *Without*, 27).

31 Arthurs, *Without*, 17–19; Polden, *A History*, 10; G. R. Rubin and D. Sugarman (eds),

Law Economy and Society, 1750–1914. Essays in the History of English Law, Abingdon: Professional Books, 1984, 380–411.

32 Freedley, *A Practical,* 46; B. Z. Khan, 'Order without law. Social capital, civil litigation and economic development', *Australian Economic History Review,* 39 (3), 1999, 179; Barbara Weiss, *The Hell of the English Bankruptcy and the Victorian Novel,* Lewisberg: Associated University Presses, 1986, 43. Imprisonment for insolvency was largely abolished in 1869 (V. M. Lester, *Victorian Insolvency,* Oxford: Clarendon, 1995, 97).

33 Weiss, *The Hell,* 42–9; Lester, *Victorian;* PP 1852–3, xxii.1, qq. 44, 273, 284, 772, 811.

34 Victor M. Batzel, 'Parliament, businessmen and bankruptcy, 1825–83. A study in middle class alienation', *Canadian Journal of History,* 18 (2), 1983, 182; Bates, *A Discourse,* 173.

35 Arthurs, *Without,* 17–19, 42, 45, 167; A. H. Manchester, *A Modern Legal History,* London: Butterworth, 1980, 18, 148; Polden, *A History,* 38, 58, 60; P. Johnson, 'Class law in Victorian England', *Past and Present,* 141, 1993, 158. In many cases, campaigners for tougher laws adopted moral arguments. Both those in favour and those against the 1842 Copyright Act, for instance, assumed a social capital standpoint. Objectors argued that the Act would prevent the diffusion of books that improved 'the moral character' (C. E. V. Bossche, 'The value of literature. Representations of print culture in the copyright debates of 1837–42', *Victorian Studies,* 38 (1), 1994, 49). Conversely, supporters claimed that, devoid of protection, authors would no longer be willing to create those important works of literature that 'form the unseen bond which links together the high and the low' (A. Alison, quoted in Bossche, 'The value', 51).

36 PP 1871 xii.523, q. 635, 637, 644; Polden, *A History,* 50, 52, 70–1; N. Wood, 'Debt credit and business strategy. The law and the local economy, 1850–1900', University of Leicester, PhD thesis, 1999, 260–2.

37 Brooks, 'Interpersonal', 367, 374; Paul Johnson, 'Small debts and economic distress in England and Wales, 1857–1913', *Economic History Review,* 46 (1), 1993, 72; PP 1912/3, lxix, 15; PP lvi.1; PP 1893/4, cv; PP 1872 lxvi, part 2; PP 1892, lxv, 5; PP 1882, liv, 51; PP 1872, l.117. The debts did not exceed £20, and the legal-administrative process experienced little alteration over the period. A similar trend was found in a study of New South Wales civil litigation during the second half of the nineteenth century (Khan, 'Order'; B. Zorina Khan, 'Commerce and co-operation. Litigation and settlement of civil disputes on the Australian frontier', *Journal of Economic History,* 64 (4), 2000, 1088–119).

A large proportion of cases were settled before they reached court and relatively few execution orders against goods were issued. In 1865 and 1912 respectively, 44 per cent and 35 per cent of cases initiated failed to reach court (Johnson, 'Small debts', 67). As previously discussed, rising real income itself boosts social capital.

In Bolton there were 4.08 cases (under-20s) per 100 residents, in Oldham 3.19, in Blackburn 2.55, in Preston 1.86 and in Burnley 2.28 (PP 1912/3, lxix.15; PP lvi.1; PP 1893/4, cv; PP 1872 lxvi, part 2; PP 1892, lxv.5; PP 1882, liv.51; PP 1872, l.117).

8 Kin and geographic trust

1 F. Fukuyama, *The Great Disruption,* London: Profile, 2000, 36; P. Laslett, *Family Life and Illicit Love in Earlier Generations,* Cambridge: Cambridge University Press, 1977; E. Lord, 'Communities of common interest. The social landscape of S.E. Surrey, 1750–1850', in C. Phythian-Adams (ed.), *Societies, Cultures and Kinship, 1580–1850,* Leicester: Leicester University Press, 1993; B. Reay, 'Kinship and the neighbourhood in nineteenth century rural England. The myth of the autonomous nuclear family', *Journal of Family History,* 21 (1), 1996; Barrett, 'Kinship', 208; S. Ruggles, *Prolonged Connections. The Rise of the Extended Family in Nineteenth*

Century England and America, Madison, Wis.: University of Wisconsin, 1987. See also D. Cooper and M. Donald, 'Households and hidden kin in early nineteenth century England. Four case studies in suburban Exeter', *Continuity and Change*, 10, 1995, 257–78. The most inter-connected kinship groups were probably non-conformists, whose social closeness promoted chain migration and inter-marriage (Barrett, 'Kinship', 207).

2 Somers, 'Citizenship', 593–601; J. Goody, J. Thirsk and E. P. Thompson (eds), *Family and Inheritance. Rural Society in Western Europe, 1200–1800*, Cambridge: Cambridge University Press, 1976, 112–56; J. Thirsk, 'Seventeenth', 84.

3 Anderson, *Family*, 116–18.

4 W. T. Griffin, *The Homes of our Country*, London, 1887, 535 quoted in Ruggles, *Prolonged*, 131; S. A. King, 'The English proto-industrial family. Old and new perspectives', *The History of the Family*, 8, 2003, 32; Anderson, *Family*, 107; M. W. Dupree, *Family Structure in the Staffordshire Potteries, 1840–80*, Oxford: Clarendon, 1995, 298, 309. In 1871, in the Lancashire towns of Turton and Salford, approximately 30 per cent of the middle class lived with extended kin as opposed to 20 per cent of the skilled and 12 per cent of the unskilled (Ruggles, *Prolonged*, 36–7).

5 Anderson, *Family*, 66, 71–2, 121; Gaskell, *Artisans*, 89; Laslett and Wall, *Household*; Field, 'From', 112. A number of historians have criticised Ruggles' research (J. E. Smith, 'Method and confusion in the study of the household', *Historical Methods*, 22, 1989, 57–60).

6 Migrant father-son relationships may have been damaged by the tendency for migrants to possess different social norms from those of their children, who were brought up and partly socialised in the urban environment.

7 Barrett, 'Kinship', 203, 213, 218.

8 Anderson, *Family*; Barrett, 'Kinship', 215, 221; L Hollen-Lees, *The Solidarities of Strangers. The English Poor Laws and the People. 1700–1948*, Cambridge: Cambridge University Press, 1998, 171.

9 Dupree, *Family*, 344–5.

10 S. Nenadic, 'The small family firm in Victorian Britain', *Business History*, 35 (4), 1993, 96; B. Preston, 'Occupations of father and son in mid-Victorian England', *Geographical Papers, University of Reading*, no. 56, 1977, 31–3. In Bolton, an analysis of 417 sons born in the first half of the century to the elite of the town and a study of 1,840 males, many self-employed, who were married from 1837 to 1846 at the parish church at Deane, Bolton shows that 60 per cent and 55 per cent of elite and non-elite sons respectively adopted the same occupation as their father. Within the elite the practice was most common among those involved in the bleaching, engineering/metals and professional/white-collar sectors, and, among the non-elite, those working in engineering/metals, other manufactures and textiles.

11 In Bolton, 55 per cent and 65 per cent of elite nephews and brothers respectively entered the same occupation as their uncles and one other brother. Of the 567 boot and shoe manufacturers that traded in the town from 1780 to 1860, 52.5 per cent possessed a surname shared by at least one other person in the trade. 59 per cent, 66 per cent and 62 per cent of elite sons whose fathers were in respectively the textile sector, bleaching and engineering/metals and who did not follow their father's trade became professionals or white collar workers.

12 Hazlitt, *Table Talk*, vol. i, 359; Parkes, *Domestic*, 28; F. Lyon, 'Trust and power in farmer-trader relations', Durham University, PhD thesis, 2000, 18; M. B. Rose, 'Beyond Buddenbrooks. The family firm and the management of succession in nineteenth century Britain', in J. Brown and M. B. Rose (eds), *Entrepreneurship, Networks and Modern Business*, Manchester: Manchester University Press, 1993, p. 130.

13 Parkes, *Domestic*, 36; Ellis, *The Women*, 56. There is also a possibility that the trustworthiness of individuals was related to their family birth position. For example, firstborn children, more likely to inherit their parents' businesses, may have enjoyed more

trust as regards financial matters than their siblings, and will have been the first to use their father's network connections. Conversely, last-born children may have possessed more competence trust, as, owing to the contributions made to the family budget by older siblings, they will have been under less pressure to find employment and therefore less likely to enter an occupation to which they were unsuited.

14 J. A. James, *The Family Monitor*, Birmingham 1828, 19–20; Tosh, *A Man's*, 139. By spending their leisure time at home, men could also ensure that no family member acted in an immoral manner. Such behaviour could both damage the family trust reputation, and, by suggesting that he possessed little patriarchal authority, weakened the household head's masculine trust status.

15 Nenadic, 'The small', 87.

16 S. Mintz, *A Prison of Expectations. The Family in Victorian Culture*, New York: New York University, 1983, 27; *Bolton Chronicle*, 16 January 1847; Anon., *The Young*, 145. Parents also influenced the generation of a sense of trust. Family behaviour determines children's ability to participate in social groups, and the failure to provide sufficient food, warmth, comfort, love and security can lead to the development of a suspicion of others (M. M. Bubolz, 'Family as source, user and builder of social capital', *Journal of Socio-Economics*, 30, 2001, 129–31).

17 Entwisle, *A Report*, 89; PP 1840, x, q. 1602–6; Kay, *The Moral*, 11; Faucher, *Manchester*, 31; PP 1850, xxiii, 571, Mining Commissioners Report 1850, 26; Holden, *Respectable*, 161. Recent research suggests that emotional and physical neglect reduces social capital, not only through the poor socialisation of trust norms, but also by changing the nature of the developing brain. Neglect causes the prefrontal cortex, the area that enables people to recognise and respond to the feelings of others, to be underdeveloped, and overstimulates that part of the brain that is linked to stress and hostile behaviour (K. Braun, E. Lange, M. Metzger and G. Poeggel, 'Maternal separation', *Neuroscience*, 95 (1), 1999, 309–18; Anon., 'Mom's neglect hurts baby's brain', *Biotechnology Newswatch*, 3 November 1997, 6–7). Brutality by fathers would have particularly affected the respect sons held for their fathers and may have increased the bonds between siblings and between mothers and children.

18 Smelser, *Social*, 188, 193, 281, 406; M. Anderson, 'Smelser revisited', *Social History*, 1, 1976, 317–34; C. Creighton, 'Richard Oastler, factory legislation and the working class family', *Journal of Historical Sociology*, 5 (3), 1992, 307–10; Gallagher, *The Industrial*, 122; D. A. Galbi, 'Through eyes in the storm. Aspects of the personal history of women workers in the industrial revolution', *Social History*, 21 (2), 1996, 147, 156.

19 Ure, *The Philosophy*, 420, 421.

20 Creighton, 'Richard', 293, 301–2; Gallagher, *The Industrial*, 123; *The Home*, 1 (1851), 93 quoted in Creighton, 'Richard', 301; J. L. Matus, *Unstable Bodies. Victorian Representations of Sexuality and Maternity*, Manchester: Manchester University Press, 1995, 58.

21 Anderson, *Family*, 71; Smelser, *Social*, 282. See also S. Horrell and J. Humphries, 'The origins and expansion of the male breadwinner family. The case of nineteenth century Britain', *International Review of Social History*, 42, 1997, supplement, 25–64.

22 Morris, 'Voluntary', 100; J. E. Winters, *The Medical Record*, 1896 quoted in Matus, *Unstable*, 161; Mintz, *A Prison*, 30–9; Parkes, *Domestic*, 37; J. Tosh, 'Authority and nurture in middle class fatherhood. The case of early and mid Victorian England', *Gender and History*, 8 (1), 1996, 52. In 1859, C. H. F. Routh wrote 'I myself have known of two cases: one of a lady suckled by a bad woman, who in youth was full of like bad passions till converted by the gospel truth; and another of a gentleman suckled by a nurse of strong sexual passions who has inherited all her propensities' (Lancet 1 (1859), 581, quoted in Matus, *Unstable*, 161).

23 PP 1840, x.1, q. 696–7; Gallagher, *The Industrial*; Tholfsen, 'The intellectual', 75;

Taylor, *Popular*, 301; J. F. Bray, *Labour's Wrongs and Labour's Remedy*, Leeds, 1839, 111–12; J. Kucich, *The Power of Lies. Transgression in Victorian Fiction*, London: Cornell University, 1994, 7–9; A. B. Seligman, *The Idea of Civil Society*, New York: Free Press, 1992, 27; Ferguson, *An Essay*, 57. By the 1830s very few young children worked full time in factories, legislation having made it illegal to employ minors under eight years of age, and by 1850 only 5 per cent of Lancashire's cotton labour force was under the age of 13 (Anderson, *Family Structure*, 23).

24 E. Gordon and G. Nair, 'The myth of the Victorian patriarchal family', *The History of the Family*, 7, 2002, 126; Tosh, *A Man's*, 126; C. B. C. Amicus, *Hints on Life and How to Rise in Society*, London, 1845, 47–8; Parkes, *Domestic*, 23; Anon., *The Young*, 201. William Cobbett particularly warned suitors against women who drank alcohol, as there had never been 'a woman who loved strong drink who was chaste', and those who were not always clean, since 'a sloven in one thing [is] a sloven in all things'. To avoid the latter, he advised prospective bridegrooms to check for dirt behind their intended's ears (William Cobbett, *Advice to Young Men*, London 1829, letter 3). The extent to which young people could choose partners from families with good trust reputations was largely depended on class, higher status singletons having a wider choice of partner (R. A. Houston, 'Marriage formation and domestic industry. Occupational endogamy in Kilmarnock, Ayrshire, 1697–1764', *Journal of Family History*, 8 (3), 1983, 216).

25 *Taylor, Popular*, 63–4; Houston, 'Marriage', 221. In Bolton, a study of 172 son-in-laws who married into elite families in the first half of the century and the 1,824 non-elite males who were wed at the parish church at Deane, Bolton from 1837 to 1846 indicate that around a third of son-in-laws were in the same occupation as their spouse's father. Within the elite, the practice was most common among those involved in the professional/white collar and textile sectors, and, among the non-elite, those employed in textiles and other manufactures.

26 A banker quoted in Alborn, 'The moral', 211; A. Stanley quoted in E. Trudgill, *Madonnas and Magdalens*, London: Heinemann, 1976, 80; Parkes, *Domestic*, 8, 10, 16, 23; J. Tosh, 'What should historians do with masculinity? Reflections in nineteenth century Britain', *History Workshop Journal*, 38, 1994, 8. The Manchester cotton factory owner Magdalin Goffin constantly bemoaned in his diaries that 'at home . . . [he had] . . . no support or sympathy', only 'dirt, rags, a mean appearance, a table wretchedly provided, linen but half washed, [and] a disgusting mixture of finery and beggarliness' (Watkin, *Absalom*, 105).

27 Through her relationships with servants, a wife and ultimately her husband, could also plug into domestic service networks, which again were carriers of much useful knowledge regarding other servant keepers.

28 Lewis, 'The working', in Lewis, *Labour*, 107; A. Fletcher, *Gender, Sex and Subordination in England, 1550–1800*, New Haven: Yale University, 1995, xvi; L. Gowing, *Domestic Dangers. Women, Words and Sex in Early Modern London*, Oxford: Clarendon, 1996, 61; S. Walby, 'From private to public patriarchy. The periodisation of British history', *Women's' Studies International Forum*, 13, (1–2), 1990, 91–104; D' Cruze, 'Women', 62. Pawning damaged trust reputations and was therefore done secretively (Johnson, *Saving*, 183).

29 Lewis, 'The working', 107; N. Tomes '"A torrent of abuse". Crimes of violence between working class men and women in London, 1849–75', *Journal of Social History*, 11, 1978, 328–45; A. Clark, 'Humanity or justice? Wife beating and the law in the eighteenth and nineteenth centuries', in C. Smart (ed.), *Regulating Womanhood. Historical Essays on Marriage, Motherhood and Sexuality*, London: Routledge, 1992, 188.

30 M. H. D. Van Leeuwen and I. Maas, 'Partner choice and homogamy in the nineteenth century. Was there a sexual revolution in Europe?', *Journal of Social History*, 36 (1), 2002, 102; Mintz, *A Prison*, 191; Shoemaker, *Gender*, 92; Elizabeth Foyster,

'Creating a veil of silence? Politeness and marital violence in the English household',
Transactions of the Royal Historical Society, 12, 2002, 399, 409; A. J. Hammerton,
'Victorian marriage and the laws of matrimonial cruelty', *Victorian Studies*, 33 (2),
1990, 277–8, 218–22, 282–3. Marriages lasted longer due to falls in the number of
women dying during pregnancy, and earlier marriage (Mintz, *A Prison*, 19). People
married at a younger age because they became economically more independent
earlier and perhaps because kinship networks, which aided the discovery of a suitable
partner, became more dense and functional, and it became more difficult to determine
negative reputations that would discourage marriage (Steven King, 'Chance encoun-
ters? Paths to household formation in early modern England', *International Review of
Social History*, 44 (1999), 23–46, 23). Men who were 'most polite in the company of
strangers', but at home threw 'aside their good manners as they do their best clothes'
were despised by the polite and respectable (Mrs Marshall, *The Child's Guide to
Good Breeding*, London 1839, 27). Their disapproval was partly related to the rise in
sensibility and the belief that women possessed sensitive and easily damaged nervous
systems (Foyster, 'Creating', 409). Nineteenth-century divorce court records show
that, over time, middle-class women were more willing to take legal action against
partners who acted in a violent manner or cruelly; resorted to violence or humiliating
acts themselves when attacked by their husbands; and, occasionally, openly defied
spouses (Hammerton, 'Victorian', 277–8). The Matrimonial Causes Act 1857 allowed
divorce without the need for a separate act of partnership. The Married Women Property Acts of 1870 and 1882 eroded the legal doctrine of couverture, which stated that
a woman's property was owned by her husband (D' Cruze, 'Women', 76). Common
law also became less unfair. By 1869, for example, charges of cruelty no longer
needed to be substantiated by evidence of violence (Hammerton, 'Victorian', 277–8,
282–3).

31 J. Tosh, 'Domesticity and manliness in the Victorian middle class', in M. Roper and
J. Tosh (eds), *Manful Assertions. Masculinities in Britain Since 1800*, London: Routledge, 1991, 53; Anon., *Business*, 55, 56, 58; Shepherd, *A Series*, 252–3. According
to a sample of the 1851 census, 31 per cent of upper-middle-class husbands were at
least five years older than their wives (Davidoff and Hall, *Family*, 323). It was
believed that if the age difference was 'more than from 5 to 8 years, it will become
next to impossible [that] there can be long continued participation in the same pleasures and pursuits' (Anon., *Business*, 51).

32 Bates, *A Discourse*, 91.

33 R. J. Dennis, 'Distance and social interaction in a Victorian city', *Journal of Historical Geography*, 3 (3), 1977, 237–50.

34 M. Tebbutt, 'Centres and peripheries. Reflections on place identity and sense of
belonging in a north Derbyshire cotton town, 1880–1990', *Manchester Region
History Review*, 13, 1999, 9, 11; L. Cuba and D. M. Hummon, 'A place to call home.
Identification with dwelling, community and region', *Sociological Quarterly*, 34 (1),
1993, 112; S. Caunce, 'Urban systems, identity and development in Lancashire and
Yorkshire', in N. Kirk (ed.), *Northern Identities. Historical Interpretations of the
North and Northerness*, Aldershot: Ashgate, 2000, 62; K. D. M. Snell, 'The culture of
local xenophobia', *Social History*, 28 (1), 2003, 24; Rodger, 'The "common"'. Place
identification was intimately related to self-identification and self-confidence
(Feldman, 'Settlement', 188). Pearson argues that sense of community was differenti-
ated by class attitudes and that the connection of community with harmony was a
middle class construct (R. Pearson, 'Knowing one's place. Perceptions of community
in the industrial suburbs of Leeds, 1790–1890', *Journal of Social History*, 27 (2),
1993, 221).

35 Bolton Archive, 'Bolton Biographical Notes' (newspaper cuttings), vol. i, 299; N.
Stirk, 'Manufacturing reputations in late eighteenth century Birmingham', *Historical
Research*, 73 (181), 2000, 142–55; J. R. Gold and S. V. Ward, *Place Promotion. The*

Use of Publicity and Marketing to sell Towns and Regions, Chichester: Wiley, 1994; Rodger, 'The "common"', 147.

36 S. Smiles, *The Life of George Stevenson*, London, 1858, v quoted in L. Otis, *Networking. Communicating with Bodies and Machines in the Nineteenth Century*, Ann Arbor: University of Michigan, 2001, 81, 120. The network nature of the new communications and the importance of networks in Von Helmholtz's research on the human nervous system and Tyndall's investigation of the behaviour of atoms caused many to apply network principles to human relations. George Eliot, for example, believed that 'railways, steam ships and electric telegraphs' demonstrated 'the interdependence of all human interests, making self-interest a duct for sympathy' (Eliot quoted in ibid., 81).

37 Anon., *Organization in Daily Life*, London, 1862, 26, 69; W. D. Rubinstein, 'Wealth elites and the class structure of modern Britain', *Past and Present*, 76, 1977, 99–126. Given the large sums of money involved, trust was essential in the City. It was also easier to generate owing to closer sector inter-connections; the geographic concentration of activities, which facilitated face to face meetings; the lack of elite division; and the greater dependence on staff honesty, which encouraged employers to develop strong trust relationships with their employees.

38 Colley, *Britons*; R. J. Morris, 'Civil society, subscriber democracies and Parliamentary government in Great Britain', in N. Bermeo, and P. Nord, *Civil Society before Democracy. Lessons from Nineteenth Century Europe*, Oxford: Rowman & Littlefield, 2000, 123; G. Morton, 'Civil society, municipal government and the state. Enshrinement, empowerment and legitimacy. Scotland, 1800–1929', *Urban History*, 25 (3), 1998, 348–67; R. F. Foster, *Modern Ireland, 1600–1972*, London: Allen Lane, 1988, 257–308.

39 S. Collini, *Public Moralists. Political Thought and Intellectual Life in Britain, 1850–1930*, Oxford: Clarendon, 1991, 134; Langford, *Englishness*, 122, 124; W. E. H. Lecky, *History of European Morals from Augustus to Charlemagne*, London, 1869, vol. 1, 144 quoted in Kucich, *The Power*, 6.

40 Thomas Russell, 1795 quoted in S. H. Jeyes, *The Russells of Birmingham in the French Revolution and in America*, London, 1911, 204–5; A. Smith, *Lectures on Justice, Police, Revenue and Arms*, New York: A. M. Kelley, 1964, 254. B. Porter, ' "Bureau and barrack." Early Victorian attitudes towards the continent', *Victorian Studies*, 27 (4), 1984, 410, 426; B. L. Kinzer, 'The unenglishness of the secret ballot', *Albion*, 10 (3), 1978, 243; D. N. Livingstone, 'The moral discourse of climate. Historical considerations on race, place and virtue', *Journal of Historical Geography*, 17 (4), 1991, 416, 419; J. Hunt, 'On ethno-climatology or the acclimatization of man', *Transactions of the Ethnological Society of London*, 2, 1863, 53. Samuel George Morton believed that the cranial capacities of Greenlanders proved that they were 'crafty, sensual, ungrateful, obstinate and unfeeling and [that] much of their affection for their children may be traced to purely selfish motives' (Samuel G. Morton, *Crania Americana*, Philadelphia, 1839, 54).

41 Tosh, 'Masculinities'; Tosh, 'Domesticity', 46; Tosh, 'What should', 185, 190.

42 Ibid.; Dennis Smith, 'Paternalism, craft and organizational rationality, 1830–1930. An exploratory model', *Urban History*, 19 (2) (1992), 215, 217–18.

43 Tosh, 'What should', 195–7; Tosh, 'Domesticity', 65. Homosexuals also symbolised a rejection of bourgeois masculinity, spending little time in the domestic sphere and often putting personal gratification above the demands of work.

Colonial imagery increasingly took on a despised feminine aspect – the dark continent possessed allure and awaited penetration, natives were docile and devious, and so on.

44 *Rifleman's Magazine*, no. 1, August 1860, 17, *The Times*, 22 September 1857 and *United Services Gazette*, 29 September 1860, quoted in P. Morton, 'A military irony. The Victorian volunteer movement', *Journal of the Royal United Services Institute*

for Defensive Studies, 131 (3), 1986, 66, 65, 68. For officers, costs of involvement were low; their counterparts in the regular army had to purchase a commission and meet a variety of expenses.

45 Davies, 'Youth', 32.

46 M. Granovetter, 'Economic action and social structure. The problem of embeddedness', *American Journal of Sociology*, 3, 1985, 481–510.

9 Business trust

1 Nickalls, *Journal*, 37–8; Freedley, *A Practical*, 4; Bates, *A Discourse*, 115; Searle, *Morality*, 78.

2 D. E. Zand, *The Leadership Triad. Knowledge, Trust and Power*, Oxford: Oxford University Press, 1997, 108; Harris, 'Social leadership', 268; J. Raven, 'English popular literature and the image of business, 1760–90', Cambridge University, PhD thesis, 1985.

3 C. Bronte, *Shirley*, Oxford: Clarendon, 1979 (originally published 1849), 186; Bates, *A Discourse*, 7, 8, 23, 21; Dymond, *Essays*, 277, 282.

4 D. Sunderland, *Managing the British Empire*, London: Boydell & Brewer, 2004, 33; D. J. Moss, 'Business and banking. Ethics and white-collar crime in Norwich, 1825–1831', *Albion*, 29 (3), 1997, 377; Defoe, *The Complete*, 175–6; Bates, *A Discourse*, 115.

5 Amicus, *Hints*, 42; Anon., *Business Life*, 36; F. Tristan, *London Journal*, London: Prior, 1980 (originally published 1840), 147; R. A. Black, 'Henry Sidgwick and the Institutionalists on the goodwill of the firm', *History of Political Economy*, 24 (1), 1992, 85; Hambly, *Competition*, 14. Goodwill was first recognised in English courts in 1743, but it was not until the end of the century and the writings of Wilhelm Roscher and H. D. Mcleod that it was treated as capital by economists (Black, 'Henry', 82).

6 Lamb, *Free*, vol. i, 95–6; J. W. Diggle, *The Lancashire Life of Bishop Fraser*, London, 1889, 133; PP 1852–3, xxii.1, q. 270; Bates, *A Discourse*, 117, 119.

7 R. Owen, *A New View of Society and Other Writings*, New York: Everyman, 1963, 122; Wood, 'Debt', 23; Field, 'From', 37; R. Church, 'Ossified or dynamic? Structure, markets and the competitive process in the British business system of the nineteenth century', *Business History*, 42 (1), 2000, 4, 15, 18; Nenadic, 'The small', 90; T. K. Hareven, *Family and Kin in Urban Communities, 1700–1930*, New York: New York University, 1977, 144–63. See also V. A. C. Gatrell, 'Labour, power and the size of firms in Lancashire cotton in the second quarter of the nineteenth century', *Economic History Review*, 30, 1977, 120 and A. Owens, 'Inheritance and the life-cycle of family firms in the early industrial revolution', *Business History*, 44 (1), 2002, 27. The advantage of using trade directories to determine firm lifespans is that they contain information not available elsewhere. Drawbacks are that they can be inaccurate and incomplete and particularly omit very small businesses (J. Newman, ' "A want of better information"? Some early trade directories of Southern England', *Southern History*, 16, 1994, 180, 182; P. Corfield, ' "Giving directions to the town". The early town directories', *Urban History Yearbook*, 1994, 22). It is therefore probable that the Bolton database underestimates the turnover of firms.

The greater competition is also reflected in price data. After the French wars, prices fell until 1850 when they stabilised. Apart from the bullion-based credit expansion of the early 1850s and the inflationary boom of 1870–3, they then remained flat until the 1890s. There is also evidence that in the first half of the century raw material prices remained relatively buoyant, which in some industries will have resulted in a profit squeeze (Church, 'Ossified', 4, 15).

8 Popp, 'Trust', 28–53; Searle, *Morality*, 99–101; Seed, 'Unitarianism', 8; G. Robb, *White Collar Crime in Modern England*, Cambridge: Cambridge University Press,

1992, 170; J. Butcher, *Instructions in Etiquette*, London, 1847, 40; Smith, *Lectures*, 254; M. Casson, *Enterprise and Competitiveness. A Systems View of International Business*, Oxford: Clarendon, 1990, 43, 109–10, 117; Hambly, *Competition*, 18, 19. See also Dr J. Watts, 'On cooperation as an economic element in society', *Transactions of the Manchester Statistical Society*, session 1872–3, 4.

9 T. Carlyle, *The Complete Works of Thomas Carlyle*, New York, 1902, vol. xii, 142; McKendrick *et al.*, *The Birth*, 211.

10 J. Hoppit, *Risk and Failure in English Business, 1700–1800*, Cambridge: Cambridge University Press, 1987; M d'Archenholz, *A Picture of England*, Dublin, 1790, 256. The creditworthiness of companies can, again, be used as a measure of town trust. Means of company credit ratings published in *The Credit Index* of 1894 suggests that Bolton was perceived as relatively highly creditworthy with an average company credit rating of 4.64 (4 = good for £2,000 to £5,000) (*The Credit Index*, London 1894).

11 Anon., *Remarks on the Facility of Obtaining Commercial Credit*, London, 1806, 7–8, 29–50.

12 Bates, *A Discourse*, 118; Anon., *Remarks*, 16–17; Freedley, *A Practical*, 235.

13 R. MacKelworth, 'Trades, crafts and credit in a Victorian village. A trading family in Milford, Surrey 1851–81', *Family and Community History*, 2 (1), 1999, 36–41; Gatrell, Labour', 124; C. H. Lee, 'Marketing organisation and policy in the cotton trade. M'Connel and Kennedy of Manchester, 1795–1835', *South African Journal of Economic History*, 8 (1), 1993, 123–31.

14 H. Thornton, *An Enquiry into the Nature and Effects of the Paper Credit of Great Britain*, London: Allen & Unwin, 1939 (originally published 1802), 187; Barton, *Historical*, vol. i, 152; J. Locke quoted in F. Ritzmann, 'Money a substitute for confidence? Vaughan to Keynes and beyond', *Journal of Economics and Sociology*, 58 (2), 1999, 168. Usually the debts of new entrants were called in first, even though these traders were not the deepest in debt. Creditors had strong trust relationships with longer established firms. These businesses were more likely to survive a downturn, and demanding repayment could therefore prove costly in terms of lost future trade. Long-established businessmen were also well liked in the community and forcing them into insolvency would damage the creditor's trust reputation.

15 Searle, *Morality*, 159; Somers, 'Citizenship', 601; Dutton and King, 'The limits', 63; Putnam, *Democracy*, 163–85; Lamb, *Free*, vol. ii, 95; Brooks, 'Interpersonal', 393–5.

16 Robb, *White*, 11, 24, 169, 172.

17 Crafts and Harley, 'Output', 704; L. O. Pike, *A History of Crime in England*, London, 1876, 477–8; N. Russell, *The Novelist and Mammon. Literary Responses to the World of Commerce in the Nineteenth Century*, Oxford: Clarendon, 1986, 10–11; S. Mariner, 'English bankruptcy records and statistics before 1850', *Economic History Review*, 33, 1980, 358. Crafts and Harley have shown that both national income per caput and the cotton industry grew less rapidly than previously assumed (Crafts and Hartley, 'Output', 703, 705; C. K. Harley, 'British industrialization before 1841: evidence of slower growth during the industrial revolution', *Journal of Economic History*, 42, 1982, 281).

18 Searle, *Morality*, 99; F. Trentmann, *Paradoxes of Civil Society. New Perspectives on Modern German and British History*, Oxford: Berghahn, 2000, 29; E. Miall, *The British Churches in Relation to the British people*, London, 1849, 296–7; Smith, *Lectures*, 253; T. Hodgskin, *The Natural and Artificial Rights of Property*, London, 1832 quoted in Jaffe, 'Commerce', 257; *The Economist*, 23 June, 1855, 671–2.

19 Mackelworth, 'Trades', 33–43; Muldrew, *The Economy*; Finn, *The Character*, 10, 76; Anon., *Remarks*, 48. Letters of reference and a willingness to provide security for another, similarly, acted as gifts, the referee damaging his reputation and the security provider losing whatever he gave as collateral if the borrower failed to pay his debt.

The repayment of a loan acted as a signal to the business community that a borrower could continue to be trusted.

20 H. S. Maine, *Ancient Law*, London, 1861, 306–7; PP 1852–3, xxii.1, q. 257–60, 272, 339, 341, 359, 360.

21 J. P. Riley, 'God unwilling and with a pang of conscience. White collar criminality and secret commissions, 1875–1916', University of Lancaster, PhD thesis, 2000, 329.

22 D. Loftus, 'Social economy. Cultures of work and community in mid-Victorian England', University of Southampton, PhD, 1998, 86, 98; PP 1850, xix, 20; *Quarterly Review*, April 1852, 406; PP 1850, xix, 85; *Westminster Review*, 6 (1853), 414; PP 1851, xviii.1, q. 576. The 1856 Companies Act did away with the cumbersome and expensive procedures that previously had to be followed to obtain limited liability. Under the new legislation, shareholders had merely to sign a memorandum of association. The Act also abolished limits on the number of shares that could be held, which theoretically enabled workingmen to invest in companies (Loftus, 'Social', 86).

It was further claimed that the introduction of limited liability, by demonstrating to people 'that the legislature were willing to give them fair facility' to build infrastructure schemes would strengthen the social contract (PP 1850, xix, 10, 17).

23 L. Newton, 'Capital networks in the Sheffield region, 1850–1855', in Wilson and Popp, *Industrial*.

24 J. F. Wilson and J. Singleton, 'The Manchester industrial district, 1750–1939', 51, 66 in Wilson and Popp, *Industrial*; D. J. Jeremy, 'Survival strategies in Lancashire textiles. Bleachers' Association Ltd to Whitecroft Plc, 1900–1980s', *Textile History*, 24 (2), 1993, 163–209.

25 J. Z. Namenwirth, 'The wheels of time and the interdependence of value change', *Journal of Interdisciplinary History*, 3, 1973, 649–83; J. Z. Namenwirth, 'Change within or of the system. An example from the history of American values', *Quantity and Quality*, 10, 1976, 145–64; R. P. Weber, 'Society and economy in the western world system', *Social Forces*, 59 (4), 1981, 1130–48; Wilson and Singleton, 'The Manchester', 66; S. Bowden and D. Higgins, 'Much ado about nothing? Regional business networks and the performance of the cotton and woollen textile industries, *c*.1919–*c*.1939', in Wilson and Popp, *Industrial*, 91, 111.

26 Granovetter, 'Economic', 481–510. In 1828/9, Bolton had 95 trading sectors and an average of 13.9 tradesmen per sector; in 1851, 144 sectors and an average of 14 tradesmen per sector, and, in 1869, 194 sectors and an average of 21.7 tradesmen per sector (Pigot, *National*; *Slater's . . . 1852*; *Slater's . . . 1869*).

27 The norms of the dominant industry would also have a disproportionate influence on the trust culture of a town.

28 Rose, *Firms*, 67; R. M. Kirk, 'The economic development of the British textile machinery industry, 1850–1939', Salford University, PhD thesis, 1983, 12.

29 BA, ZHE 35/34.

30 Burchell and Wilkinson, 'Trust', 218.

31 G. George, D Robley-Wood Jnr and R. Khan, 'Networking strategy of boards. Implications for small and medium-sized enterprises', *Entrepreneurship & Regional Development*, 13, 2001, 273; Nenadic, 'The small', 87.

32 Anon., *The Young*, 243; Anon., *Business*, 31; Hoppit, *Risk*, 165.

33 See also Nenadic, 'The small', 95.

34 J. M. Barbalet, *Emotion, Social Theory and Social Structure*, Cambridge: Cambridge University Press, 1998, 90; Benabou and Tirole, 'Self-confidence', 4; Binney, *Is it*, 31; Hazlitt, *Table*, 364; Anon., *Essays on Social Subjects from the Saturday Reviews*, London, 1864, 365; Smith, *The Theory*, 303; Smiles, *Self*, 202.

35 Anon., *Essays Written in the Intervals of Business*, London, 1853, 87; Freedley, *A Practical*, 56; Anon., *Business*, 35; Lamb, *Free*, vol. i, 202.

36 Freedley, *A Practical*, 40; Defoe, *The Complete*, 66; W. Scott, *A Sermon on Bankruptcy*, London, 1773, 2; Anon., *The Young*, 368; F. Robertson, 'The aesthetics of

authenticity. Printed banknotes as industrial currency', *Technology and Culture*, 46, 2005, 31–50.

37 Boyce, 'Network', 52–76. There were also post-negotiation routines covering the buyer's monitoring of the manufacturing process, the resolution of disagreements and the delivery of the finished product. Disputes were usually resolved by 'splitting the difference'. Delivery of large items sometimes involved a handing over ceremony, which allowed each side to advertise his relationship with his opposite number, and the manufacturer to signal the successful completion of the contract to his customer's satisfaction. Such ceremonies were also attended by the families of both traders, leading to the development of inter-family trust; local notables, who added to the principals' trust reputations; those who worked on the project, which increased employer–employee trust; and inevitably local newspaper reporters.

38 Field, 'From', 35–6; BA, Poll book, 1832, 1841.

39 Gunn, *The Public*, 40; E. Jones, *Industrial Architecture in Britain, 1750–1939*, London: Batsford, 1985, 147, 141; Morgan, *Manners*, 104.

40 Crawforth, 'Evidence'; A. Offer, 'The mask of intimacy. Advertising and the quality of life', in A. Offer (ed.), *In Pursuit of the Quality of Life*, Oxford: Oxford University Press, 1996, 218–27.

41 J. J. Fenstermaker, 'Using Dickens to market morality. Popular reading materials in the Nickleby "Advertiser"', *Journal of Popular Culture*, 28 (3), 1994, 9–17; D. Garrioch, 'House names, shop signs and social organization in Western European cities, 1500–1900', *Urban History*, 21 (1), 1994, 27, 31; Crawforth, 'Evidence', 484.

42 N. F. Koehn, *Brand New. How Entrepreneurs Earned Consumers' Trust From Wedgwood to Dell*, Boston: Harvard Business School, 1995, 35, 327. High sales in themselves were often an indicator of quality. Salesmen could also monitor the creditworthiness of retailers.

43 Bolton Archive, ZHH.

44 Hoppit, *Risk*, 163. From 1815–72, clog and patten makers had an average lifespan of 4.2 years in Bolton, 8.3 years in Oldham and 6.9 years in Preston; iron and brass founders had an average lifespan of 9.3 years in Bolton, 7.9 years in Oldham and 7.4 years in Preston; and wheelwrights had an average lifespan of 6.7 years in Bolton, 8.3 years in Oldham and 6.3 years in Preston.

45 Gatrell, 'Labour', 98; R. Lloyd-Jones and A. A. Le Roux, 'Marshall and the birth and death of firms. The growth and size distribution of firms in the early nineteenth century cotton industry', *Business History*, 24, 1982, 141–55; C. Young, 'The economic characteristics of businesses in rural lowland Perthshire', *Business History*, 36, 1994, 35–52.

46 Gatrell, 'Labour', 98, 107–8, 117; Hoppit, *Risk*, 26, 165; R. Mackie, 'Best for the family. Researching families and businessmen', *Family and Community History*, 4 (1), 2001, 39; N. Abercrombie, S. Hill and B. S. Turner, *Sovereign Individuals of Capitalism*, London: Allen & Unwin, 1986, 96. Eliot's Silas Marner, *Middlemarch*'s Bulstrode, *Bleak House*'s Richard Jarndyce and *Oliver Twists*'s Fagin are all examples of the corrupting power of greed. Many of the money obsessed are cheats and swindlers – Uriah Heep in *David Copperfield*, Carker in *Dombey and Son*, the Chadbands in *Bleak House*, and Bulstrode in *Middlemarch*. Some, such as Silas Marner and Mr Dombey, become cut off from human company. Others, for example the narrator of Tennyson's *Maud*, descend into madness (V. Cunningham, 'Goodness and goods. Victorian literature and values for the middle class reader', *Proceedings of the British Academy*, 78, 1992, 109–27).

47 B. Hilton, *The Age of Atonement. The Influence of Evangelicalism on Social and Economic Thought, 1795–1865*, Oxford: Oxford University Press, 1988, 107, 119; PP 1852–3, xxii.1, qq. 291, 293; *Bolton Chronicle*, 16 October 1847; The cotton mill owner H. Houldsworth quoted in Gatrell, 'Labour', 117; Defoe, *The Complete*, 70.

48 D. A. Collier, 'A comparative history of the development of the leading stationary

steam engine manufacturers of Lancashire, 1800–1939', University of Manchester, PhD thesis, 1951, 189; Freedly, *A Practical*, 36; Anon., *The Young*, 368.

49 S. Nenadic, 'Businessmen, the urban middle classes and the dominance of manufacturers in nineteenth century Britain', *Economic History Review*, 44 (1), 1991, 68; Winder, *A Life's*.

50 Nenadic, 'Businessmen', 68; B. Harrison, *Drink and the Victorians. The Temperance Question in England, 1815–1872*, Keele: Keele University Press, 1994, 53.

51 Anon., *Business*, 194; PP 1852–3, xxii.1, qq. 49–50, 166, 765; Defoe, *The Complete*, 85–6; Anon., *The Management and Economy of Trade*, London, 1783, 28; J. Nicholls and E. Doyle, *Nicholls' Practice in Insolvency in the Courts of Bankruptcy*, London, 1845, xix; *The Spectator*, vol. iv, 6; E. Gibbon, *Memoirs of my Life*, Harmondsworth: Penguin, 1984, 153.

52 Owens, 'Inheritance'.

53 Wilson and Popp, *Industrial*, 12.

54 McIvor, *Organised*, 38, 136; F. Carnevali, '"Crooks, thieves and receivers." Transaction costs in nineteenth century Birmingham', *Economic History Review*, 62 (3), 2004, 533–50.

55 PP 1834, x, q. 4686; Church, 'Ossified', 5, 6.

56 McIvor, *Organised*, 42; A. Yarmie, 'Employers' organizations in mid-Victorian England', *International Review of Social History*, 25 (2), 1980, 212, 221.

57 Wood, 'Debt', 27, 30–1; Morgan, *Manners*, 133–7; Alborn, 'The moral', 207.

58 O. Westall, 'The competitive environment in British business', in M. Kirby and M. B. Rose (eds), *Business Enterprise in Modern Britain from the Eighteenth to the Twentieth Centuries*, London: Routledge, 1994, 209. Collusion was made possible by the small number of local firms present and high transport costs, inefficient information flows and strong local tastes and preferences, all of which prevented geographically distant firms entering such markets.

59 L. Newton, 'Regional bank–industry relations during the mid nineteenth century. Links between bankers and manufacturers in Sheffield 1850–85', *Business History*, 38 (3), 1996, 64–81; Newton, 'Trust', 177, 187, 189.

60 To ensure high-value networking and to avoid the appointment of the dishonest, some banks required their directors to hold a minimum number of shares in the company and not to be a bankrupt.

10 Employer–employee trust

1 W. Cobbett, *Rural Rides*, London, 1830, 100; R. Southey, *Essays. Moral and Political*, London, 1812, 112–13; A. Fox, *History and Heritage. The Social Origins of the British Industrial Relations System*, London: Allen & Unwin, 1985, 3–10; M. R. Somers, 'Citizenship and the place of the public sphere. Law community and political culture in the transition to democracy', *American Sociological Review*, 58, 1993, 597–600.

2 T. Moore, *Utopia*, 130 quoted in Fox, *History*, 10; Fox, *History*, 7–10

3 Somers, 'Citizenship', 601–5; J. Kent, 'The English village constable, 1580–1642', *Journal of British Studies*, 20, 1981, 29; M. Davies, *The Enforcement of English Apprenticeship, 1563–1642*, Cambridge: Cambridge University Press, 1956, 175, 177, 255; J. Bohstedt, *Riots and Community Politics in England and Wales, 1790–1810*, Cambridge, Mass.: Harvard University Press, 1983, 41–2.

4 PP 1834, x, q. 6356, 5359, 6349; Huberman, *Escape*, 10.

5 Smelser, *Social*, 65; PP 1834, x, q. 4367, 4937.

6 Smelser, *Social*, 65, 80; G. Unwin, *Samuel Oldknow and the Arkwrights*, London: Longman, 1924, 49.

7 PP 1802–3, viii, pp. 3–4, 10, 31; PP 1834, x, q. 5297, 5645, 5033, 5854, 6349–57.

8 Ibid., 4570, 4389.

9 Huberman, *Escape*, 22. Gender division of labour will have raised intra-gender trust, but weakened inter-gender relations.

10 G. H. Wood, *The History of Wages in the Cotton Trade*, Manchester, 1910, 14, 15, 28; Joyce, 'The factory', 546; PP 1834, xxxvi, appendix b2, parts 3, 4 and 5, q. 51. Depicted in the press as lawlessness, Luddism also generated general distrust. Where employer exploitation of workers was great, the Stockholm syndrome may have operated. Employees may have developed positive feelings of trust towards their exploiters as a coping strategy (S. M. Auerbach, D. J. Kiesler, T. Strentz, J. Schmidt and C. Senior, 'Impersonal impacts and adjustment to the stress of simulated captivity', *Journal of Social and Clinical Psychology*, 13 (2), 1994, 207–9).

11 Taylor, 'The new', 28; Dutton and King, 'The limits', 7, 65; D. C. Woods, 'The operation of the Master and Servant Acts in the Black country, 1858–1875', *Midland History*, 7, 1982, 94. In the 1770s, before the introduction of power relationships, courts occasionally sought to contribute to the re-establishment of trust relationships though the provision of lenient sentences (A. Charlesworth, 'From the moral economy of Devon to the political economy of Manchester, 1790–1812', *Social History*, 18 (2), 1993, 215).

12 Smelser, *Social*, 105; Rose, *Firms*, 113–14; Holden, *Respectable*, 56.

13 PP 1852–3, lxviii (1), pp. lxxvii–lxxviii and county entries; PP1867/8, xxxix, 83; Fletcher, 'Moral', 213; Mintz, *A Prison*, 15; Ball and Sunderland, *An Economic*, chapter 12.

14 Quoted in Huberman, *Escape*, 53.

15 C. Calhoun, 'Transition in social foundations for collective action', *Social Science History*, 4 (4), 1980, 443.

16 Huberman, *Escape*, 55; B. Love, *The Handbook of Manchester*, Manchester, 1842, 85; Poole, 'Popular', 4; Taylor, 'The new', 12.

17 Clegg, *Annals*, 7; Taylor, 'The new', 50. The greater level of conflict in Oldham has been blamed on that town's militant radicalism, and the relative peace of Bolton has been related to the religious and political divisions within the elite, which obstructed the development of employer trust (Rose, *Firms*, 126).

18 Factory Inspectors reports, 1837–1870; R. Gray, *The Factory Question and Industrial England*, 1830–60, Cambridge: Cambridge University Press, 1996, 168, 178.

19 Rose, *Firms*, 125; Joyce, *Work*, 68; Huberman, *Escape*, 13, 20, 134; PP 1834, x, q. 4404; Ure, *The Philosophy*, 417. Kirk and Taylor argue that conflict continued at least until the 1870s (Kirk, *The Growth*, chapter 6; Taylor, *Popular*, 13). Foster believes that the collapse of militancy was the result of skilled workers being drawn into the authority structure of the factory. Joyce argues that a culture of subordination developed (Foster, *Class*; Joyce, *Work*).

According to Huberman, mule spinners failed to operate new machinery to its full potential, because they feared that employers would cut piece rates if they realised its optimum output. The thesis depends on the questionable assumption that all workers would willingly sacrifice higher wages in the short term merely on the possibility of higher long-term incomes. The theory is based on the supposed actions of the workers of just one firm, McConnel and Kennedy.

20 D. Philips, *Crime and Authority in Victorian England*, London: Croom Helm, 1997, 223; Ure, *The Philosophy*, 416.

21 Ure, *The Philosophy,* 363; Huberman, 'The economic', 179–80.

22 Loftus, 'Social', 45; PP 1847–8, xxvi, 10; PP 1850, xxiii, 41; PP 1844, xvi.1, 68; PP 1849, xxii.395, 23; Bates, *A Discourse*, 130; Ure, *The Philosophy*, 418.

23 Ure, *The Philosophy*, 353; Taylor, *Popular*, 182, 221; W. Cobbett, *Two Penny Trash*, 9 March 1831, 204; quote from the Bolton Spinners Union, *Bolton Chronicle*, 26 June 1830.

24 Huberman, *Escape*, 135, 138; Rose, *Firms*, 126; Wood, *The History*, 3. Arbitration generated 'between masters and workmen' 'a more intimate acquaintanceship of each

others views and a knowledge of the laws which regulate trade, commerce, capital and labour', and thus created 'goodwill ... confidence and sympathy' (PP 1856, xiii, xv).

25 Freedley, *A Practical*, 87; PP 1849, xxii., 395, 7; Ure, *The Philosophy*, 366; Faucher, *Manchester*, 130.

26 Dutton and King, 'The limits', 59–73; Kirk, *The Growth*, 22; Taylor, 'The new'; *Bolton Chronicle*, 16 October 1869, ibid., 22 August 1874.

27 H. Ashworth, *The Preston Strike. An Enquiry into its Causes and Consequences*, Manchester, 1854, 96; *Bolton Chronicle*, 9 August 1845.

28 Boyer, 'Poor', 71; *Bolton Chronicle*, 9 March 1861; Lamb, *Free*, vol. ii, 357; Huberman, *Escape*, 125; W. O. Henderson, *The Lancashire Cotton Famine, 1861–65*, Manchester: Manchester University Press, 1934, 69.

29 Taylor, *Popular*, 204–7; Seed, 'Unitarianism', 8; Hewitt, *The Emergence*, 6. The ten-hour campaign was supported by the major manufacturers, operatives and a range of professionals, shopkeepers and clergymen. It thus itself promoted much employer–employee and inter- and intra-class trust.

30 Anon., *Business*, 43; J. Garnett and A. C. Howe, 'Churchmen and cotton masters in Victorian England', in D. J. Jeremy (ed.), *Business and Religion in Britain*, Aldershot: Gower, 1988, 76; Bolton Archive, ZAH 11/4, Halliwell Bleach Works, July 1857, 'List of persons employed'; Holden, *Respectable*, 183, 421; R. M. Fernandez *et al.*, 'Social capital at work', *American Journal of Sociology*, 105 (5), 2001, 1291–8; Freedley, *A Practical*, 86.

31 *Bolton Chronicle*, 31 May 1845; Bolton Archive, ZAH 11/4. Knowles and Son employed 253 staff and the Halliwell bleachworks 574. Length of service and employee age varied between departments and gender. The average age and length of employment of those working in the Halliwell Bleachwork's calendaring department, for example, was 55 years and 41 years respectively, as compared with 27 years and 14 years for those employed in the Jaconet room. The average age and length of service of women workers was 20 years and 6 years respectively, but 38 years and 25 years for male staff (ZAH 11/4).

32 Faucher, *Manchester*, 39; Wright, *Some*, 85, 86, 92; *Bolton Chronicle*, 14 September 1861; Lamb, *Free*, vol. ii, 363.

33 R. Harrison, *Before the Socialists. Studies in Labour and Politics, 1861–81*, London: Routledge, 1965, 6; Taylor, *Popular*, 14; Kirk, *The Growth*, 11; *Bolton Chronicle*, 26 June 1830; 1874 miners leader quoted in E. F. Biagini, 'British trade unions and popular political economy, 1860–80', *The Historical Journal*, 30 (4), 1987, 834; K. Burgess, *The Origins of British Industrial Relations*, London: Croom Helm, 1975, 254–5.

34 Joyce, *Work, Society*; S. Lukes, *Power. A Radical View*, London: MacMillan, 1974, 23–4; Anon., *Samuel*, 67; 'Special report by the directors', *Quarterly Review*, December 1852, 8.

35 Rose, *Firms*, 103.

36 Taylor, *Popular*, 187; *Bolton Chronicle*, 7 January 1865; ibid., 2 November 1850; ibid., 5 August 1865.

37 Clegg, *Annals*, 84, 117; *Bolton Chronicle*, 31 May 1845; *Fortnightly Review*, October 1868, 437; ibid., December 1868, 690; Lamb, *Free*, vol. ii, p. 294.

38 PP 1849, xxii (1017), Factory Inspector's Report, 18; *Bradshaw's Handbook to the Manufacturing Districts of Great Britain, 1854*, London, 1854, 98; Heyes, 'Leisure', 26; Howe, *The Cotton*, 307–9; Taylor, *Popular*, 187. Trust among team members will have facilitated the co-ordination of tasks, fostered co-operation and increased efficiency and productivity. Co-ordination will have been raised as team members will have been more certain that colleagues would complete their part of the production process. Higher efficiency will have resulted from greater discussion among workers of production problems. Productivity will have improved because individual

employees will have been more willing to direct their efforts towards the group task, confident that their colleagues would not take advantage of them or prove unpredictable (K. T. Dirks, 'The effects of interpersonal trust on work group performance', *Journal of Applied Psychology*, 84 (3), 1999, 448).

It could be argued that greater community social capital would have been produced if employers had invested their time and money in leisure facilities for the whole community rather than merely for their own workers.

39 Dutton and King, 'The limits', 59, 61; *Bolton Chronicle*, 27 October 1855; ibid., 19 March 1859; Taylor, *Popular*, 190. A further reason for worker apathy may have been the 'the spirit of jealous suspicion with which everything set in foot by the masters is regarded' (PP 1850 xxiii.571, 50).

40 Taylor, *Popular*, 186; *Bolton Chronicle*, 7 September 1850; ibid., 21 May 1859; ibid., 17 March 1860.

41 Anon., *The Young*, 191; T. M. McBride, *The Domestic Revolution. The Modernisation of Household Service in England and France*, New York: Holmes & Meier, 1976, 120; T. Griffiths, 'Work, class and community. The structures and values of working class life in coal and cotton Lancashire with particular reference to Bolton and Wigan, 1880–1930', Oxford University, DPhil. thesis, 1994, 313; A. Trod, 'Household spies. The servant and the plot in Victorian fiction', *Literature and History*, 13 (2), 1987, 176; Phillips, 'The social', 444; J. Barber, 'Stolen goods. The sexual harassment of female servants in West Wales during the nineteenth century', *Rural History*, 4 (2), 1993, 123–36.

42 Finn, *The Character*, 76, 82, 84; Bates, *A Discourse*, 129; Anon., *The Young*, 194; L. Schwarz, 'English servants and their employers during the eighteenth and nineteenth centuries', *Economic History Review*, 52 (2), 1999, 253.

43 1853 *North British Review* article quoted in B. W. Mccuskey, 'The kitchen police. Servant surveillance and middle class transgression', *Victorian Literature and Culture*, 28 (2), 2000, 362. The belief that servants constantly watched employers was fuelled by novels of the period, for example Mary Elizabth Braddon's *Lady Audley's Secret* and Wilkie Collins' *The Moonstone*.

Conclusion

1 R. Dawkins, *The Selfish Gene*, London: Paladin, 1978, 21; Becker, 'Altruism'; Holland, *Thoughts*, 9; *Illustrated London News*, 2 December 1843. See also N. B. Ferris, 'An American diplomatist confronts Victorian society', *History Today*, 15 (8) (1965), 557.

2 The share of Englishmen living in towns with more than 10,000 inhabitants rose from 16 per cent in 1750 to 33 per cent in 1831 (Jan de Vries, *European Urbanization, 1500–1800*, London: Methuen, 1984, 44).

3 Freedley, *A Practical*, 123.

4 H. Fielding, *Enquiry into the Causes of the Late Increase in Robbers*, London, 1751, 6; Morgan, *Manners*, 42–6.

5 Owen, *A New*, 122.

6 Britain's early industrialisation was related to its strong property rights, which raised the return on and promoted innovation; its well-established civil society; its widespread credit networks, which forced traders to trust each other and brought communities together; and its many ethical non-conformist sects. It also possessed a culture that valued and trusted wealth and status (North, *Institutions*; J. Habermas, *The Structural Transformation of the Public Sphere*, Cambridge: Polity, 1989; Muldrew, *The Economy*; Perkin, *The Origins*).

7 Lamb, *Free*, vol. i, 38; A. W. Ryley, *The Itinerant*, London, 1817. See also Joyce, *Work,*, 68 and Kirk, *The Growth*, 45. Oldham's low social capital continues to this day, as evinced by the 2001 'race' riots in the town.

8 Rota's 'measurements' of international social capital suggest that UK social capital fell from 1,529 in 1870 to 1,511 in 1890 (M. F. Rota, 'Is social capital persistent? Comparative measurement in the nineteenth and twentieth centuries', paper presented at the Economic Society, annual meeting, 2005).

9 Analysis of the themes of American presidential campaign party platforms from 1844 to 1964 and speeches delivered at the opening of each British parliamentary session from 1798 to 1972 suggest that during upswings in the Kondratieff cycle governments develop a preoccupation with social reform that is absent during downturns (Namenwirth, 'The wheels'; Namenwirth, 'Change'; Weber, 'Society'; E. O. Wright, *Class, Crisis and the State*, London: NLB, 1978). If excessive trust does not bring about downturns, it will, at least, amplify other causes. Other suggested reasons for falls in the Kondratieff cycle include the exhaustion of the economic benefits of new technological innovations, under-consumption and a rise in the organic composition of capital, that is falling profit rates due to greater capital intensity (Wright, *Class*).

10 In 1959, 61 per cent of those under 40 were trusting, but in 1990 just 40 per cent. Only 32 per cent of those between the ages of 18 and 20 years now express faith in the honesty of their fellow citizens (Hall, 'Social', 431–2). See also R. Putnam, 'Bowling alone. America's declining social capital', *Journal of Democracy*, 6 (1), 1995, 65–78; Putnam, *Bowling*. The average Briton now watches 2.5 hours of television each day. The Internet, by encouraging interaction, albeit of a disconnected kind, may promote trust.

11 Holland, *Thoughts*, 11.

Index

abstemiousness 169
accent 7, 17, 83, 96, 149, 150
accountancy associations 183, 233n13
accounts 169
Acts of Settlement 198
advertisements 91–2, 103, 171–3
adult education 83–4
adulteration of food 91–2, 155
affluence trust 93, 94, 95, 146, 167, 170,
    173, 204, 228nn23, 250n6; definition 6,
    7; education and 82–3; middle class 27,
    29, 215n15; networks and 54, 57, 60;
    philanthropy and 70
age 7, 11, 36, 62, 85, 96, 98, 105, 139,
    148, 167, 241n31
Alkali and Explosives Acts (1880/1) 111
American War of Independence 170
Americans 151
Anglicanism 11, 73, 77, 78, 79, 118,
    217n38, 225n27
anthropometric cartography 151
Anti-Corn Law League 48, 117
anti-Poor Law movement 48, 83, 102, 117
appearance 7, 16–17, 20–1, 34, 71, 78,
    104, 167, 214n15
apprenticeships 42–3, 78, 81, 85, 96, 160,
    182, 186, 189
arable regions 108, 187
arbitration 111, 124, 134, 197
architecture 99
Arnold, Thomas 82
artisans 43
ascribed distrust 19
ascribed trust 11, 45, 49, 90, 97, 104, 115,
    148, 168, 204; definition 6–7; education
    and 80, 81, 82–3; middle class 15, 16,
    17, 23, 27; networks and 56, 60, 62
Ashton, Thomas 94

Bagehot, Walter 19, 112

bailiffs 134
balls 28
bankruptcy 132–3, 158, 166, 167, 178–9,
    183
bankruptcy court 133
banks and bankers 2, 111, 124, 155, 183–4
Baptists 11
barristers 125
beer houses 89
Bentham, Jeremy 99, 145, 162
bible societies 63, 75, 76
Birmingham 229n25, 235n16
Blackburn 223n1, 226n3, 227n11–12,
    233n16–17, 237n37
bleachers 164, 171
blood sports 38, 87, 130
Boards of Health 116
boards of trade 189
Boards of Trustees 116
Bolton 3, 13, 100, 102–3, 206, 228n24,
    237n37, 238n10–11, 240n25; business
    trust 157–8, 164, 166, 167–8, 170,
    171–2, 174–5, 176–9, 244n10, 245n26,
    246n44; crime 120–1, 235n16;
    education provision 225n32;
    employer–employee trust 188, 191–2,
    195, 197, 199, 200; networks 50–2,
    60–2, 64–6, 221n13; philanthropy 68–9,
    70, 223n1; politics 233n16, 233n22,
    234n24; pubs 227n11–12; religion 73–4,
    75, 77, 78, 225n24
books 104–5, 142, 147, 155, 167, 173,
    175, 193
Booth, Charles 72
borough councils 115, 126
Bourdieu, Pierre 2
Braddon, Mary Elizabeth 250n43
Braidley, Benjamin 65
brands 173
brass bands 40, 55, 58